The Story of Human Rights

Marcello Flores

Translated by Benjamin Ginsborg

Kingston University Press Ltd
Main Building
Kingston University
Penrhyn Road
Kingston upon Thames
KT1 2EE
Email: KUPLtd@hotmail.co.uk

ISBN 978-1-899999-49-1

Set in 11/14 Palatino Linotype by Yorkshire Editorial Services

Printed by Lightning Source
Cover designed by July3rdDesigns. Design Consultant: Robert Mann

The translation of this work by Benjamin Ginsborg has been funded by SEPS SEGRETARIATO EUROPEO PER LE PUBBLICAZIONI SCIENTIFICHE.

Via Val d'Aposa 7 - 40123 Bologna - Italy
seps@seps.it - www.seps.it

Contents

Preface

Marcello Flores' *The Story of Human Rights*, which Kingston University Press is pleased to bring to English-speaking readers in this vivid translation, tells what is in many ways a dramatic tale, ranging far and wide across continents, borders and boundaries. It weaves together an account of how understandings of human rights have evolved with the critical struggles that courageous men and women have waged against various forms of tyranny, oppression and exploitation over the past few centuries. This has not, as he tells us, been a smooth, even or linear process – far from it. There have been reversals, defeats and setbacks alongside great victories and triumphs. Sometimes the setbacks have been severe, even to the point of the most fundamental rights disappearing entirely, even what Hannah Arendt once identified as the right to have rights at all. Sometimes it seems that the darkest days have been just before the dawn: if one thinks, for example, about the violent assault conducted (not so long ago) by Nazi Germany on an entire group, the Jews (and on many others too), in their bid to refashion humanity itself, followed as it was by what Flores calls the miracle of the Universal Declaration of Human Rights and by the Genocide Convention. Each time, ordinary men and women, and some extraordinary men and women too, have gathered their courage, their wits and their imagination to think, fight and demand their rights anew, not just those they have lost and been denied but those they have now come to see as equally urgent and imperative.

It is this intimate, if complex, connection between thought and action which is in many ways the most striking feature of this book. The reader will find here a clear and lucid account of the contributions of a long list of thinkers, from Grotius to Locke to Beccaria and on to Paine and Wollstonecraft. But he or she will be riveted too by accounts of the great struggles from below against slavery, against racism, for the rights of women, of workers, of children, of civilians and citizens and peoples across an increasingly inter-connected world.

For the story of human rights is not only a Western one, as Flores makes clear from the outset. It may have begun in one form in the West, for particular, historically conditioned reasons but was never confined to just one part of the world. Many thinkers and many activists from across the globe have played and continue to play their part, not least in formulating the Universal Declaration itself which owes so much, as he shows, to the clear and resolute thinking of a Lebanese philosopher, Charles Malik. It is fashionable in some quarters these days to query the idea that human rights really are universal, to suggest that actually they are culturally specific and that we should be sceptical about their supposedly exclusively Western origins. But Flores shows how disingenuous such claims are, and how often those who argue along these lines turn out to be those who want to deny rights to their own peoples. He challenges too the notion that cultures are themselves fixed, or immutable or immovable, in the West or anywhere else. For the history of human rights has in many ways involved an effort to change cultures, received wisdom, ways of thinking and acting that keep people in various forms of subjection and misery. As he points out, for centuries most Western societies enjoyed no traditions of human rights whatsoever. It was those who challenged prevailing ways of thinking and organising who developed ideas about human rights. They did not always do so consistently, for sure. Part of the intensely human fascination about his story is how people could demand some rights but not others, how people could be blind at times to other injustices going on around them. But part of the story too is how people did make connections, how women who fought against slavery for example came to fight for the rights of women, and vice versa. It is a story of how people came to see that if you argue for rights for some people, it makes no sense to deny them to others.

Logic alone is of course never enough. There has to be a felt involvement, an emotional engagement which (and here he draws on the important work of the American historian Lynn Hunt) makes people see that human rights are so important. This is then not a dry, purely analytical or philosophical analysis, though there is plenty of theory here. The arguments are serious, often complex, sometimes difficult, and need to be thought about and examined carefully and rigorously. But they are arguments which also appeal and motivate, leading people to take action, to make history themselves, as they have done in so many places over the past three hundred years or more.

The story that Flores tells here is, however, clearly unfinished. There are still arguments to be had, issues to resolve, rights to be won (or lost). It is a story which, we think, will appeal to many different kinds of readers, academic and non-academic, students and the general reader, as do all KUP books. It is one which, in translating, we wanted to bring to a new English- speaking readership, who we think will enjoy it as much as its many Italian readers have done. Our hope is that you will come away as enthralled as they have been and perhaps enthused too with the optimism with which Marcello Flores finishes his work. He thinks, as I do myself, not just that the story is unfinished but that we may be standing on the eve of another revolution in human rights, where we have the greatest opportunity as citizens of the world to achieve freedom, equality and justice for all. Whether you share his optimism is of course up to you but, if nothing else, we hope you enjoy the story he tells of the journey so far.

Professor Philip Spencer, Director of the Helen Bamber Centre for the Study of Rights, Conflict and Mass Violence at Kingston University

About the Author

Marcello Flores is Professor of Contemporary and Comparative History and coordinator of the European Master in Human Rights and Genocide Studies at the University of Siena. He has published extensively on human rights and genocide, totalitarianism, history of communism.

Introduction

Much attention is given to human rights today. Some say too much, with the attendant risk of creating a 'rhetoric' that can only devalue the profound meaning of a culture aiming for a certain degree of universality and shared recognition. The fact that nowadays everyone is a declared supporter of human rights – apart from a few lovers of paradox or certain ideologists seeking polemical effects – does not actually mean that everyone is speaking about the same thing, nor that everyone has in mind the same strategies, objectives and timing when it comes to transforming human rights into a widespread reality. Today the culture of human rights is typified by great debates, by somewhat less-than-homogeneous opinions, by deep tensions and contradictions which make it one of the most intellectually dynamic sectors of our era. Yet it is also a field affected by over-simplifications, clichés, banalities, even genuine misunderstandings; and above all by exploitative practices, often conscious ones, which confuse public opinion.

In any case the question of human rights cannot voluntarily be ignored: the cultural battles and political practices (both on an international level and within single states) at play are capable of strongly influencing the life of every single person in the world. Thus the promotion of the knowledge of human rights and the dissemination of information which establishes their role in a contemporary globalised society become truly useful objectives.

Obviously human rights have been confronted mostly within the juridical world. It was jurists, or philosophers of law, who provided the most articulate and complete formulations on the argument, and who contributed to the understanding, codification, classification and development of human rights onto a level of theoretical reflections and normative proposals, by considering the question of principles and values as well as norms and their implementation.

A historian's point of view is of course different. This is partly due to the fact that so far no historical reconstruction of human rights has simultaneously analysed the succession of ideas and theoretical proposals, and the practical and organisational itineraries of those groups and individuals seeking to transform reality in the name of the discriminated, the marginalised, the oppressed and all those suffering due to the denial of some or even all rights. The historical reconstructions we have are, in most cases, compendiums of histories of ideas or histories of the juridical norms regarding human rights, which focus primarily on the two crucial moments in which human rights fell under the historical spotlight: the middle of the eighteenth century and the middle of the twentieth century, the two periods during which 'declarations' of rights became central and indelible moments of history in general.

Tensions have always characterised the history of human rights: between its universalistic premise and ambitions and its heavily partial practical capacity; between moral and political values and regulations codified by laws; between declared principles and behaviour which often contradicts them. Such a distance between theory and practice, sometimes resulting in the shrinking of the former within the latter, has been considered a weakness of the human rights culture, although this very same argument is also valid when speaking of freedom, equality and justice, which are the fundamental pillars of the human rights culture, alongside the recognition of the dignity inherent in every human being.

A historical approach may indeed prove itself to be useful in an attempt to clarify the contradictions and aporias within the theory and practice of rights. History may help solve the major, centuries-old debate, once again relevant, over the 'natural' or 'positive' nature of human rights. Human rights are, indeed, 'historical rights', not just because they were born in particular circumstances, evolved in defined contexts or were characterised by widespread battles for freedom and equality recurring in diverse and articulated ways over the course of time. Human rights are 'historical rights' because the religious or secular, political or positive ideas they were born from have transformed through time, have known different declinations, have been influenced by previous and concurrent historical events and have contributed to influence successive ones. A universalistic view of rights has always intertwined, at least until a few decades ago, with a particularistic reading. Claim rights have always been rights of specific groups appealing to universal characteristics in order to strengthen their demands. This ambivalence of rights is, in some way, the same as the ambivalence within power, and it is no coincidence that the reciprocal legitimisation of power and rights is one of the fundamental aspects of the modern state and of democracy.

The reciprocal limits, the potential balance, the reasons for violations and, when possible, the realisation of the principles and values which embody human rights – dignity, justice, freedom, equality – are all rooted in history. A history formed by ideas and theory, by the institutions which proved instrumental to their material realisation, but also, and perhaps above all, by those people and movements who contributed to making possible the passage from theory to practice; those who attempted to realise the diffused, recognised and shared principles and values, and who helped this passage to be seen as inevitable in certain historical moments. Even the most far-seeing or courageous, the most enlightened or combative, capable or sensitive personalities who fought for human rights displayed certain inconsistencies and contradictions, due more to their own time than to personal weaknesses and limits. These failings should, however, not be forgotten.

This text's basic choice is to interlace, as much as possible, the evolution of ideas regarding human rights with a significant, yet certainly arbitrary, selection of the struggles and organisations which allowed them to become established in concrete reality. Thus we will pay particular attention to a number of personalities, some more and some less known, who distinguished themselves by placing certain rights at the centre of the public's attention. The first chapter aims to offer the historical background – from ancient times to the eighteenth century – leading to the elaboration of concepts and to the deepening of debates destined to merge, from the eighteenth century onwards, into what may be called the true history of human rights. The great turning point of the eighteenth century belongs equally to the world of ideas and to that of organised actions aimed at improving human conditions and the abolition of aberrant and discriminatory behaviour. As a historian I cannot avoid considering the roles of Cesare Beccaria and Granville Sharp first, and of John Stuart Mill and Henri Dunant later, as complementary cases, without privileging the ideas of the first two and yet also underlining their role in the formation of the latter two's personalities. In many ways the history of human rights has been more a history of practical attempts than of conceptual development, even if the political and juridical battles surrounding rights have always contributed important clarifications and theoretical elaborations.

The history of human rights is the itinerary through which moral principles and values have transformed into political objectives and into laws and juridical institutions, as well as into common sense and shared opinions. This has been due to cultural mobilisation and to the daily actions of all who felt the urgency of realising these rights. This itinerary was hardly linear or evolutionary, characterised as it was by accidents and obstacles, by moments of stasis and of acceleration. As part of a fundamentally universal history, even if for many centuries rooted mainly in the Western world's experience, human rights followed the stages and forms of that process of internationalisation, cosmopolitism and globalisation which characterises all human history, in particular from the sixteenth century onwards.

As an instrument to restrain and transform power, in harmony with ideas of freedom and justice, equality and personal dignity, the battle for human rights has almost always been a form of mobilisation from below, although it often required the help and interventions of powerful players in order to achieve its goals. A historically sensitive account of events regarding human rights, more inclined to comprehension than to judgement, may be useful in order not to reduce their complexity to simple political or ideological positions. Human rights represent a filter which is certainly only partial for the observation of the history of the last three centuries, yet it may also allow us to centre our attention on previously overlooked aspects. This hope and objective motivated the writing of this book, which does not claim to discover new truths or propose original interpretations, but which aims rather to reorganise a vast and diverse subject and recompose it, not without difficulties, within a unitary piece of work.

In my particular course of studies and research, the question of human rights has become ever more central since the end of the eighties. It was then that the transitional process towards democracy, forged in that decade and in the following one, radically transformed the global scenario. This change had at its heart the crisis and fall of Eastern communist and Latin American military regimes, as well as many authoritarian and racist regimes shamefully symbolised on a world scale by South African apartheid. The interest surrounding these events, expressed by the multiplication of studies into totalitarianism, violence and genocide, was accompanied by a need to observe human rights through a different approach from the – prevalent and necessary – juridical one.

A fundamental element in this process was the institution, less than a decade ago, of a Masters Degree in Human Rights and Humanitarian Action at the University of Siena, where the contacts between diverse disciplines and different competences led to significant cultural exchanges between Italian and international colleagues, as well as the European institution of a Masters Degree in Human Rights and Genocide Studies. It was within this ambit that the multiple volume work on human rights published by the Italian publishing house Utet in 2007 was conceived and coordinated.

During the preparation of this work, as on previous occasions, I received help, support, criticism and participation from many people. I hope not to offend anyone who contributed in one way or another to my own cultural development if I only mention those who had a more direct relationship with this history of human rights. First of all the long-standing colleagues and friends with whom I have frequented and exchanged ideas – Tommaso Detti, Giovanni Gozzini, Maurizio Bettini, Franco Cazzola, Marco Mayer, Marco Ventura – all of whom read the whole or parts of the manuscript and suggested modifications and improvements. The colleagues who have been by my side during the years of the Masters programme have been an unfailing source of input, discussions, elaborations and enlightenment on aspects of human rights I would otherwise not have considered. The same is true of those friends with whom I debated and discussed during various initiatives regarding human rights, and the colleagues within the Doctorate in Anthropology and History and within the European research group on the Strasbourg Court: Tania Groppi, Riccardo Pisillo Mazzeschi, Wiktor Osiatynski, Aryeh Neier, Andrea Bartoli, Antonio Donini, Philip Spencer, Antonio Cassese, Farian Sabahi, Paola Gaeta, Stefano Nespor, Anthony Dworkin, Ruti Teitel, Joanne Mariner, Glenda Wildschut, Jacques Semelin, Ben Kiernan, Tzvetan Todorov, Carola Carazzone, Adolfo Ceretti, Alberto Cutillo, Andrea de Guttry, Giovanna Ceccatelli Gurrieri, Massimo Toschi, Laura Boldrini, Marina Calloni, Dia Anagnostou, Evangelia Psychogiopoulou, Amaya Ubeda. Many female colleagues and younger female collaborators gave me important suggestions and indicated crucial corrections. Their careful, critical and friendly readings allowed me to modify and improve the manuscript, even if I probably have not fully lived up to their expectations: Isabella Pierangeli Borletti, Maddalena Carli, Ilaria Favretto, Valeria Galimi, Barbara Montesi, Valentina Cioncolini, Marialaura Marinozzi.

I would like to dedicate a special thanks to Paul Ginsborg and Ayşe Saraçgil who allowed me to write the last chapter and review the entire manuscript in their lovely house at Vinca in the Apuan Alps. And to Ugo Berti who has always expressed the sort of confidence and appreciation which any author would love to receive from his/her publisher. Once again Stefania's patience, encouragement and critical help have been fundamental. I dedicate this work to our grandchildren Alchimia, Leon, Nausicaa and Aqua, with the hope that theirs may truly be the century of human rights.

Chapter One
From Duties to Rights

1. *Religions and values*

Two of the most important philosophers of law of our times, Norberto Bobbio and Peces-Barba Martínez, have written that human rights are 'historical rights', born of specific contexts and circumstances, amidst many struggles for recognition, as an effect of both the development of new ideas and changes in political and social reality. According to Bobbio it was during the eighteenth century that 'a radical change of perspective, characteristic of the modern state's formation' took place, following a process in which 'the individualistic conception of society slowly shifted from the recognition of the rights of the citizen of one single nation to the recognition of the rights of the citizens of the world'.[1]

The idea of dating the origins of human rights, some might say their 'invention', to the eighteenth century is a widespread one.[2] Yet it is useful to trace – even if in brief and by observing only a few illustrative moments – the ideas and landmarks which in some ways make human rights a constant element of human history. This is particularly true today, since:

> human rights have become so ubiquitous in the present time that they seem to require an equally capacious history. Greek ideas about the individual person, Roman notions of law and rights, Christian doctrine of the soul... the risk is that the history of human rights becomes the history of Western civilisation or now, sometimes, the history of the entire world. Do not ancient Babylon, Hinduism, Buddhism and Islam also make their contributions, too? How then do we account for the sudden crystallisation of human rights which is claimed at the end of the eighteenth century?[3]

Law has retained a central role since ancient times. *The Code of Hammurabi* – the Babylonian king who died in 1750 BC – now in the Louvre museum, is considered by many scholars to be the first example of government norms based on principles of justice. The code is the first complete and organic compilation of laws to apply to citizens while distinguishing them from non-citizens and slaves, and lays down a strict yet stern justice, to be applied according to the juridical status of both the victim and the accused and by following the *lex talionis*, which established consistent rules for each social category. The laws promulgated by the Babylonian king represent the first attempt to abolish individual vengeance and to emphasise the value of the individual as a person: the code determines when to apply the *lex talionis*[4] – for bodily damage and injuries – and when on the contrary an economic compensation is sufficient, yet it also includes norms regarding marriage and divorce, agricultural practices and peasants' salaries, doctors' and sailors' duties. However, these laws were determined by the king and were thus considered to derive from divinity, and were not applied according to the inherent value of each individual, based as they were on the social roles given to each person by the aristocratic political order.

In ancient Greece the relationship between law and government was central to the thoughts of the great philosophers. Both Plato and Aristotle viewed the former as the instrument that defined the tasks and limits of the latter, no matter what form of government (monarchic, aristocratic, democratic) one was wishing to privilege. Thus Bobbio wrote that 'the true hero of the classic world is the great legislator: Minos, Licurgus, Solon'.[5]

Alongside the law, however, are values, precepts for wise actions, moral principles that should guide man's behaviour. These are mainly found in religions, from the ancient ones to the great monotheistic religions, the so-called 'religions of the book' which entrust the truth revealed by the only God to a sacred text. The first sacred texts we know about are probably the ritual writings of the Vedas (from the Sanskrit *vid*, to know) dating back to the second millennium before Christ; in addition to these we should also mention other sacred Hindu texts such as the Upanishad, which are commentaries and developments of the Vedas, or the Āgamas, all of which:

> address the existence of good and evil, wisdom, the necessity for moral behaviour and especially the importance of duty (*dharma*) and good conduct (*sadâchâra*) toward others, those suffering in need. They enjoin believers to fulfil faithfully their earthly responsibilities to all

people beyond the self or family without distinctions by practicing selfless concern for their pain, particularly charity and compassion for the hungry, the sick, the homeless, and the unfortunate, as discussed in the *Manava Dharma Sûtra* (Treatise on Human Duties).[6]

Judaism speaks, in a different manner but with the same force, of a brotherhood of men united in God, about the holy nature of human life and responsibilities towards fellow human beings. It is not by coincidence that a biblical phrase – Cain's guilty declaration, 'Am I my brother's keeper?' – once reversed into an affirmative statement, became one of the most famous mottos as well as a model for many movements for rights throughout history. Aside from the values of equality and justice that may be found in the sacred texts, it must however be noted that 'the Judaic language has no authentic word to indicate rights. The present term meaning right (*z'khut*) originally indicated purity, virtue, innocence; it was used to describe privileges received or even deserved [...] Judaism knows not rights, but duties, all of which are ultimately due to God.'[7]

Over two thousand years ago Buddhism spread universalistic principles regarding the value of every human being's life, compassion toward pain, brotherhood and equality, refusing all differences between social castes and roles and endorsing ethics that underlined the right to think, to speak, to act and to be responsible toward all human beings. The concepts of *anatma* (altruism) and *duhkha* (innate individual suffering) should guide believers toward feelings of universal compassion, that Buddha himself moved toward a detachment from the world, a journey of self-renunciation leading to freedom from pain and suffering in the Nirvana. Buddhism also speaks of solidarity, as an instrument for the salvation of other human beings and the achievement of the individual's greater internal freedom. Next to negative obligations (do not kill, do not steal) are positive rights (regarding property) and connected duties (such as the redistribution of one's riches).

Confucius's doctrine dates back to the same historic period as Buddhism:

The basic ethic concept of Chinese social and political relationships is the fulfilment of duties toward one's similar, rather than a demand for rights. The idea of reciprocal obligations has been considered Confucianism's main teaching. The five basic social relationships described by Confucius and his followers are those between (1) governors and subjects, (2) parents and children, (3) husband and wife, (4) elder and younger brothers and (5) friends. Instead of demanding rights, Chinese ethic teachings emphasised the sympathetic attitude of considering other human beings to have the same desires, and thus the same rights, that anybody would want for him/herself.[8]

The aphorisms and anecdotes of the *Lún Yǔ* are a guideline for human conduct, the Path, characterised by efforts to realise the self and to follow a path of right and proper altruism. The conviction that education may awaken human qualities (rational, emotional, aesthetic, political, transcendent) in all men, and that social interaction contributes to the self-realisation of the individual, places the doctrine's attention on social wealth and on the unity of the family, of the community and of the state, based upon security, stability and peace. Instructions on how to avoid the possible vices of command and how to govern positively are further moral prescriptions, which may allow governors to earn the trust of their subjects, if followed respectfully. Alongside these prescriptions Confucianism also provides indications regarding an equal distribution of resources, the refusal of power and riches as dominating values and the respect of stability and harmony as foundations of peace and social growth.

The search for the possible roots of human rights within religions and great ancient law systems can go no further than the recognition of similarities or associations between analogous values. The contexts are too diverse for us – both one from the other and in relation to the modern world in which human rights were 'invented' – to speak about a real derivation. Yet we should not underestimate the presence, in all major religions, of references to personal dignity and to respect for other human beings, as well as appeals for equality and justice.

These rules, 'essentially imperative, negative or positive', 'which aim to obtain desired behaviour and avoid undesired behaviour by resorting to celestial and earthly sanctions',[9] with their differences and their even stronger similarities, formed the moral code of humanity within all ancient civilisations, religions, moral and juridical systems.

2. *Laws and morality in the classical age*

Only recently was an attempt made, with regard to the classical age, to 'individuate the specific cultural forms in which the Greeks and the Romans confronted problems that were somewhat equivalent to what we now define as 'human rights': thought categories, terms and modalities that may find a correspondence in modernity.'[10] The subject of rights in the ancient world has been examined more often than not from an actualising perspective, linking present interpretations and modern conceptions of the world to possible references within the Greek and Roman cultures.

One of the most discussed classical texts, as well as one of the strongest examples of this 'actualisation' of classical references, is Sophocles' tragedy *Antigone*, written in Athens in 442 BC. Indeed the sensitivity of our modern culture of human rights interlaces with past interpretations of this tragedy, first by Hegel, then Alfieri, then by Jean Anouilh in 1944 and Bertolt Brecht in 1948, up to the feminist interpretations of the 1980s.

The tragedy, often viewed as a clash between moral law and the laws of the state, as first interpreted by Hegel, narrates Antigone's struggle to bury her brother Polynices (murdered by her other sibling Eteocles), against the veto declared by King Creon. Moved by familiar and religious *pietas*, Antigone disobeys earthly law (the king's veto), and is condemned by Creon who has her buried alive in a cave. The tragedy comes to its climax with a series of suicides – Antigone hangs herself; her lover Haemon, Creon's son, throws himself upon his own sword; Eurydice, wife of Creon, cannot stand her son's death and kills herself immediately afterwards.

The more philological interpretations underline how Antigone's behaviour was inspired by love for her brother and by a strong sense of family identity, rather than by the appeal of an unwritten law or some sort of universal morality represented by a 'divine law'. Hers is a morality 'of blood', not a 'universal' one, a bond with her clan rather than a rebellious act against the tyrant. It has also been noted that 'Antigone speaks of the divine "laws of God" not "natural laws"; furthermore the divine laws she invokes concern bloody loyalty among family members, not "human rights" in some general and universal sense'.[11]

The greatness of classical texts, however, also lies in their capacity to offer new interpretations according to the cultural necessities and social needs of each historical epoch. Hegel identified in Antigone a clash between moral law and the laws of the state, Alfieri saw in her a courageous opposition against tyranny, Anouilh read the text as a para-existentialist study of beauty, folly, sexuality and death, while Brecht actualised and politicised the tragedy, by opposing a Creon-Hitler to an Antigone who is a heroine of the Resistance, and the Living Theatre later interpreted the text as a representation of public and individual cruelty.

A human rights-inspired reading cannot, as suggested by Gustavo Zagrebelsky, avoid the dilemma of justice and law: in the tragedy justice contradicts the law and vice-versa. Creon's laws are positive, written ones; Antigone's laws are perennial ones, fundamental moral precepts which transcend law as an expression of power. It is the intrinsic limits of these two visions – positive law versus natural law – that define *Antigone*'s reality, in the effects of their parallel absoluteness and reciprocal closure to each other's reasons. 'The double nature of rights illustrated by Antigone may be obscured. We live in an obscurantist era and no longer see natural rights. These can however emerge within constitutions: summaries of the political, social and ethic history of a country'.[12] It is indeed not by coincidence that constitutions – from the revolutionary American and French ones to those of the nineteenth and twentieth centuries – emerge in the same epoch in which human rights were 'invented', while in earlier times, even when they were called constitutions, their basic role was to summarise promulgated laws.

With regard to the classical age, Maurizio Bettini underlined the existence of a *ius gentium* as a 'common cistern which single communities' rights draw upon', yet also as a 'nucleus of rather archaic norms, which identify in certain elementary obligations what will later be efficaciously defined by Seneca *humanum officium*, "the duties of men toward men" (*Letters to Lucilio*, 95, 50-53)'.[13] These are obligations for all populations, which are useful for those who receive them and harmless for those who observe them, and are often called communia: the most well-known and frequent are to give water to the thirsty and food to the hungry, to be merciful toward one's enemies, not to offend prisoners or women. In the classical age human rights are still contained within a 'religious context', as demonstrated by an annual ceremony in Attica, during which 'priests, belonging to the Bouzúgai (literally the "ox subjugators") family, would cast curses against those who refused to concede fire or water to the needful, to show the right path to passer-bys or who left a body unburied'.[14] Within the religious sphere, inviolable rights deserve a form of guarantee. It is religion that somehow protects humans from 'impiety' (*impietas*) by preventing men from committing an excessive amount of impious acts. Thus Priam asks Achilles to 'respect the gods' by allowing him to bury his son Hector, in the same way that Antigone appeals to the 'law of the gods' to justify her disobedience toward Creon. Those who feel their rights have been violated demand a form of punishment for such acts of impiety toward the gods; and those who have suffered because of cruel, ferocious or treacherous acts demand forms of punishment for the powerful populations (Sparta, Athens, Rome) who have behaved – or obliged their smaller allies to behave – in a fashion that opposes the 'common rights of men'.

In the classical world, however, moral values did not only exist within religion. Bettini, following Benveniste's research, indicates how the term *philantropía* – a concept widespread in Greece thanks to Xenophon and

Demosthenes, and especially during the fourth century BC at the time of a particularly brutal and violent crisis – had a strong social connotation, referring to 'he who recognises the human being, in general, as a member of his own social group'. Bettini also underlines how, from the first century BC, the Romans used the equivalent term *humanitas*, even if in this case the educational and cultural connotations prevail over the social aspect.

Like the Greeks' *philantropía*, Roman *humanitas* establishes a tight connection between the notion of 'man' on one side, and of 'moderate, fair, comprehensive' behaviour on the other; this connection is a profound one, capable of installing itself within 'language', where expressions deriving from the notion of 'man' (*philantropía, humanitas*) are also used to indicate 'fairness', 'generosity', 'moderation' in behaviour. This is an extremely relevant cultural passage. Essentially the notion of 'man' becomes 'translatable' as 'fairness, moderation', and thus a human being is only to be considered a man when he behaves moderately and generously toward other human beings. Such linguistic and cultural presuppositions precisely constitute the preparatory basis for juridical configurations such as modern 'human rights'.[15]

These notions still remain, predominantly, within the field of moral qualities, desirable yet not binding, especially with regard to powerful individuals and governors. What is more, we must still acknowledge a strong ambiguity between an inner circle (family members, friends, cities) and a more general identity (the human race, comprising other individuals, possible enemies). The parameter of vicinity and the connected parameter of language are still what allow individuals to enter the 'society' towards which they are considered to have uniform and constant obligations.

It was probably above all the Stoics who philosophised about a more universal dimension of relationships between men. Diogenes the Cynic defined himself as a 'citizen of the world' while Zeno believed that all men were inhabitants of the same *pólis* and of the same community. Seneca went even further, by claiming that nature:

> generated us as relatives (*cognati*), as we were created with the same elements and tend toward the same end. [...] May we always wear in our hearts and upon our lips the famous verse: *homo sum: humani nihil a me alienum puto*. May we convince ourselves of the fact that we were born to exist together (*in commune*). Our society is like a stone vault, capable of standing only because each stone supports the next, for if they didn't it would collapse (*Letters to Lucilio*, 95, 51-53).[16]

In Stoic philosophy the system of nature was both physical and moral, and included respect for one's similar. However, the further one moved away from 'society', his family or city, the more complex things became. Even Seneca, the classical age's most severe critic of slavery, wrote that slaves should be considered as 'men', 'house companions', 'humble friends', without hypothesising any possible abolitionist steps.

Many contradictions were also present in judgements regarding allies and enemies, close and distant populations, according to circumstances and to the relationships between populations at specific historical moments. From this perspective the themes of war and of the *ius gentium* are particularly instructive with regard to the centuries to come.

3. *Between the law of nature and the divine law*

In the fifth book of the history of Rome Livy recalls how some Roman ambassadors had been asked to act as intermediaries during the negotiations between the Gauls and the city of Chiusi, which they were holding under siege. When faced with the Gauls' demand – a spurious one according to the ambassadors – to obtain part of Chiusi's territory, the ambassadors took up arms and allied with the besieged city. In the thirty-first volume of his *Ab urbe condita*, Livy defines Philip V's behaviour against the Athenians and the destruction of Cinosarges a sacrilege, because 'everything consecrated and pleasant that existed near the city was burnt, houses and tombs were destroyed, and nothing was saved from the rampant rage, not out of respect for divine laws or for human laws'. [17]

In this case the profanation of sacred locations and of tombs went far beyond the necessary cruelty of the laws of war, which did admit the burning of fields and the destruction of houses, as well as the confiscation of men and cattle. As in the case of Antigone, it is the violation of divine laws and the conflict with the *religio* and *pietas* that constitute the condemned example of inhumanity: cruelty and violence are no longer interpreted as physical or material as they are transformed into symbols of a violation of the *ius humanum* and of the *ius gentium*.

Appian's narration of the destruction of Carthage by Scipio Aemilianus's legions in 146 BC is extremely detailed:

Then more horrifying scenes took place. The fire spread out and destroyed everything, and the soldiers didn't destroy just a few buildings at a time, preferring to demolish them all at once. These collapses made an increasing amount of noise, and many people fell under the stones amongst the dead. Others survived, mainly elderly people, women and children, who had hidden in the farthest corners of the buildings, some of them wounded, others burnt and screaming horribly. Others still who had fell from above together with stones, wooden beams and fire, were decomposed in horrible ways, squashed and crushed [...] [Roman soldiers] threw the dead and the alive into holes in the ground, dragging them like sticks and stones or turning them over with iron tools, while a man was used to fill the holes with earth. Some were thrown in with their head inside, while their legs, sticking out of the ground, would twist about for quite some time. Others would fall in the holes with their feet buried and their head still above the ground. Horses would tread on them, crushing their faces and craniums, not as a premeditated act, but as a consequence of the hurried confusion [...] Six days and six nights passed in this agitated way.[18]

In an observation of past history through present categories the destruction of Carthage has been considered similar to genocide, given the determination to follow Cato's reiterated appeals and to intentionally destroy an entire nation. Cato, who had recently driven the sceptic philosopher Carneades out of Rome, complained about the Roman tendency to give in to Greek luxury and laxity. Thus the combination of fear of external aggression (from Carthage, a city which had rapidly returned to its ancient strength and was expanding dangerously) with an internal degeneration led him to envision the possibility of returning Rome to its ancient authority by annihilating the ancient rival.

Publius Cornelius Scipio Aemilianus, during the years preceding his African campaign, had contributed to the protection and patronage of Publius Terence Afer, a Carthage native slave, and later a freed man, who was the author of six successful comedies before he died in a shipwreck ten years before the campaign that lead to Carthage's destruction. It was Terence who wrote that 'paradigmatic phrase, which over the course of our cultural history has so often been a foundation for the very characterisation of what is human' (*homo sum: humani nihil a me alienum puto*), even if it was originally conceived – in the *Self-tormentor (Heautontimorumenos)* – 'as an invitation not just to communication, but even to indiscretion'.[19]

Was Scipio, the patron of Terence – the first artist to summarise, in an extremely popular phrase, the invitation to 'overcome the barriers between men in the name of common "humanity"'[20] – then a forerunner, as the destroyer of Carthage, of the genocidal behaviour of the twentieth century? The discussions between historians, jurists and scholars of human sciences, who, with regard to the ancient world, have mostly concentrated upon

the Athenian massacre of the inhabitants of Melos and the destruction
of Carthage, are yet another demonstration of how problems regarding
present human rights are creating a growing interest in history, sometimes interpreted in debatable ways, which may however often contain
significant elements for further analysis. This interest in history has often
been expressed by attempts to adapt contemporary concepts to episodes
from the past – for example the destruction of Carthage has often been
reinterpreted through the filter of the 1948 Convention for the Prevention
and Punishment of Genocide[21] – which have somewhat underestimated
the importance of identifying the equivalent elements, in the classic age,
of what we now call human rights or violations of human rights.

The law of nature, according to Cicero, and above all Seneca and the
Stoics, is a universal fact upon which the possibility of justice is founded,
even if in actual Roman history 'the law of nature does not serve to reject
positive law'.[22] What then is the true value of:

> [a] superior and eternal (Cicero also defined it as *aeternum quiddam*)
> law, based on the sense of justice, which also becomes a parameter
> for distinguishing between fair and unfair laws: *nos legem bonam
> a mala nulla alia nisi naturae norma dividere possumus* ('we cannot
> distinguish a good law from a bad law if not through the norms of
> nature')?[23]

It has been noted that:

> certain Roman jurists considered the *ius gentium* as a form of
> inherent rights of men in function of the social relations which exist
> within a community; in this case it should be seen as a form of
> rights that articulate as a subset within the vaster ambit of the law
> of nature, which is valid for men as much as it is for animals. Other
> juridical texts consider the 'people's rights' as the common system
> of institutions and practices of all populations, regardless of their
> degree of adherence to the law of nature.[24]

Plato, when speaking of war, identified in the *Republic* a set of rules (the
prohibition of conflicts amongst Greek populations, moderation toward
the defeated) which Romans later forged into more coherent and rational
laws concerning the principle of the 'painful' necessity of war. In the *De
officiis* Cicero summarises these ideas by observing how one must 'be
moderate in revenge and punishment; the Republic must respect the laws
of war; dialogue, which belongs to the human being, should be preferred

to the use of force, which is typical of animals; one should only resort to force when dialogue fails to solve a conflict;.[25]

4. *Christianity and human rights*

Certainly the 'great change' described by Bobbio, 'beginning in the Western world with the Christian conception of life, which states that all men are brothers, as they are all children of God',[26] is a suggestive idea, although it is more historically correct to state that:

> Christianity's contribution to human rights is a rich and articulated one, yet also profoundly contaminated (by Jewish and Greek influences above all) and bivalent. Christianity is not just a positive factor for development in the struggles for human rights. If Christian theories and procedures founded and supported the development of rights, Christian theories and procedures also have represented an obstacle for such development. Both violations and redemptions are Christian. The history of human rights is for the most part a history of fights between Christians.[27]

In Christian theology and philosophy, in the practices through which the Church proceeded to spread the new religion, in the Church's hierarchic organisation – which led its history to entwine with the history of the empire – we can observe appeals for human dignity and for universality, yet also justifications for their denial. Certainly the values inherited through time, which constitute the tradition that has survived up to now, are based upon equality and solidarity in an absolutely un-rhetorical fashion. If in the Gospel of Mark the 'next person' to be loved corresponds to the Jewish tradition's 'neighbour', he who belongs to the same community, in the Gospel of Luke, the 'neighbour' becomes he who has, in the Samaritan parable, taken care of the wounded 'following a philanthropic attitude. Mark's "neighbour" is truly becoming the "next" to receive the Gospel'.[28]

Certainly the profoundly anti-state nature of Christian tradition, the centrality of the person and, to an even larger degree, of the family and of the community of believers, create fertile grounds for a reflection on the limits of power and for a recovery of the classical theory regarding the law of nature. Indeed the law of nature, based on its divine derivation, became central to a new philosophic era, whose major figures were Saint Augustine and Thomas Aquinas. The role of the Church was essential for the destabilisation of hierarchies and in offering a vision of a community more universal than even the great cosmopolitan cities; as

Paul claimed, 'in Christ there are no Jews or Greeks, males or females, slaves or free men'.

It was principally through the new institution of the Church, which claimed to embody universal values for all, that Greek and Roman philosophers, whose most coherent formulation was to be discerned in Stoic philosophy, identified a common ground for their diffusion in society. Indeed it is certainly true that 'without the utilisation of Greek and Roman philosophic categories to express and refine the ethical universalism of Hebraic tradition, Christianity might have remained an esoteric cult in the Mediterranean basin, ill-equipped to make its way into the marketplace of ideas in several cultures'.[29]

The primitive Christian church constitutes both an institutional and a social terrain for the formation of ethics based on universal values that do not, and can not, coincide with any political regime; indeed the Church often placed itself at a distance from political powers. Alongside the equality based on all men being 'created in God's likeness' we find the freedom manifested by the Church during the first phase of its existence – as an institution based upon universal values, as a place for resistance against states' absolutist demands, yet also against certain partial demands such as familiar, ethnic and political ones. However, freedom and equality never belong to every human being; indeed Augustine claims that both values may only be achieved by entering the Church and embracing true faith.

Scholars who have confronted the problem of the origins of human rights in the Middle Ages have for the most part claimed that these should be dated between the fourteenth and fifteenth century; even if some scholars suggested a continuity with the ancient theory of natural rights. When speaking of the laws of nature, such studies do not often refer to claims born from an objective common morality, from shared ethics, from the participation in an objective moral order constituted by a world dominated by Christianity and the Church. The possibility of identifying in Thomas Aquinas a medieval doctrine of human rights has been debated at length and the opinion of the more renowned[30] scholars is that it is indeed a possible option, yet only:

> If we assume that natural rights are equivalent to natural duties. [...] Aquinas has a concept of the natural rights, or *ius*, an objective order of equality established by nature, but he does not speak in terms of rights inhering in individuals, which give rise to duties in other (*Summa theologiae* II-II 57.1,2) human beings. In other words Aquinas has a concept of the right, and he apparently also has a concept

of claims emerging out of a particular set of social arrangements more or less equivalent to our concept of civil rights, but he does not appear to have a concept of natural rights in the strong sense.[31]

However, the affinity between natural rights theoreticians and medieval philosophers may lead to the recognition that 'there is no sharp break between the high middle ages and early modernity on this issue'.[32]

Thomas's frequent appeal to *dignitas humana* and to every individual's autonomous capacity to make moral choices did not prevent him from legitimising slavery, just as Aristotle did before him and as Thomas Jefferson, one of the fathers of American rights, would do later.

The chronological coincidence between the Fourth Council of the Lateran and the granting of the *Magna Carta libertatum* – both in 1215 – demonstrates, even if we must of course consider the great differences between the two events, how the relationship between politics and religion was now addressing the question of which authority should prevail and what relations should be built between the two universal powers, the papacy and the empire. This also demonstrates the increasing demands for a recognition of the right to freedom, and consequently for a limitation of absolute powers. This question involved, in different ways, the relationship between the monarch and the lords and the relations between the lords and their subjects. Political relationships, and the rights which followed their juridical institutionalisation, provided the context for confrontations between those moral values that were at the basis of promulgated laws.

The rights of this period still have a corporative nature, as they related to groups, not individuals: the first beneficiaries of the king's renunciation of certain rights in the *Magna Carta* were actually the barons. The system of bans and guarantees regarding possible abuses by the ruler formalised a right to freedom that, although extended only to its beneficiaries and not always possible in reality, did constitute a principle that other wider groups would appeal to successively.

The declaration made during the seventeenth-century English revolution by British *common law* codifier Sir Edward Coke, according to whom the *Magna Carta* represented a form of protection for all English men born free, was not just a rhetorical exaggeration.

The attribution of political objectives considered at the time to be essential (peace, freedom, rights) to a fundamental law – that would later materialise in the form of constitutions – involved every relevant social group and laid the foundations for the birth of the modern state. Such foundations were also strongly influenced by the theories and governmental practices of the Italian communes, in which citizen rights were born and the legitimisation of the ruler's power was attributed to the will of citizens – as a community of free men.

5. *Humanism and Renaissance*

The relationship between rights and politics found a clearer, even if not linear, configuration starting from the thirteenth century, up until the birth and affirmation of the modern state between the fifteenth and seventeenth century. It was the Tuscan and Lombard communes, which had become independent republics, who, from the thirteenth century, began formalising their systems of self-government and justice through written constitutions. The communes felt a need to legitimise their autonomy from the empire through a juridical connotation. This claim to autonomy is the basis of the civil ideology Quentin Skinner dates back to the start of Humanism; Skinner also considers this civil ideology to be a heritage more of the Roman republican virtues of Seneca, successively reinterpreted by pre-humanist philosophers and by Niccolò Machiavelli, than of Greek ideas and Aristotelism.

The most complete works of this epoch regarding urban government were Brunetto Latini's *Livres du Trésor*, published in 1266. The explicit objectives of these treatise are civil concordance and the prevalence of common well-being over individual egoisms and sectarian particularisms, so that 'the city, governed only according to law and truth, where everybody owns what they deserve, will certainly grow and multiply its inhabitants and its goods, and will maintain its peace, for its own honour and that of its allies'.[33]

Skinner analysed in a masterly fashion what he considered the 'most memorable contribution' to the debate on republican ideas and forms of self-government: the *Allegory of Good Government* painted by Ambrogio Lorenzetti, between 1337 and 1339, in the Hall of the Nine of Siena. In this representation, ideological and artistic, philosophical and symbolic, political and narrative, Seneca and Cicero's influence is far more evident than Aristotle or Thomas's. Peace occupies the central area of the painting, as the most important value of civil existence: the powerful have the duty of avoiding particular ambitions that may bring harm to public well-being. Next to peace is justice, which is the fundamental bond of human society and is conceived by Lorenzetti, as in Brunetto Latini, as the capacity to correct conditions of injustice and inequality. Authors writing about urban self-government emphasise the limited role of the governors, whose position is chronologically determined and whose powers are established by the law: 'The Senese *Breves* begin by describing officers as "bound" to their duties and to "their mandate". Analogously the 1309-10 Senese constitution establishes in almost all sections regarding the Nine that "sieno tenuti et debiano" (literally, they should be obliged) to act as indicated by the constitution.'[34] This unprecedented conception of citizenship, which 'owes much more to Rome than to Greece',[35] later merged into the Renaissance civic Humanism and inspired both Guicciardini and Machiavelli.

Even Petrarca, in the second half of the fourteenth century, considered the objective of good government to be the achievement of its goals in such a way that 'every citizen may live freely and safely, without any innocent blood being spilled'[36] ; while Machiavelli, in the second decade of the sixteenth century, wondered how to ensure the prevalence of virtue in public life, given the fact that egoism and corruption constitute the individual's 'natural' tendency. In Machiavelli only the binding and iron-strong power of law can restrain the vices to which completely free citizens would abandon themselves; and amongst laws the ones with general characteristics, the constitutions, are the most important in ensuring a balanced government. Thus the Florentine author theorised his conception of 'realism', and identified the 'virtuous prince' in he who 'will instead be distinguished by an unfailing intuition, capable of showing him when to respect justice's dictates and when to ignore them. He will substantially be guided by necessity rather than by justice'.[37]

The reflection upon the source of power and self-government which developed between the thirteenth and fifteenth century ran parallel to the theological and philosophical one regarding natural rights. One of the most important thinkers of the fourteenth century, William of Ockham, is widely considered[38] to be the father of the theory of natural rights. Even if granted by God, these rights are bound to each person, who may not renounce them even if he may choose not to exercise them. In his works alongside a contribution on natural rights, the English philosopher re-elaborated the ideas on power of Marsilius of Padua. In the *Defensor Pacis*, written at the beginning of the fifteenth century, Marsilius took Italian communes as an example and identified civic assemblies as the source of law and as the governance destined to bind the ruler himself. The law, produced by the social body (citizen assemblies), concurrently protects and binds every individual belonging to society: just as Ambrogio Lorenzetti depicted so admirably, by representing citizens 'bound' by holding the double string which constitutes the rope of justice.

The thirteenth century's canonic rights had developed the concept of *ius naturale*, thus envisioning a sphere of rights founded on a natural moral law, and conceiving 'a view of individual human persons as free, endowed with reason, capable of moral discernment, and from a consideration of the ties of justice and charity that bound each individuals to one another'.[39] This basis was also strongly influential for the increase, within the fifteenth-century council movement, in criticisms of religious power and for the defence of a contractual idea accompanied by the right of resistance.

The Church's internal debate, culminating in the 1415 Council of Constance, attempted to address the question of papal authority as well as the problem of the diffusion and growth of heretic movements, in particular the one founded by Jan Hus, which was strongly connected to the birth of certain Christian 'nationalisms' favoured by the European political context of the period. This is the ambit in which the Church felt the urge to indicate a universal moral law all human beings should abide by.

> Human duties and human rights were not to differ according to national interest or ethnic traditions, nor according to religious 'preferences', political positions or even ecclesiastical offices. To assure that everyone understood their view, they deposed the Pope, John XXIII (the first), and claimed the moral superiority of a gathered representative body, of many spirits, over any single claimant to spiritual leadership.[40]

John Neville Figgis called the Council of Constance's Decree 'the most revolutionary official document in world history'.[41] However, the decree did not achieve the objectives the Council had set beforehand, nor did it succeed in spreading the moral vision it had approved . In this period the Church, seeking to impose its moral vision, legitimised its existing power upon realistic foundations, and was incapable of blocking the increasing national divisions. The existing clash between rulers, communes, assemblies and intermediaries – those military powers which had become partially autonomous – certainly did not facilitate the universalistic perspective of a sole institution, even a renewed one guided by a collegial organ. This was the political and institutional – and cultural – context that would set the historical scene for the Reformation, destined to split the Church into factions and to shock Europe.

The struggle for religious freedom, historically the most significant corollary of the Reformation's conflict between doctrines and of the clash between Luther, Calvin and the Roman Church, has often been considered to be the origin of natural rights and even of human rights altogether. Two different interpretations of this co-exist: on one side are those who believe the influence of single reformers led to the rights of man and on the other are those who instead deny that human rights share any affinity whatsoever with the Reformation's spiritual patrimony. It is however impossible to deny that Protestant sects and Calvinism had a fundamental role, through their struggles, in encouraging an intellectual climate that would be far more well-disposed to the birth of human rights.

The emphasis placed by the Reformation on the single, autonomous and responsible, person favoured the tendency toward individualism concurrently expressed in the fields of art and philosophy, science and literature, and which placed man at the centre of the universe, progressively subtracting the human being from the privileged yet subordinate relationship with God. On a political level the Reformation accentuated the need to obey authority, yet also guaranteed the possibility of opposing it when it operated illicitly, by trying to recognise, especially in Calvin's case, the reciprocal obligations that may strengthen the relations between citizens and power.

The appeal to traditional rights and to the principles of Scripture represented an important aspect of the peasant civil war that broke out in Germany immediately after the Reformation. Each freedom that the various revolts demanded was a particular one (be it freedom of movement, established by the 1525 Ortenau treaty, the religious community's freedom to elect and dismiss its pastors, or the freedom to emigrate for religious reasons included in the 1555 Peace of Augsburg), yet the more revolutionary fringes of the movement – represented by the Anabaptists – fought bitterly for religious freedom as a political claim. The Peace of Augsburg introduced the *ius reformandi*, which allowed rulers to decide which confession the citizens of their territory should follow (*cuius regio eius religio* – whose realm, his religion). These changes would conclude a century later with the Peace of Westphalia (1648), which granted – through the *ius emigrationis* – anyone the right to abandon a country incapable of guaranteeing public celebration of their religious faith.[42]

6. *Conquest and equality*

The year in which Christopher Columbus discovered America on behalf of the rulers of Spain – 1492 – is also the year of the Christian victory over the Arabs in Grenada and the year of the Jewish expulsion from Spain. It is a key date for European identity, for Europe's relations with non-Christian realities, for testing Christianity's universal reach, built by the humanist world upon Greek-Roman foundations and by ignoring Oriental influences (from Babylon to Egypt to India). After all it was precisely in Spain that Arab culture, which was now being politically erased, had produced an indelible moment for that renovation of science and philosophy – exemplified by Ibn Rushd (Averroes) – that spread from the Middle East across Europe starting in the ninth and tenth century.

It was during this period that religious justifications were first accompanied by the concept of *limpieza de sangre*, racial purity: 'Christianity and race. This is the double legacy that serves to legitimise the conquest of America.'[43] Columbus and Cortés are, to a certain degree, the symbols of this double identity: the former, an extremely capable and religious sailor, wished to carry Christianity to new populations; the latter was instead moved by the era's ruthless military logic, and despised the 'barbarians' who refused to submit to his conquest. Four centuries later, in a completely different context, this same duality would attend Rudyard Kipling's thoughtful and ambiguous reflection upon colonialism and Lord Kitchener's ferocious actions, when British colonialism was characterised by both the 'white man's burden' and the 'rational' and cynical use of the Maxim machine-gun.

Todorov, who considered the problem of 'the other' by analysing events and documents concerning the Conquest, asked how:

> can Columbus be associated with these two apparently contradictory myths, the one where the Other is a 'good-natured savage' (when observed from a distance) and the one where he is a 'dirty dog', a potential slave? The fact is that both myths are based on common foundations, the disregard of the Indians and the refusal to consider them as subjects that may share our same rights yet are different. Columbus discovered America, not the Americans.[44]

This difficulty of recognising a strong diversity without appealing to an equally consolidated hierarchical conception was part of the cultural context of the time, although it did not generate uniform behaviour. As indeed happened and continued to occur in the relations that Europe and white Christian men built with American, and later Asian and African, populations, this hierarchic conception may be based on diverse motivations, on discordant values and principles, and may produce different policies: in any case it still remains the foundation of an ideology of domination – natural or historical, religious or cultural – which eventually was bound to clash with the culture of human rights.

In Aztec culture the pre-eminence of social and community elements over personal and individual ones was far more extreme and radical than in the European Middle Ages. Aztec law formalised problems of etiquette and style, centring its attention on the relationship between man and the world, filtered by the mediation of priests or fortune-tellers, rather than on interactions between human beings. This logic welcomed human sacrifice, because 'the benefits of submission to the community's rules are far more important than the loss of an individual. Thus the victims of sacrifices would accept their fate if not joyfully, at least not with desperation, like soldiers on the battlefield: their blood would be spilled to contribute to the maintenance of society'.[45] The symbolic and ethic context within which such supremacy of society over individuals was manifested is certainly different, yet the violent and arbitrary character of the deaths cruelly inflicted on the Indians by Spanish conquerors, often for no other purpose than pleasure or full exercise of their power, are similar.

Todorov refuses the simple equation between the violence and cruelty of Aztec society and the atrocities of the Spanish conquest; he instead attempts to analyse the differences between the two societies and the reasons behind the former society privileging rituals and the latter improvisation, the former society acting upon a code and the latter according to the context; his conclusions 'speak of a society of sacrifice and a society of massacre, represented by the Aztecs and the Spanish conquerors of the Sixteenth century'.[46] Sacrifice appears to be a religious crime which involves its own community, and is committed in front of everybody in order to celebrate the official ideology; massacre is an atheist crime, carried out in distant locations and against individuals associated with beasts.

In sixteenth century Spain, theological and juridical discussions and reflections regarding the equality or inequality of all men developed, due to the practical results of the Conquest; these arguments connect directly to the doctrines of human rights, of limited sovereignty and of the contractual foundation of the state.

In 1514 the Requerimiento, written by jurist Palacios Rubios, was published, in order to inform the Indians (indeed the conquerors were supposedly obliged to read the text to the local population before each military act of conquest) of the Spanish monarchy's intention to act on the basis of both a religious and juridical legitimisation. Only by accepting the text and by adhering to its values (the fact that the Pope donated America to the Spanish crown) could the natives escape a destiny of slavery, which was described as inevitable and terrible. The memoirs left by the conquistadores concerning their actions tell that often the Requerimiento was not actually read or translated, thus arbitrarily authorising single commanders to decide whether to proceed by negotiating the conquest or by immediately and brutally subjugating local inhabitants.

Bartolomé de Las Casas was certainly the most famous opponent of the idea of inequality between men (between the Spanish and the Indians) based upon a strongly egalitarian doctrine such as Christianity, and defined the Requerimiento as an 'absurdity'. The debate between supporters of equality and those who believed in an irreconcilable difference between Spanish and American Indians took place during the first half of the sixteenth century, climaxing in 1550 in Valladolid, on the occasion of the clash between Bartolomé de Las Casas and Ginés de Sepúlveda, who had been forbidden to print a pamphlet pleading the lawfulness and legitimacy of a war against the Indians.

The immediate context for the debate was set by the conflicts and controversies which had surrounded, during the preceding two decades, military expeditions subsequent to Columbus's discovery and which involved the different forms of power structures, exploitation of human resources, territorial expansion and possession of local riches in the conquered regions. Before a commission composed of theologians and jurists Las Casas acted as prosecutor and evidently his long closing speech – which lasted five days – must have been a convincing one. Although no explicit judgement was expressed, it resulted in a ban on the publication of Sepúlveda's text.

The text referred to Aristotle's politics and to the distinction between men born free and slaves by nature, identifying in hierarchy mankind's natural character and in domination by the superior role the source of correct behaviour. Thus Sepúlveda believed it was legitimate to subjugate the inferior, to fight cannibalism and human sacrifice by any means necessary and to promote Christian religion amongst the indigenous populations through the use of military operations.

This last aspect is actually the most important characteristic of Sepúlveda's position. The act of winning over souls to the true faith has an absolute value and a social meaning that is superior to the destiny of single individuals and thus to the death of even a large number of 'faithless human beings'. Theological justification of massacre – which dates back to Saint Augustine and pervaded the whole Middle Ages – once again counters (as in the case of Aztec human sacrifices) society's common well-being, in this case European Christian society expanding to new territories, against the rights or value of single individuals.

Las Casas's Christianity was based more upon Christ than Aristotle, and summarised early Christianity's egalitarian aspects, which in the past had so strongly helped the religion to spread. His was a Christianity in which death is not justified by salvation and in which murdering somebody to save his/her soul is a mortal sin. The equality introduced by Christianity is the reason for Las Casas's opposition to slavery, which had also been condemned by the Spanish monarchy; Carlos V had declared the practice inadmissible in a 1530 ordinance and Paul III had prohibited slavery in a 1537 papal bill, stating that Indians were 'men like all others'.

7. *Theology and philosophy between war and peace*

The 1550 Valladolid discussion was strongly inspired, on a theological and juridical level, by the views of the most important Spanish theoretician of the time, Francisco de Vitoria. His thought is centred on the problem of the right war, which he considered extensively in the two *relectiones* dedicated to the Conquest, the *Relectio de Indis* (1538) and the *Relectio de iure belli* (1539), as well as in the lectures he held in Salamanca, the headquarters of the 'second Spanish school', which strongly influenced public opinion before and even after Valladolid.

As evidenced by Sepúlveda's positions, war can be considered necessary and natural, or, as in Erasmus, Thomas More and in some ways also in Luther, it may be seen as opposed to Christian doctrine and thus a solution that should be avoided in every possible way. Vitoria, while recognising the complexity of the theme, attempted to restore, with unprecedented depth of analysis, the tradition of 'right war', by studying the limits that exist when starting a war and the bonds that involve those who fight it. It is not by coincidence that today his works have regained much attention and that many attempts have been made to actualise his positions.

> While it is traditional to examine Vitoria's thought in terms of the development of theories of the just war, it is also possible to deal with his work in terms of what we would now call humanitarian intervention, that is the right, perhaps even the responsibility, of Christians to punish violations of the natural law or to raise a primitive society to civilised status, in other words to intervene in another state for the welfare of those who live there.[47]

Vitoria's complex arguments for the Spanish conquerors' right to subjugate the Indians, the opportunity that they have to rebel, and the authority that should determine solutions for complicated moral and juridical questions constitute problems that concern 'conflicting rights and responsibilities [...] if the value of humanitarian good imposed outweighs the costs involved'.[48] The Salamanca theologian's convictions that human beings formed a single community and that the Pope[49] had no rights over secular questions, that the emperor was not *dominus totius orbis* and that there was no such thing as the right to discovery, did not prevent him from accepting that 'in lawful defence of the innocent from unjust death, even without the pope's authority the Spaniards may prohibit the barbarians from practicing any nefarious costume or rite'.[50]

However the interpretation of these arguments as 'a universal responsibility for each for the well being of one another and, apparently, the right to intervene whenever other people are engaging in practices deemed "nefarious"'[51] appears to owe too much to actualisation, and may lead to a misunderstanding of the meaning of Vitoria's reflections and of the conscious complexity and ambiguity of his statements. Massacre, as Todorov stated, is no less 'ill-omened' than human sacrifice or even cannibalism (considered, unlike sacrifice, 'unnatural') yet is justified within a different moral and symbolic order. Vitoria deems possible a right to defend those who, because of craziness or stupidity, like the Indians, have not been capable of governing and have led many innocent people to death. The basic problem lies in the fact that the judgement of craziness or innocence, stupidity or tyranny, is not founded upon objective and verifiable parameters, but instead on postulates and criteria determined, in this case, by the Spanish. Thus the conquerors – as Vitoria states in what is probably the weakest point of his reflections – become the judges of a conflict they themselves are involved in, yet it is their own ideological horizon that deems human sacrifice worse than the massacres they have indiscriminately committed.

Certainly Vitoria appears uncertain as to whether he can justify the Spanish intervention, yet he also believes it is impossible to condemn his state's claim to conquer the New World. Thus, once again according to an actualising interpretation of his works, 'his discussion underscored the great gulf between morally acceptable justifications for intervention and the actual consequences on the ground. It also reflected the gulf between intellectual theorising about the responsibilities of an imperial power and the actual practices of the agents of the empire on the frontier.'[52]

Vitoria's views, which refuse to consider the rejection of Christian faith or the practice of acts against nature (cannibalism, incest, sodomy) sufficient justifications for war, are highly original in their attribution 'to states of the role of subjects of international law', and in identifying the guiding principle of the *ius gentium* in 'the right to free circulation of people and goods', in the name of a 'universal degree of kinship' between men. Alongside the right to commerce Vitoria speaks of the right to preach and announce the Gospel, although the former is a natural right, while the latter is a divine right. 'Vitoria introduces the concept of right war in this context of rights of people intended as populations – not as individuals - which must maintain reciprocal relations, based upon natural friendship and mutual interest, in order to exchange riches, persons and ideas'.[53]

In recognising that every republic and prince has the power to declare a war, Vitoria lists the causes that are not sufficient for the proclamation of a conflict (religious diversity, territorial conquest, personal ambition and glory), maintaining as a possible justification the avenging of an insult; he also states that in war only one side fights legitimately. As for the modalities of combat (*ius in bello*), he enumerates possible actions and confronts delicate questions such as the killing of innocent people (allowed if not intentional), the extermination of the enemy (legitimate in certain cases), the killing of prisoners (excluded from the list of acceptable actions) and the customs of looting and sacking conquered cities (tolerated in certain circumstances). Thus his works 'fit in the realm of right war's tradition because of arguments that clearly distinguish him from "pacifists" such as Erasmus yet also from "war-mongers" such as Sepúlveda', and identify the decisive element in the *'vindicta iniuriam acceptam* which, despite Vitoria's declared intentions of reducing war's excesses and horrors, may become a strong instrument to legitimise war itself'.[54]

The Salamanca school founded its position on a concept of universality which included the right of nature, owned by Christians as much as by barbarians. The right of nature was conceived as an inherent property of man that not even the lack or the refusal of faith could destroy. This was considered the basis of equality between all men, the foundation of their parity and of the comprehensive unity of mankind.

> 'Thus Vitoria's reflection places itself somewhere between the medieval *ius gentium* and the *ius publicum europeum* of the new-born states: it recognises the existence of moral and theological bonds that are more than merely political to the Prince's actions, yet it does not identify an authority with the *vis et auctoritas* to make such principles and bonds respected.'[55]

The recognition of the lack of an international juridical power, a judge *super partes* – solved unconvincingly by Vitoria by assigning all judgement upon the legitimacy of a right war to the king himself – marks the crisis of a model based upon the authority of the Church. This was the era of the Conquest of the New World, yet also the era of the Reformation, of the clash between Christian powers for religious motivations and because of rising nationalisms (the conflict between Carlos V and Francis I), the era of the sack of Rome by 'barbarian landsknechts' serving Christian princes and of the menace of Ottoman expansion.

> The abandonment of the theological-moral and cosmopolitical premises of the medieval doctrine of *iustum bellum* created the context for the affirmation, in seventeenth-century Europe, of an 'interstate international law'. Seeing that the absence of a universal moral authority would lead all contenders to consider their war a right war – *bellum utriquem iustum* – interstate (and no longer cosmopolitan) law concentrated its attention exclusively on formal and procedural regulations.[56]

8. *Natural law and international law*

It was during the seventeenth century, the so-called 'iron century', that the culture of human rights accelerated in its development, thus moving toward its more coherent expressions in the following century. At the very beginning of the seventeenth century a young Delft-born lawyer, twenty-one year old Hugo de Groot – later known as Hugo Grotius – who had been practicing for only five years, was asked to defend the United Company of Amsterdam. One of the Company's captains, Jacob van Heemskerk, had captured the *Santa Catarina*, a Portuguese vessel, because he was convinced that, even without an authorisation from the Company or from his government, the war between the Netherlands on the one side and Spain and Portugal on the other authorised the use of military strength.

During 1604 and 1605 Grotius prepared a treatise (*De Indis*) which, starting from this particular case, aimed to identify the general foundations of the laws of war. The work was not printed because the Company won the case and had no further interest in seeing it published. Five years later, however, the treatise merged into a new text (*Mare liberum*), devoted to the principle of 'freedom of the seas', an idea which reflected the hopes of Dutch merchants, who were interested in exploiting their nautical possibilities and in interrupting the other major powers' (Britain above all) monopoly. It was an Englishman, John Selden, who most vehemently attempted to oppose the idea that the sea could be conquered like any other territory (*Mare clausum*). It was, however, only at the beginning of the eighteenth century that Cornelius Bynkershoek, in his *De dominio maris* (1702), established that the sea tract under each state's dominion was to be considered only the water that could be reached by cannon fire, and thus defended.

Grotius's career proceeded, as a general lawyer for the Dutch tax office and later as mayor of Rotterdam, until his legal opinion was requested once more, this time regarding the religious dispute between Jacobus Arminius, a theologian in Leiden, and the reformed Calvinist Church represented by Franciscus Gomarus. The result was the 1613 edict that temporarily halted the conflict: basing himself on a principle of tolerance, which had been present for at least a century in the United Provinces, Grotius stated that each private conscience could choose its own doctrine, as long as public faith in the existence of God and his Providence was guaranteed.

Although Grotius's position was victorious on a juridical level it was defeated politically when the prince of Orange, Maurice of Nassau, decided to break the truce: his adversary, Oldenbarnevelt, was put to death and Grotius was condemned to a life sentence in the castle of Loevestein. He escaped to Paris in 1621, hidden in a crate full of books, and after obtaining a pension from Louis XIII he published the apologetic text *De veritate religionis christianae* and continued to write the first three books of the *De iure belli ac pacis*, which he had began to work upon during his imprisonment. In 1625 the Dutch jurist 'put forward a notion of rights that was applicable to all of mankind, not just one country or legal tradition. He defined "natural rights" as something self-possessed and conceivable separately from God's will. He also suggested that people could use their rights – unaided by religion – to establish the contractual foundations of social life.'[57]

According to Grotius, natural rights give birth to civil rights. They are an indissoluble part of man's ethic and rational nature, and would remain such even if God did not exist. Through the state contract man delegates to law a relevant, yet not absolute, part of his freedom. The law – *ius* – relates to every individual, although it is above all through the state, which men have trusted to contractually manage their natural rights, that fundamental rights are guaranteed and protected. Political authority is no longer legitimised by God – directly through Scriptures or via the Church – as it is now based upon a union of individuals, whose natural rights have been partially transferred to the state, allowing it to create laws and transform the inherent natural rights of all men into civil rights for its citizens. Amongst these rights is property, the paradigm for equality between men; yet in Grotius the most important rights are life, the body, freedom and honour.

The Thirty Years' War between the Netherlands and Spain and between European Catholic and Protestant nations forms the background for Grotius's reflections on war. By developing Vitoria's position within a more open contextual and historical situation,

Grotius elaborates the theory of right war, which he conceives as legitimate for reasons of self-defence, for avenging insults and as a form of punishment: the Dutch jurist analyses the behavioural regulations governments should undertake which should be observed and respected by all contenders.

Samuel Pufendorf, a German student of Grotius who became the first teacher of 'natural law' within the University of Heidelberg, in 'his most important work, the *De iure naturae et gentium* (1672), defined man as 'an ethically free being and as the bearer of a dignity that associates him with all other human beings.'[58] Dignity allows man to reach a state different from all other living beings and is an integral part of the freedom man owns upon being born into the state of nature, as an equal to all other men. Dignity and equality necessarily create a form of sociability between human beings that leads to each man permitting or demanding the same treatment he would expect for himself, and to cooperating with other men in each situation that does not imply an individual disadvantage for him.

Grotius, a citizen of the United Provinces, was particularly concerned with questions related to maritime commerce and religious tolerance, and with the conflicts caused by these issues; Pufendorf, a citizen of the empire trying to influence the enlightened Germanic bureaucracy, is concerned with the conciliation of imperial unity with the Princes' partial autonomy from the Emperor. Thus he believes that on an institutional level the search for cooperation – the only solution for man to maintain peace – is inevitable, just like sociability between individuals.

Both in relationships with his citizens and with other states, the ruler must conform to the fundamental laws deriving from natural rights (for example with regard to the freedom of religious conscience), although he may intervene, if necessary, within the sphere of individual freedom (censorship, taxation, even expropriation). If the objective is the peaceful coexistence between men and states, the law must protect and promote this goal through a system made up of reciprocal duties and rights. Thus 'the strong impact of Pufendorf's works upon the reflections on human rights and rights of citizens is evident, for example, within the codes of enlightened absolutism and in the juridical and political thoughts it gave birth to in eighteenth century Europe.'[59]

This interweaving of natural law theories and contractual ones found its turning point in the works of John Locke. Individual freedom, even if limited by law, cannot coincide with an organic vision of society, as qualitatively superior to its members and thus able to subjugate them and excessively bind their freedom. If all individuals, independently from their social or cultural conditions, own 'perfect freedom' and 'uncontrolled enjoyment' of rights and privileges given by the law of nature, in a way that is 'equal to all other men', this principle must be true for populations as well, and thus no population can be superior to another.

Thus it is the governments that must safeguard and protect the rights of single individuals, for this was the purpose of men forming societies and contractually instituting the state. The government's eventual non-fulfilment of this objective gives birth to the right to resist, as a governmental violation of natural rights immediately dissolves the contract with the citizens. 'Such an argument for individual freedom rights, of course, was not only revolutionary in an age of entrenched privilege, but remains so in much of the world to this day.'[60]

9. *Rights and revolution*

In 1679 Locke began writing 'one of the most influential political treatises of all times'.[61] This was the *Second Tract of Government*, in which he most thoroughly summarised the idea of the state of nature and consequent political theory. During that same year the Habeas Corpus Act was promulgated in England, which elaborated, in modern terms, the protection and forms of guarantee citizens could enjoy upon being arrested or being submitted to a criminal trial. In absence of a written order nobody could be arrested, and the longest period of imprisonment before appearing in front of a judge was declared to be 20 days. Around 50 years earlier, in 1628, many revolts and protests had surrounded the Petition of Right, strongly supported by Sir Edward Coke, which protested, in the name of the common man, against arbitrary arrests and demanded parliamentary consensus for the institution of new taxes, the defence of Habeas Corpus and the end of arbitrary interferences in the rights to property. This was the beginning of the English revolution, of a socially and religiously characterised civil war, of violent confrontations between groups and factions and of a questioning of royal authority which would culminate in the execution of King Charles I in 1649. The country then went from parliamentary power to Oliver Cromwell's dictatorship, initially legitimated by Parliament itself, to the eventual restoration of Charles II. These were the fundamental landmarks of a conflict involving a bitter and in-depth argument about power and regulations, law and authority. The 1647 'Putney debates' on universal suffrage and popular sovereignty still appear extremely modern today. The debates gave birth, within Cromwell's New Model Army, to a democratic-radical group, the Levellers, which took the conviction regarding human equality to its extreme consequences: their goal was a society in which all men shared the same rights and duties, first of all on a political level, without any census-based or religious forms of discrimination.

Ten years after the Habeas Corpus Act, in 1689, the Bill of Rights was published, the conclusive moment of the 'glorious revolution' that gave birth to the reformatory principles later included in every constitution and declaration of rights. The principles expressed so concretely and coherently in the bill were innovative ones: limits to the power of a monarchy that was to be subjected to parliamentary decisions, certainty and impartiality of law and security of property, free elections to create a representative government, freedom of speech and religious tolerance, fair trials in the presence of a jury and the prohibition of cruel and unusual punishments. The document also referred, both for rhetorical reasons and the necessity of legitimisation, to those ancient and unquestionable rights English citizens had already obtained, which were now being protected from violations by the state's rulers. The guarantee of impunity for citizens who signed petitions also constituted a fundamental land-mark in guaranteeing free citizens' participation in parliamentary works and political life in general.

The request for religious freedom by different sects, in a continent struck by religious wars, was somewhat inevitable; the push to realise the theory of natural rights within a request for an active electorate, capable of ratifying the proclaimed equality, was instead far less obvious. Amongst the figures who strengthened the link between demands for religious tolerance and the request for civil rights was the poet John Milton, a Puritan and a humanist, as well as Cromwell's collaborator and tutor.

> Milton proclaimed man's right to self-determination. The objective of the 'limited contract' was, in his opinion, the protection of rights as much as the well-being of the community. The state found its limit in law, superimposed upon it. Milton defined various civil and religious rights of freedom, organically connected to each other. The triad of life, freedom and property, which every English free man had enjoyed since remote times, in virtue of the founding con-tract of the state (stipulated between the king and his subjects), was integrated by the request for a freedom of religion and of conscience that was no longer to include only Catholics.[62]

During the first English revolution, Thomas Hobbes also addressed the issue of natural rights, providing a very different interpretation, especially in the conclusions he drew. In reality the difference lies within the type of pact – or contract – Hobbes believed each man has established with other men. The submission to the ruler, required by the pact, is accompanied by the loss of natural rights in the name of self-conservation of the species and of single individuals, although each citizen may refuse to obey orders contrary to morality and nature. Thus in Hobbes the contractual state becomes an absolute state, where the ruler has full authority even if he must protect his citizens, who may feel free from the pact if the king does not fulfil his duties. Natural rights are not inalienable, as they were in Grotius or Milton; indeed citizens must entrust such rights to an entity other than themselves (the state, the ruler) if they are to become a part of a civil and political community. The social contract is the moment in which man dispossesses himself of his *status naturalis* in order to live in society, and is accompanied by the loss of natural rights, which are collectively transferred to the state.

However, the importance Hobbes attributed to the individual led him to also hypothesise a subjective right that could coexist – as a guarantee – with the absolute state's coercive public sphere, as established by the law. It was upon this individualistic vision of rights that Locke insisted, deeming – differently from Hobbes – that natural law remains binding even after the social contract's stipulation. 'Property' is, in Locke, the synthesis of the right of nature, as it includes life and freedom, as well as patrimony; yet as it is valid for free men, it is not compatible with slavery, if the slaves have been subjugated during a 'right' war.

It is clear that the context of the 'iron century', with its civil and religious conflicts, influenced the philosophical and juridical debate; yet the debate was also strongly influenced by the rapid ascendancy of a bourgeoisie which based its rights of property upon work and enterprise rather than on hereditary succession. Thus the setting for the realisation of seventeenth-century rights theories was created by social changes which accompanied the rise of the small nobility and of the rural bourgeoisie, the so-called *gentry*, as well as by cultural changes, represented in Britain by the Puritans, who were later to lead the revolution.

10. *Modern state and absolute state*

The modern state, which emerged in Europe between the seventeenth and eighteenth centuries, saw a strengthening of the rulers' prerogatives and the development and growth of public institutions (the army, tax offices and the monopoly of violence in the name of citizens' security). The modern state did not have a unique model and the way it developed in England was different from France, just as the Dutch experience was different from the German one. The push toward absolutism came less from theories and ideas – which, on the contrary, were more often oriented to limit the ruler's powers – than from the necessity of a state organisation capable of simultaneously bearing the weight of internal clashes and international conflicts; even if the English case demonstrates how dangerous it can be to upset the balance of relationships of power between various degrees of authority, and how social transformations are reflected inevitably within political battles and introduce new historical actors.

Even in its most coherent and compact expressions, the absolute state is a state 'limited' by law, by rights, by the *iura et privilegia* of individuals, of social classes, of bodies; ancient regime societies are not the realms of that will that certain antique 'liberal' apologetics opposed to the new 'rational' order of nineteenth-century codes. There is no longer a confrontation between non-reason and reason, disorder and order: instead profoundly diverse attitudes and values come in contact with each other and clash: between the seventeenth and eighteenth century a new vision of the subject, of rights and of sovereignty started to develop and a new 'discourse of citizenship' gave birth to a condition of insurgence, the foundation of the expression 'state of law'.[63]

Within absolute states, the seventeenth and eighteenth centuries marked not only the introduction of powerful and articulated thoughts, which Kant, defining the Enlightenment, called 'humanity's exit from intellectual minority'; this period also saw the creation of a civil society capable of interacting with high culture and with political and international options, a society whose public opinion was forged in theatres and squares, in marketplaces and in courtrooms. Lynn Hunt, in her exceptional reconstruction of the 'invention' of human rights questioned how 'these men, living in societies built on slavery, subordination and seemingly natural subservience, ever come to imagine men not at all like them and, in some cases, women too, as equals?'[64] The self-evidence of equality between human beings, reaffirmed in all major declarations preceding the 1948 Universal one, was born on a historical level in the context of the absolute state and of Enlightenment, of the English revolution and of the 'iron century' conflicts. If on one hand the consideration of rights as founded upon nature appears comprehensible, especially if we think of the role of Christianity, on the other it was hard to imagine that such rights would be considered the same for everyone and valid in any location, given that the society of the time was based on strong hierarchies, exclusion, discrimination and marginalisation that affected large portions of the population.

Hunt states that, in order to gain a common language and shared feelings, equality between human beings, and thus between the rights they could and should enjoy, had to affect more than just the intellect.

> Human rights are difficult to pin down because their definition, indeed their very existence, depends on emotions as much as on reason. The claim of self-evidence relies ultimately on an emotional appeal; it is convincing if it strikes a chord within each person [...] Philosophical ideas, legal traditions, and revolutionary politics had to have this kind of inner emotional reference point for human rights to be truly self-evident.[65]

By analysing a large number of studies concerning the high and low literature of the period, the American historian identified an increasing presence, in the most widespread texts of the time, of autonomy and empathy, characteristics that we may find in the protagonists of short stories and novels of that particular historical moment, yet also features that could probably be observed in daily life. 'I believe that social and political change – in this case, human rights – comes about because many individuals had similar experiences, not because they all inhabited the same social context but because through their interactions with each other and with their reading and viewing, they actually created a new social context.'[66] These few words clarify how complex, articulated, yet fundamentally unitary history's progress is: new and original ideas, great personalities and exceptional situations would mean nothing if their influence and role were not based upon a vast and widespread social and cultural foundation, capable of acknowledging and communicating elaborated ideas and projects.

The English, the French and the British settlers in America now had far more opportunities to come into contact with a culture of rights, because of the increasing importance particular rights (English free men for example) were earning; but also due to the fact that they could recognise themselves in other people's experiences, shared aspirations, worries, anxieties and desires for freedom and self-realisation. This profound social and cultural, even psychological, result of that individualistic culture, born in the seventeenth century, is what allowed the slow, uncertain and as yet incomplete, shift towards the conviction of equality in front of God and to the acceptance of equal rights to be shared on earth.

The culture of rights is the result, and at the same time the accelerator, of a time which saw the birth of capitalism and the affirmation of the bourgeoisie and middle classes – to begin with in the cultural and economic spheres, and successively in the institutional and political ones; a time in which the public sphere gave increasing importance, in the press and in its salons, to the demands of the emerging classes; in which the nuclear family was, slowly yet decisively, substituted in cities by patriarchal families, thus feeding an individualism which also affected the condition of women. The moral emulation created by literature in this new, well-read, emerging class aimed to reconcile the construction of a new ethical horizon with the daily practices of civil life. 'Readers learned to appreciate the emotional intensity of the ordinary and the capacity of people like themselves to create on their own a moral world. Human rights grew out of the seedbed sowed by these feelings. Human rights could only flourish when people learned to think of others as their equals, as like them in a certain fundamental fashion.'[67]

Personal autonomy in daily life was the equivalent of the individualism theorised by Locke and Milton, inserted into a no longer medieval idea of community: a modern one, which found its cohesion in work and social relations, rather than uniquely in religion. This community aspired, as in the English revolution, to be both represented and recognised. Thus 'the individual is lifted from the logics of belonging, of connection to other bodies, so that he may be represented as a unitary subject with needs and rights, defined by the parameters of freedom and equality'.[68] It is no co-incidence that Voltaire's *Traité sur la Tolérance à l'occasion de la mort de Jean Calas* (1763), which in Europe soon became a manifesto for enlightened ideas on human rights, was written in relation to an event still strongly anchored to the question of the body – the death sentence and torture of a Toulouse citizen accused of murdering his son to prohibit him from converting to Catholicism.

Law is the foundation of power only if it does not preclude the development of freedom; this became even clearer in Montesquieu, who identified the division of powers as the most efficacious instrument to guarantee maximum freedom within the law. To treat man as a man in every circumstance: this was the maxim by which Montesquieu fought slavery and studied limitations to the right of war. In many of the *Encyclopédie*'s entries we can find, even if not defined explicitly, the fundamental rights Mirabeau would soon summarise in the development of the person, of property, of economic freedom and of security before the law.

Chapter Two
The Discovery of Rights

1. The defence of the body

Midway through the eighteenth century, the twenty-six year old Milanese Marquis Cesare Beccaria upset the world of justice and penal organisation with a short and powerful text, destined to endure through time and maintain its real and polemical strength even today. *On Crimes and Punishment*, first published in 1764, is the finest contribution of the Lombard Enlightenment to the European intellectual world, as well as the only Italian book of the time comparable to the works of Voltaire and the French Enlightenment writers, whose success certainly contributed to its dissemination.

In eighteenth century Europe the juridical system, penal law and treatment of criminals were still dominated by a ferociously repressive culture, permeated by arbitrary decisions and barbarity. Deprivations of personal freedom – sometimes of property and even of one's life – were based in most cases on evidence that was hardly solid, such as anonymous accusations or dubious testimonies; the judges' discretion was practically total, as was their tendency to be corrupted and to judge on the basis of social class affiliations. The punishment of criminals was a bloody public spectacle, in which the excess of violence served to exalt the power of justice, frightening spectators and warning them not to challenge the law's vengeance and punishments.

Habeas corpus – the protection against arbitrary arrests and the guarantee to be judged by a trial of equal citizens and on the basis of certain laws – although included as a principle in the *Magna Carta* by John of England (1215) and by Henry III (1225), and actually introduced only in 1679 (Habeas Corpus Act), was in truth still unapplied in the whole of continental Europe and largely unused even in England, where it had been codified. It must also be noted that habeas corpus was not, however, an idealised defence of the body and its sacredness – at the time only the king's body was considered sacred – but rather a protection against arbitrary behaviour by the police, guaranteed by a magistrate system that had only partially freed itself from political power.

Beccaria wrote his short treatise against the mechanisms of the epoch's juridical system and penal law, against abuses and cruelties, arbitrary behaviour and caprices, against a lack of rationality which horrified and disturbed enlightened thinkers. Even though he had earned a law degree in Pavia six years earlier, in 1758, the young Beccaria was not an expert on juridical questions, nor did he have an in-depth knowledge of the penitentiary system. It was Pietro Verri, economist and philosopher, as well as founder of the *Accademia dei Pugni* and of the journal *Il Caffè* – which owed its name to the meeting place and centre of the Italian Enlightenment – who advised him during his work on the text. Beccaria was also helped by Pietro's brother, Alessandro Verri, also a founder and participant in the famous Milanese circle, who worked as a 'protector of prisoners' and was thus able to provide his friend with important information and suggestions.

Three years after obtaining his degree Cesare Beccaria had broken off relations with his family, as a result of his marriage to a girl of humble origins, Teresa Blasco, with whom he would later have a daughter, Giulia - Alessandro Manzoni's mother. The friendship with the Verri brothers (later on Pietro would also help Cesare partially to repair his family relationships) was cemented by their common battle for the spread of enlightened ideas, as well as by relationships and fertile intellectual exchanges with the French *philosophes* who were revolutionising contemporary culture through the *Encyclopédie* of D'Alembert and Diderot, and who were trying to make radical reforms, courageous changes and ambitious transformations to political life.

On Crimes and Punishment is not a theoretical reflection; it is a systematic criticism of the prevalent systems for the administration of justice in the eighteenth century. Beccaria's strongest intellectual debt, which he explicitly references in the introduction, is to Montesquieu (his *Esprit des Lois* had been published in 1748 and revised in 1758), yet he also makes constant reference to the *Contrat Social* by Jean-Jacques Rousseau, which had been published a year before Cesare began writing *On Crimes and Punishment* (1762). According to the rational and utilitarian vision he adhered to, in Beccaria the objective of the law is to guarantee freedom and security to the greatest number of people possible. This position is clearly bound to the conviction, shared by all eighteenth century reformers, that power should realise the common interest, exemplified by the search for public happiness.

Thus the punishment of criminals should not be characterised, as it was for many centuries, by a vindictive, violent and spectacular nature.

Punishment is founded upon the 'need to defend the deposit of public well-being from particular usurpations',[69] and only the legislator – not a judge's arbitrary decision – may 'decree punishments for crimes'.[70] There must be a balance between crimes and punishments, which should be measured by the damage caused to the community ('to the nation') rather than by criminal intent. This is why, according to Beccaria, the most serious crimes are the ones involving 'lese-majesty' (betrayal of or revolt against the state), followed by those 'against the security' and property of individuals; the least serious are those which menace citizens' social peace and tranquility.

The object of punishment should be the prevention of further crimes. The deterrent character of punishment should not derive from its violent and terrorising form – as the public's horror in the face of the condemned criminals' sufferings fades away after just a few days – and should instead be based upon its certainty and inevitability, as well as on the rapidity of its execution. Potential criminals are discouraged less by 'the cruelty of punishments' than by 'their inevitability'.[71]

Within this context, and starting from the position that 'the goal of punishment is not to torment and afflict a living being, nor to undo a crime that has already been committed,[72] Beccaria considers two questions that are still central today in the debate over human rights: torture and the death sentence.

Torture, 'a cruelty consecrated by use in most nations', cannot solve the basic dilemma of justice in any way: 'whether the crime is certain or it is uncertain; if it is certain, the only correct punishment is established by the law, and all further torments are useless, because the culprit's confession is useless; if it is uncertain, an innocent person should not be tormented, as according to the law he is a man whose crimes have not been proven to exist'.[73] Just as the idea that torture may prevent further crimes, or help to discover accomplices to criminal acts, is undemonstrated and actually contradicted by experience, so is the irregular search for the culprit's confession absurd and in reality not aided by torture, given the fact that an individual is 'so barely free to speak the truth between spasms and suffering'.[74] In this 'infamous' search for truth Beccaria sees a legacy of the 'primitive' legislation of the times arising from the judgement of God; just as the conviction that torture may purge an individual of infamy, the idea that a confession of sins is part of the 'mysterious tribunal of penitence' also derives from religion. In truth 'torture itself is a real infamy towards its victim. Thus this method will cancel one infamy through another infamy'.[75] Beccaria reminds his readers that the ancient Romans only allowed torture to be carried out on slaves, who were denied dignity as persons and citizens; and that in contemporary Europe torture was prohibited in England by common law and had been abolished in Sweden (for common crimes, not for political ones) as well as by 'one of the wisest rulers of Europe', Frederick II of Prussia, a friend and correspondent of the *philosophes*, who, in 1740, had effectively abolished torture upon ascending to the throne at only twenty-eight.

Regarding the death sentence, Beccaria does not consider it to be legitimate or necessary, nor does he view it as useful or right. He states that it may be considered necessary only in two exceptional cases: to safeguard national security and as a defence against a 'dangerous revolution', in those moments in which 'the nation recovers or loses its freedom, or during a time of anarchy, when disorders themselves act as laws'. Laws are the result of small deprivations of individual freedom, in order to represent 'the general will, which is the aggregate of particulars. Whoever wants to leave the arbitrary decision to murder himself to other men? How can the sacrifice of the greatest of all goods, life, be included in the minimum sacrifice of each individual's freedom?[76] Beccaria does not agree with the hypothesis, based on logic and secular experience, that the death sentence may 'dissuade others from committing crimes', as in reality it 'becomes a spectacle for many and an object of compassion and indignation for others; both such feelings occupy spectators' souls more than the healthy terror the law seeks to inspire'.[77]

The death sentence is an atrocity that adds to the spilling of blood during periods of war, when the task of the laws should be to favour moderation, 'to lead men to the maximum happiness or to the minimum unhappiness possible'.[78] For the deterrence of potential crimes, deprivation of freedom is far more useful than the death sentence, given that 'the intention of perpetual slavery, substituted for the death sentence, has all that is necessary to remove any determined disposition'.[79]

In Beccaria prevention is far better than punishment, and thus well-organised governments should invest in education rather than in repression. His passionate – though expressed in logical and rational language – aversion to torture and the death sentence, in the name of public utility and happiness, merges into the more general struggle against arbitrary juridical decisions and in favour of a law built around man; a law taken out of any claimed sacredness, and based on the simple but explosive statement that 'there is no freedom every time the law allows a man to stop being a person and to become a thing in relation to certain events'.[80]

2. *The enlightened ideas*

Beccaria's attempt to separate, once and for all, crimes and punishments from the idea of sin and atonement, remains one of the most significant moments of the Enlightenment's struggle to transform political and social reality; to translate into real reforms the ideas, values and principles that enlightened thinkers fought for all over Europe, against the conservatism and privileges of the nobility and against the obscurantism of a Church which now feared for its ideological and moral supremacy. Of course it was no coincidence that these powers (the aristocracy and the Church) were extremely hostile to Beccaria's text and any realisation of his proposals.

The last thirty years of the eighteenth century and the first decades of the nineteenth century were distinguished by many significant experiments in the field of penal law reform, which certainly owed much to Cesare Beccaria's ideas, and, more generally, to the cultural climate the Enlightenment created in the European and North American societies and within some of the more dynamic courts of the old continent. The strongest example was the penal code introduced, in 1786, in the Grand Duchy of Tuscany by Leopold II – the ninth son of Maria Theresa of Austria and Francis I – which completely eliminated torture and for the first time abolished the death sentence, even for murderers and crimes of lese-majesty.

It was mainly thanks to the Enlightenment, which favoured a historic vision of man and his nature on one hand and of rights and their formulations on the other, that the language of rights became increasingly widespread in the second half of the eighteenth century. Man, removed from divine arbitration, was placed in the natural world, where he was considered to be capable of building his own culture and history. By elaborating upon the results gained in the seventeenth century from 'natural' law and with the construction of the modern state, the Enlightenment accentuated the idea of man as a subject of rights, and attempted to dispose of the theory of the divine right of kings and of national interest as predominant over the 'interests' and rights of citizens.

The long journey towards freedom of conscience, which had begun with the struggle for religious tolerance, had a new important landmark in Voltaire's Enlightenment: not only because tolerance was indicated as the foundation of all human rights, but also because the separation of the political sphere from the religious one was denoted a prerequisite for peace and progress. In Voltaire freedom of opinion and expression became the concrete realisations of the more general and abstract principle of freedom as recognition of individual diversities. However, the freedom of individuals, which guarantees the transformation from subjects to citizens, must also apply to the public sphere. 'Thus the exercise of freedom is limited by the need for *universality* and the sacred, which left behind dogmas and relics, and is now entrapped in these newly recognised "rights of man" [...] The request for equality derives from universality.'[81]

It is no coincidence that Montesquieu's constitutionalist struggle for the division of powers, Beccaria's battle for the centrality of the law and Voltaire's fight for tolerance and individual rights were all part of a new discourse on rights – that should also include Rousseau's reflections on the general will and popular sovereignty – which was transforming eighteenth century thoughts and customs and was destined to find its explosive, yet ambiguous and contradictory, realisation in the great revolutions (the American and French) at the end of the century. Rousseau opposes a *general will*, which 'acknowledges differences' and that should be 'understood as equality before the law'[82] to the *will of everyone*, a sum of particular wills expected to be unanimous – and according to him this 'will of everybody contains the seed of a totalitarian intention'.

The *philosophes'* ideas were also strongly related to the scientific debates of the period, whose protagonists were Linneo (whose *Sistema naturae* was published in 1735) and Buffon (whose *Histoire naturelle* was published in 36 volumes between 1749 and 1789), with their classification of man within the natural world and the historicising of nature itself. Their findings greatly contributed to the expulsion of the divine and the metaphysical from reflections on humanity, the dignity of the person and the rights of men and citizens.

The idea of a universal process of civilisation through which, in the progression from a savage condition to a civil one, mankind slowly conquers his essence, was a widespread conviction amongst enlightened thinkers – despite differences in the interpretation of the idea of a 'state of nature' preceding human history and society. Enlightened thinkers also shared the idea that during this civilising process mankind historicises and makes cultural a 'nature' which is transformed and contextualised within this journey towards progress as a result of the social contract.

The freedom of each individual to satisfy his own needs, in the state of nature, signifies that only subjective rights exist, yet there is no objective right that is universally valid. These subjective rights (the private sphere) are those that mankind must – partially – give up, in the social contract, in order to have a ruler, or a state (the legal sphere) capable of guaranteeing self-conservation and the search for peace amongst men. The construction of the political system and of the law – objective rights – guarantees the widest enjoyment of each individual's natural or subjective rights. Between these two spheres, a third one exists:

public or social, strongly characterised by norms and values, which however concede a certain degree of freedom [...] for example moral rules, pressures exercised by fashion or by the spirit of the times, or even religious prescriptions (thus it represents the same area once dominated by spiritual power). The map of these three areas changes according to each country and historical period, yet everyone agrees on the necessity to distinguish them and to establish their limits.[83]

The birth of civil rights is, substantially, the way in which the political system (the state) guarantees rights (both natural and subjective) of freedom and property thanks to the law, within an increasingly complex world, characterised, due to progress and evolution within the social contract, by an increasing inequality between men. The modern state, in truth the 'revolutionary state' of the late eighteenth century, will offer a 'positive' guarantee, represented by the law, of the natural subjective rights of a larger number of persons; such a 'positive' guarantee is potentially universal.

The social contract, as interpreted by Locke, constituted the voluntary union of men – equal in the state of nature – willing to give up part of their freedom in order to receive protection of their lives, their freedom and their property from the government. The Scottish Enlightenment thinkers (Francis Hutcheson and Thomas Reid) instead presupposed the existence of a hierarchic society, in which inequality was necessary for the underlining of each individual's duties and the moral obligations that favour and strengthen social harmony.

If in the Scottish Enlightenment's ideas the 'unequal' character of development (the increase in social and cultural inequalities) is a structural element of the process of civilisation – which necessitates a strategy of education and progress in order to guarantee social balance and the spread of rights for everyone – in Rousseau's radicalism the social contract must make a further step, guaranteeing and creating equality between all who have adhered to it by transferring their rights (totally or partially) to the community and the state. 'In other words, the state substitutes the natural equality lost by mankind in the historical process with a moral equality. In this situation, the common condition of individuals, who are both subjects and citizens, guarantees the same rights to everyone.'[84]

Thus it is within the political context, the horizon of the state, that rights are individuated and realised, and that precise answers are formulated with regard to the need for freedom and property in general, with all the consequences implied by the institution with clear limits against violations of other individuals' rights. The source of the law, however, remains human society, and inalienable rights – indicated by the various 'revolutions' or by philosophical and juridical proposals – are based on the premise of human equality and on a universal 'reason' shared by all men: human beings are born equal, enjoy the same natural rights, belong to the same order of nature and to the same species.

The defence of freedom, the foundation of civil societies, cannot be solved within a single state order, or in a single nation. This is what pushed Kant to go beyond the political horizon and speak of *ius cosmopoliticum*, within which anyone, even the Other, even citizens of other states or nations, becomes a recognised owner of the same rights, a 'subject' of rights on our own level, on the basis of the principle of universal hospitality. The new enlightened concept of 'human dignity' is that of personal freedom, of the independence and autonomy of each person, guaranteed by its own essence and by the agreement between all men (the social contract), rather than by God and by religions. Its consequence is the legitimacy, almost the necessity, of struggles to eliminate all forms of slavery, servitude, submission, dependency, yet also all privileges, immunities, concessions and advantages. Freedom cannot be realised without being given to everyone, or without equality.

The widespread diffusion of the language of rights, of a culture based on rights and of the twin ideals of freedom and equality, required a radical transformation of ideas, which would soon translate into a revolution of pre-existing institutions and laws, carried out through a mutual exchange of thoughts and action: the mobilisation against the *status quo* of privileges and arbitrary actions certainly interacted with the freedom, granted to reason, to guide all human decisions and behaviour. Within this struggle against mental obscurantism and against the injustices of past laws and institutions, the Enlightenment and the late eighteenth century revolutions provided a fundamental contribution to a new definition and realisation of human rights.

This new culture of rights put an end to an entire historic phase and inaugurated a new one, raising the level of expectations and at the same time spawning new contradictions, some of which became visible almost immediately. Amongst the more relevant ones: the question of women's equality in the sphere of 'man's' rights, the problem of slavery as a social practice and an economic interest, the treatment of minorities and 'foreigners' within a state; the tendency to not recognise that citizens of 'enemy' nations might enjoy the same rights and the developing of a classificatory tendency that, based on some of the epoch's scientific discoveries, contributed to the construction of the idea of race and the justification of colonialism. Two co-existing aspects of Western culture led men to fight privileges and arbitrary decisions in the name of freedom and equality, while at the same time allowing a part of mankind to suffer because of violations of those very same principles.

The history of human rights does not provide a definitive result: it is a gradual process – in which nothing is definitively guaranteed – toward the enrichment, clarification and comprehension of what humanity and personal dignity really mean.

3. *Against the slave trade*

While the *philosophes* were debating and spreading their ideas – destined to transform modern culture and strongly influence the political and institutional revolutions of the late eighteenth century – a group of courageous men and women, whose name is still widely unknown, fought for an equally significant cultural and juridical revolution.

On 22 May 1787 twelve men met in the printing house and bookstore owned by James Phillips in Clapham, a village on the south-west of London. Nine were Quakers – including James and his cousin Richard Phillips; one was a lawyer; another one, William Dillwyn, was a businessman from Pennsylvania; while F.Mussard was a dancing and fencing teacher. The last three were Anglicans, including Granville Sharp, who had recently turned fifty, and Thomas Clarkson, who was only twenty-seven: these last two men would be, alongside William Wilberforce – one year older than Clarkson and a member of the House of Commons for Kingston upon Hull – the most well-known figures of the twenty-year battle which led to the February 1807 parliamentary abolition of the slave trade.

Amongst enlightened thinkers the strongest condemnations of slavery were pronounced by Montesquieu in 1748 (in the fifth chapter of book XV of the *Esprit des lois*) and by Voltaire in 1756 (in his *Essai sur le moeurs*), while in 1770 Father Guillaume-Thomas Raynal had expressed (in the *Histoire philosophique et politique des établissement et du commerce des Européens dans les deux Indes*) a position that, despite the support of the Abbés Antoine-François Prévost and Henri Grégoire, was destined to remain a minority opinion within the Church. Certainly the explanations of the theologians Germain Fromageau (1698) and Jean Bellon de Saint-Quentin (1764), who claimed that the trading of slaves conformed to natural law and holy texts,[85] were still strongly influential in the Church.

If the Enlightenment was doubtless the movement of thought responsible for a turnaround of eighteenth-century moral and political values and philosophical beliefs concerning human equality, it was mainly religious groups, or strongly religious men and women, who gave life to the movement that would fight for the abolition of the slave trade and, later, of slavery itself.

Since the last decades of the sixteenth century, the Quakers – the 'Society of Friends' George Fox had founded in the middle of the century, motivated by the belief that Protestant religion had betrayed biblical teachings – had denounced the trade of slaves as immoral, even if within the movement some people were in favour of slavery. In 1688, *Oroonoko or the History of the Royal Slave* by Aphra Behn, the first English woman writer to use her own name rather than a male pseudonym, enjoyed widespread success. The book narrates the story of an African prince who is sold as a slave in Suriname, anticipating the figure of the 'noble savage' that would later be elaborated by Voltaire and Rousseau, and predating the character of Friday in Daniel Defoe's *Robinson Crusoe* (1719).

It has often been emphasised that the attitude toward slavery, even on the part of those who condemned it, was often ambiguous, pietistic or paternalistic, characterised by the idea of the superiority of the white race and of Western civilisation. Thus it is even more important to understand how the anti-slavery ideas of just a few people were spread and managed to convince a majority in such a brief period of time. Abolitionist attitudes found their ideal motivations in Christianity and in Enlightenment philosophy, yet were obstructed by the logic of colonial conquest, by commercial interests and by the apparent utility of slavery in a time of industrial expansion.

In the eighteenth century the idea of 'tolerance', a growing sympathy for the figure of the slave and a willingness to emancipate him, even if gradually, co-existed with the economic understanding of a practice many deemed as immoral despite the wealth it could produce. So what motivated thousands of people, over the course of just a few years, to sign petitions which were the very backbone of the later parliamentary battles against slavery?

Even if we must obviously avoid any mono-causal explanation, a decisive factor in this phenomenon was the moral and religious influence upon social classes that had little in common with the enlightened intellectual groups. Granville Sharp, a public officer who had studied law, a son and nephew of religious people (his grandfather had been the Archbishop of York), was living with his brother in east London when he decided to take care of Jonathan Strong, a sixteen year old slave who had been beaten by his owner, David Lisle, and left on the street in agony. Two years later, Jonathan, who had temporarily recovered his health, was sold by Lisle – who had paid two men to recapture him – to a new owner. Sharp, apprised of this fact by a letter from his protégé, decided to bring the case before the Lord Mayor of London, claiming that in England a slave could not be considered as such, and that any man walking on English soil should be considered a free man. Jonathan Strong, declared a free man, would die three years later from his wounds.

Following this first judicial victory, publicised by the press, Granville Sharp became the defender of blacks and of slaves: a role which certainly radicalised his position against slavery, as well as on other issues, such as the struggle to raise the salaries of day labourers or solidarity for the American colonists' fight for independence. Having returned to his law studies, Sharp attempted to refute the doctrine established in 1729 by the judges Yorke and Talbot, which declared that slaves, even if converted to Christianity and brought to England, were to remain the property of their owners. A couple of years later, in 1771, the James Somerset case would push Sharp into the public spotlight once more.

Somerset, the slave of a Boston customs officer, escaped two years after his arrival in England, but was recaptured and imprisoned on a ship leaving for Jamaica, which was then a British colony – as was Massachusetts. Sharp's intervention forced the ship's captain to bring Somerset before a king's magistrate, the president of the High Court Lord Mansfield, who adjourned the case for a few months. Only on 22 June 1772, after hearing five lawyers in defence of the fugitive slave and two in favour of his owner, did Judge Mansfield establish that 'here no owner has permission to take a slave by force in order to sell him abroad because he deserted his services, nor for any other reason'.

What did the eighteenth century slave trade consist of? How had it developed and what phase of its existence was it going through? The advanced research by historians, demographers and statisticians now allows us to study reconstructions that, although incomplete, are very close to the truth.

Over the course of almost four centuries (from the beginning of the sixteenth century to the middle of the nineteenth century) the sale of people from Africa to Europe, and above all to the American continent – the 'western' trade – involved around ten million people. A large part of this number, over eight million, were deported after the start of the eighteenth century, when the development of the plantation economy made the slave trade useful for the development of English, French, Portuguese and Dutch colonies. The West Indies and Brazil were the privileged objectives of slave traders' traffic, and were dominated by English, Portuguese, French and Dutch vessels, crews and ports. Liverpool and Bristol were the ports where slaves from Africa would be sent toward Barbados or Jamaica; these two ports managed about 70% of a traffic involving almost six thousand slave ships – the stylised illustration of these ships became an important tool of anti-slavery propaganda. 'Whatever scale we choose for our analysis, slave trading peaked in terms of concentration and importance between 1720 and 1760. During this period two states dominated the traffic: England, which controlled 50% of the trades, and France, with about 20-25%.'[86]

In the same year as Granville Sharp's success in the Somerset case, one of the most important books for the anti-slavery movement was published: *Some Historical Account of Guinea*. The author, Anthony Benezet, was born in Saint-Quentin, in Eastern France, to a Huguenot family, and had soon migrated to London and then to Philadelphia, the capital of the English colony of Pennsylvania. Here Benezet met the first Quakers and joined them, creating a school for slave children in 1750 and the first public school for girls in 1754. In 1770, after spending twenty years teaching, writing and convincing Quaker slave owners to abandon this anti-Christian practice, he founded the Philadelphia 'Negro School'.

Some Historical Account of Guinea did not influence only Granville Sharp; it was indeed fundamental reading for John Wesley, the founder of the Methodist Church, and led him to join the anti-slavery struggle by publishing his *Thoughts upon Slavery* in 1774. The pamphlet passionately accused the slave-mongers while trying to convince them to abandon their inhuman commerce: 'Are you man? Then you should have a human heart. But have you indeed? What is your heart made of? Is there no such principle as compassion there? Do you ever feel another's pain? Have you no sympathy, no sense of human woe, no pity for the miserable?'[87]

During his last years (he died in 1791) Wesley was a preacher in Bristol and in the main slave-exporting ports; in the August of 1787 he wrote to the Committee for Abolition asking them to hold strong and offering to republish his booklet. Although *Thoughts upon Slavery* was out of print, it had been read by Thomas Clarkson, who was strongly inspired by the pamphlet, and by Benezet, when he wrote the Latin essay (*Anne liceat invitos in servitutem dare*) – in response to the question 'if it is legitimate to enslave others against their will' – which won the 1785 Cambridge University Prize. The following year the text was published in English (*An Essay on the Slavery and Commerce of the Human Species, Particularly the African*) and distributed on a vast scale, and its author soon came in contact with many other figures of the anti-slavery struggle, including Granville Sharp.

Clarkson was the youngest of the twelve men who founded, in May 1787, the Committee for the Abolition of the Slave Trade, soon officially named the Society to Effect the Abolition of the Slave Trade. The committee was one of the very first voluntary moral and humanitarian associations to be created in modern society, a predecessor of the many that would be founded in the following centuries. Built upon a moral and religious impulse, Sharp and Clarkson's Society would confront the intensity and contradictions of a problem – slavery and the slave trade – strongly influenced by a world in transformation, caught between the Enlightenment and capitalism.

4. *The American Revolution*

The Declaration of Independence of the United States of America (*The Unanimous Declaration of the Thirteen United States of America*), ratified in Philadelphia on 4 July 1776, begins with a strong and formal appeal to the rights of man and to the necessity and legitimacy of the colonists' revolution against the British crown. The text as we know it – written by Thomas Jefferson with the assistance of another four men (John Adams, Benjamin Franklin, Robert Livingston, Roger Sherman) – was corrected eighty-six times before achieving the clarity the authors were seeking. The initial appeal 'We hold these truths to be sacred and unquestionable; that all men are created equal and independent' was changed into 'We hold these truths to be self-evident, that all men are created equal'.

The use of the term 'declaration' rather than the more usual, at that time, 'petition', 'charter' or 'bill' – as would be used in France thirteen years later – underlined the sovereignty and legitimacy of the act. It was not by coincidence that the Declaration began with a historical justification[88] preceding the list of self-evident rights that submission to King George III appeared to obstruct, identified in a clear and strong fashion as 'life, liberty and the pursuit of happiness'.

To declare as evident the equality of man – not only 'citizens', or 'British' – meant on one hand to affirm a principle that everyone should already have recognised, and on the other to judge as blinded by prejudice all those who refused this assertion, in the past and in the present. It meant the beginning of a struggle against all those who, in order to defend their power and privileges, would not accept a self-evident truth.

Certainly the beginning of the Declaration of Independence was influenced by the theory of natural rights, although it also claimed that men are given inalienable rights and equality 'by the Creator'. In the Declaration, the universal character of fundamental rights such as life and freedom, and the pursuit of happiness intended as complete self-realisation, is not yet explicit. What is clear is that by using the word *man*, as in France *homme*, the text underlines how these inalienable rights relate to every *person* as a member of the human society (or race), although the political translation of these fundamental rights was later to encounter many obstacles with regard to gender and race. 'At some time between 1689 and 1776 rights that had been mostly considered to belong to particular persons – English men born free, for example – were transformed into human rights, into universal natural rights.'[89]

The ideas of the Enlightenment, assimilated into Republican ideals and into a growing debate on democracy within the American territory, had a determining role in the battle that the thirteen British colonies[90] fought against their motherland from 1775 and 1781 – ending with the military victory of the patriots of independence. France played an important (historians are still debating whether decisive or not) role by offering military and economic aid to strengthen the defensive and offensive capacities of the colonists; and further, by renouncing any demand on the British colonies from the 1860s, the French pushed the British government to impose a series of taxes to force the colonies to finance their own defence. These measures provoked protests by a population not represented in the British Parliament which had passed such oppressive and unpopular decisions. The practice of boycotts under the slogan *no taxation without representation* was the first sign of rebellion.

Starting in Boston, the War of Independence opposed local 'militia' to British troops, sent from England to put down the rebellion and capable of controlling only a few cities on the coast and no more than 10-20% of the total territory. The first battle took place in Concord, Massachusetts. The Second Continental Congress, which from 1775 united 65 representatives from the assemblies of the 13 colonies, acted as a national government, especially following the ratification of the Declaration in 1776 and the temporary constitution of the Confederation (*Articles of Confederation and Perpetual Union*) approved in 1777 in York, Pennsylvania – eleven years before the definitive Confederation was formed, on 21 June 1788.

The alliance made by the Congress with France in 1778 opened the path for a military reinforcement which led to the victory in Yorktown in 1781. The following Treaty of Paris (1783) fixed the borders of the new state: in the north bordered with Canada, in the south with Spanish Florida, and in the west with the Mississippi river.

The right of a population to overthrow rulers who behaved as tyrants was now a principle, inherited from Locke and later from Rousseau, which certainly was joined with the denunciation of the British crown's betrayal of the rights of the colonists in their quality as 'Englishmen'. For many colonists the anti-British polemic was one and the same as an anti-royalist position: some of the 'founding fathers' – the 65 members of the Congress – shared a clear republican orientation, yet the majority, led by John Dickinson, appeared to be open to reconciliation with the crown. The last attempt in this direction was made in 1775, when a petition – written by Thomas Jefferson and revised by Dickinson, who had found it too offensive – was sent to the King: it denied the resolve to win independence and hoped for negotiations to solve the dispute regarding taxes.

The refusal of George III to resume the dialogue with the 'traitors' and 'rebels' who had opposed the crown inevitably favoured the more radical and republican ideas of John Adams and his followers. Once the war began it was fundamental to render explicit a definitive break with the motherland and to clarify the reasons for independence. A minority of the colonies' citizens remained loyal to Britain (about 20%), while others maintained a neutral position, as did the Quakers, who opted for this solution both because of their refusal of violence and their peaceable vision of relations between states, and because they hoped to continue their profitable commerce with England. This choice earned them accusations of sabotaging the revolution.

During the months preceding the Declaration of Independence, some states (including Virginia) decided to declare independence separately and established their own constitutions. The 13 colonies finally declared independence on 2 July 1776, two days before the Declaration was ratified.

It is quite obvious that the American Revolution – just as with all revolutions and great events that hasten historical transformations and changes – was motivated by ideals as well as by concrete demands. However, historians still debate whether the cultural reasons (moral, religious, political, juridical) were more important than the economic and social ones. The republican ideology which conquered the hegemony of the anti-British struggle, expressed concretely in the Declaration of Independence, was strongly related to British Whig culture: in England the Whigs were the strongest supporters of constitutional ideas, struggles against absolutism and privileges, civil virtues, the condemnation of corruption, as well as of the diffusion and defence of natural rights, as theorised by the Enlightenment.

It was not by chance that the main author of the American Declaration of Independence, Thomas Jefferson, after having tried to realise the Declaration's principles as governor of Virginia between 1779 and 1784, and after having prepared a law proposal regarding religious freedom – approved in 1786 – was sent to France in 1785 to replace Benjamin Franklin as the representative of the government of the United States; here he participated in the episodes preceding the outbreak of the French

Revolution with interest and sympathy. Jefferson, like enlightened thinkers, considered man to be a rational animal, provided by nature with rights and an inherent sense of justice. 'Natural rights – he wrote to James Monroe in 1797 – are those whose protection motivates the formation of society and the establishment of municipal laws.'[91]

During the years Jefferson was in Paris he was also visited occasionally by Tom Paine, an Englishman who had moved to Philadelphia in 1774 and in January 1776 had published a pamphlet which went on to sell one hundred and twenty thousand copies in just three months. This pamphlet, at first published anonymously, was called *Common Sense*, and within it Paine expressed the colonists' need to forcefully, and without compromises, obtain independence from Britain. A radical statement – which also contained the proposal to call the new nation the United States of America – which was destined to influence both George Washington and John Adams.

5. *From the Declaration of Independence to the Declaration of the Rights of Man and of the Citizen*

The growing spread of a new idea of human rights, certainly encouraged by enlightened culture, was the source of an acceleration – especially in the face of significant and unexpected political events – of the practical definition, organisation and transformation of such rights into laws. During the American Revolution a rapid, sometimes even unnoticed, passage from a particularistic vision of rights (the colonists' rights as colonists or as British men) to a universalistic one (the rights of colonists as men and people) took place.

What allowed this transition to succeed – between 1774 and 1776 – was the combination of the diffusion and discussion of enlightened ideas regarding the existence and defence of natural rights with the actual resistance of the American colonists against the British authorities, fully expressed in Tom Paine's *Common Sense*. Richard Price's pamphlet, *Observations on the Nature of Civil Liberty, the Principles of Government, and the Justice and Policy of the War with America*, which was also published in 1776 in England, was equally influential, and earned the author criticisms from Edmund Burke and John Wesley, as well as the accusation of his being a traitor because of his defence of American colonists, even if only as regards to the most 'inalienable rights of human nature'.

The political and philosophical discussion surrounding Price's pamphlet was certainly a very interesting one, and related to a question, partially anticipated by the political-philosophical positions of Hobbes and Locke, that would later be addressed in every debate on human rights. Price accepted the existence of 'natural' rights inherent to every individual, yet he stated that the formation of the state through a social contract also meant renouncing one's will as a condition of freedom. The 'natural' freedom which made all men equal, according to those enlightened ideas inscribed within the American Declaration of Independence, was now opposed to a 'civil' freedom whose limits and borders had to be established by the state, in order for society to be organised in a balanced fashion.

This opposition to 'natural rights', which found its political supporters in defenders of the *status quo*, was also articulated by Jeremy Bentham, who would soon disseminate the principles of utilitarianism, including the objective of the 'greatest happiness for the largest number' – a principle first formulated, as we have seen, by Cesare Beccaria. Despite his opposition to natural rights, which he considered (in the French version of the *Declaration of the Rights of Man*) 'simple nonsense; natural and inalienable rights, rhetorical nonsense,'[92] Bentham was a radical reformer as well as a supporter of the rights of women, of the abolition of slavery and the end to the corporal punishment of children, the end of discrimination against homosexuality and even, up to a certain point, of animal rights.

This philosophical and juridical antagonism toward natural rights, which opposed supporters and opponents of reforms and of the American and French revolutions, partially explains the increasingly frequent transition – from the middle of the eighteenth century – towards the use of terms such as 'rights of humanity' or 'rights of man' as substitutes for 'natural rights'.

If we exclude the Virginia Declaration of Rights, which was approved 20 days before and certainly influenced the American Declaration of Independence, none of the constitutions approved during the war against Britain and after the peace treaties (the 1777 Articles of Confederation and the 1787 Constitution) contain an actual list of rights, a Bill of Rights like the 1689 English one; consisting of the first ten amendments of the constitution, the American list of rights was approved only in 1791.

The attention given to the 'rights of man', although opposed by defenders of privileges, now strongly bound the two sides of the Atlantic: this explains the huge interest with which Europeans followed the American revolution – not only in Britain, but also in France, in the Netherlands and elsewhere – as well as the large number of Americans who participated in, or followed with interest, the events which led to the French Revolution and to the Declaration of the Rights of Man and of the Citizen on 26 August 1789.

A constitutional crisis, within a more general economic and social one, provided the conditions for both these events: the revolution, which lasted longer in chronological terms, and the Declaration, which however had a far more lasting influence.

As France faced bankruptcy, due to the economic support given to the American colonists and to repeated failures to reform its financial system, the convocation of the States-General,[93] which had last been called in 1614 by Louis XIV, was refused by the Minister of Finances Charles Alexandre de Calonne, nominated in 1783, and later by his successor and antagonist, the Arch-Bishop of Toulouse Etienne-Charles de Loménie de Brienne, in power from 1787. At the end of 1787 Louis XVI promised that the States-General would be called within five years, yet faced with the worsening of the situation in the August of 1788 he ordered their convocation for 5 May 1789.

In preparation for the States-General the three 'estates' were supposed to both elect their delegates and summarise in a series of *cahiers de doléance* (books of complaints) the problems that needed to be solved urgently. The third estate, which included the entire population from the bourgeoisie to the peasants, excluding only the nobility and the clergy, obtained permission to have twice the delegates of the other estates, given the fact that it represented 98% of the population, but the king's silence made it uncertain if votes would be assigned 'per head' or 'per order', which would have made the double delegation of the third state completely useless.

The *cahiers de doléance* frequently included requests related to the 'rights of man' which spoke of dignity or freedom, and sometimes even of the necessity to adopt a declaration of rights, which were listed in different ways yet always dealt with the right to associate, the freedom of the press and of expression, religious freedom, equality before the law and fiscal justice.

The States-General were blocked for a few weeks by procedural problems and by the debate over the verification of powers. On 17 June the delegates of the third estate reunited autonomously and proclaimed themselves the National Assembly, inviting the other orders to follow them. The monarchy attempted to stop the activities of the National Assembly by refusing to let it use the Hall of States, and later even the Tennis Court Hall, where the delegates had sworn to remain until a written constitution was approved. Ultimately the church of Saint-Louis hosted the Assembly and a constitutional battle began – between the king, who demanded that the Assembly return to monarchic legality, and the delegates, who proclaimed themselves, on 9 July, the National Constituent Assembly – and the rebel delegates were threatened with direct and indirect violence to repress their activities. On 13 July a large popular demonstration took place in Paris, to protest against the convocation of the King's Council, but it was charged by German soldiers following the orders of Louis XVI. On the following day sixty thousand citizens took to the streets, looted the arsenal and headed towards the Bastille, where around one hundred demonstrators were killed; the others managed to overcome the guards and began to demolish the prison, a symbol of royalist power.

At this point the king was forced to accept the situation and to participate in the Assembly, thus recognising its authority. It was during the second half of July that the discussion regarding what type of declaration was necessary, and what relationship it would have with the soon-to-be-enacted constitution, was resumed. A decision in this direction had been made at the beginning of July, with the creation of a Committee for the Constitution which had expressed its intention to write a declaration regarding the 'natural and inalienable rights of man'. The Assembly transformed this into a solemn objective on 4 August, by establishing that it would be a declaration of rights that would not include any indication of duties, just as the supporters of a constitutional reform of the monarchy had hoped for.

The American case, which was constantly quoted during those days, was a demonstration that a declaration 'of rights' signified a frontal opposition to the previous power structure. The discussion regarding the 24 articles, proposed by a 40-member committee, was a confused and agitated one; after a week, and following the presentation of many amendments, only 17 articles had been approved. On 26 August the National Constituent Assembly approved the *Déclaration des droits de l'homme et du citoyen*, and the following day it decided to postpone the discussion on the remaining articles until after the enactment of the constitution. The basic text of the Declaration had been written by the Marquis de Lafayette, who had been nominated Commander of the National Guard the day after the events of the Bastille. Amongst his advisers was Thomas Jefferson, who was at the time the United States' representative in Paris.

6. *The rights of man*

The 17 articles of the Declaration of the Rights of Man and of the Citizen – the fruit of a revolutionary political act by an entire nation and its representatives – were a summary of the principles and values of the new culture of the fifteenth and sixteenth centuries, first disseminated by natural law and later by the Enlightenment. If the idea of a division of powers, as theorised by Locke and Montesquieu, constituted the basis for the new rules of government, the theories regarding equality, derived from reflections on the social contract, paved the way for a new relationship with citizens. Indeed the *Déclaration des droits de l'homme et du citoyen* confirmed the principle of equality and indicated as 'inalienable rights of man' freedom, property, safety and resistance against oppression. The principle of sovereignty, which derives from the nation, is incarnated by the law, the expression of the general will formed by all citizens via their representatives. The law also dictates the rules of justice and punishment for those who commit crimes against the common well-being, and guarantees the presumption of innocence until a citizen is declared guilty. Every opinion, even if religious, is admitted and must be defended, as with freedom of speech and communication. To guarantee public powers in order to safeguard the listed rights and equal taxation, proportional to each citizen's abilities, is indispensible. Nobody can be deprived of property except for public necessity, in which case he must be compensated fairly.

The era of revolutions would appear to have reached a point of no return, in which the language of rights had now found an indelible place and role, at least in the consciences of a growing number of individuals. In November 1789, Richard Price, a Scottish philosopher and preacher who had supported the American Revolution and the 'rights of humanity', summed up his happiness about these great transformations in a sermon:

> I lived the possibility of seeing the rights of man be understood far better than in the past, and nations craving a freedom they had appeared incapable of even imagining. […] After sharing the benefits of a revolution [the 1688 Second English Revolution], I had the possibility of witnessing another two revolutions, and both were glorious.[94]

Two men had the privilege of not only witnessing, but actually participating in both the American and French revolutions. The Marquis de Lafayette, a French nobleman who had become a General, and Tom Paine, a British post office worker, son of a Quaker, who was to become the most read political thinker of the late eighteenth and early nineteenth century. Paine had arrived in the United States, on Benjamin Franklin's suggestion, at the end of 1774, and, about a year later, inflamed and radicalised American patriots with his successful pamphlet *Common Sense*.

The French events leading to the constitution of the National Assembly and the attack on the Bastille tore Tom Paine away from his main activity of the time: he was a bridge designer who hoped to soon build bridges over the Seine. Between November 1789 and March 1790 Paine stayed in the French capital, in the Hotel de la Monnaie, whose guests included Adam Smith and Benjamin Franklin, Thomas Jefferson and Cesare Beccaria: here Paine began working on a reflection on the French Revolution that would later become a book in two parts – *The Rights of Man* – destined to be the most impressive editorial success of the time.

While Paine was in Paris the revolution carried on. On 5 October 1789, pressured by an increasingly restless population, Louis XVI was forced to approve the Declaration of the Rights of Man and of the Citizen, which had just been voted upon by the National Assembly. The following day the king sought refuge in Versailles. Meanwhile the revolution was characterised by an increasing number of disagreements and contradictions, above all regarding the crucial question of which citizens could vote and who could be elected. The existing limit was an economic one: whoever paid taxes corresponding to three days of work could be an active elector, while whoever paid a Gold Mark (circa 44 days of work) could also be elected. In January 1790, when the National Assembly confirmed this electoral principle, many protests and demonstrations took place, leading to Lafayette's entrance in the Cordeliers district with 3,000 guards to arrest Jean-Paul Marat. It was the firm reaction by the district's president Georges-Jacques Danton that allowed Marat to escape arrest. This electoral rule was quite evidently a limitation for the 1789 Declaration, as the nation, embodied by the population, was to be represented only by those who could vote. This anomaly would be solved by the universal suffrage act introduced by the Jacobins, alas accompanied by the Reign of Terror.

In the meantime Paine wrote to his friend in London, Edmund Burke, recounting the French events and hoping the revolution would spread to the rest of Europe. The silence of his friend, with whom he had shared the battle for American independence, led Paine to deduce that their respective positions on the revolution were no longer similar; he hoped to further understand his friend's position from a soon-to-be-printed book on the argument, which had already been announced by Burke's editor. At the end of October 1790 Paine returned to Paris to carry the American flag during the ceremony celebrating the new French constitution. He got back to London just in time to buy one of the first copies of Edmund Burke's *Reflections of the Revolution in France*, which would sell 12,000 copies in the first month after publication, and 19,000 in its first year.

Paine read Burke's work with a growing sense of astonishment and concern, as he found himself criticised and ridiculed for the abstract nature and ingenuity which, according to the author, characterised the 'new doctors of the rights of men', for whom the conquests of the 'glorious revolution' and of the 1689 British Declaration of rights fixed the insurmountable terms of legality and democracy. Thus Paine transformed the book he was writing – or at least the first part of it – into a reply to Burke, addressing on one hand the French events and on the other the English perspectives, within a more general reflection upon the only institutions, a democratic republic and government, which according to his views could guarantee the rights of man and avoid wars.

Civil rights, which form the heart of Paine's defence of the French revolution, are based on the assumption of a condition which precedes the formation of governments: the existence of 'natural' rights to equality and freedom. Only governments, however, can realise these natural rights, transforming them into civil rights, made unassailable in the face of despotic temptations (not just of a monarch, but also of a majority of citizens) by a written constitution that protects all citizens and through parliamentary dynamics which guarantee the representation of all parts of society. If citizens have rights, governments have duties towards them: Paine was overturning the pre-revolutionary paradigm of the duties of subjects and rights of rulers. Thus the division between civil society and political institutions becomes a necessary element to strengthen – as well as render actual, defended and verifiable – the efficacy of the constitution, the division of powers, the freedom of the press and of information.

On 29 January 1791, the day of his fifty-fourth birthday, Paine finished writing the first part of *The Rights of Man*, which was published on 13 March. A few months earlier, on 14 July 1790, Lafayette had celebrated the first anniversary of the revolution alongside the king and queen, who had sworn in the recently approved constitution. The attempted escape by the king, a few months later, ushered in a new phase of the revolution, characterised by the conflict between supporters of a constitutional monarchy and the advocates of a democratic republic. The huge demonstration that took place, in July 1791, in the Champ de Mars, bloodily suppressed with Lafayette's order – to the national guard – to shoot on the crowd, marked a decisive breaking point, although the situation and the revolution's future path remained uncertain for over a year.

In England the publication of *The Rights of Man* was a major political and cultural event: in two months the book sold 50,000 copies; within ten years it would go on to sell a record number of 500,000 copies (to a population which only had four million literate citizens). Although many associations, including the Society for Constitutional Information, appreciated Paine's work, it was also heavily and frequently criticised; the government itself appeared to accuse the book of sedition – something it would openly do later over the second part of the book – yet the risk of turning the author into a victim and a hero made silence a preferable strategy for the time being.

During April Paine returned to Paris, before stopping in Versailles between May and June to write the second part of his book. It was his friend Lafayette who warned him of the king's escape; Paine reacted with a ferocious accusation towards constitutional monarchy, in which Lafayette still believed. After being directly involved in a series of violent acts with the rebellious crowd, Paine justified them in a letter to the Marquis de Condorcet, with whom he shared many political views:

> During the first period of a revolution mistakes are very probable, on a theoretical or practical level, or perhaps on both the theoretical and practical level. [...] When men are in the first phase of their freedom they are not sufficiently educated to keep each other informed of their reciprocal opinions [...] We have observed the symptoms of this imperfection at the beginning of this revolution. Fortunately they were manifested before the constitution was fully introduced, so that every mistake may still be amended.[95]

Convinced as he was that the French revolution would soon find the 'American' path towards a democratic republic, although not a federal one, Paine returned to London with the intention of stirring up a revolutionary tide in his own country; yet he immediately had to face angry and violent pro-royalist demonstrations – which destroyed, for example, the house, books and property of scientist and theologian Joseph Priestley, who was forced to escape to the United States. Paine also appeared to have to escape from the country after the publication of the second part of *The Rights of Man*, in February 1792: 'the most brilliant and powerful political rocket of English history had been launched'.[96] In just one year over 200,000 copies of the book were sold in Britain, and over 100,000 copies were sold in the United States. The enthusiasm of a minority was opposed by an unprecedented offensive led by the government itself, which on 21 May announced a proclamation against seditious and sinful texts. The second part of *The Rights of Man* was described in Parliament as an 'attack upon hereditary nobility, which aims to destroy the monarchy and religion and aims to totally subvert all recognised forms of government'. [97]

Agents of the crown searched and closed down bookstores and publishing houses; they also fined, legally prosecuted and sometimes arrested anyone who was involved in the circulation of the book: Richard Phillips, the owner of the print shop where the Society against the slave trade was born, was amongst the people arrested. On the same day that the Royal Proclamation was announced, Paine was prosecuted for having written a seditious text. In truth, by threatening and prosecuting him, the government aimed to force Paine to leave the country. On 13 September, after suffering further accusations and intimidations, the author left for France, just in time to escape a trial that began, in his absence, in December.

7. *Terror and rights*

Just a few days before he arrived in Calais, Tom Paine's name was included by the Bordeaux Girondin leader, Elie Guadet, amongst the foreign candidates to be presented for the legislative assembly, alongside William Wilberforce, Joseph Priestley, Thomas Clarkson, James Mackintosh and David Williams. During the September elections for the National Convention, four departments voted for Paine, who decided to become the deputy of Pas-de-Calais. On 20 September 1792, while on the fields of Valmy, as Goethe immediately wrote, 'a new era in world history was beginning', the Convention reunited for the first time and two days later it proclaimed the republic.

The revolution's first military victory, which forced the Prussians and Austrians to retreat, coincided with the start of the new Convention's activities, and hastened the republican creation of a commission to write a new constitution. This commission was composed of four Girondins and two Jacobins, as well as three independent deputies who were respected for their intellectual and moral qualities in the field of political philosophy: the Marquis de Condorcet, Emmanuel-Joseph Sieyès and Tom Paine.

The constitutional project that was presented to the Convention on 15 February was considered to be excessively long; by 29 May only six of its 368 articles had been approved. During the following night the Jacobins created the Revolutionary Central Committee that was to guide the insurrection against the Parliament, which was in majority composed of Girondins. In the meantime a lengthy and dramatic debate on the faults of the monarchy and the fate of Louis XVI had taken place. Paine had intervened repeatedly, helped by translators, in favour of the condemnation of the king, but against the desire for vengeance that characterised the majority of the assembly. His proposal of an exile in the United States was defeated by just a few votes, and it was decided that the king should be executed.

By now the revolution had taken a different direction from Paine's hopes, and its inability to agree a new constitution was yet another demonstration of this fact. His Girondins friends were defeated while the Jacobin dictatorship was unable to realise the constitution, approved in July and already suspended by 10 August. The expulsion of Danton, the strong man of the Public Health Committee, by Robespierre; the murder of Marat; the radical actions by the Parisian Sans-Culottes led by Jacques-René Hébert and Jacques Roux; the law of military service and the war against the Vendée rebels: these were the main events that accompanied the increasing use of the guillotine, which was first used on 25 April 1792 and was soon to become the symbol of the merciless logic of the revolution.

On 20 October 1793, two weeks after the Jacobin deputy André Amar had accused him before the Convention of being a supporter of the Girondin leader Brissot, and of having tried to rouse the United States against the republican government, Tom Paine wrote a heartfelt letter to Thomas Jefferson, who was at the time the Secretary of State for President Washington. The farcical trial of the revolutionary tribunal against the Girondin Party began five days before this letter was sent; it would end with the death sentence for almost all the accused. Paine wrote to Jefferson that 'there is now no prospect of France carrying the revolution to Europe'. [98]

In this new phase of the revolution Paine returned to writing and revised a pamphlet which was first published anonymously in French (*Le siècle de la raison, ou le sens commun des droits de l'homme*) and later, in 1794, became *The Age of Reason* in an expanded English edition. The heart of this work was religion, in the very moment when the Jacobins were carrying out their program of de-Christianisation and attempting to constitute a homeland religion.

Paine's pamphlet was too consistent with his reflection on the rights of man to be understood in a time when, after the triumph of the *Declaration of the Rights of Man and of the Citizen*, factious battles and the conquest and safeguard of power had become so central for the revolution. While his name was already on the blacklist of a xenophobe such as Robespierre, and according to the 'law of suspicion' he could easily be considered a certain victim of future repressions by the Jacobins, in England Paine was accused of writing an attack on religion and Christianity, although the pamphlet was a commercial success on both sides of the Atlantic.

It is certain that on this point – Paine wrote in The Age of Reason – all nations and religions agree: that all of them believe in God.

> What makes them different are the redundancies connected to this
> faith [...] Adam, if a similar man ever existed, was created a Deist;
> in the meantime let us allow every man to follow, as is his right, the
> religion and cult he may prefer.[99]

Consistent with his vision of rights, Paine believed that the choice of a
religious creed was a fundamental right of all citizens and that there was
no contradiction between the principles and truths of major religions.
He repeated this once more, in a postscript to *The Age of Reason*, while
he was already in the Luxembourg prison, where he was imprisoned on
Christmas day in 1793 (two days after his parliamentary immunity had
expired): 'I have always inexhaustibly supported the right of every man
to his own opinions, no matter how different from my own. He who denies
another person this right renders himself a slave to his present opinion,
as he keeps himself from changing it.'[100]

While he was in prison Paine observed the dramatic succession of
prisoners in nearby cells, arrested and tried with no possibility of defending themselves, and then executed rapidly to avoid popular reactions:
first the followers of Hebert and then Danton suffered this fate. In June
(*Prairial* according to the new calendar) a law was proclaimed giving the
revolutionary tribunal the power to punish all enemies of the revolution, without any regard to their rights, with the only possible outcome
of absolution or the death sentence. According to the broad definition
given by article 6, anybody could be accused of being 'an enemy of the
population'. By now thirty 'enemies' were being executed every day, and
Paine's doom appeared to be inevitable.

On the night of 24 July 1794, as Paine himself wrote later on, 'the angel
of destruction overlooked me', and allowed the author to live for another
fifteen years. The squadron that had been entrusted to mark the number
of prisoners to be executed on the door of each cell did this on the internal
part of the door, as the prisoners had been allowed to keep the door open
due to the heat. When at night the execution squadron came to take the
prisoners away, they skipped Paine's cell, believing it empty. Three days
later, before the mistake could be discovered, Robespierre was arrested
and Thermidor began.

Before the Reign of Terror the revolution had tried – sometimes
successfully – to make the passage from the universal and general terrain
of the Declaration towards a concrete specification of rights, to be ratified
by governments and with specific laws. Although many people criticised
the revolution for its abstractness, in truth its internal dynamics were capable
of identifying and enlarging the categories of the holders of rights to be

included in the Declaration's general category of 'man' or 'person'.

One of the most relevant cases concerned a theme Paine had already indicated as crucial, and which he had written about during his terrible days in the Luxembourg prison: religious freedom. When the National Assembly had begun legislating electoral rights, the principle of equality before the law led to a debate on existing limits and on limits to be imposed, not only in relation to personal income and wealth. Protestants – or rather Protestant men – were granted the same political rights as Catholics in December 1789, while Jewish men earned these rights almost two years later, on 27 September 1791. Obviously we are referring to revolutionary France: in Britain this process was much slower. The right to be admitted into the army, to attend a university and to become judges were ratified for Catholics in 1793, while Jews were conceded these rights only in 1845. As for political rights, and for the prospect of being elected in the British Parliament, Jews were granted these rights respectively in 1829 and in 1858.

In the United States, although the Federal Constitution adopted in 1791 established complete religious freedom, the process of ratifying this in each separate state's constitution and legislation was a long and contorted one. Christians, for example, were granted rights in Massachusetts in 1780, yet other religions were not recognised in this state until 1833.

Obviously equality before the law did not change the fact that the path towards a substantial recognition of rights was filled with difficulties and obstacles, not to mention the existence of discriminatory prejudices, which survived their legislative denial for many decades or centuries to come.

The problems regarding gender rights and slave rights, or the rights of enslaved or colonised populations, were even more complex than the religious question. When on 10 August 1792 France gave the right to vote to all men, women were still denied their 'natural' rights, as were servants and unemployed people, not to mention slaves: only much later would it be established that, on principle, slaves were to be treated as 'persons'.

8. *Marie: the rights of woman citizens*

Within the space of one year, two short texts upset French, British and American societies, and planted the seeds for an ongoing debate that is still very much alive today. The first, by Marie Gouze, better known by the name Olympe de Gouges, appeared in 1791, in the middle of the French revolution; the second, by English writer Mary Wollstonecraft, was published in 1792. The two titles – *Déclaration des droits et de la citoyenne* and *A Vindication of the Rights of Women* – immediately reveal their debt to the previous two decades' debate on human rights and to the political and legislative gains of the late eighteenth century revolutions. Both published during the more exciting days of the French revolution, and preceding its more dramatic moments, the *Declaration of the rights of woman and of woman citizens* presents itself as a female version of the August 1789 Declaration, while *A Vindication of the Rights of Women* introduced all women and men of the time, in a clear, innovative and direct fashion, to the basic problems of the 'female question', whose foundations were firmly rooted in the past, and destined to last.

During the years of the *ancien regime* French women, like all European women, enjoyed practically no public rights. With no control over their own person or on any of their possessions, they passed directly from paternal to marital authority and were confined – in the case of women who were not aristocratic or bourgeois – to domestic service or underpaid heavy labour. As for political rights, if we exclude women belonging to religious orders (who could send representatives to the French States-General) and widows who could participate in the Third Estate primary assemblies, women enjoyed none.

Enlightenment philosophers were the first to explicitly introduce the question of relations between sexes and of their equality and differences, by examining the costumes and laws – marriage above all – that excluded women from public life and institutions, and strongly influenced their condition. Montesquieu and Voltaire had identified the Salic law – that excluded women from succession to the throne in France – as the true symbol of discrimination, while Diderot protested against the Statute that placed women in an analogous situation to that of children or of the insane. However, even amongst these thinkers, the view of women as overwhelmingly victims of emotions, passions and superstitions, whose behaviour was dictated by instinct as much as men's was dictated by reason, was a widespread opinion. Diderot himself warned mothers to protect their daughters' honesty by preventing them from behaving too 'indiscreetly', while Montesquieu claimed that only 'modesty' could reinforce female resistance to male assaults, considering promiscuity a violation of nature's laws.

Education was considered by all to be a crucial aspect of the 'female question'. Here the views expressed by Rousseau in *Emile* had a wide following, even amongst women.

Thus the entire education of women should be in function of men.

To be pleasant and useful to men, to be loved and honoured by them, to foster them as children, take care of them as adults, to advise them, to make their life pleasant and sweet: these are women's duties in every stage of life, and this is what they should be taught since infancy. (…) Women's power is made of sweetness, attention, complacency, her orders are caresses, her menaces are sighs. She must dominate within the household as a minister does within the state: by allowing herself to be ordered to do what she desires. Certainly the best examples of familiar harmony are the cases in which woman's authority is stronger. Yet when she does not listen to the head of the family, when she aims to usurp his rights and exercise leadership, the results are simply misery, scandal, dishonour.[101]

The Marquis de Condorcet, who was probably the only Enlightenment thinker and protagonist of the French revolution to coherently attribute to women the same prerogatives the revolution aimed to gain and defend for men, expressed his complaints about Rousseau's success amongst women, which according to him made women ill-prepared for a discussion on rights that included the right to vote. Condorcet spoke in the name of the numerous pamphlets and *cahiers de doléances*, written by women, which were circulating in revolutionary France and being discussed in Parisian political clubs and intellectual salons. The focus on education and economic subordination evidently did not overshadow the need for laws against paternal and marital despotism, in favour of divorce, an age of majority, and equal economic rights.

For a while the *Journal des droits de l'homme* wrote about the rights of women, until protests by male readers led its director to abandon the argument. The theme was addressed more generally within the pages of the female journal *Etrennes nationales des dames* and in the political club Cercle Social, where at the end of 1790 Condorcet shared his defence of the rights of women with Etta Palm, a Dutch woman who hoped for a 'second revolution' of customs and mentality. Palm attempted, unsuccessfully, to create a federation of female groups demanding equality in the fields of education, work, politics and law. The context however was hardly a favourable one. In July 1789 the Abbé Sieyès had summed up the widespread belief of the more open and progressive sectors of French society: 'Women, at least for the time being, with children, foreigners, in other words all those who contribute nothing to the public well-being, should have no direct influence on the government'.[102]

The *Declaration* of Olympe de Gouges incisively summarised the radical female perspective within the debates and participation of women in political clubs and in revolutionary publications. As a playwright Olympe had earned a certain degree of notoriety in 1785, when she presented, in the Comédie Française, a text later published under the title *L'esclavage des noirs*; in 1788 she published the pamphlet *Réflexions sur les hommes nègres* and in 1790 the theatrical play *Le marché des noirs*. These works allowed her to be included in the Société des Amis des Noirs, founded one year before the revolution by Jacques Pierre Brissot, the Girondin leader and friend of Tom Paine guillotined in October 1793. Initially a supporter of the constitutional monarchy, Olympe had become a republican after frequenting Madame Helvetius's literary salon and under the influence of Condorcet and the Girondins, who she had joined in 1792. Like Tom Paine, she was opposed to the execution of the king, and in 1792 had obtained the permission for women to participate in the *fête de la loi* on 3 June and in the celebration of the events of the Bastille on 14 July.

Following a preface filled with sharp and ironic phrases ('Man, do you know how to be fair? A woman is asking you: surely you don't want to deny her this right. Tell me, who gave you the superior power to oppress my gender? Your strength? Your capacities?'), the *Declaration*'s list of rights of women was similar to the list of rights of men, although it meticulously demanded an equality that, while generally accepted in terms of 'natural rights', nobody appeared inclined to recognise within the field of civil and – above all – political rights. Article 6 stated that:

> The law must be the expression of the general will: all male Citizens and female Citizens must concur personally or via their representatives in its formation; it must be the same for all: all female citizens and male citizens, being equal before the law, must be equally admitted to all public forms of dignity, locations and workplaces, according to their capacities and according to no further distinction than their virtues and talents.

Article 10 claimed that 'nobody should be molested because of their opinions, and if women have the right to be publicly executed, they should also have the right to speak publicly, as long as their demonstrations do not disturb public order as established by the Law'.[103]

Olympe was doomed by her closeness to the Girondins but above all by her attacks on Robespierre. On 9 June 1793 she courageously sent a letter full of indignation over the attack led by the Convention against the Girondin party on 2 June; destined, according to her, to disgrace all the democratic principles of the revolution. She was arrested on 6 August and accused of disputing, in a federalist-inspired article, the idea of the unique and indivisible republic. While being transferred between various prisons, Olympe managed to publish two clandestine testimonies (*Olympe de Gouges au Tribunal révolutionnaire* and *Une patriote persécutée*), but on 2 November she was sent to the guillotine which had, just a few days earlier, killed Brissot and most of the Girondin leaders.

A few months earlier a woman from the Beaurepaire section had pronounced these words before the Convention:

> Legislator citizens, you have given men a constitution; now they enjoy all the rights of free beings, yet women are far away from sharing these glories. Women count for nothing in the political system. We ask for primary assemblies and, just as the constitution is based on the Rights of Man, we now ask for the full exercise of such rights for ourselves too.[104]

How could it be that the execution of the most renowned champion of the rights of women was welcomed by the gazette *Feuille du salut public* with the words: 'it would appear that the law punished this conspirator for forgetting the virtues that suit her gender'?[105]

Marie-Olympe was not the only woman who paid for her ideas: the revolution would not allow the struggle for the rights of women to interrupt or obstruct its projects. Thus, while the intervention by the woman from Beaurepaire had been paternalistically praised by the President of the Convention, who then quickly dismissed the argument, a far worse destiny awaited Anne Terwagne, better known as Théroigne de Méricourt, who had participated in the assault on the Tuileries and struggled to create a female militia. Savagely beaten by the women of a Jacobin club in the spring of 1793 because of her sympathy towards the Girondin position, Théroigne went insane as a result of the violence and spent the last years of her life in an asylum.

Amongst the female clubs born during the revolution, the most famous was the Citoyennes républicaines révolutionnaires, founded in the spring of 1793 and directed by the actress Claire Lacombe and by the 'chocolate-maker' Pauline Léon. The club represented the most explicit case of women sympathising with the more radical aspects of the revolution. The Citoyennes were in favour of the fall of the Girondins and soon even abandoned the Jacobins by joining the cause of the 'enragés' and focusing their attention on economic and social objectives, rather than on political and civil equality. It was the Jacobins, who had executed Olympe de Gouges, who decided to close female clubs, which they considered instruments of the extremist 'counter-revolution' led by Jacques Roux and Théophile Leclerc (who was arrested in April 1794, along with his wife, Pauline Léon, and his former mistress Claire Lacombe).

In October 1793 André Amar presented the Convention with a report on behalf of the Public Health Committee, which denied women the opportunity of exercising political rights and of partaking in the constitution of the government, as well as the right to unite within political associations:

> their [of women] presence within the *sociétés populaires* would concede an active role in the government to persons who are far more inclined to mistakes and seduction than men are. May we also add that women, by nature, are more open to an excitement that may reveal itself as menacing within the public sphere. The interests of the state would soon be sacrificed in favour of all the kinds of dismemberments and disorders such hysteria could produce.[106]

All female clubs were closed and vetoed by a Convention vote, during the days when Olympe de Gouges was executed and Théroigne de Méricourt was taken into an asylum. The reasons seem to correspond to the logic of a political battle between various revolutionary factions, but in truth the fear that women – as such and as a group – could demand and gain citizenship and political rights was too strong a threat for those who were by that time fighting to enforce their positions. Many years would appear to have passed (in fact it was only 1790) since Condorcet had written: 'the rights of men derive only from the fact that they are sentient, capable of acquiring ideas and of reasoning about these ideas. Since women share these same qualities, they necessarily enjoy the same rights'.[107] By now the prevalent mentality was instead summarised in the final appeal to 'virtue' of the *procureur* of the Paris *Commune*, Anaxagoras Chaumette, when speaking to a delegation of women protesting against the closure of female political clubs:

> Women! Do you wish to be republicans? Dress in simple fashion, work hard within your homes, do not go to popular assemblies with the intention to speak. Do allow, however, your occasional presence to encourage your sons. If you act in this way your home-land will bless you, as you will have done all it can expect from you.[108]

9. *Mary: the rights of men and women*

In France the revolution had blocked and rejected the political aspirations of women. Following the closure of female clubs, in 1795 the Convention allowed women to attend its meetings only if accompanied by a male citizen, and prohibited them from exiting their home or meeting ingroups of more than five. On the civic and private level things were however improving: equality was obtained for heritage, debts, wills, divorce and partially for the administration of possessions and decisions about their children. The Napoleonic civil code – considered one of the most civilised of all times in many aspects – established, in article 213, that 'La femme doit obéissance au mari'.

What impeded the possible progress of women towards the acquisition of their rights in revolutionary France? Was it the political battle between various currents and the politicisation and fragmentation into diverse parties of the struggle for rights? Was it the prevalent Enlightenment culture that maintained an ambiguous attitude to the female question? Or was it the lack of articulate and courageous men – if we exclude Condorcet and, in some ways, Jacques Roux – capable of overcoming the dominant misogyny and the widespread idea that women belonged 'naturally' in the household? The view of the 'family' as the centre of female interest was an integral part of the bourgeoisie mentality (liberal or conservative, moderate or progressive) of the time. It was indeed medium-rich classes that lived the sociological condition of the nuclear family which was to become the model for the nineteenth century: a model within which women have a central role and responsibilities, as well as limited freedom and opportunities to become interested in the public sphere without damaging the private one.

The results, often conservative on a social level, of an explosive political event such as the revolution, must not be considered a simple contradiction or lack of coherence. The changes of mentality and customs, on one hand, and of economic and social transformations, on the other, hardly ever coincide with the accelerated political changes carried through by revolutions or events involving radical institutional or legislative transformations. In the case of women, however, it is important to not only identify this chronological gap, which became even wider as the revolution proceeded; but to underline how the theoretical logic, implied by the affirmation of natural rights and of the rights of man, and the practicality, inherent to the revolutionary legitimacy of overturning all existing norms, laid the foundations for the aspirations of women to remain on the rights agenda in the following decades and centuries.

Within this process Mary Wollstonecraft's book played a far more important part, in terms of circulation and influence, than the declarations and writings of French feminists. Her work was far more exhaustive in confronting the freedom enjoyed by men, and in demanding rights as a counterpart to duties or the supposed benefits granted to women when they demanded equal prerogatives.

With both the American and French declarations of rights, the era of revolutions affirmed the equality of all human beings, with the corollary that every person is a bearer of natural rights that belong to the entire human race. The debate on rights of the last two decades of the eighteenth century was destined to progressively erode the limits – above all political, but also cultural – set by powerful players and philosophical, juridical and scientific theories for the realisation of its objectives. It was the radical nature of the language of rights that allowed it to successively evolve, according to the phases permitted by each country's politics and culture, within an increasingly interconnected world.

In the Anglo-Saxon world, one of the first characters to openly demand the right to vote for women had been James Otis, the Massachusetts lawyer who coined the successful phrase 'taxation without representation is tyranny'. His position on female rights, analogous to those of Condorcet, were widely ignored or disregarded during the American Revolution, which fundamentally left the political condition of women unaltered. A *Vindication of the Rights of Woman* became the most formidable tool for the diffusion of women's expectations, with regard to their rights and to the possibility of a revolution 'in female ways', capable of offering greater professional opportunities, guarantees about the upbringing of children and participation in public life.

Mary Wollstonecraft addressed the problem in a simple manner. If natural rights are universal, as was claimed by all supporters of the theory of natural rights from the Enlightenment up to Paine, then they must also apply to women: since 'the rights of humanity have been limited to the male line from Adam onwards', female reality should be verified according to the same method as male reality. 'I truly believe' – Mary stated – 'that women should have their own representatives, rather than be governed arbitrarily without a direct action allowing them to participate in the deliberations of the government.' Women, at least 'in a political and civil sense, are slaves, although they indirectly obtain an excessive degree of power and are degraded by their efforts to obtain an illicit dominion'. The only possibility is to 'set them free, and they will soon become wise and virtuous, as will men; this evolution must be reciprocal, or the injustice half the human race is forced to suffer will turn against its oppressor, and the virtue of men will be eroded by the insect it holds beneath its feet'.[109]

In many cities of the United States *A Vindication of the Rights of Woman* sold as many copies as Tom Paine's *The Rights of Man*. Although they were the centre of persistent attacks against her 'immoral' conduct, Mary's ideas and the content of her polemical book continued to find an audience of careful and interested female readers and to progressively influence the male world at the same time. Mother of two daughters, one of whom was openly admitted to be a 'bastard child', Wollstonecraft had enjoyed many relationships, which her husband William Godwin, a rational philosopher, described in the memoirs he wrote after Mary's death in 1797 – she died while giving birth – which scandalised the defenders of the family and of female 'virtues'. Twenty years later, the girl who was born as Mary died, who became the wife of the poet and writer Percy Bysshe Shelley, published her novel *Frankenstein*.

Even the supporters of natural rights and the defenders of equality mostly shared an ambiguous attitude towards the full participation of women in the universality of rights. Although the reasons for this may be cultural or economic, individual or because of the state, influenced by the mentality and social reality of the historic period, the justifications for this tendency should be sought in the multiple and contradictory origins of the theories of rights of the seventeenth and eighteenth century. The coexistence, amongst the followers of natural rights and of utilitarianism, of a Scottish branch and a French one, of traditions referring to Grotius and Pufendorf as well as to Locke, or Rousseau, allows too for the coexistence of universality of rights and gender differences.

This meant the acceptance of the recognition that women had rights, yet that such rights were considered to be based in the world of virtue, in the moral code established by the community rather than in individual freedom attributed to the autonomy of each person. This declination of the theory of rights into two distinct forms is due to the incoherent, often confused and transversal relationship between supporters (and antagonists) of natural rights and the followers of the theory of the social contract. Convictions regarding existing regulations, the preference for a republic or for a constitutional monarchy, the legitimacy of a revolutionary outburst or the stubborn defence of social balance: these are also fundamental elements for individual interpretations of the theory of rights, which vary from person to person, be they philosophers or politicians, citizens or women aiming to obtain citizenship. Only Tom Paine, who did not write much in defence of women, demonstrated how it was possible to change one's institutional or political convictions coherently with a clear vision of rights.

In the cultural context of the late eighteenth century the rights of women could be considered the logical and evident consequence of attributing natural rights to women as 'persons'; yet it was also possible to deny them in the name of the 'real rights' of women (the maintenance of their children and of their husband) and of the difference between genders. The defence of family virtues, above all in the post-revolutionary United States, was carried forth in a positive key: as a 're-establishment' of female rights shadowed by male arbitrariness and despotism.

In the 1780s, William Loughton Smith, a deputy from South Carolina, told a female crowd: 'Although you are excluded from participation within our political institutions nature has given you worthy and healthy rights, which are beyond their [of men] control. To delight, civilise and improve humanity, *these are the precious rights of women!*'[110]

The fear that the rights of women, from education to the right to vote, could threaten male supremacy in the public sphere, and men's authority in the private sphere, was certainly one of the reasons behind the lack of support for such prerogatives. Indeed the lack of radical and coherent positions amongst women themselves reveals how the 'exchange' between more power within the family and participation in the public space was widely accepted in the mentality of the time.

However the fact that nobody denied that women were bearers of rights would become the Trojan horse for the struggles to follow. Radical positions were intrinsic to the very language of rights, to the egalitarian and universalistic notions it contained, even when it was denying the rights of single groups or, as in this case, of an entire half of humanity. At the end of the eighteenth century these radical positions were not yet fully understood, if not by just a few, and thus found limited space for expression. The refusal of the political rights of women appears to be the limit, beyond which an acceptance of the natural rights of every person was still incapable of going. However this refusal was historical, contingent, not inherent to the theory of rights of the period; it is more the result of mentality and customs than of reason and morality. Interests and convictions, often no more than prejudices, temporarily halted the culture of rights. Yet this culture had time and reason on its side. This would be demonstrated by the other great question which emerged alongside the gender problem: the question of slavery.

Chapter Three
The Humanitarian Rules

1. *Toussaint and the independence of slaves*

On 22 August 1791, at ten o'clock in the evening, on the island of Santo-Domingo – from 1627 the most important French colony – the rhythm of drums spread out across the sugar cane plantations. This was the signal for the rebellion of the slaves. Armed with hooks and machetes, they angrily and violently attacked cultivated fields, farmhouses and bakeries, leaving behind destroyed vehicles and raped women. 'If the Negroes of Santo-Domingo have committed this amount of crimes' – wrote Madame Germaine de Staël in 1818, replying to François-René de Chateaubriand who had asked 'who will dare to still defend the cause of the Black Folk after the crimes they have committed?' – 'it is because they were even more oppressed. The fury of revolts reveals the extent of the vices of in-stitutions'.[111]

Just a few days before the approval of the constitution, and coinciding with the clash between moderates and radicals – which had exploded with the Champ-de-Mars massacre on 17 July – the French revolution faced an unexpected problem: the revolt of thousands of slaves in French territories, incited by the rumours, promises and hopes coming from Paris after the events of the Bastille and the proclamation of the Declaration of the Rights of Man. In truth it was the beginning of a new revolution that would last for twelve years, which in 1938 was summarised as followed by CLR James, a Trinidad-born cricket journalist and Trotskyist revolutionary, as well as a supporter of independence for the West Indies:

> The slaves defeated in turn the local whites and the soldiers of the French monarchy, a Spanish invasion, a British expedition of some 60,000 men, and a French expedition of similar size under Bonaparte's brother-in-law. The defeat of Bonaparte's expedition

in 1803 resulted in the establishment of the Negro State of Haiti which has lasted to this day. The revolt is the only successful slave revolt in history.[112]

The revolt's leader was Toussaint Louverture – a recently freed slave, herdsman and coachman, veterinarian and herbalist, who owned slaves himself, although he was not a mulatto but allegedly descended from the Chief of a Western African tribe. Were his followers really *black Jacobins*? And did they act because of the harsh conditions under which they lived or because they were conscious of their rights as 'persons', which were being debated in enlightened and revolutionary France?

During a meeting in Paris in August 1789, the Comte de Mirabeau had told Thomas Clarkson, the leader of the struggle against the slave trade, that he believed the white colonists of Santo-Domingo were living as if they were 'below the slopes of the Vesuvius', awaiting an inevitable eruption. When news of the events of 22 August arrived in Paris, the Convention was still debating the protests and proposals of colonists united in the club Messiac. Opposition to the decision, approved on 15 May 1791, to grant the rights of citizenship to mulattos born of free parents, forced a change of attitude and a transfer of power concerning these issues to colonial assemblies. On 24 September 1791 Antoine Barnave tried to defend, in a sophisticated and somewhat captious fashion, both the motivations of the colonists and the principles of equality established by the National Assembly:

> Prejudices are the safeguard of White existence in the colonies. This regime is absurd yet it is constituted and can not be modified bluntly without provoking the greatest disorder; this regime is oppressive yet it allows millions of men to live in France; this regime is barbaric yet an attempt to change it without the necessary knowledge would cause even greater barbarism: the blood of a numerous generation will be spilled because of your imprudence.[113]

The Santo-Domingo revolt soon spread to the entire island. In the North the leader of the movement was Toussaint Louverture, while in the South the revolt had involved mulattos as well, and was led by André Rigaud. The return of the colony's governor to Paris, where he was guillotined, paved the way for a civil war between white colonists themselves, divided into monarchists and republicans – just as in France. The Legislative Assembly overturned its previous judgement and on 4 April 1792 granted political rights to mulattos and black slaves. The slaves of the most important French colony were now the most coherent supporters of the ideals of freedom and equality, clashing with revolutionary France, which faced one of its most profound contradictions over these very issues.

In the meantime the violence escalated; brutality and barbarity characterised behaviour on both sides, each of which justified its actions in the name of freedom. At the time Santo-Domingo produced 30% of the world's sugar, and half of its coffee: William Pitt, the British Prime Minister, had called it 'the Eden of the West', while the French called it 'the pearl of the Antilles'. The island was also the most active market for the Atlantic slave trade. Over a territory as vast as all the British colonies of the Caribbean put together, 40,000 white colonists subjugated half a million slaves.

As sometimes happens in these critical moments of history, it was one man who acted as a detonator for the situation, dominated by violence and seemingly unresolvable. Léger-Félicité Sonthonax, who had been sent to the island as a commissar to implement the April 1792 decree and to win back the control of the situation in the name of the French government, was a Girondin who belonged, as did Brissot, to the Society of the Friends of Black People. He soon realised he did not have sufficient forces to maintain order on the island, which was ravaged by the slaves' rebellion and by the fierce clash between republican and monarchist colonists. The monarchists were the majority and were paying great attention to events taking place in Jamaica, a British colony which had declared war against revolutionary France in February. On 29 August 1793 Sonthonax proclaimed, on his own initiative, the end of slavery on the island of Santo-Domingo.

While the French government, by then controlled by the Committee of Public Safety, was preparing to legitimise a decision which had already been proclaimed without its consent – on 4 February 1794 the Convention voted unanimously for the liberation of slaves in all French colonies, making France the first European country to abolish slavery – the Santo-Domingo colonists turned their hopes to Britain, which was currently at war with their homeland. Henry Dundas, the War Minister of the British government, declared that the battle to conquer the French island was 'a war for security', that needed to be fought to prevent Jamaica and other islands of the Caribbean discovering the temptations of anti-slavery revolts.

In September 1793 the first British soldiers disembarked on the Southern beaches of Santo-Domingo, where they were met with the unexpected resistance of a mulatto army. Nonetheless, they quickly managed to conquer the capital Port-au-Prince. Believing they had already won the war, the British did not realise that in Toussaint Louverture they were up against a brilliant military strategist, and that the freed slaves were prepared to face any ordeal to prevent a return to oppression. Their guerrilla warfare spread fear and death amongst the British troops, aided by outbursts of malaria and yellow fever, whose destructive and horrific effects generated even more terror and insecurity amongst the invaders. The British, on the other hand, were not only fighting in Santo-Domingo, but in the whole of the Caribbean, given the fact that the slaves of many other colonies were attempting to emulate the exploits of their French brothers: in Grenada, in Barbados, in Jamaica and in Guadalupe, which had been removed from French dominion and was now inhabited by freed slaves. In addition, they had to face an increasing number of desertions by the soldiers who had been sent to the colonies to suppress the slave rebellions.

While in France most of the Friends of Black People had been guillotined, victims of the Jacobin Reign of Terror, an English fleet – 20,000 men and 200 ships - set sail for Santo-Domingo. The island was by then split in two: on one side were the British and the monarchist French colonists, while the other was occupied by the freed slaves and the republican colonists. The invaders were being fought by the army of Toussaint in the North and by Rigaud's forces in the South, a black man and a mulatto born – as the *London Gazette* wrote – 'to vindicate the claims of this species and to show that the character of men is independent of exterior colour'.[114]

Half of the 90,000 British soldiers fighting in the West Indies between 1793 and 1801 died in battle or of tropical diseases; 15,000 were injured and abandoned the battle; 20,000 sailors died on Her Majesty's ships travelling between England and the Caribbean. The total number of troops sent to fight this war was greater than that used against the American colonists and the number of victims was also higher.

The impossibility of victory and these continuous losses led to the British abandoning Santo-Domingo. On 31 August 1798 General Maitland signed an agreement with Toussaint himself, ignoring proposals by General Hédouville, the pacifier of the Vendée, who had been sent by the Directory to re-establish French sovereignty on the island. Toussaint agreed not to intervene, either militarily or via propaganda, in Jamaica and in the other British islands. The occupation had ended and yet the conflict now continued between the troops of Toussaint and those led by Rigaud, nominated General Commander by Hédouville, who had left the island in October. Thus began the 'war of knives' or 'war of races', in which most of the white colonists sided with the mulatto general while most of the black population supported Toussaint Louverture.

This civil war, if possible, was even more brutal than the previous ones, and took place while France was undergoing the experience of the Directory, followed by the Napoleonic *coup d'état* on 18 Brumaire 1799 (9 November). Toussaint defeated Rigaud, who escaped to France, and instituted a military regime that was later opposed by his very own adoptive son, Moïse, who was in favour of a division of land amongst freed slaves. Louverture appeared to now be in control of the situation, having pacified the island and sacrificing his own family during this process, and wrote to Napoleon as 'the leader of the black people' to 'the leader of white people' (ignoring the Ajaccio general's own anti-abolitionist convictions and the slave driver origins of his wife Joséphine, whose father owned a plantation in Martinique).

At the beginning of 1802 30,000 French soldiers landed in Santo-Domingo. Initially the invasion did not appear to be successful against Toussaint's guerrilla tactics and the technique of scorched earth he used to render the enemy victories useless. However when some of his generals, tired of fighting and attracted by French promises, swapped sides, Toussaint decided to negotiate. General Charles Leclerc, the head of the expedition, promised Toussaint would receive the title of General and that slavery would not be re-introduced. Deceived and captured, he was sent to France in chains and imprisoned in the Fort de Joux on the Swiss border. Napoleon reinstated slavery and the trade in slaves and denied mulattos the equality of rights that the French revolution had given them.

As soon as the news, carried by slaves escaping from Guadalupe, that slavery had been reinstated as a French law spread to the colony, a new rebellion began in Santo-Domingo. Leclerc informed Paris that the black soldiers were fighting fanatically and that he believed the only way to win the war was to kill all men and women, allowing only children under twelve to survive. In the meantime he ordered the fight against the rebels to continue with as much determination and brutality as possible. A long series of atrocities took place: naked prisoners were left to be eaten by starving mastiffs and Molossian dogs; some were forced to watch their children drown; black people and mulattos were imprisoned in ship holds and suffocated slowly by fumes of burning sulphur.

Now that Napoleon was at war with them, the British began to praise Toussaint and his heroism. In April 1802 William Wordsworth dedicated a short poem to him, calling him 'the unhappiest of men'.[115] On 7 April

1803 Louverture died, just a few months before the French troops were forced to abandon Santo-Domingo, defeated, just as the British had been before them, and after losing 50,000 men.

On 1 January 1804 the Republic of Haiti was born, under the ancient name given to the island by the Arawak Indians: after three centuries of slavery the inhabitants were finally free and independent, and proclaimed a constitution which allowed any black person or Indian to acquire citizenship.

2. *The abolition of the slave trade*

Twenty years after the first meeting in James Phillips's print shop, the British Parliament abolished the slave trade. It wasn't the first act of this kind to take place in the European and American continents, yet it was certainly the most significant as a reversal of tendencies concerning the commerce of human beings; the decision of the Parliament strengthened the struggle against the very idea of slavery.

Denmark was the first country to abolish the trade in 1792, after a governmental commission had demonstrated its limited commercial value and economic convenience. The country first established a transitional regime, based on the procreation of existing slaves within the colonies rather than the introduction of new ones. The trade was finally abolished in 1803, yet in these colonies the end of slavery only arrived in 1848.

Following its initial hesitations and contradictions over the problem of slavery, revolutionary France was incapable of protecting and stabilising its 1794 abolition, except in Haiti, where it was the former slaves who fought for independence. The 1802 Napoleonic reintroduction of slavery and of slave trades was suspended by the emperor himself, once he regained power after his hundred-day exile on the island of Elba. Louis XVIII and Talleyrand, reinstated by the British after the victory at Waterloo, tried to circumvent the British order to abolish the trade, consenting to a formal but ineffective repression of their slave ships, in reality letting Nantes play the role that Bristol had before the victory of English abolitionism. The 1827 French abolitionist law hardly had any consequences and only a third law, dated 1831, achieved any tangible results.

In the United States, Massachusetts, Connecticut, New York and Pennsylvania prohibited the slave trade in 1788. A few years later, only Georgia still legally traded slaves, until Thomas Jefferson convinced the congress, in 1807 – the same year as the British abolition – to ban the importing of slaves throughout the entire American territories. As in

France, this law was widely ignored in the United States, until such a point was reached that in 1820 the trading of slaves was declared equal to piracy, so that it could be suppressed more severely. However, the fact that many Southern captains, who were strong supporters of slavery, led the Union's ships, made this action widely unsuccessful until 1840. Only the civil war, which broke out in 1861, made a significant difference to the trade, and gave birth to the anti-slavery struggle.

The abolitionist movement was far slower in Spain; the government intended to defend its Cuban plantations – where a slave revolt had taken place in 1844 – and consequently failed to respect the international agreements it had signed. A first abolitionist law, proclaimed in 1845, was followed by a second and definitive one in 1867, the year in which the very last slave ship travelled to Cuba. Abolitionism was equally contested and complex in Portugal; the country had signed agreements with Britain yet still decided to award the most successful slave-mongers of the following years with titles of nobility.

What allowed the English Parliament in February 1807 to abolish the slave trade, with only six votes against in the House of Commons and a 75% majority in the House of Lords? The attempts by William Wilberforce, the parliamentary representative of abolitionist groups – who had obtained an initial rejection in 1791 and the approval of a gradualist proposal in 1792 (which was rejected by the House of Lords) – faced significant difficulties after the Santo-Domingo revolts, which appeared to block the expansion of the movement started by the 'Clapham saints' in 1787. However, over the course of two or three years, Granville Sharp, Thomas Clarkson, the Phillips cousins and the other advocates of the struggle against the slave trade managed to obtain hundreds of thousands of signatures for their parliamentary petitions, mobilising all social classes and involving women and indeed the entire population by using new and effective communicative strategies. Churches joined the battle, while the press often acted as an unexpected and welcome source of resonance; badges featuring the slogan 'Am I not a man and a brother?', above a kneeling black man in chains, were distributed amongst the nobility and bourgeoisie, while other parts of the population were won over by drawings of slave ships or by tales of the violence, deprivations and humiliations the slaves had to suffer during journeys from Africa to the Caribbean and to America. The drawing of the Brookes, the vessel whose schematised section was found by Clarkson in Liverpool, with the image of almost 500 men imprisoned within tiny spaces, travelled across Europe and America alongside texts by Mirabeau, Condorcet and the Abbé Raynal, as well as others by Tom Paine and Olympe de Gouges in defence of the 'natural' freedom of each person. In those same years theatrical works like Madame de Staël's *Mirza*, Victor Hugo's *Bug Jargal* and *Tamango* by Prosper Mérimée addressed the issue of slavery and transformed it into a subject of debate amongst the bourgeoisie, often contributing to the formation of the myths of innocence and violent nature of slaves. Other works, though less important on a literary level, were strongly influential on the general population – *Ourika* by Claire de Duras and Sophie Doin's *La famille noire* (not coincidentally works by women); and also *Lebao, le nègre* by Hippolyte Demolière and Jules Chardon – and offered hints of social explanations and psychological justifications for the contradictory and 'emotional' behaviour of enslaved men.

The abolitionist movement was aided in its diffusion and growth by its humanitarian objective, by the religious context within which it was initially organised and by the egalitarian conscience that the Enlightenment had, for various parts of society, transmuted into common sense. However, the movement was also helped by the novelised stories of its protagonists and by the attention both high and low forms of literature devoted to the issue of slavery: these literary works had a phenomenal effect on problems which just a few years earlier seemed to interest only minority groups. Samuel Taylor Coleridge described the 'moral beauty' of Thomas Clarkson, comparing him to Napoleon and Alexander; certainly these literary recognitions were yet another incentive to struggle on in a battle that was still far from over when the anti-trade law was approved in 1807.

Amid the enthusiasm following Napoleon's defeat in 1814, the British government granted the French five further years of slave trading in the Caribbean. Within a few weeks Clarkson managed to collect more than 700,000 signatures – from a population of 12 million – on a petition asking the government to change the peace treaty with regard to allowing further trading. Shortly after these events, during the Easter of 1816, the slaves of Barbados rebelled – amongst their leaders was a housemaid who used to read leaflets and proclamations to her companions – claiming they had discovered that Wilberforce had freed them.

After brutally suppressing the rebellion, Britain did not proceed, as Clarkson hoped, along the road towards the new goal of full emancipation. In 1823 the survivors of the first struggles against the slave trade, encouraged by their younger supporters, met in the King's Head Tavern and founded the London Society for Mitigating and Gradually Abolishing the State of Slavery throughout the British Dominions. Soon the society could count on 230 branches across Britain, and was extremely active in organising meetings and demonstrations, as well as presenting over

700 petitions to Parliament, which were received by MPs with vague assurances, and proposing laws to improve the life and instruction of slaves and to forbid the use of whips against women.

At this point it was in fact women who proved themselves determinant, by leading and attempting to radicalise the next phase in the movement's evolution. It must of course be stressed that women had already participated in abolitionist efforts during the previous years. In the 1750s Rebecca Jones, Catherine Phillips and Mary Peisley had travelled for thousands of miles, in the North and South of the United States, to convince their co-religionists – Quakers – to free their slaves; and during the 1780s they travelled once more, in England and Ireland, to participate in the abolitionist campaign. In 1788 over two hundred women had joined the 'Clapham twelve', including Hannah More and Lady Margaret Middleton, friends and wives of MPs and influential members – often conservative and evangelical – of the upper classes, as well as authors of poems and stories which drew the compassion of their fellow citizens. Nor was the movement short of teachers, including Anna Laetitia Barbauld and Helen Maria Williams, friends of Mary Wollstonecraft, who were the first to denounce the suffering and humiliation of women slaves. And it was a woman, Mary Birkett, who proposed the boycott of slave-produced sugar which began in 1791 and involved aristocratic and bourgeois women as well as female servants and members of the lower classes.

Thirty years later it was once more a woman who proposed the boycott of sugar in the county of Leicester. A teacher who had converted to Quakerism, her name was Elizabeth Heyrick and in 1824 she wrote the pamphlet *Immediate, not Gradual Abolition*, speaking in the name of over 70 female anti-slavery societies instituted during the previous years. In the elections of 1826 these groups asked for immediate emancipation and proposed to vote only for men who agreed to reject gradualism. They also distributed badges featuring the writing 'Am I not a woman and a sister?' above a black woman in chains. In some locations the boycotts also targeted bakers using sugar produced in slave plantations, while women-only demonstrations took place in most English cities. Wilberforce, who had now retired after 40 years in Parliament, described the behaviour of these women as unbefitting feminine nature as described in the sacred texts.

Why, asked Elizabeth Heyrick, were the revolts of the West Indian slaves not considered 'heroic and deserving' like the Greek battles for independence against the Ottoman Empire? Nobody appeared to be able to answer the simple question asked by this courageous woman who, although she did not enjoy the right to vote herself, fought for slaves – as

well as women – to be considered as people. Certainly she would receive
no reply from William IV, the new English king, viewed by Clarkson as
one of the worst enemies of slave emancipation. It was however during
his brief reign (1830-37) that in 1833, ten years after the founding of the
new society, the Slavery Abolition Act established the end of slavery in
the entire British Empire.

3. *Nations and nationalisms*

> Breathes there the man with soul so dead
> Who never to himself hath said:
> This is my own, my Native land?[116]

Thus begins the first of Walter Scott's narrative poems – *The Lay of the Last
Minstrel* – to reach a wide audience, in 1805. Patriotism, as depicted in his
first historical novel (*Waverley*) and later in the medieval myth of *Ivanhoe* and
his Scottish tales (*Rob Roy, The Bride of Lammermoor, A Legend of Montrose*),
lay at the heart of the author's Romanticism. Scott, who had also translated
into English Goethe's *Götz von Berlichingen*, gave his tales an adventurous
and heroic dimension in which national identities play an important role.
The bond to the homeland represented, at the beginning of the nineteenth
century, the emotional and passionate aspect of the liberal political ideal
of nation-states. National identity appealed to the collective feelings of the
bourgeoisie and 'revolutionary' social classes of the late eighteenth century
and early nineteenth century. They opposed the reigning dynasties in the
name of the people, of a civic nationalism and of the rights of citizens. The
nation was the modern declination of the concept of the homeland. It met the
demand for territorial and political unity, and accounted for the necessary
transformation of communities in the era of the major economical, social and
cultural transformations of developing capitalism. These communities reacted to such changes by creating collective representations and narratives
in order to preserve their identities, reinforce them or even build them from
scratch, while demanding to become autonomous states. The nation became
the primary and recognised objective of nineteenth century international
politics, as well as the terrain where, ever since the French revolution, the
masses were transformed into individuals belonging to nations, and were
accompanied by the nation-state in their journey – more cultural than social
– from 'peasants' to 'citizens'.[117]

The rights of man were mainly signified by his individual freedom
and his equality before the law, while those of the citizen mainly
concerned political rights and inclusion in the nation. Thus, in the case of

a violated or oppressed nation, these rights coincided with the possibility of gaining identity through a battle for autonomy and independence. If each man has the right to a nation, each nation has a right to existence, and should therefore liberate itself from the bonds which prevent its realisation and become separate from the state entities which deny such a possibility.

This was the ideal that pushed many men, patriots and soldiers, and especially poets and artists, to fight for the independence of a nation. One such was the Englishman George Gordon Byron, who died in 1824 near Patras, where he was helping the Greek population rebel against the oppression he had written about with desperation in the last stanza of *The Isles of Greece*:

Place me on Sunium's marbled steep,
Where nothing, save the waves and I,
May hear our mutual murmurs sweep;
There, swanlike, let me sing and die:
A land of slaves shall ne'er be mine--
Dash down yon cup of Samian wine![118]

'My dear David' – wrote Diderot to David Hume in 1768, in an exaltation of cosmopolitanism – 'you belong to all nations and will never ask an unfortunate soul for his baptism certificate. I am proud to be, as you are, a citizen of the great city of the world'.[119] Half a century later the sense of belonging to the human race was no weaker, at least among the more generous (and combative) personalities, yet appeared to be summarised in every person's right to own a baptism certificate, to see their home-land recognised and their own nation established. The 'revolution' of the Enlightenment and the Romantic 'nation' – the two collective ideals which succeeded each other in the eighteenth and nineteenth centuries – found their model, which fascinated Europeans above all, in Greece, giv-en the country's legacy of a classical culture in which the right to freedom had first been consecrated. In the New World it was instead the Latin Ameri-can countries that gave rise to hopes and worries, as we can read in the following letter, from Thomas Jefferson to Alexander von Humboldt: 'I think it most fortunate that your travels in those countries were so timed as to make them known to the world in the moment they were about to become actors on its stage. That they will throw off their European dependence I have no doubt; but in what kind of government their revolution will end I am not so certain. History, I believe, furnishes no example of a priest-ridden people maintaining a free civil government.[120]

Between 1810 and 1830, between the climax of the Napoleonic era and the July revolution in France (which terminated the main line of the Bourbon dynasty), almost all Latin American countries gained their independence from the colonial domination of Spain and Portugal. The first ones to rebel against Madrid had been the 60,000 Indios from Peru under the leadership of José Gabriel Condorcanqui, known as Tupac Amaru II – a descendant of the last Inca emperor who had led the resistance against the Spanish invasion. Despite their failure – in 1781 Tupac Amaru II was decapitated in Plaza de Armas in Cusco – their revolt was soon imitated by the Indios in Venezuela, who were also brutally repressed by the Spanish. The local populations, apart from the richer and privileged élites bound to the Spanish crown, were inspired by the echoes of American independence and of the French revolution. Thus, in 1808, they took advantage of the Napoleonic invasion of Spain to begin their war for liberation. Led by Simón Bolívar and Francisco de Paula Santander, José de San Martín and Antonio José de Sucre, the patriotic juntas of Caracas and Quito, Bogotá and Buenos Aires proclaimed their independence in 1816. This event marked the beginning of a complex battle – involving social and border-related struggles – against the Spanish, which eventually resulted in the establishment of the national states of Colombia (1819), Venezuela (1819), Argentina (1816), Chile (1818), Peru (1821), Mexico (1821), Brazil (1822), Bolivia (1824) and Uruguay (1825).

Independence was not always accompanied by political freedom and civil rights for all; the dictatorial and Caudilist tendencies which have characterised the history of the Latin American continent were already present in the years of the wars for independence. What was important, at the beginning of the nineteenth century, was the correlation between the individual and the nation, between the rights of the person and those of a collectivity united by a common identity. Each population recognised it had its own singular and unrepeatable history and, as a consequence, the right to a common territory (the nation) where it could exercise its sovereignty (as a state).

The major multinational empires of the nineteenth century (Hapsburg, Tsarist and Ottoman) had to face many difficulties with regard to the question of nationalities. The British ideals of civic and economic freedom (in 1800 England had incorporated Ireland and created the United Kingdom) were now accompanied by the ideals of political freedom and independence spread across the world by the French and American revolutions. After the end of the war between Napoleonic France and England, the battle for the freedom of populations became a central argument in Europe, where the Congress of Vienna (1815) had succeeded in restoring ancient powers only on a formal level.

As we have seen Greece was the most important example of such struggles for freedom. The death of Selim III (1807), the last reformist Sultan, marked the beginning of the decline of the Ottoman Empire, which would continue for the entire nineteenth century (and beyond) and was characterised by a constant loss of territories and power in its dominions. In 1811 the Egyptian Pasha Mehmet Ali, who had been named governor by the Sultan in 1805 and had later defeated the Mamluks, proclaimed Egypt's autonomy from the Ottoman Empire, although he agreed to take part in the battle of Navarino, where the Ottoman fleet was defeated by the Europeans. Having started in 1821, the insurrection of the Greek patriots soon extended to the islands and to continental Greece, although it was forced to retreat during the following years, in the face of the Ottoman response backed by Egyptian troops. The final battle for Greek independence took place in the port of the Peloponnese; the nation's independence was established by the Treaty of Adrianople (1829) and, definitively, by the Protocol of London (1830).

The revolutions which took place in 1848, not by coincidence dubbed 'the springtime of the peoples', were the first to successfully combine the struggle for freedom with the fight for independence, the civil and political rights of individuals with the rights of citizens to have their own nation and a representative state for their national community. The first population to rebel was the Sicilians, who demanded and secured independence for their island, obtaining a constitution from their Bourbon rulers; in March the inhabitants of Piedmont also secured the constitution known as the Statuto Albertino. However it was Paris, once again, that was destined to be the epicentre of a revolt that would soon spread to the whole of Europe: on 22 February the revolution which led to the Second Republic began; on 13 March Vienna rebelled against the Hapsburg rulers and Budapest did the same two days later, demanding independence from Austria. In the German Confederation Berlin rebelled and obtained the universal male suffrage; on 22 March Venice proclaimed the Republic of San Marco and in the same period the Five Days of Milanese insurrection against the Austrian occupation took place. On 23 March the Kingdom of Sardinia declared war against Austria, only to be defeated at Custoza in August, after the victories in Goito and Peschiera. In November Rome also rebelled and in 1849 the Roman Republic was formed.

In contrast to the previous Latin American events, all the European revolts ended in defeat: the 'springtime of the peoples' was followed by a winter of restoration. The end of the German parliamentary assembly; the defeat of the Hungarian population; the repression of the Austrian,

Calabrese and Sicilian revolts; the 1849 suppression of the Republics of Venice[121] and Rome; the abrogation of all the statutes and constitutions which had been conceded in order to stop the revolts: all these events could not, however, turn back the clock of history and erase the rights of citizens and nations. At the time 1848 appeared to have been a failure and a futile bloodbath. In the following decades, however, the push for national independence would be victorious in Germany and Italy, while constitutional reforms were accepted, with diverse results and effects, in numerous other European countries.

It was not by coincidence that, just after these convulsive decades, Renan provided us with what was destined to become the most classical and well-known definition of a nation: 'A nation is a soul, a spiritual principle [...] The possession in common of a rich legacy of memories [...] consent, the clearly expressed desire to continue a common life [...] a daily plebiscite'.[122]

Amongst the reasons for the failures of 1848, alongside the ruling monarchies' will to restore and repress, we should certainly mention the conflicts between the patriots themselves: on one side was a more moderate and constitutional faction, on the other a more radical one, thirsty for political changes that could lead to deeper social transformations. It was probably no coincidence that during the same year as the 'springtime of the peoples' a pamphlet that anticipated the themes of social revolution and was destined to influence the following decades, was published: *The Communist Manifesto* by Karl Marx and Friedrich Engels. In that very same year, as we shall see, on the other side of the Atlantic, a document which probably marked the dawn of the feminist movement was signed.

An important figure for emerging nationalisms was certainly Pasquale Stanislao Mancini, who held the first professorial chair of international law in Turin (1850) and was the author, one year later, of an inaugural essay – *Nationality as the source of the rights of people* – that would become an essential juridical reference for the Italian Risorgimento. 'He stated that the actual subjects of the international community should be Nations (human groups united by a common language and culture, by common traditions and customs) and not states, as each sovereign state should embrace within its borders only one nation'.[123]

4. *The declaration of Seneca Falls*

At the end of July 1848, while the European 'springtime of the peoples' was at its most lively, the first Convention for the Rights of Women was taking place in the United States, in Seneca Falls, New York.[124]

In the United States the 1830s and 1840s were a period in which demand for reforms and profound changes coalesced into associations and organisations; these groups, widely inspired by religious movements, identified a series of concrete goals to be achieved through mobilisation, propaganda and political activities. Plenty of the associations were marked by a strong degree of female participation, while many were composed exclusively of women. The post-revolutionary period was characterised by the contradiction between the recognition of the equality of persons (and thus of genders) and the persistent subordination of women to men. The success, in the United States, of Mary Wollstonecraft's *A Vindication of the Rights of Woman* – thanks in large part to literary periodicals and female journals, which were gaining an ever-wider public during those very years[125] – allowed women to consider the matter of their rights in terms that were increasingly pertinent to daily life, by questioning the disparity between their recognised roles in private and public life.

The revolution 'in female forms' that Wollstonecraft had announced found its strongest arguments in the fields of education and of professional opportunities for women, which constituted the privileged terrain upon which they could reinforce their existence as 'bearers' of rights participating in the natural rights of humanity. Thus, just as small proprietors and artisans, labourers and unemployed men had entered the political community created by the American Revolution, women now aimed to take advantage of the culture of natural rights which 'invited inquiry, not simply into the rights which human beings possessed but into those rights which, given their nature, they *ought* to possess'.[126] The objective of all those who addressed these arguments between the end of the eighteenth century and the beginning of the nineteenth century, women included, would appear to be the conciliation of the *theoretical* rights of women with their *practical* subordination to men. The fear that a denunciation of the gender *status quo* might trigger conflicts and social transformations, which could contradict the social models which emerged from the attainment of independence, prevailed mainly due to a conservatism that was not only political or social, but, on an even deeper level, cultural. The fear of domestic rebellions and of a crisis of the institution of the family, the pivot of communal existence, led to an emphasis on a spiritual and moral equality between genders. There emerged the proposal of an *equal* right to education that in reality was *different* because its aim was to prepare women for their roles as wives and mothers. Commenting upon the proposal advanced by Bridget Bearwell on 31 October 1801 in the 'Lady's Monitor', to confer exactly the same duties, roles and positions to men and women, the 'Mercury and New-England Palladium' concluded that 'nothing was more dangerous to the rights of men than when it took possession in the *home department*' and that 'when women leave their character, and assume the character and rights of men, they relinquish their own rights, and are to be regarded, and treated, as men'.[127]

Whether indicating a biological difference between men and women, or a psychological or cultural one, nobody at this time seemed to deny the *right* of women to have rights. Both men and women were considered bearers of rights, but distinct ones; among the *real rights* of women were first of all the upbringing of children and support of the husband, while political freedom and personal autonomy were not yet considered as such. The fact that women had been recognised as bearers of rights, however, made it difficult to contrast, on a theoretical level, the appeal by women to access spheres of society beyond the domestic. When, in 1822, Elizabeth Bartlett was nominated cadastral inspector of the county of Middlesex, in Massachusetts, women showed their appreciation for this decision, although they also wondered if it had only happened because Bartlett was unmarried. What would have happened, some asked, if she had decided to marry: 'if a lady be eligible as a Register of Deeds, is she not also as a Governor, Senator, Representative, Overseer of the poor or other public office?'[128]

The denial of the political rights of women was one of the main limits of post-revolutionary America's application – the other, equally important one, regarded the black minority – of a culture of rights that was accepted, or rather demanded, on a theoretical level. Was this exclusion due to an entrenched gender discrimination, the conviction that women carried some kind of inferiority (biological and inherent, historical and cultural, psychological) when compared to men? Or was it instead the contingent result of an era in which theoretical principles (in this case the rights of the person) had difficulty in being translated into concrete facts, because they faced a social structure and mentality which still considered gender hierarchy too significant an obstacle? Historical reasons would appear to indicate the prevailing of a gender-based division of human rights, which led, in the United States more obviously than elsewhere, to the elaboration of an ideology based on 'separate spheres'.[129]

The 1830s saw a notable increase in the number of women involved in organisations working for the improvement of the life conditions of deprived persons, from the mentally ill to the incarcerated, from cholera victims to uneducated children. In 1834 the Female Reform Society was founded in New York, an exclusively female association, led by Lydia Finney. It was created with the objective of saving prostitutes from being exploited and marginalised. Lydia was the wife of a pastor who was an active member of the Protestant Evangelical Church the Second Great Awakening, a religious movement which advocated – via itinerant preachers, universal redemption, the fundamental role of personal pity and the centrality of the values of work – temperance and frugality. The movement was also socially active in trying to reform prisoners, alcoholics and prostitutes, and in supporting women's right to vote and the abolition of slavery.

The occasion for the Seneca Falls meeting originated in the 1840 London World Convention against Slavery, whose participants included Elizabeth Cady Stanton and Lucretia Mott. The former, influenced by Charles Finney and travelling in Britain on her honeymoon, supported the latter, a Quaker minister and anti-slavery militant, who was taking on the men of the Convention, who were refusing to let women participate, even if – as in Lucretia's case – they were delegates elected by their respective organisations. Forced to follow the assembly from the guest balcony, the New York-born twenty-five year old and the forty-seven year old from Massachusetts became close friends and later decided to organise a Convention to discuss the rights of women in Seneca Falls, the town to which Elizabeth had just moved.

Although the first session was supposed to include only women, the arrival of many men altered the situation. Indeed, alongside 68 women, 32 men also signed the Convention's conclusive document, the Declaration of Sentiments, which, in its opening section, purposely echoed the 1776 Declaration of Independence: 'We hold these truths to be self-evident: that all men and women are created equal'. The most relevant part of the Declaration, which rightfully transformed it into the first ever feminist document, were the incisive assertions following the statement that '[t]he history of mankind is a history of repeated injuries and usurpations on the part of man toward woman, having in direct object the establishment of an absolute tyranny over her'.[130] In conclusion, and to overcome this 'fraudulent' deprivation, the Convention demanded for women the 'immediate admission to all the rights and privileges which belong to them as citizens of the United States'.

Some called the document 'the most unnatural and shocking event ever to take place in the history of women',[131] but many supported it as a 'basis to conquer the civil, social, political and religious rights of women'.[132] Amongst these supporters was the journal edited by Frederick Douglass, the leader of the abolitionist movement – and advisor to Abraham Lincoln during the Civil War – who had, in 1840, sat next to Elizabeth Stanton and Lucretia Mott in the London Convention to protest against the exclusion of women by the conservative wing of the anti-slavery movement. At that time, women's right to vote was guaranteed only in the island of Pitcairn, according to an 1838 decision, established when the island had become a British colony.[133]

5. *From Geneva to The Hague, via Solferino*

The poor wounded men that were being picked up all day long were ghastly pale and exhausted. Some, who had been the most badly hurt, had a stupefied look as though they could not grasp what was said to them; they stared at one out of haggard eyes, but their apparent prostration did not prevent them from feeling their pain. Others were anxious and excited by nervous strain and shaken by spasmodic trembling. Some, who had gaping wounds already beginning to show infection, were almost crazed with suffering. They begged to be put out of their misery, and writhed with faces distorted in the grip of the death-struggle.

There were poor fellows who had not only been hit by bullets or knocked down by shell splinters, but whose arms and legs had been broken by artillery wheels passing over them. The impact of a cylindrical bullet shatters bones into a thousand pieces, and wounds of this kind are always very serious. Shell-splinters and conical bullets also cause agonizingly painful fractures, and often frightful internal injuries. All kinds of splinters, pieces of bone, scraps of clothing, equipment or footgear, dirt or pieces of lead, often aggravate the severity of a wound and double the suffering that must be borne.

Anyone crossing the vast theatre of the previous day's fighting could see at every step, in the midst of chaotic disorder, despair unspeakable and misery of every kind.[134]

Three years had passed since Jean Henri Dunant had observed the images he described in the above-quoted pamphlet: they refer to the battle of Solferino, where, on 24 June 1859, French and Piedmont soldiers on one side, and Austrians on the other, fought the bloodiest battle since Waterloo, involving 300,000 men and resulting in 40,000 deaths. Born in Geneva, with commercial interests in North Africa and a company based in Algiers, at the age of twenty-seven Dunant had participated, in 1855 in Paris, in the foundation of the Unions Chrétiennes de Jeunes Gens (Young Men's Christian Association, YMCA), whose manifesto he wrote himself. Four years later, dressed in white linen for protection against the heat of the Mantuan summer, he was seeking out the Emperor Napoleon III, with important letters of presentation, in order to gain assistance for the development of certain agricultural properties in Algeria, where he hoped to achieve the emancipation of peasants and the modernisation of the countryside.

Having entered Castiglione delle Stiviere, he found himself surrounded by thousands of wounded soldiers who had been carried into town from the battlefield and chaotically abandoned without any form of assistance. Aided by the local population Dunant transformed the Chiesa Maggiore into an improvised hospital for over 500 victims, giving them water to drink and attending to their dying wishes. Two other men were making a similar humanitarian commitment in Castiglione during those days: Philippe Suchard, the founder of the company of the same name and innovator in the field of chocolate production techniques, and Louis Appia, a doctor from Geneva who had financed a group of Italian and French colleagues to help war victims. The experience of the aftermath of the battle of Solferino haunted Dunant, distracting him from his business. He returned to Geneva and wrote *Un souvenir de Solferino*, which immediately gained attention and provoked concern amongst politicians and writers, religious figures and even members of the army. After finishing the pamphlet he joined the Société Genevoise d'utilité Publique, directed by Gustave Moynier; Louis Appia and General Dufour was also members of this organisation. A commission of the Société, having carefully studied his account regarding Solferino, became the International and Permanent Commission for the Aid of Soldiers Wounded in War, which would later, in 1875, become the International Commission of the Red Cross. Dunant was the secretary and animator of the Commission, as he conceived of ways to organise continuous and immediate aid and identified the basis for future activities in the neutral role of medical personnel – and regarding the neutrality of the wounded themselves.

The idea that a wounded soldier could cease to be an 'enemy' in the eyes of his adversaries, and could thus return to being a needful human being, required the consensus of states and governments in order to become the premise for a transformation, if only a partial one, of battlefields and battles themselves. Dunant became an ambassador and a diplomat, and tried to convince major and minor countries to participate in an international conference organised by a committee composed of five Genevans. He cleverly presented his ideas in the Berlin Congress of Statistics and from there sent out a circular letter which called for the organisation of the Geneva conference, in order to address the theme of the neutrality of military medical staff and groups of volunteers. On 26 October 1863, when the conference was inaugurated in Geneva, fourteen states had sent official delegates, who approved ten resolutions and declared three 'votes': that every country was to protect the National Committee, that nurses were to be considered neutral and could not be held as prisoners, and that all military medical staff should wear the same distinctive symbol.

On 22 August 1864, following a series of meetings between delegates from 16 nations summoned by the Swiss government, 12 states signed the Geneva Convention for the Amelioration of the Condition of the Wounded and Sick in Armed Forces in the Field, which confirmed the ten points established a few months earlier and proclaimed that a red cross on white background (the inverted colours of the host country, the Swiss Confederation) was to become the symbol of the neutrality and protection conferred on combatants at an international level. Over the course of the following two years 19 nations signed the Convention, and in 1867 Empress Eugenia, the wife of Napoleon III, personally asked Dunant to extend the protection conferred on soldiers to sailors also.

In the months in which the Red Cross was established in Geneva – providing hope for a new era of partially humanised military conflicts – on the other side of the Atlantic the civil war was at its climax. The president of the United States Abraham Lincoln included, amongst the 1863 General Orders, the 'Instructions for the government of armies of the United States in the field'. The author, jurist Francis Lieber – the instructions were dubbed 'Lieber code' – detailed, in over one hundred and fifty pages, the customary conduct in war, in order to make it as consistent as possible with the principles upon which the American nation was founded.

It has often been claimed, perhaps over-emphatically, that the result was a 'war code inspired by humanitarian ideas'.[135] It is probably more truthful to consider the Lieber code as 'the final product of the eighteenth-century movement to humanise war through the application of reason'; differently from the ideas of Dunant, which 'represent a nineteenth-century Romantic approach to limiting war', an attempt to go beyond reason by 'engaging emotions' and trying 'to shock the public into humanitarian action, through gritty descriptions of individual sufferings after Solferino'.[136]

In the absence of other considerations and codified regulations, the principle of 'military necessity' was to be the juridical and moral limit to the violence of war, leaving considerable space for arbitrariness and confusion. Article 14 of the Instructions synthesised the question by explaining that 'Military necessity, as understood by modern civilised nations, consists in the necessity of those measures which are indispensable for securing the ends of the war, and which are lawful according to the modern law and usages of war.'[137] Thus the destruction of 'armed' enemies was acceptable, as was the 'incidentally inevitable' destruction of other persons caused by the conflict (art.15), while the code prohibited:

> cruelty--that is, the infliction of suffering for the sake of suffering or for revenge, nor of maiming or wounding except in fight, nor of torture to extort confessions. It does not admit of the use of poison in any way, nor of the wanton devastation of a district. It admits of deception, but disclaims acts of perfidy; and, in general, military necessity does not include any act of hostility which makes the return to peace unnecessarily difficult.[138]

In 1868, during the Congress of Saint Petersburg convened by Tsar Alexander II, it was established that the only legitimate objective of war is the weakening of the enemy's military power. Weapons that caused useless additional suffering, such as explosive bullets or those which contained inflammable substances, were banned. In 1874 another international conference was convened in Brussels to establish the rights and duties of neutral nations. On a conceptual level, it would appear that the road had been paved for coherent and definitive conclusions that could be respected by the entire international community.

Although the rules of war were established unequivocally only a few decades later, by the conferences at The Hague, the practical actions by groups and individuals aiming to help the victims of armed conflicts, epidemics, natural catastrophes, social inequality and industrial 'progress', developed in different ways, yet with the same conviction of a human brotherhood capable of embracing every person.

6. *The Lady with the Lamp*

A few years before the battle of Solferino led Jean Henri Dunant to create the International Red Cross, and before the debate on the rules of war laid the basis for the Conventions of The Hague, another conflict led to a series of initiatives – as always by both individuals and small organised groups – which were destined to alter the landscape of humanitarian aid. The occasion this time was the Crimean War, fought between 1854 and 1856 by Russia against a coalition of European states (including England and France, supported by the small Kingdom of Sardinia), who were allies of the Ottoman Empire and deeply worried by its ongoing weakness and decline. Anglo-French troops led by Saint-Arnaud and Lord Raglan landed in Crimea in September 1854 and, following a series of military victories, laid siege to Sevastopol. Before the anti-Russian coalition was joined by Cavour and Victor Emmanuel II the famous British cavalry 'charge of the six hundred', led by Lord Cardigan, took place in Balaclava, on 25 October. It resulted in half of the British hussars, lancers and dragoons being killed or wounded. [139]

The high number of victims and the terrible condition of the wounded led the Minister of War, Sir Sidney Herbert, to send a team of about forty female nurses to Crimea. In November they arrived in Shkoder, five hundred kilometres from Balaclava, where the British army's field hospital was situated. The leader of the nurses, whom she had trained in the previous months, was a thirty-five year old woman, described as follows in an 1855 article in *The Times*:

> She is a "ministering angel" without any exaggeration in these hospitals, and as her slender form glides quietly along each corridor, every poor fellow's face softens with gratitude at the sight of her. When all the medical officers have retired for the night and silence and darkness have settled down upon those miles of prostrate sick, she may be observed alone, with a little lamp in her hand, making her solitary rounds.[140]

The 'Lady with the Lamp' was named Florence, after the Tuscan city where she was born in 1820 into a rich family – the Nightingales. At the age of twenty-four, following a public scandal involving a nurse from a London workhouse, she decided to dedicate her life to the aid of the sick and to the improvement of general sanitary conditions, against the will of her family, who would have rather seen her quietly married. Florence, instead, rejected the pressing courtship of Richard Milnes, Baron of Houghton, and decided to become a nurse, in an era in which such a decision was taken only by women belonging to the poorer classes. In the meantime she made the acquaintance of Sidney Herbert, who had been Minister of War and would return to office during the Crimean conflict. It was indeed Herbert who accepted and favoured Florence's request to travel to the front to aid the wounded soldiers.

The hospital of Shkoder was in a state of abandonment: many medicines were missing, hygiene was non-existent, and the hospital had very little food. Soldiers dying from infections were ten times more in number than those dying of their wounds (this proportion was even worse for the Sardinian and Piedmont soldiers: during the battle of the Chernaya river every twenty victims of the war were matched by two thousand deaths caused by cholera). Florence was convinced that poor nutrition and fatigue were decimating the British army, yet it was only after reports by a sanitary commission from London – which suggested improvements to the ventilation system, as well as emptying the sewers and giving soldiers guaranteed drinkable water only – that the mortality rate began to drop radically.

Besides taking care of the health and well-being of soldiers, Nurse Nightingale was responsible for the general sanitary organisation of the hospital. She replaced all previous medical officers in this role and collected data and information she would then use, once back in England, to create a much-discussed statistical diagram. A member of the Unitarian Church, Florence believed that humanity could evolve by using its reason to improve its existence: the statistical data she provided to scholars and to the public demonstrated the saving of human lives made possible by improvements in hygiene, by comparing soldiers in Crimea and England with citizens of the surrounding areas. The results, which are still used today as evidence of the war in Crimea – with regard to the fact that soldiers died mainly because of diseases and that the mortality rate dropped radically after the improvement of hygienic conditions – were the fruit of Florence's statistical diligence. Though not irreproachable as a mathematician, just as she was not always perfect as a sanitary organiser,[141] she was without doubt a notable symbol of humanitarian commitment and of an unprecedented passion for helping suffering human beings.

When she returned to London in August 1857,[142] Florence was welcomed as a heroine and, through the Nightingale Fund, dedicated her efforts to the professional formation of nurses and to the enhancing of their role within hospitals, public institutions and the civil sphere. During her long life – which lasted enough to see four different changes upon the English throne – she received honours and prizes, and became one of the most famous women of the Victorian Age. Her commitment to the humanitarian cause of the sick, while remaining central in her existence, entwined with the themes of electoral and political reforms and with the question of the rights of women. The option of becoming a medical officer was a significant corollary of such emerging rights.

Florence Nightingale and Elizabeth Blackwell, the first female doctor of the United States, were friends and collaborators, although these two women – who were born and died in exactly the same years – 'had different, at times antagonistic, missions that sometimes resulted in mutual criticism and that critically influenced the role of women in medicine'.[143] While Florence returned to London after being in the Crimea, Elizabeth opened the Infirmary for Women and Children in New York, the first hospital to be fully managed by women and in which women could study and practice medicine. The attempt to unite their two different goals – a nurses' school and a medicine course for women – was unsuccessful, as Florence explicitly wrote to Elizabeth: 'We are on two different roads, although to the same object. You to educate a few highly cultivated ones – I to diffuse as much knowledge as possible.'[144] Teaching a doctor to cure diseases was not the same as offering basic courses in public hygiene and sanitation: on one hand the stake at play was women's chance to access specialist instruction; on the other was an unprecedented approach to public health and preventive medicine. This was the most evident difference between the two women, on top of which lay Florence's uncertainty over the struggle for women to become doctors, summarised in an 1860 letter to John Stuart Mill:

> I refer to an American World, consisting of female M.D.s etc., and led by a Dr. Elizabeth Blackwell, and, though the latter is a dear and intimate and valued friend of mine, I reassert that her world talks a "jargon", and a very mischievous one – that their female M.D.s have taken up the worst part of a male M.D. ship, of 30 years ago – and that, while medical education is what it is – a subject upon which I may talk with some *conaissance de cause* – instead of wishing to see more Doctors made by women joining what there are, I wish to see as few Doctors, either male or female as possible for, mark you, the women have made no improvement – they have only tried to be "men" and they have only succeeded in being third-rate men. They will not fail in getting their own livelihood, but they will fail in doing good and improving therapeutics. I am only stating a matter of fact. I am not reasoning, as you suppose. Let all women try. These women have, in my opinion, failed. But this is a no *a priori* conclusion against the principle.[145]

During her brief and occasional correspondence with John Stuart Mill, Florence Nightingale demonstrated how an emancipated, autonomous and professionally successful woman did not feel the urge to join the struggle for women's political emancipation and for the acquisition of the same rights as men. In 1866 Florence refused to sign the petition for women that Mill had presented to the House of Commons, as well as the option of joining the London National Society for Women's Suffrage. Yet she never appeared hostile to the views expressed by the author of a System of Logic, whom she appreciated and held in high regard. In her letters she expressed her aversion to the 'jargon' which identified 'the rights of women which urges women to do all men do, including the medical and other professions, merely because men do it, and without regard to whether this is the best women can do'. However, she also expressed dislike for the 'slang' that prevented women from attempting masculine activities 'merely because they are women and should be "recalled to a sense of their duty" and because "this is women's work" and "that is men's" and "there are things which women should not do", which is all assertion and nothing more'.[146]

A strong believer that women were more successful as nurses and obstetricians, a field inappropriate for men, Florence wrote a short text, *Cassandra*,[147] describing the restrictions imposed on women by social conventions, the oppressive atmosphere they were forced to live in, and presenting 'in a few pages a scathing indictment of a society which reduced women to spiritually and mentally impoverished creatures with no control over their lives'.[148] The centre of her reflections – which were partially referred to by Mill in his 1869 work, *On the Subjection of Women* – was the fundamental difference between men and women regarding the use of time:

> women are never supposed to have occupation of sufficient importance not to be interrupted, except "suckling their fools"; and women themselves have accepted this, have written books to support it, and have trained themselves so as to consider whatever they do not of such value to the world or to others, but that they can throw it up at the first claim of social life.[149]

Despite different attitudes and points of view – the one was formed by theoretical studies, the other by individual experience – John Stuart Mill and Florence Nightingale agreed on the 'tyranny' of the family. From 1860 onwards they did not correspond for seven years. However, in 1867 John decided to contact Florence to ask her to support the London National Society for Women's Suffrage and the amendment on women's suffrage he had presented to the Second Reform Bill on 20 May. Following a harsh criticism of women who refused to accept their political responsibilities and of men who prevented them from doing so, Mill proposed as the only solution 'to either make men perfect or to give women equal voice in their matters'.[150]

Although she was still convinced that women suffered worse limitations than the inability to vote, Florence decided to place her signature at the top of the fifty-thousand strong petition presented by Mill in the House of Commons in 1868, and agreed to become a member of the London National Society for Women's Suffrage, even if she never dedicated herself to the organisation's activities.

7. *Industrial revolution and rights of the population*

Coming as it did halfway through the nineteenth century the 'springtime of the peoples' was the expression of bourgeois and national revolutions destined, despite their defeat, to mark a new consciousness in the identification of and demands for collective rights. In that very same period the industrial revolution was widening its regions of expansion, where it imposed its rhythms and modalities for development, its criteria for judgement and its moral values. By then England was no longer the only country to experience the operation of mills and factories, of mines and cotton-spinning workshops, and the brutal conditions of suffering, instability and humiliation which accompanied urbanisation, mitigated only in part by the progress and greater wealth of industrialised 'nations'.

At the time a worker faced an average working week of 41 hours.[151] While five-year old boys and eight-year old girls transported sacks of coal or sewed in the gloom, women and men worked shifts of 15 straight hours, in dangerous conditions and without any type of protection, suffering from cold, humidity, harmful fumes and asphyxiating heat. The novels of Charles Dickens (*Oliver Twist*, which refers to his work experience in a factory at the age of twelve – for ten hours per day – was published in 1839; *Little Dorrit*, which describes the great social differences between the rich and the poor, as well as the harsh experience of English prisons, was written between 1855 and 1857) or those of Honoré de Balzac (*Eugénie Grandet* was published in 1833, *Père Goriot* in 1835, *Les Paysans* was written in 1844 though published after the author's death in 1855: all are ferocious and realistic portraits of an unprecedented social transformation). They told unaware or indifferent bourgeois readers about the poverty which was introducing, in major capitals and European industrial cities, the 'social question' destined to last for many decades of the nineteenth century and beyond. In those same years, Friedrich Engels, less distinguished on a literary level, but strengthened by his study of economics and knowledge of industrial relations, published *The Condition of the Working Class in England* (1845), which soon became for many workers a revelatory text on their condition and the need to change it.

At the beginning of the century England had already experienced, on the occasion of the Peterloo massacre, the degree of violence which could accompany political and social conflicts, increasingly entwined and inextricable as urbanised workers gradually learnt of their condition and began to demand their first rights. About 80,000 people had met, on 16

August 1819, to demand universal suffrage as well as the abolition of the Corn Laws which had imposed heavy tolls on farmers and peasants, leading to a rise in the price of grain and bread. The Manchester Patriotic Union Society, which was close to the more radical members of the House of Commons, had summoned a public assembly which the local magistrate had decided to disperse. The charges by the militia and horse-guards killed 11 people and wounded 500, including around 100 women. These events inspired Percy Bysshe Shelley to write his great poem *The Masque of Anarchy*:

> Men of England, heirs of Glory,
> Heroes of unwritten story,
> Nurslings of one mighty Mother,
> Hopes of her, and one another;
> Rise like Lions after slumber
> In unvanquishable number,
> Shake your chains to earth like dew
> Which in sleep had fallen on you-
> Ye are many — they are few.[152]

England was the cradle of new industrial development and of the working class, and attempted – on the basis of political objectives – to respond to the needs of this new exploited social class and to its demand for rights. These were transformed by exploitation into requests for freedom. The first organised movement – Chartism – was inspired by the electoral reform of 1832. This reform was strongly supported by the Whigs – the parliamentary minority – and opposed by the Tories, who had a majority in the House of Lords, and was thus constantly rejected or delayed. In the end the pressure of public opinion subdued the aristocratic resistance. The reform allowed over 650,000 men to vote (out of a population of 14 million, of which four million were adult males): more than double the previous amount and with a distribution of constituencies that, despite maintaining notable disproportions (Liverpool had 11,000 electors, while many other constituencies only had a few hundred), allowed major industrial cities to participate in the vote for the first time.

Workers were still almost totally excluded from the suffrage. Yet so too were many sectors of the lower middle class, and they would join the more conscious elements of the working class in their demands for an electoral reform more responsive to contemporary social transformations. The prominent idea, based on the diffusion of rights during the previous century, was that through democratic participation workers could obtain the economic and social reforms which they believed could no longer be delayed. Thus the workers followed the debate regarding the Reform Act with great attention, and were deeply disappointed by the form it took when it was approved in 1832. Their disappointment turned into indignation and rage when, two years later, the same government introduced a further law. The Poor Law, besides greatly reducing welfare contributions and funds for the poor, created a new system – both inside and outside workhouses – that favoured competition between workers in the job market, without considering the resulting social effects.

This system of homes for poor and unemployed people (workhouses) comprised degraded and almost unsustainable life-conditions with regard to hygiene and comfort, as well as disciplinary measures, punishments and rules to discourage anyone from choosing to be 'assisted'. It aimed to push people back into the job market at any given price.

These 'prisons for the poor', as they were called by Richard Oastler – a Tory supporter of the abolition of slavery and of the reduction of working hours to ten – cleaned the streets of beggars and reduced the cost of welfare, encouraging the poor to find personal solutions for their return to the mechanisms of work and exploitation. For many English workers the prospect of ending up in a workhouse was no different than the idea of being sent to jail.

Disappointment regarding the Reform Act and rage about the Poor Law led the more conscious workers to unite their demands for universal suffrage for men above twenty-one, for the secret ballot, a reform of constituencies, salaries for deputies and their yearly election, the abolition of property and other qualifications for candidates. These were the objectives of the 1838 People's Charter proposed by a committee of six radical parliamentary members and six workers from the London Working Men's Association, which had been founded two years earlier. The most representative figure of the committee was William Lovett, who was elected secretary of the movement during its first congress in London, on 4 February 1839, while a campaign was being carried out across the country to collect signatures in a petition asking for the Parliament to recognise the *People's Charter*.

The assemblies which took place in all major cities led to the collection of one million and 280,000 signatures, and in May the Congress moved to Birmingham to discuss the possibility of arranging collective actions such as cancellations of bank deposits or the organisation of strikes in factories. The petition was presented to the House of Commons in June, and was rejected by 235 votes to 46. Lovett was arrested after taking responsibility for a series of offensive slogans against the police, and the movement was split between supporters of the use of moral force (persuasion, campaigns, petitions) and those who believed in carrying out violent and revolutionary activities – indeed such initiatives began to take place in English cities and led to around 20 deaths in London.

Having served his time in prison, in July 1840 Lovett tried, unsuccessfully, to impose the supremacy of moral force within the association, yet once he realised the more radical positions were triumphing, he decided to withdraw from politics and form an educational movement for workers and their children. In May 1842 a new petition, signed by three and a half million people, asked for the abrogation of the Poor Law and for the end of macroscopic injustices – even including an attack against Queen Victoria – and was rejected just as the preceding one had been, by 287 votes to 47. Strikes and demonstrations – some of which were violent – spread across the industrial districts and Prime Minister Robert Peel, after an initial phase of non-intervention, was pressured into a repressive response which led to the arrest of 1,500 Chartist workers and all the leaders of the movement, including the advocate of the radical line Feargus O'Connor, founder of the *Morning Star* newspaper. In 1843 O'Connor suggested the formation of the National Land Company: workers were supposed to buy shares of the company in order for it to acquire lands which would be divided into tiny lots to be divided amongst the shareholders, drawn by lot. The plan failed because of its financial incongruence and in 1848 O'Connor presented a new petition in Parliament, featuring almost six million signatures: most of these turned out to be false, with fewer than two million real signatures.

The end of Chartism progressively alienated the movement's social base from its political objectives. These objectives were taken up by radical members of Parliament, some of whom joined certain fringes of the Whigs and Tories leading to the formation, in 1859, of the Liberal Party. In 1866 the leader of this new party, William Gladstone, proposed a Reform Bill which would double the number of electors; it was approved one year later by a minority Conservative government led by Benjamin Disraeli. The struggles of the workers, while often protesting in forms that appeared to replicate the strikes and demonstrations of the Chartist years, were already proceeding along the path that would lead to the centrality of trade unions and the creation of new political parties. The revolutions of 1848 can be read as a premise of this process, while the *Manifesto* by Marx and Engels was its most far-sighted and efficacious expression.

William Cobbett, who at the start of the century had founded the *Political Register*, soon to become the most read newspaper by artisans and workers, entered the House of Commons after the 1832 Reform Act and openly accused the government of stealing from workers the 'right to have a living out of the land of our birth in exchange for our labour duly and honestly performed; the right, in case we fell into distress, to have our wants sufficiently relieved out of the produce of the land, whether that distress arose from sickness, from decrepitude, from old age, or from inability to find employment'.[153] This marked the beginning of a new battle for economic-social rights, destined to accompany – and sometimes oppose – the struggle for civil and political rights born one century earlier.

8. *Second generation rights*

The first phase of the industrial revolution ended around 1850 in England, and around 1880 in the other European countries to have started a similar process of economic and technological development. Between these two dates a second agricultural revolution took place, due to the introduction of machinery and chemical fertilizers in the countryside, as well as the development of new productions, aided by technological innovations (steel, chemistry, electricity, petrol): these changes characterised the last quarter of the nineteenth century and the first years of the twentieth century, up to the First World War.

The huge progress in productivity, transport and international commercial exchanges, accompanied by improvements in terms of life expectancy and educational opportunities, had evident human and social costs: a marked inequality in the distribution of earnings; an increase in the number of poor people; the effective condition of slavery of those children forced to work unlimited amounts of hours for shameful salaries; the fatigue and frustration of workers living in environments and hygienic conditions typical of savage urbanisation.

The most tragic and scandalous situation concerned children: the first legislative social act of the new industrial age, the 1833 Factory Act, established that workers were to be older than nine years old, that children between nine and fourteen could work a maximum of eight hours a day, and those between fourteen and eighteen a maximum of twelve. This law, initially applied only in the textile sector, was widened so it could incorporate other industrial segments only twenty years later. In 1860 boys under sixteen still represented one-fifth of mineworkers, and twenty years later, in some regions, 10% were still under fourteen. Thus much of the social legislation of the nineteenth century was quite inadequate as a response to the terrible life conditions imposed on millions of people by the transformations of the industrial revolution. If we exclude the changes achieved during the Chartist period, these results are an aspect of the more general struggle for democracy and rights which took place in Europe during the second part of the nineteenth century, after the defeats of the 'springtime of the peoples' in 1848-49. In order to have a clear view of the general social situation, we must remember that the level of salaries 'of fifteenth century Britain would only be achieved again after 1875-85'.[154]

Social laws were the result of an intertwining, varying from country to country, between the philanthropic attitude of parts of the ruling classes (generally entrepreneurs with strong religious convictions or who came from worker-artisan backgrounds, and members of the medical profession), demands by the more conscious groups of workers, and a more general popular protest (particularly in post-revolutionary France). The extension of the 1833 Factory Act to the entire industrial sector was agreed only in 1878, while in 1867 it was established that children under eight could not work in the fields. The working hours for adults stabilised around twelve hours a day, and in 1854 Saturday working hours were halved: work was to end at two in the afternoon.

Germany, or rather Prussia, had made important social changes from the beginning of the nineteenth century, abolishing serfdom and organising jobs into corporations in 1807. In 1839 its first industrial law vetoed work by children under nine, night shifts and work on Sundays for anyone under sixteen, and introduced a three-year apprenticeship for children. In 1853 the law extended the veto to children under twelve, with three obligatory daily hours of instruction for all children. Following the unification of Germany it was Bismarck's government that established a more complete social legislation – in the very same years when it also produced its anti-socialist laws – than in any other country of the time. From social security, introduced in 1881, to forms of insurance for illness (1883), from legislations on work accidents (1884) to pensions for invalid and elderly people (1889) 'it can be rightfully stated that the system created by Bismarck constituted the beginning of what would later become the social state'.[155]

In France the 1848 revolution had achieved, alongside some of its political objectives, many social measures. These included the limitation of adult working hours, in conformity with the maximum of twelve working hours for children between twelve and sixteen; the abolition of the Le Chapelier law which, from 1791, had prohibited the formation of workers' associations; the introduction of funds to aid cooperatives and to discourage work by children and elderly people. However it was only in 1874 that a law allowed the creation of a body of inspectors, to ensure that the laws regarding working conditions were actually being respected.

Not in all countries was there a connection between social legislation and the eighteenth century process of democratisation. In Switzerland, for example, work by children under twelve was prohibited in 1837 and work by adults was limited to twelve hours a day in 1864, yet pensions for invalids and elderly people were introduced only in 1946. In terms of the right to vote, male universal suffrage was obtained in 1848, yet women were allowed to vote only in 1971. In Tsarist Russia, alongside an 1845 law for the protection of work by minors, extremely modern norms – apparently in contrast with the Romanov autocratic regime – were established in the 1880s for night work shifts, work by women and minors, and daily working hours.

Starting in the 1860s, 'liberal constitutionalism registered an impressive international growth through the reorganisation of states and recognition of popular rights, most important in relation to the vote but also including limited legalisation of trade unions on a local and national scale, from Spain to the Hapsburg Empire, from Britain to Greece'.[156] During the course of the 1848 revolutions a split took place between liberal forces and radical democratic ones over citizenship, the right to vote, civil and political rights. This was also true for social issues, which led to the first workers' organisations joining the supporters of democracy in order to achieve objectives more advanced than monarchist constitutionalism. In the second part of the nineteenth century, during a period of political reforms linked to the growth of national states (the 1860s were characterised by the unifications of Italy and Germany), the first enduring worker organisations were formed, destined to influence the 'social question' of the time across the whole of Europe.

Social legislation and social and economical rights – later dubbed 'second generation' rights, to distinguish them from the civil and political ones of the late eighteenth century – were the result of a deep transformation in Europe, which prompted new responses by the more open and far-sighted sectors of the 'establishment' and by new organisations, born from below to defend the workers' life and work conditions. In truth it is still incorrect to speak of stable or coherent human rights when referring to the nineteenth century. The political reforms in Britain in 1867 (the doubling of male voters, from one to two million out of a total of five), in France in 1871 (with the Third Republic replacing the Second Empire), in the Hapsburg Empire in 1867 (the compromise between the Hungarian nobility and the Hapsburg monarchy gave Hungary a strong autonomy and significant self-government), in Spain in 1868 (the dethronement of Isabella II, the revolution and the new 1869 constitution), in Greece in

1864 (the constitutional reforms relegating the king to a merely formal role) and in Russia with the 1861-61 reforms of Alexander II (the abolition of serfdom, the new judiciary system, the new penal code, the law on local self-government via elective assemblies) established the coordinates of a constitutional liberalism that appeared to grow unimpeded, incorporating the activities of workers' organisations and trade unions, on a local and national scale, seeking to make gains in the name of the workers themselves.

In the inaugural speech for the International Working Men's Association, in 1864, Karl Marx began by stating that the 'misery of the working masses has not diminished between 1848 and 1864, yet this has been an unprecedented period in terms of the development of the industry and the growth of its commerce'.[157] He then went on to claim that after thirty years of battles the English working class had obtained a law regarding the maximum of ten daily hours of work; and concluded by affirming the necessity of international solidarity (in that moment above all towards Poland) and the need for an active participation within foreign politics to become an integral part of the struggle for workers' emancipation.

Two years later, during its first Congress in Geneva, the International Working Men's Association approved a resolution for the limitation of the maximum daily working hours to eight, which soon became the most important and unifying objective of the working class struggle. The eight -hour day had already been obtained in New Zealand and Australia, although not in a generalised form, during the 1850s, and was granted to the workers of Chicago in 1867, even if the law in question proved widely ineffective; the eight-hour day became the main goal of the working class movement of the 1870s and of socialist and anarchic organisations; and was the reason behind the 80,000 person strong demonstration in Chicago on 10 May 1886, which gave birth to strikes in 1200 factories involving over 350,000 workers. In July 1899 the founding Congress of the Second International, in Paris, established that the following 10 May was to be the date on which to ask all public authorities to reduce daily working hours to a maximum of eight.

However the eight-hour objective was fully achieved only in the following century, after the end of the First World War (in Germany, England and Italy) and in some cases just before the Second World War (in France).

9. *Keeping the war away*

After the great revolutionary period of the late eighteenth century, which led to the consideration of civil and political rights as a basis for the more general rights of man, the nineteenth century saw the reforms that were supposed to consolidate such rights, coming face-to-face with all the difficulties, obstacles and oppositions involved. The affirmation of the natural equality between men – i.e. persons – was at the root of the philosophical reflections and political demands regarding the end of slavery, the rights of women, the need to give the condition of 'states' to violated national identities, as well as the safeguarding of minorities and the need for citizens and victims to enjoy adequate forms of protection during wars. All these problems were solved only in an extremely partial way, yet gained much attention and introduced the constant presence, in the public arena, of a new, burgeoning culture of rights. When, during the second half of the century, the gravity of the social question and the profound inequalities of the industrial revolution appeared to monopolise the attention of reformers and philanthropists – as well as that of all the workers' associations and political parties of the time – the interlacing and overlapping of many rights that were the objects of theoretical debates and legislative proposals indicate a complex, intricate and contradictory reality.

The consideration of these different types of rights and the attempts to understand them globally, in order to include them in a unique political project, still faced great difficulties. Indeed the great universalistic attempt of this period came with Socialism, which subordinated the French Revolution values of freedom, brotherhood and equality to a political and social revolution projected towards an uncertain future. According to Marx, the most lucid and innovative theoretician of his time – destined to become the most important name for the entire Socialist/Communist ideology, as well as for its many organisations – the 1789 Declaration of the Rights of Man consecrated the rights of the bourgeoisie, of the proprietors separated and isolated from the majority of men – the proletarians – who remained slaves within the social and economical sphere despite their apparent equality in the political and civil areas. This 'Marxist criticism did not capture the essential aspect of the proclamation of rights: they were the expression of a request for limitations to the excessive powers of the state, a request that, although when it was made probably did help the bourgeoisie above all, still maintained a universal value'.[158] The contraposition of a supposedly individualistic vision versus a collective vision of rights raises the risk of the re-emergence of organicist ideas, in which society comes before – and is more significant – than its parts, individuals; as well as the risk of not realising how modern democracy was born precisely from an individualistic conception of society. 'Nowadays the very concept of democracy is inseparable from the rights of man. Eliminate an individualistic conception of society. You will no longer be able to justify democracy as a form of government. What better definition of democracy could there be, if not the idea that individuals, all individuals, partake in the sovereignty?'[159]

In a historical moment in which civil and political rights were often still bound to wealth, and in which the number of individuals forced to live in conditions of exploitation, humiliation, dehumanisation and loss of dignity was constantly increasing, it was difficult for the defence of the rights of each person to find adequate expression in the newly formed workers' organisations, which combined solidarity and struggles, economical objectives and political pressures. For example, the disinterest of the socialist movement in taking on as a priority the rights of women was certainly a demonstration of the predominantly economical and class-related vision it had of the process of workers' emancipation. This conception tended to postpone – after the male achievement of universal suffrage and of economical and social rights – the prospect of women achieving the same results, conceiving of them as 'individuals' who belonged to a gender of less importance within the process. Alongside the limits of the materialistic and organic conceptions belonging to the socialist tradition, this incomprehension of the rights of women was also due to the historical characteristics of the time: from the traditional ideology of male superiority to the role of the family, from the prejudices of the dominant value system to the gendered division of work imposed by authorities and the market; not to mention the stereotypes and convictions regarding female weakness and fragility, and women's 'natural' role within the family, supported by the scientific theories of the time.

The years in which the International Working Men's Association began it brief but intense existence – which ended in 1876 after the failure of the Paris Commune and the debates which followed, and the increasingly bitter clash between the followers of Marx and those of Proudhon and Bakunin – coincided with the Atlantic slave trades being officially terminated: the last slave-ship travelling to Cuba was discovered and stopped in 1867. Spain, in 1886, was the last European country to abolish slavery in its territories, and was followed, two years later, by Brazil, which concluded the emancipation process of the American continents (the last country in the world to officially abolish slavery was Mauritania, in 1980). In December 1865, eight months after the end of the civil war between the Northern States Union and the Southern States Confederacy, the thirteenth amendment of the American constitution declared that 'Neither slavery nor involuntary servitude, except as a punishment for crime whereof the party shall have been duly convicted, shall exist within the United States, or any place subject to their jurisdiction'.

The world of the late nineteenth century was a world of empires, measuring their military and economic power in order to increase their dominion and extend their territory. The conflicts of the last quarter of the century were not just social ones caused by the progress of industrialisation, political ones such as the European 1848 struggles or civil ones such as the events of the 1860s in the United States; they were also international conflicts between states and expansionist wars in the African and Asian colonies. The 1870s began with the Franco-Prussian war, which ended with the French defeat and the Paris Commune epilogue, and with the German unification around the central core of Prussia; and proceeded with the conflict between Russians and Ottomans, concluded by the Treaty of San Stefano. The defeated Ottoman Empire recognised the independence of Romania, Serbia, Montenegro, of the new state of Bulgaria, and the autonomy of Bosnia and Herzegovina. Three months later, in Berlin, the Great Powers decided to reduce Russian expansionism, which was menacing Constantinople, by returning some territories to the Sublime Porte and by creating an autonomous Bulgarian Principality under the formal sovereignty of the Ottoman Empire.

While many problems remained unsolved on the Ottoman and Balkan front – destined to heighten conflicts between European powers up to the outbreak of the First World War – the colonisation process led to confrontations between major European states over Africa. In 1884-85 another conference in Berlin attempted to reconcile all existing appetites and competitions, establishing the relative spheres of influence of each country and dividing Africa according to a new geopolitical map, the prelude to its complete conquest by European colonists. France was assigned control over West Africa, while Britain obtained control of East and South Africa. Germany could count upon four colonies, one in each region of the continent, and the Portuguese owned two vast colonies in the South and one small one in West Africa. The king of Belgium, Leopold II, made sure that the territories in the Congo basin – the Free State of Congo – were assigned to the Congo International Association which he had just recently founded: thus he gained the new colony as a personal property by promising in exchange to favour scientific explorations, to introduce civilisation, to Christianise the indigenous populations and to protect them from the more brutal effects of colonialism.

In 1899, a conference in The Hague was organised by Tsar Alexander II. It was an unexpected event if we consider the relationships between states at that time – just one year earlier the French and British had almost clashed in Fashoda, in Sudan – and the race for armaments that was heavily weighing on all the finances of all the major countries. The conference was to discuss possible measures of disarmament, the maintenance of peace and the regulations of war, based upon the previous 1874 Brussels conference, which had been nullified in its results by the continuous succession of military conflicts. The conference involved 26 states, including two American (USA and Brazil) and four Asian ones (China, Japan, Siam and Persia), and was attended by numerous international pacifist associations.

The basis for the conference was the document outlined twenty years earlier in Brussels; the participants went on to agree a list of prohibited actions in war (the use of gases and poisons, the bombing of undefended cities, artistic or religious buildings and hospitals, the use of weapons, bullets or substances created to cause unnecessary sufferings) and added a declaration which prohibited the use of the explosive Dum-Dum bullets, built for the British army in Calcutta (the English delegate, Sir John Ardagh, tried, to no avail, to convince his colleagues that wounds caused by these bullets were no worse than those due to explosions of different kinds of pellets). Indeed it was claimed that these military instruments did not simply neutralise enemies (by killing or wounding them) like 'traditional' bullets did, but caused 'terrible sufferings that didn't appear to be justified in relation to the objective of war: to impede the participation of as many enemy soldiers as possible in the conflict'.[160] Norms were also established regarding the characteristics of armies and of volunteer associations, the treatment of prisoners of war and, in the Preamble of the Convention, it was decided that civil populations and belligerent armies were to remain 'under the protection and empire of the principles of the rights of people, as they result from the customs established between civil populations, from the laws of humanity and from the dictates of public conscience'.

This 'Martens clause', taken from the name of the German jurist who suggested it – although some claimed that the idea was originally conceived by a Belgian delegate – 'allowed the Regulations of The Hague to enter the Twentieth century with some instruments of power, aimed at containing war's worst forms of violence and inhumanity'.[161]

If we look closer, however, the strictly humanitarian significance of these instruments of international law was rather limited. The codifying Conventions of military conflicts (the Conventions of The Hague), although motivated by the intention of limiting sufferings caused by war, aimed above all to defend the states involved in conflicts rather than the individuals. Furthermore, they only applied to international military conflicts (conflicts between states, not ones that were internal to states); thus their conception was still the traditional one, according to which individuals are considered to be matters of the state.[162]

Chapter Four
Principles and Reality

1. The racial hierarchy

The end of the slave trade, and later of slavery as such, seemed to have spread, during the nineteenth century, the idea of a universal equality for all. In fact, at the very moment in which the most passionate debates were taking place over the rights of workers, women, exploited children, victims and prisoners of war – debates that were often unable to find solutions capable of being translated into laws or customs acceptable to public opinion – the context was provided for the development of a new idea of difference, or of a hierarchy of civilisations and races (meaning groups of individuals belonging to homogeneous populations and categorised by easily recognisable exterior elements: colour of the skin, hair, size and length of the nose, cranial configuration, height).

From ancient times, enemy populations, especially distant ones, had been identified as barbarians and in some cases considered inferior in terms of civilisation, morality and customs. The changes which followed the conquest of the New World reinforced the idea of underdeveloped or intrinsically different populations, whose territories 'deserved' to be conquered and Christianised. This was the period that saw the beginning of the process of elimination, in Western culture, of the composite influences which, during the Middle Ages, had interwoven Greek-Roman traditions with certain instances from Oriental cultures. It was however only during the nineteenth century that the seventeenth century ideas of racial purity were added to a discussion which found its principle source of legitimacy in new scientific discoveries. And it was precisely at the end of this century that the 'paradox of the Western world' took on a distinct form and became more refined, in its capacity to:

produce universals and make them into absolute values, to violate the principles it traced with a fascinating systemic spirit and to feel to need to elaborate theoretical justifications for such violations. The planetary character of its hegemony, the constant and obstinate construction of its justification, was built across the centuries through the use of a sophisticated cultural instrumentation which relentlessly referred to the universal.[163]

The idea of race is the result of a particular historical context in which the influences of high culture and its simplification as 'common sense' constantly overlapped. The idea of a hierarchy of communities – as a result of the different development of each single community – was perceived as natural because it was endorsed by science. The popularisation and trivialisation of the great scientific revolution, bound above all to the name of Charles Darwin, would appear to attribute natural and hereditary characters to each population, which would supposedly constitute their essence and culture. The myth of the Nation State which found its validation at the very same period – that the state is the most natural manifestation of a nation – appeared to reconcile historical itineraries and make sense of a diversity of destiny, geography, demography and international positions with a hierarchical vision of populations and nations, and thus also of the races which compose them. This was also a period of great dynamism produced by the second industrial revolution, in which the extreme transformations in the social landscape – within European countries – were accompanied by a violent and arbitrary territorial conquest in other parts of the world: a period which is summarily termed colonialism and represents an essential chapter in the history of human rights.

The beginning of the twentieth century coincided with the achievement of the limits of colonial expansion and with the widespread conviction at all social levels of the need for and usefulness of the construction or maintenance of an empire. This was most evident in Britain, where the enthusiasm for the conquest of Khartoum (initiated with the 1898 battle of Omdurman, during which the rifles of Lord Kitchener's men killed 11,000 Dervishes, while the British lost only 48 men) or for the liberation of Mafeking (the decisive episode of the war against the Boers in South Africa, as well as the origin of the Scout movement founded by General Baden-Powell) signified moments of collective pride and of popular participation in the imperial identity. In Europe the empire coincided with the consciousness of a nation's strength, as well as of its mission. When writer Rudyard Kipling, the bard of imperial Romanticism, as well as the first British Nobel Prize winner for literature, asked Americans to take up 'the White Man's burden' and intervene in the Philippines, he was expressing the hope that the United States also believed in the civilising character of Western intervention. Published in February 1899 in the *McClure's Magazine*, Kipling's poem appeared while a vigorous debate on imperialism was taking place in the United States, caused by the war against the Philippines which had begun on 4 February.

The first verse, often trivialised as a hypocritical example of the Western world's greed and yearning for power, goes as follows:

Take up the White Man's burden
Send forth the best ye breed
Go bind your sons to exile
To serve your captives' need;
To wait in heavy harness,
On fluttered folk and wild
Your new-caught, sullen peoples,
Half-devil and half-child.[164]

The text contains no resentment, nor indeed hate, for the subjected or yet-to-be-conquered populations who, 'fluttered' and 'new-caught', may perhaps even cause fear, and who are to be overcome through a heroic effort and proper sacrifice. If it is necessary to send abroad 'the best' and force the nation's sons to 'exile', if the goal is to 'serve' the needs of the conquered, with a risk that involves a 'heavy harness', it is because the civilisation mission is both necessary and inevitable. Subjected people are not savage, they are 'wild', and they have the opportunity to progress along the path of civilisation with the aid of those who are further developed and are lending them a hand to bring them up to their own level. Just as with children, who are to be encouraged or punished (when they unwittingly behave as 'devils'), with the knowledge that the manner and occasion of their maturity depend on the education we can give them.

The paternalism expressed by Kipling, who had a deep knowledge of India and of the relationship between the British *master* and the proud local populations, was different to Kitchener's blind and conceited use of force, but relates however to a widespread and common conviction which would sometimes be expressed in violent and humiliating forms – although on other occasions it was expressed in a more indulgent and understanding way.

As a result of an intellectual period in which high culture tended to unify the elaboration of every thought into the influence of exact sciences, Social Darwinism, once popularised and simplified, became one of the cornerstones of popular culture and of the stereotypes and prejudices which supported it. The 'survival of the fittest', the 'struggle for existence', the 'menace of extinction' and the 'dominance of the strong' are some of the concepts attributed to Darwin, even if they were actually invented by Herbert Spencer. These ideas used the revolutionary and innovative idea of natural selection and the theory of evolution by mechanically applying such concepts within the social context of the time.

The common aspect of the explanations of Social Darwinism, above all those of the Europeans, was the organic vision of the diseases which had accompanied the age of modernity and undermined the solidity of the Western world. Nor was the pessimistic current, which included Oswald Spengler and Ortega y Gasset, different in its vision of the decline and crisis of Western civilisation in its inability to understand the entry of the masses into the public arena and their new needs, born of modernisation's great technological, social and cultural transformations.[165] In the culture of Social Darwinism, however, ambiguous or even 'degenerative' reactions to urbanisation and colonial expansion, or to the entrance of the masses into politics and the possibility of future revolutions were pinpointed and scientifically 'explained' by referring to *blood*, which soon became the prevailing element for connoting national, racial and cultural identities.

The antagonism between the individual and the masses, the irreducibility of the individual to the masses and his psychological transformation when becoming a part of them were central elements of the cultural debate and its transmission.

The *soul* of the masses – studied at the end of the century by Gustave Le Bon, with strong comparisons to the *soul* of the 'underdeveloped' races – was modelled and analysed on the basis on the concept of folly, which negated an individual identity's consciousness of itself and favoured the emotional behaviour used (or suggested) by the 'prestige' of the leader through 'mental contamination'. The crowd became a category that was no longer social, but psychopathological; and the masses supposedly found their identity in disorderly emotions and dangerous passions.[166]

The idea of science as the elite's conscious control over society was fully expressed by eugenics, a sort of upside-down Darwinism: the state was supposed to carry out what natural selection was incapable of doing, removing the unfit and the obstacles to evolution through controlled social selection. Preoccupation surrounding the condition of the health of the British soldiers during the Boer War led to the creation of the Parliamentary Commission on Physical Deterioration, while in 1905 the Racial Hygiene Society was founded in Germany.

Eugenics did not share the same qualities in all nations: proposals to sterilise or segregate the sick or even the *undeserving poor* – as they were called by the English Charity Organisation Society – were accompanied by supporters of egalitarian eugenics, capable of destroying class barriers, or by feminist movements aimed at controlling births through 'positive' eugenics. The identification of a common denominator in theories by Galton and the eugenistic and Socialist aspirations of H.G. Wells is not helpful. However, it was the idea of race that created the basis for an evaluation of potential adulteration, and thus for the elimination or marginalisation of whoever was considered to be alien as against the 'norm'. This evaluation found its origins in the taxonomic classifications of natural sciences, in the cultural hierarchies established by anthropology, in the ambiguous formulations of Social Darwinism: in other words in the political use the adversaries of democracy and of human rights made of science and in the – sometimes direct – scientific endorsement of the legitimisation, popularisation and simplification of cultural prejudices artificially emphasised by patriotic education and the proud claims of national belonging.

The racist and nationalist current of Social Darwinism did not only involve the countries conquered by the Western world and the populations it colonised. It also spread across Europe, into the very heart of the most advanced civilisations and democracies, obstructing the already complicated progress of the culture of rights. Two prominent cases, one in France and the other in Britain, demonstrated how strong prejudice was in an era characterised by significant historical transformations and by the need to gain the approval of the masses.

The Dreyfus *affaire*, which began in France in 1894 and lasted for over a decade during the Third Republic,[167] was a signal of how anti-Semitism could become an important political and ideological weapon, yet also openly marked the entry of intellectuals into the public arena and their stronger cultural involvement in problems related to human rights. The second and contemporary case was the trial taking place in Britain of the writer Oscar Wilde, who was accused of gross indecency within a homosexual relationship. He was sentenced to two years of forced labour, ostracised, financially ruined and psychologically debilitated to the point that he would die just a few years later. If analysed side by side, the two trials which took place at the end of the nineteenth century in the two major European democracies, nations that were pioneers in the field of human rights, are testament to the conjunction between public and private spheres that modernisation and mass society had rendered irreversible; and of a new, even more complex and contradictory phase in the battle for rights.

It was not by chance that the first organisation to be explicitly dedicated to the defence of human rights – the French Ligue des Droits de l'Homme – was founded in June 1898, in the midst of the Dreyfus *affaire*, with the explicit objective of defending the innocent Jewish captain from the accusation of treason. The Ligue acted above all against a State capable of violating individual rights, and during the first twenty years of its existence it was committed to defending the freedom of expression of each citizen and the right of trade unions to organise workers' activities in order to improve their working conditions.

2. *The rise of pacifism*

At the beginning of the twentieth century, on the occasion of the tenth Universal Congress for Peace, the following optimistic statement was issued: 'Arbitration is becoming a worldwide custom, both in the form of permanent and general treaties and as specific treaties dealing with particular cases. We can say that this is a precise marking of the superior civilisation which has developed at the end of the Nineteenth century'.[168] Ten more congresses would follow this one, which took place in Glasgow in 1901, and the twentieth – the first to take place in The Hague in 1913 – was destined to be the last of an almost uninterrupted series which had begun in 1899. The congresses would only be revived eight years later, after the First World War.

The author of such an optimistic reflection was Frédéric Passy, an economist and jurist who, in 1867, had founded the Ligue Internationale et Permanente de la Paix. After the Franco-Prussian war the Ligue became the Société Française des Amis de la Paix. Passy, alongside the English-man William Randall Cremer, was the promoter, in 1889, of the conference which involved 96 parliamentary members from nine nations and gave rise to the Inter-Parliamentary Union. The date was no coincidence: the organisers decided that peace should be declared a priority and crucial objective in the context of the celebrations of the hundredth anniversary of the French Revolution. The meeting of pacifist parliamentarians was accompanied, that same year, by the first Congrès International de la Paix, which involved 300 delegates of associations of the 'friends of peace' from Europe and the United States. The preponderance of French citizens – 135 – was in part due to the location of the congress, but above all to the fact that French pacifism was, at least until the Great War, the most numerous and active in the world. In 1891 the association's third congress, which took place in Rome (the second was in London) decided to create a Bureau International de la Paix, based in Bern.

The creation of the Inter-Parliamentary Union was the realisation of Passy's conviction that civil society should support all European political representatives who declared themselves to be in favour of arbitration as a way to resolve disputes between states and nations. International peace was to be considered more important than any other objective. His was not the only point of view within the vast and composite pacifist arena at the end of the nineteenth century. In the same year (1867) of the creation, in Paris, of the Ligue Internationale et Permanente de la Paix, the Ligue Internationale de la Paix et de la Liberté was founded in Geneva by Charles Lemonnier, a Saint-Simonian who offered Giuseppe Garibaldi the honorary presidency of the new-born association, which soon included Victor Hugo and John Stuart Mill among its members.

In Lemonnier's view peace was to be founded upon Republican ideals and human rights, according to the Kantian conviction that politics should be guided by morality and by 'the respect of the autonomy and independence of populations. The premise of freedom is followed by those of equality which, in a progressive evolution, lead to the solidarity of interests and to the brotherhood of truly civilised populations. Consequently, war between civilised countries is a crime.' [169]

International pacifism, at the time of its institutionalisation (in the Paris congress and above all with the creation of the Bern Bureau), was divided between those who proposed the 'pragmatic' solution of arbitration and those who instead favoured struggles for national unification and universal male suffrage and against absolutism, motivated by the belief that only democratic republics could avoid war. During the following two decades, however, both positions proved incapable of comprehending a reality that was analysed by an unusual scholar, Polish banker Ivan Bloch, in a six-volume work published in 1898, *La guerre future*.[170]

Driven by pacifist preoccupations, yet also by a positivist approach, Bloch was not interested in contesting the legitimacy of armed conflicts, and instead concentrated his theories on how modern warfare, as a result of the profound technological changes which had taken place, was bound to lead to a stalemate situation which would have dramatic consequences for the order and balance of the entire European continent. The innovations of rifles, grenades and new artillery devices would impose a defensive war marked by an endless series of trenches. Consequently, victory would depend on each state's economic potential, with the chance that the collapse of internal fronts – for example in Germany – might cause Anarchic or Socialist revolts. Militarism, thanks to the new technology of war, could lead to Socialism: it was therefore imperative for each state that war be avoided. These convictions led Bloch to participate in the first conference on peace in The Hague, in 1899, proposed by Tsar Nicholas II.

The term 'pacifism' was first used by Emile Arnaud in 1901, according to a letter by Dennis Myers, secretary and librarian of the World Peace Foundation, to the *New York Times*, published on 23 March 1918. One year earlier, during a meeting of the Bureau, Fredrik Bajer, from the Danish Peace Society, had proposed the use – as opposed to 'belligerent' – of the term 'pacigerent', which had already been used during the Glasgow congress. Later Arnaud would coin the linguistically more convincing 'pacifist'. The term was initially known mainly in France, where in 1904 Giard & Brière began publishing a *Bibliothèque Pacifiste Internationale*.

Although they were divided into factions – beside the two aforementioned currents there were also absolute pacifists, against any sort of war and opposed to the use of violence on any occasion – pacifists were not anti-patriotic, or at least they defended themselves energetically from such an accusation. At the beginning of the century pacifist initiatives increasingly overlapped with the Ligue des Droits de l'Homme, which had gained much credit after the Dreyfus trial. Pacifist organisations, however, abstained from participating in the struggle for rights which took place in France and later in the rest of Europe. Amongst the most important figures who intervened in favour of peace, in France, were the Grand Master of the Grande Orient Lucien Le Foyer, a radical deputy; the writer Anatole France, who held many conferences during the Russo-Japanese war in order to collect funds for the victims; and sociologist Emile Durkheim, who organised meetings on international issues in the Sorbonne.

Teachers constituted the largest group actively involved in initiatives for peace (and, during the Dreyfus *affaire*, also for civil rights) and animatedly discussed the role of the teaching of history, and the need to convey different patriotic ideals from the traditionally bellicose (and anti-German) ones encouraged by ministerial directives. In 1910 the Société d'Education Pacifique, which prepared intercultural didactic material, could count on over 10,000 members.

During the French congress of 1904, which took place in Nîmes before the world congress in Boston, controversy engulfed Gustave Hervé, a Socialist and radical leader who had always expressed anti-militarist and anti-patriotic positions. Hervé, who in 1919 would found the Fascist-inspired Parti Socialiste National, invoked civil war, insurrection and revolution during a trial in which he was accused of anti-patriotism, thus encouraging a press campaign which attacked – in a general and indiscriminate manner – pacifism in all its forms. During the sixteenth universal peace congress (Monaco, 1907), to avoid being represented by the positions of a small minority, the doctor-physiologist Charles Richet (who in 1913 would win the Nobel prize for medicine for his studies on anaphylaxis) proposed a motion to demonstrate pacifists' 'love of country' and repudiate those 'men who dare to declare they will plant the flag in a pile of dung or use their arms, in the case of a mobilisation, against their own governments'.[171]

The congress approved a more general resolution, which declared that pacifism was alien to anti-patriotism and to struggles against obligatory military service, but did not resolve the questions, which would indeed remain for years to come: what position should be taken with regard to disarmament? How to intervene in populations' struggles for independence and self-determination? What to do about human rights and their violation? How to address the problems of colonialism and the rights of natives? Was pacifism to support, fight or ignore the tendency to obligatory military service that had spread to almost the whole of Europe?

On top of these problems French pacifism had to face the tricky question of Alsace-Lorraine. The attempt to find a German counterpart – within the pacifist movement – to work with in identifying 'creative solutions' and carrying on an anti-nationalistic propaganda campaign amongst the bourgeois and popular social classes did not however result in actual mobilisation. The insistence on self-determination of populations, which many deemed a prerequisite for international peace, led Léon Bourgeois – a radical and former Prime Minister who was considered to be very close to the pacifist movement – to propose, in 1909, a sort of declaration of the rights and duties of the nation, based on the concept of the 'independence and dignity of the nation'.[172]

During the eighteenth universal congress which took place the following year in Stockholm, Arnaud proposed and managed to make the congress approve, despite resistance from German and English deputies, a *Code de la Paix* in 145 articles. National independence was considered an inalienable right, equal to the right to life, individual freedom and work; and the consequent corollary, the possibility of defending national independence, also assumed the connotations of a universal right. The Italian delegation in Stockholm had insisted on the inclusion of the right to revolution for the achievement of national independence, but the proposal had been rejected.

Instead, for the first time pacifists addressed, in an international congress, the problem of the rights of the natives of European colonies: the rights of the inhabitants of the Congo – probably the most urgent – and those of the populations of Morocco and the Sudan, as well as in the Asian South-East.

3. *The Congo situation*

The largest and most significant humanitarian movement to develop in late Victorian and Edwardian England, at the climax of the imperial era, was the campaign for the reform of the Congo: a campaign that brought together various and limited protests against the new slavery which had accompanied European colonialism in Africa. The main inspirers and organisers of the movement were very different people, often divided over the objectives and forms of organisation, who had extremely dissimilar individual stories and diverse opinions regarding colonialism and the role of the West, both on a political and ideological level. Yet all of them found the way the 'philanthropist' Belgian king Leopold II was treating the inhabitants of Congo intolerable, and urged Britain and other major European countries to intervene.

During the 1884-85 conference in Berlin the king of Belgium had acquired the territories of the Congo basin as his personal property, and had in exchange promised to promote scientific exploration and to Christianise the indigenous populations while protecting them from the more brutal aspects of colonialism. In the 1889-90 conference on slavery, weapons and the traffic of alcohol in Africa, which he hosted in Brussels, the king agreed a tax on Congo imports; in the next decade, however, he became the object of increasing criticism, due to his termination of free trade (one of the cornerstones of the Berlin agreement) and the creation of an increasingly violent system of forced labour. According to calculations over three million Congolese people died between 1895 and 1905, while the wealth accumulated by Leopold II, thanks to the extraction of rubber and to the trading of ivory, supposedly amounted to the equivalent of 500 million Euros.

On 18 November 1895 *The Times* published the first humanitarian protest against what was happening in the Congo: it was an account by Reverend John Murphy, from the Bolenge station of the American Baptist Missionary Union (ABMU), which described the custom of chopping off the hands and feet of victims to prove to the Congo Free State officials that a good job had been done. A similar testimony was presented two years later by a member of Murphy's confraternity during a meeting organised by the Aborigines' Protection Society in London. A guard had shot an old man who had stopped collecting rubber and decided to go fishing, and had ordered a young boy to cut off his right hand: 'The man was not dead yet and when he felt the knife he tried to withdraw his hand. The boy, with difficulty, eventually managed to cut his hand off and left it next to a fallen tree. Some time later the hand was placed on a fire and smoked before being sent to the commissary'.[173]

Over 200 missionaries were in the Congo, yet only a minority openly expressed their concerns over the violence and the forced labour system instituted by Leopold II. Other more urgent international problems in North and South Africa (the Fashoda crisis in 1898 and the war between the British and the Boers in 1899-1902) appeared to overshadow the situation in the Etat Indépendent du Congo, which was at the centre of two distinct groups' attention, partially converging in their desire to expose the Congolese scandal, and in part motivated by different inspirations and objectives.

On one hand were the missionaries – the great explorer David Livingstone was himself a missionary – in particular the Protestants, who believed they could fight the slave trade by promoting legitimate forms of commerce, according to the binomial 'commerce and Christianity'. The newly-married John and Alice Harris arrived in the Congo Balolo Mission of the Region Beyond Missionary Union (RBMU), led by Harry Grattan Guinness, in the spring of 1896. For ten years they were witnesses to and protagonists of the battle over 'Congo atrocities'; once they returned to England they continued their fight within the anti-slavery movement and became central figures in its development.

On the other hand was a group which became known by the name of the 'Liverpool Sect', mainly consisting of merchants from Liverpool, Manchester and London, who were interested in defending British commercial rights, believing these rights were an important method of guaranteeing, in Africa, the minimum 'natural' human rights that were inherent to each individual. Among the group's inspirers was H.R. Fox Bourne, the secretary of the Aborigines' Protection Society, founded in 1837 to fight slavery in all its forms and to guarantee the natives' right to their land as a foundation for their full emancipation. Another important advocate was Mary Henrietta Kingsley, a writer and explorer who in 1893, at the age of thirty, arrived in Angola and travelled across various regions of the continent meeting tribes, collecting naturalistic material, studying customs and languages and becoming, in the last decade of the nineteenth century, a key figure in understanding Africa.

Mary energetically fought the 'African' stereotypes created by missionaries and merchants, which were widely shared by the Foreign Office. But above all she refused to accept a policy which destroyed indigenous states and African establishments and replacing them with unworkable Western and Catholic family models and an administration system that was far too expensive in terms of men and resources, as well as inept and ignorant because of its excessive dependence on London's political environment. Consequently Mary Kingsley became the spokeswoman for the merchants and their combined interest in free commerce and the rights of the natives, while trying at the same time to rid them of the missionaries' influence and to guide them towards a sort of cultural relativism that would be spread by a few ethnographic and anthropological societies. She often declared that the missionaries' 'civilisation' was the cause of African 'degeneration', because it weakened the traditional order of African society; yet she was also convinced that, in the relationships between white men and Africans, 'the mental difference between the two races is very similar to that between men and women amongst ourselves. A great woman, either mentally or physically, will excel an indifferent man, but no woman ever equals a really great man'.[174]

In 1899 the novel *Heart of Darkness* described Africa in an even more anti-conformist fashion than Kingsley had. Joseph Conrad, a naturalised Pole (his real name was Józef Teodor Nałńcz Konrad Korzeniowski), had visited the Congo Free State in 1889-90 as captain of a ship, and had observed the miseries, violence and barbarianism which would be related during the following years by missionaries, human rights activists and governmental agents. The protagonist of the novel, Charlie Marlow, before narrating his journey down the Congo River, begins with a series of more general reflections:

> The conquest of the earth, which mostly means the taking it away from those who have a different complexion or slightly flatter noses than ourselves, is not a pretty thing when you look into it too much. What redeems it is the idea only. An idea at the back of it; not a sentimental pretence but an idea; and an unselfish belief in the idea -- something you can set up, and bow down before, and offer a sacrifice to. . . [175]

The anti-colonial criticism in Conrad's novel and his meticulous portrayal of the differences between Leopold's ignominy and the more 'thoughtful' British arrogance, did not lead the writer to imagine a scenario without the European presence and tutelage in the continent; yet, 'by dating imperialism, Conrad demonstrated its contingent nature, recorded its illusions, terrible violence and destructions, and gave his readers the possibility of imagining something different from an Africa split into dozens of European colonies, although he had no idea of how it might become'.[176]

The most important figure of the Liverpool Sect, although completely alien to the world of philosophical contributions or theoretical reflections, was Edmund Morel, the son of a Quaker mother and a French father. After becoming, in 1890, an employee of Elder Dempster, the sea trade empire led by Alfred Jones, he married Mary Richardson and after five years obtained British naturalisation. He began writing articles against French protectionism but was soon sent to the Congo by his firm (Alfred Jones was the Congo Free State Consul in Liverpool), and specialised in commercial problems in Central and Western Africa. Morel became increasingly critical of the situation in the Congo and from 1901 he began writing anonymous and extremely polemic articles in *The Speaker*, which caught the eye of Fox Bourne from the Aborigines' Prevention Society. He gave up his job at Elder Dempster, while maintaining a good relationship with the owners, and became the vice-director of the *African Mail*. In the meantime, thanks to Mary Kingsley, he had met John Holt, a merchant from Liverpool who helped him become an important figure within the Sect, which Morel called the 'third party'. In April 1902 he expressed the opinion of the merchants' lobby in the pages of the *Liverpool Daily Post*:

> The right of the native to his land and to the fruits of his land; his right to sell those fruits to whomsoever he will; his right as a free man to his freedom – those are the real principles at stake. The British merchant, in fighting primarily for himself, is indirectly fighting the new form of slavery which has been introduced into Africa with such fatal results by the Sovereign of the Congo State, and in taking the stand he has done the British merchant is rendering a great service to humanity. [177]

One year later, supported by Holt, Jones and other Liverpool merchants, Morel founded the *West African Mail*, which was soon to become the newspaper most involved in the battle against Leopold II's Congo and in favour of a radical reform of the state's conditions. The end of the war between the English and the Boers appeared to lead to the involvement of the Foreign Office, which in March 1902 recognised, through a functionary, that some of the accusations Fox Bourne had published in *The Times* were 'moderately veracious'; while Leopold II himself asked the newspaper's director not to publish any further correspondence from Fox Bourne, who spoke of continuous violations both to free commerce and to the well-being of the indigenous people, the two cornerstones of the Berlin conference agreement.

4. *The crimes of colonialism*

The 'third party', as its members called the 'Liverpool sect', 'was a school which saw the administration of the negroid races of Africa as a challenging problem of world importance, demanding justice and wisdom but above all an appreciation of ethnological facts'.[178] Its main enemies were the 'racist school', based on the inferiority of the Negro race and on the natives' inability to become land-owners, which forced them to accept the role of a labour-force for the white race; and the alliance between the missionary world and the philanthropic one, which, despite the good intentions of bringing aid and sustenance to colonised populations, often produced the opposite effects.

> It was a school of thought which saw the preservation of the Western African land for him and his descendants; in a system of education which shall not anglicise; in technical instruction; in assisting and encouraging agriculture, local industries and scientific forestry; in introducing labour-saving appliances and in strengthening all that is best, materially and spiritually, in aborigine institutions, the highest duties of our Imperial rule.[179]

The determination of the 'Liverpool sect' to influence and modify the attitude of the British Colonial Office, and thus to be heard by the government or the House of Commons, did not weaken its conviction – both moral and political – that it should divulge facts regarding the violations of the natives' rights in Western Africa and the punitive expeditions that were often organised in those regions, justified by the belief that these were for the victims' own good. Morel and Fox Bourne decided to contact the missionaries, who they had previously so openly criticised, in order to obtain information and documentation regarding the violence they had witnessed. After an initial refusal, due to the concern that a public protest might endanger the long-term evangelisation goals of the missionary presence in Africa, the director of the Congo Balolo Mission, Harry Guinness, accepted this temporary and practical alliance, and decided to provide the information his Mission had collected.

The strength of the campaign on the Congo, which was about to begin in 1903, was not only owing to the associations and institutions which led it; its effectiveness was also the result of the continuous and growing use of photographic material, capable, more than any discourse, motion, article or book, of unsettling public opinion and arousing its emotions and imagination. The introduction, in 1888, of the Kodak photographic snap camera, equipped with a 100 shot film for 25 dollars which gradually replaced pre-sensitised dry plates, made George Eastman's invention a formidable tool for the collecting of images in the field. Once the film was finished the camera had to be sent back to Kodak, together with the exposed film, where the images were developed and printed, and the camera itself was recharged with a new film. In 1900 Kodak launched the Brownie camera, which was sold for just one dollar.

Morel's journalistic campaign, the work of Fox Bourne's Aborigines' Society and the pressures from merchant associations and parts of the missionary world led to a first parliamentary debate, which began on 20 May 1903, thanks to the initiative of a young liberal deputy, Herbert Samuel, and five of his colleagues. The motion, addressed to Prime Minister Arthur Balfour, asked the government to adopt, alongside the other states which had signed the Berlin agreements, a series of measures to eliminate the 'prevalent evil' in the state of Congo. The motion was supported by statistics and testimonies provided by Morel and Fox Bourne, as well as by missionaries. Samuel stated that the British government should intervene against the violation of commercial freedom committed in the Congo Free State and against the violation of the Africans' rights. After declaring that he was not 'one of those short-sighted philanthropists who thought that the natives must be treated in all respects on equal terms with white men', he however added that 'there were certain rights which must be common to humanity. The rights of liberty and of just treatment should be common to all humanity'.[180]

In order to grant consistency to the motion approved by the House of Commons, the Foreign Office sought to obtain certain and direct proof regarding the Congo, instead of having to rely only on the French, Belgian and English press and their 'indirect evidence'. Roger Casement, a British colonial administration official since 1892 – who had worked for private commercial companies in Africa for many years and had been the British Consul in the Congo since 1900 – was sent by the Foreign Office on a expedition in Leopold II's state to collect 'authentic information' on its misgovernment and on reported violence. Casement left in June 1903 and on 2 July arrived in Stanley Pool – the station of departure for internal travel – where he would return after spending two and a half months along the Congo, Lolongo and Lopori Rivers, the central area where the rubber production was most widespread. During his journey he became increasingly indignant and enraged as he listened to direct testimonies and personally saw the victims of terrible and savage violence, in particular among younger natives; he confessed to Lord Lansdowne, the Secretary of State in the Foreign Ministry, that on 'the subject of the treatment of the natives under the rubber regime, my indignation would carry me beyond the limits of official courtesy'.[181] Directly after returning to Stanley Pool, the British Consul wrote to the General Governor of the Congo stating that he was 'amazed and confounded at what I have both seen and heard' and asking 'how can they, poor panic-stricken fugitives . . . turn for justice to their oppressor.'[182]

Casement's report to the Foreign Office, 40 pages of precise and documented information, narrated and explained the impoverishment, malnutrition, intensive exploitation, depopulation of villages and mortality of cattle that had taken place over the course of the previous decade in the territory of the Congo: in a 20-page long appendix were the testimonies and terrible stories of murders, mutilations, kidnappings, beatings and cruel violence against women, children and men by the soldiers of Bula Matadi (the local name given to Leopold II, 'he who breaks rocks').

The King of Belgium, troubled by news of the report, began a pressing diplomatic offensive. Disagreements were taking place within the Foreign Office: the conclusion, on 12 February 1904, was the publication of the Casement report without references to names and locations, allowing Brussels to react by claiming it was filled with errors and well-intentioned mystifications. In the meantime, in December 1903, Casement had met Morel in London. This encounter, and the two men's shared conviction that in the Congo an 'extraordinary violation of fundamental human rights' was taking place, led to their common aim 'to unite in one Body the various influences at work against Leopoldianism ... ; to appeal to a wide public on a single issue; to incorporate all men whose hearts were touched, whatever their standing, profession, political opinion and religious beliefs '.[183] This is how the Congo Reform Association was founded, with the advantage of being able to act with greater freedom and determination than the Foreign Office could or would.

In Britain the association founded by Morel and Casement did not receive the support it had expected. Fox Bourne decided not to participate, viewing the Congo Reform Association as competition for the Aborigines' Protection Society, and nor did many others, worried that the association might be seen as a lobbyist manoeuvre by British merchants to achieve their own objectives. However, while the Foreign Office was still awaiting results from the international investigation commission Leopold II was cunning enough to create, Morel managed to gain attention, space, interest and support for the new association, from numerous social groups.

Among the supporters Morel was able to involve in his battle for the reform of the Congo were two the great (and extremely popular) writers, Mark Twain and Arthur Conan Doyle. The American writer, who had been vice-president of the Anti-Imperialist League since 1901 and had condemned the American intervention in Cuba and in the Philippines, as well as the British campaigns in South Africa and China, published a satirical pamphlet, *King Leopold's Soliloquy*, which was extremely successful. On one page, King Leopold II angrily reads a passage from Casement's report, where it tells of 6,000 people killed over the course of six months in the zone of the Mambogo River, and comments as follows:

> When the subtle consul thinks silence will be more effective than words, he employs it. Here he leaves it to be recognised that a thousand killings and mutilations a month is a large out-put for so small a region as the Mambogo River concession, silently indicating the dimensions of it by accompanying his report with a map of the prodigious Congo State, in which there is not room for so small an object as that river. That silence is intended to say, "If it is a thousand a month in this little corner, imagine the output of the whole vast State!"
>
> A gentleman would not descend to these furtivenesses. [...] The Kodak has been a sore calamity to us! A most powerful enemy that has confronted us, indeed. In the early years we had no trouble in getting the press to "expose" the tales of the mutilations as slanders, lies, inventions of busy-body American missionaries and exasperated foreigners who had found the "open door" of the Berlin-Congo charter closed against them when they innocently went out there to trade; and by the press's help we got the Christian nations everywhere to turn an irritated and unbelieving ear to those tales and say hard things about the tellers of them. Yes, all things went harmoniously and pleasantly in those good days, and I was looked up to as the benefactor of a down-trodden and friendless people. Then all of a sudden came the crash! That is to say, the incorruptible Kodak — and all the harmony went to hell! The only witness I have encountered in my long experience that I couldn't bribe. Every Yankee missionary and every interrupted trader sent home and got one.
>
> And now — oh, well, the pictures get sneaked around everywhere, in spite of all we can do to ferret them out and suppress them. Ten thousand pulpits and ten thousand presses are saying the good word for me all the time and placidly and convincingly denying the mutilations. Then that trivial little Kodak, that a child can carry in its pocket, gets up, uttering never a word, and knocks them dumb. [184]

When the battle of the Congo Reform Association had been partially won – in 1908 Leopold II was forced by repeated formal accusations from almost all major European powers to surrender the Congo to the Belgian state - Conan Doyle wrote *The Crime of Congo*, carrying information that was previously known by just a few people into every home. The book begins with a series of photographs of the victims of mutilations, and goes on to tell the story of the region and how Leopold, thanks to the work of two-thousand agents entrusted with the rubber production, had built the forced labour system of which he was later accused.

And now, the two thousand agents being in place and eager to enforce the collection of rubber upon very unwilling natives, how did the system intend that they should set about it? The method was as efficient as it was absolutely diabolical. Each agent was given control over a certain number of savages, drawn from the wild tribes, but armed with firearms. One or more of these was placed in each village to ensure that the villagers should do their task. These are the men who are called "Capitas" or head-men in the accounts, and who are the actual though not the moral, perpetrators of so many horrible deeds. Imagine the nightmare which lay upon each village while this barbarian squatted in the midst of it. Day or night they could never get away from him. He called for palm wine. He called for women. He beat them, mutilated them, and shot them down at his pleasure. He enforced public incest in order to amuse himself by the sight. Sometimes they plucked up spirit and killed him. The Belgian Commission records that 142 capitas had been killed in seven months in a single district. Then came the punitive expedition, and the destruction of the whole community. The more terror the Capita inspired, the more useful he was, the more eagerly the villagers obeyed him, and the more rubber yielded its commission to the agent. When the amount fell off, then the Capita was himself made to feel some of those physical pains which he had inflicted upon others. Often the white agent far exceeded in cruelty the barbarian who carried out his commissions. Often, too, the white man pushed the black aside, and acted himself as torturer and executioner. As a rule, however, the relationship was as I have stated, the outrages being actually committed by the Capitas, but with the approval, and often in the presence of their white employers.[185]

It was predominantly in Britain between the nineteenth and twentieth centuries that the question of human rights became entwined with colonial politics, yet also indirectly with internal problems, confronting problems of race, class and gender in ambiguous and contradictory ways. The battle for the reform of the Congo, whose epicentre was in Britain, demonstrated the lack of a linear process for the winning of rights, the impossibility, for anyone, of providing a coherent vision of their confirmation and the distance between principles and reality as well as between those who were theorising rights and those attempting to apply them. The partial and reductive way in which rights were theorised and violations to be fought were identified, was not the result of a more or less conscious plan to defend and justify the colonial adventure and the principles of Western capitalism upon which it was based. The divisions and overlaps between the different ideas, strategies, projects and objectives of similar and contrasting groups seem instead to indicate a world dominated by absolute ideological conceptions, which were completely inadequate for understanding the complex future to which modernisation was leading.

When speaking of rights the distinction between their supporters, those who show no interest in them and those who violate them may appear a simple one. However, even among the supporters of rights motivations are often very different: they overlap with interests that do not in fact coincide, and on many occasions form a utilitarian background which does not impede them from fighting important battles. For example, not all those who were struggling in favour of the rights of natives actually considered them to be equal to white men, just as not all were equally committed to defending the rights of workers and women in their own homeland. Yet this consideration can easily be overlooked, and demonstrates a real form of confusion – or of contradictions – which accompanied a still incoherent understanding of the values and principles of fundamental rights. The course of human rights, which had begun a century and a half earlier, still appeared to be a complicated one even in the eyes of its most attentive paladins.

5. *Concentration camps*

Some time before the First World War transformed the landscape of violence, during the period between the 1899 conference in The Hague and the 1906 one in Geneva, colonial powers had already invented an early version of concentration camps, an instrument that would become a trademark of the entire twentieth century. The first country to make use of them would appear to have been Spain, which set up concentration camps during the war against the Cuban supporters of independence (1896-98). General Valeriano Weyler issued orders for the *concentración* of civilians (or *pacificos*, as the non-rebels were called) within cities occupied by the Spanish, thus forcing them to abandon their houses, food and supplies, which were all confiscated and destroyed in order to prevent the rebels from using them. The thousands of 'refugees' enclosed within the cities had very little food and water and were forced to live in appalling sanitation conditions. Within just a few weeks mortality rates increased out of all proportion, especially of children and the elderly. The Americans, who were tempted to intervene in favour of the Cubans – something they did in 1898 – dubbed Weyler *the butcher* and some newspapers considered him 'the most brutal and heartless soldier to be found in a so-called civil country'.[186]

The initiative by British authorities during the war against the Boers (1899-1902) was a more organic one. The construction of a series of concentration camps was aimed at separating and isolating rebels from their families, thus making sure they could receive no aid whatsoever. *Concentration camps* were the other side of a military strategy which led the British to burn 30,000 farms and destroy many villages in order to drive out the Boers, who had chosen the system of guerrilla warfare and sabotage. The camps contained hundreds of huts where thousands of women, children, elderly people and a few men lived in dreadful conditions, and were surrounded by barbed-wire – invented in 1874 by an American to surround farmers' lands – and water turrets.

Initially used to protect the families of the Boers who had chosen to surrender, in 1901 the camps enclosed all civilians from areas involved in the war, as well as those who had escaped the military round-ups and fires. Over 40 camps were constructed when, in 1900, Lord Kitchener replaced Lord Roberts as commander of the British forces. The *laagers* (an Boer term meaning 'camp') for refugees were located near train routes and left under the supervision of just a few men: an intendant, a doctor, two nurses and a few armed guards. In the meantime the news of their existence was severely criticised back in the United Kingdom by a small group of human rights activists. Leonard Courtney, a liberal deputy who supported the rights of women and the Boers' position regarding the recent conflict, asked Emily Hobhouse, who was then thirty-nine, to lead the female sector of the South African Conciliation Committee. Emily left for South Africa in December 1900, while in Parliament a group of members from the liberal opposition denounced the Port Elizabeth camp and forced the Minister of War John Brodrick to ask Kitchener for a report on the South African events.

While Emily Hobhouse was visiting the camps with the British authorities' approval – when she arrived there were already 34 functional camps – the liberal deputy John Ellis (from Nottinghamshire, Rushcliffe)

was the first to use the term *concentration camp* during his questioning of
Parliament on 1 March 1901: 'I ask the secretary of state for War if there
was any revocation regarding the policy of placing women and children,
whose husbands and children are fighting, within concentration camps
in South Africa with reduced food rations; or if this policy is still in
function'. In his reply the Minister stated that 'the great majority of women
and children entered the camps on their own initiative. I am not responsible
for the reasons that led them to do so. I have as yet not received full
information, but Lord Kitchener has informed me that a sufficient level
of indemnity is conceded to all families within the camps and that they
are satisfied and comfortable'.[187]

On the 8 May 1901 Emily Hobhouse found herself, while returning
to Britain, on the same ship – *the Saxon* – as the high commissioner for
South Africa, Lord Milner, who was returning to England on holiday.
The representative of Her Majesty's Government refused to meet such
a 'troublemaker' and supporter of the Boer cause. Emily, as soon as
she arrived in London, met the Minister of War Brodrick and the leaders
of the opposition, including John Ellis, and distributed amongst them a
twelve-page pamphlet, *Brunt of War*. In June, during a new parliamentary
debate, the liberal leader of the opposition answered the rhetorical question
'When is a War no longer a War?' as follows: 'When it is fought with the
barbaric methods of South Africa'. When intervening in the debate over
the mortality rates in British detention camps, after listing the official
statistics, Lloyd George claimed that:

> For the love of the credit and good name of this country we must
> do something to end a state of affairs that is going from bad to
> worse. [...] This lady (E.H.) has provided information on what is
> happening in the best of these camps – the best equipped and those
> that have been instituted for the longest time – and they are
> in sufficiently deplorable conditions. These are not camps of
> warriors, but of women, many of whom are in weak conditions,
> and children. [...] The mortality rate of children – and I believe this
> is the most shameful aspect of the entire situation – is superior to
> the mortality rate amongst soldiers. [...] Mortality for women and
> children is 450 every one thousand and we do not have the right to
> place women and children in these conditions.[188]

In July the results of a more reliable statistic enquiry came through, and
confirmed Emily Hobhouse's worst fears. At the end of 1901 the government decided to transfer the responsibility of the camps to civilians, and

to implement measures to improve the life conditions and hygiene in the laagers. Amongst the dead 'at least' 20,000 were white people and 12,000 'coloured' people. In May 1902, when the Boer leaders decided to meet the British and accept the conditions imposed by the Treaty of Vereeniging, which ended the war, many of them stated that 'our families live in miserable conditions and the enemy uses our families to force us to surrender'.[189]

The South African events demonstrate how the attitude towards war was changing, among both military and civilian circles. It was military authorities, supported by political powers, who built the camps in the name of military efficiency and in order to hasten the enemy's defeat. Yet the British government also allowed, thanks to its democratic institutions, the camps to be inspected and that non-official reports – like that of Emily Hobhouse – could circulate and strongly influence parliamentary debates and public opinion, eventually leading to drastic changes on previous decisions. The ambiguity of the government's behaviour (the spread of lies regarding the situation in the camps co-existed with the permission to visit them) was due to contingent conditions and individual choices, yet it was also the demonstration of a changing relationship between military and civil powers, as evidenced by colonial wars.

If the development of war appeared to necessarily concern military authorities – increasingly so, given the progress of technology and weapons – politicians were in charge of strategic objectives and had the right to intervene when necessary. Indeed it was politicians who, according to international agreements, were in a position to clarify and reinforce the rules of military behaviour during war. Alongside the new involvement of civilians in South Africa, the 1904-05 war between Russia and Japan revived a set of problems which had been addressed at the end of the nineteenth century but were as yet unsolved.

In June 1906 a new Convention was signed in Geneva with regard to the wounded and sick in the army, making improvements to the text approved in 1864. The new Convention clarified the 'neutral' status of voluntary aid associations and members of medical and paramedic staff, who were given privileges and protection:

The Geneva conference of 1906 recognised that anaesthetics, anti-septic surgery, sterilisation, the hospital ships and the hospital train, were essential incidents in the modern treatment of wounds and in the prevention of camp diseases. The framers of the old convention adapted their work to existing needs: they knew that the wounded soldier was not a neutral, and in applying the term to the wounded and sick in time of war they were attempting to describe the immunity to which they were entitled, and the consideration which they desired should be shown to the victims of wounds and disease.[190]

A year later, during the second peace conference in The Hague, which involved 44 countries, the new Convention on laws and customs of land war was ratified, clarifying the norms approved in 1899. Humanitarian international rights in time of war (*ius in bello*) had reached a new phase in their evolution. Naval warfare norms were also analysed, especially due to the impact on public opinion of the naval battle of Tsushima, where the Russian fleet, after being defeated by the Japanese, had been abandoned to its own fate with thousands of wounded and shipwrecked soldiers. That very event had led the Geneva conference of the previous year to assign the protection and rescue of shipwrecked and wounded soldiers at sea to the International Red Cross. The conference in The Hague also confirmed and amplified the prohibition regarding the bombing of undefended civil buildings, as well as the protection of culturally, scientifically and religiously important buildings and the safeguard of museums and public institutions.

The attention devoted to historical monuments and buildings dedicated to religion, art, science and charitable organisations did not consider the parallel development of aeronautic technology and the changes it would lead to, just a few years later and before the First World War, especially in aerial bombardments.

6. *The defeat of pacifism*

The last winner, in 1913, of a Nobel Prize for Peace before the First World War broke out was the Belgian Henri La Fontaine, who at the time was the president of the Bureau International Permanente de la Paix in Bern. The organisation had already received the prize in 1910, while in 1908 the winner had been Fredrik Bajer, La Fontaine's predecessor as leader of the international pacifist movement.

Established on the basis of the third and last testament of Swedish industrialist Alfred Nobel, this prize was dedicated 'to the person who shall have done the most or the best work for fraternity between nations, for the abolition or reduction of standing armies and for the holding and promotion of peace congresses.'[191] The award was assigned – in contrast to those for literature, medicine, chemistry and physics – in Oslo, rather than Stockholm. Indeed the Norwegian Parliament, the *Storting*, was selected as the judge of the competition, as in 1895, the year in which his will was written, Nobel considered it more suitable than the Swedish government (Sweden had annexed Norway in 1814 and held it until 1905) with regard to a theme such as peace. The testament of Nobel, who would die the following year in San Remo, in Italy, was disclosed to the public in 1897 and the prizes in his name were established in 1901.

The first man to win the prize was Henri Dunant, the author of the 'memories' of Solferino and founder of the International Red Cross, who shared the award with Frédéric Passy; two years later the winner was William Randal Cremer. The next year the prize went to the Institut de Droit International, founded in Belgium in 1873 to contribute to the development of international law (the war between France and Prussia in 1870-71 had shown just how insufficient the existing Conventions were) and of its actions in favour of arbitration between states, as a peaceful instrument for the regulation of conflicts. In 1905 the Nobel Prize was won by one of the most representative figures of pacifism's first years, Bertha von Suttner, born in Paris in 1843. Bertha was the governess of the daughters of Baron Karl von Suttner, and was forced to leave her job because of a love affair with the Baron's youngest son. She then worked as a secretary in Alfred Nobel's firm in Paris. In 1876 she married her beloved and moved to the Caucasus, where they lived for about a decade and witnessed the war between Russia and the Turks. Having returned to Vienna and after being forgiven by Arthur's family, she travelled to Paris and participated in the activities of the International Association for Arbitration and Peace. Once she returned to Vienna she began collecting material for a novel, while participating in the work of the Red Cross and helping to establish the truth regarding Henri Dunant's role in its creation.

Die Waffen nieder! ('Lay Down your Arms!') was published in 1889, the same year as the Universal Expo and as the anniversary of the French Revolution, as well as the first Universal Congress for Peace. Just like Dunant's *A Memory of Solferino*, the book was a great editorial success, and was translated into 20 languages. In 1891 Bertha founded the Österreichische Friedensgesellschaft and the following year the Deutsche Friedensgesellschaft; a few years later she helped to convince Nicholas II to organise the conference in The Hague for disarmament and peace. At the conference, alongside Passy, she represented the Bureau. Despite the rapid succession of wars (between Spain and Cuba, in the Philippines, in South Africa and between the Russians and Japanese) her pacifist struggle continued, and during those years she founded the Monaco Peace Institute and spoke at many conferences in Europe and in the United States.

From 1909 she dedicated her activities to painting and to the production of pacifist films. She was well known and loved by many (according to a German survey dated 1903, she was the most famous woman alive), yet she was also opposed by the Socialists who did not forgive her for keeping pacifism separate from the social question. Her point of view was clear: 'First we must free the world from the menace of war and of arms races, later we can address and solve social questions with greater ease and equality'.[192] Bertha von Suttner participated in the twentieth congress in 1913 in The Hague, where she was acclaimed as the leader of the pacifist movement; she died ten months later, one week before the Sarajevo assassination.

Two further winners of the Nobel Prize for Peace before the War are also worthy of mention: Alfred Hermann Fried and Ernesto Teodoro Moneta. The former, an Austrian who had moved to Berlin, had been since 1899 the publisher of the periodical *Die Friedenswarte*; Norman Angell was the author of the bestseller *The Great Illusion*, of which two million copies were sold between 1910 and 1913, and which was translated into 25 languages – and was defined as the most influential pacifist periodical in the world. The latter, a patriot during the Five Days of Milan and a soldier under Garibaldi, abandoned his military career in 1866 and dedicated his life to studying (his book *Le guerre, le insurrezioni e la pace nel XIX secolo* was published in four volumes) and to pacifist activity (since 1890 he had published the almanac *L'amico della pace*). In 1895 he became the Italian representative in the Bureau. In 1906, one year before receiving the Nobel Prize, he presided over the fifteenth universal congress in Milan.

The pacifist movement worked simultaneously for the identification of practical proposals for governments and international diplomacy, and for the construction of a super-national ideology based on the refusal of offensive violence and of the Social Darwinist idea of a selfish human nature, classifiable on the basis of different stages of development and civilisation. Its practical influence, if compared to the two great ideological and political currents of the time, Socialism and Nationalism, was certainly very small. Yet it was the only voice to speak up about particular issues – for example the need for reform in the colonial territories. The divisions within the movement, which had been there since its origins, were accentuated when the urgencies of social problems led some pacifists to bind more solidly with Socialism; after all the Socialists too were increasingly worried by the arms race and by the threat it posed to peace: 'the entire social question was dominated by the problem of peace and war; the war would open the path for any catastrophe while armed peace would jeopardise any reform'.[193]

During the Balkan wars, Lucien Le Foyer, the Grand Maestro and, from 1913, also the leader of the French pacifist movement, proposed the abolition of secret treaties in order to dilute the atmosphere of terror intensifying in anticipation of an imminent conflict. At the same time the French and Germans met in Basel, while the association La Paix par le Droit stirred up violent reactions to the Action Français and Camelots du roi, with its proposal to use the conflict over Alsace-Lorraine to build a link between French and German cultures; it also claimed that the Alsatians would rather obtain civil rights in Germany than see the outbreak of a war.

Religious pacifist positions, which had been associated for many years with the name of Tolstoy, appeared to be quite distant from the majority of the pacifist movement, especially now that the possibility of a European conflict was becoming more apparent : 'Kill or be killed, this is war. It is a necessary evil yet it can be controlled'.[194] Between June and July 1914, pacifist and Socialist European leaders tried, to no avail, to find a solution for the growing tensions between governments and military commands. On 31 July, in a last meeting between the major European pacifist associations, the German delegate Ludwig Quidde, who would obtain a Nobel Prize for Peace in 1927, declared that in Germany nobody really wanted a war against France. He did not know that Max Weber had spoken of a 'great and marvellous' war, and could not imagine that soon Mann would write in his *Thoughts in War*: 'Why should the artist, the soldier in the artist, not have praised God for the downfall of a world of peace that he could truly stand no more? War! What we felt was sacred purification, liberation and huge hope'.[195] Quidde also had no idea that Rudyard Kipling, the winner of the Nobel Prize for literature in the same year in which Ernesto Moneta and Louis Renault had won the award for Peace (1907), would write, just as the war broke out (a war that would deprive him of his elder son John at the battle of Loos): 'For all we have and are / For all our children's fate / Stand up and take the war / The Hun is at the gate.'

Within two or three years the patriotic feelings surrounding the war would be replaced by disillusion, desperation, rage, feelings of impotency and pain for the number of victims, earning the war's generation the adjective 'lost'. The English poet Siegfried Sassoon wrote:

> I am making this statement as an act of wilful defiance of military authority, because I believe that the war is being deliberately prolonged by those who have the power to end it.. […] I have seen and endured the sufferings of the troops, and I can no longer be a party

to prolong these sufferings for ends which I believe to be evil and unjust.

I am not protesting against the conduct of the war, but against the political errors and insincerities for which the fighting men are being sacrificed.[196]

After the beginning of the war, at the end of April 1915, over one thousand women from twelve different countries met in The Hague. Their journeys to reach the city were often difficult and adventurous, especially because the authorities of the belligerent countries tried to prevent them from travelling (only three English women made it to the meeting). The instigator of the event was Aletta Jacobs, the first woman doctor of the Netherlands, who had, at the beginning of the century, become one of the leaders of the association for female suffrage. She received positive responses from German jurist Lyda Gustava Heymann and feminist Anita Augspurg, who took care of the organisation of the meeting. The Women's Peace Congress embraced the ideas of the most homogenous and important group, the American Woman's Peace Party, led by Jane Addams, which proposed the creation of an international organisation and somewhat anticipated the fourteen points enunciated by President Wilson in January 1917. The congress elected a Permanent International Committee of Women for Peace which would later participate, at the end of the war, in the Paris Peace Conference. The second congress, which took place in Zurich in 1919, was dominated by an energetic and detailed criticism of the Treaty of Versailles, condemned as 'vindictive'. The organisation took on a new name, Women's International League for Peace and Freedom, and relocated to Geneva, next to the League of Nations.

7. *Women's right to vote*

In November 1913 an article was published in an important political sciences periodical, regarding the English movement for female suffrage. It began as follows: 'At present neither the prospect of *home rule* [for Ireland] nor the danger from Germany menace, nor the mighty design of imperial federation assails the public mood of England so insistently as much as the demand for the enfranchisement of women'.[197]

The brief essay listed the most important landmarks of the struggle for female suffrage, from the end of the seventeenth to the first half of the eighteenth century and beyond, underlining the progress made within the fields of economic freedom and intellectual liberty through education.

At the beginning of the twentieth century there were one million more British women than men (1,200,000 by the time the article was published). The grim predictions which had accompanied the growth of the electoral body before each previous reform (in 1832, 1867 and 1884) had been widely contradicted. Yet those who opposed women's right to vote now did so mainly on the basis that 'when women vote they will never be content until they hold office. Then, since there is a majority of women, females will rule, and then will men suffer petticoat domination in the government which once they created'.[198]

During the final years of the nineteenth century, the union of two different groups created the National Union of Women's Suffrage Societies (NUWSS), led by Millicent Fawcett. In 1886 Fawcett had contributed to the abolition of the Contagious Diseases Acts (1864, 1866 and 1869)[199] and in 1901 she led the commission which investigated concentration camps in South Africa. By 1903, however, the new association was already split in half: some of the members, led by Emmeline Pankhurst, who would soon be joined by her daughters Christabel and Sylvia, founded the Women's Social and Political Union (WSPU). In contrast to the NUWSS, which was a more moderate and pacifist association, the WSPU, whose slogan was 'Facts, not words', was a militant organisation and worked alongside the Independent Labour Party and its radical social proposals.

The divergences between the two groups, however, were not only organisational ones: while Fawcett believed constitutional methods were the most appropriate way of gradually securing women's rights, Pankhurst opted for a different strategy. From 1905, when a proposed law regarding female suffrage was not even discussed in Parliament, the WSPU decided to oppose all political parties and began a campaign which involved interruptions of parliamentary speeches and meetings, irruptions into ministers' houses and the headquarters of parliamentary groups, and some members chaining themselves to public buildings and forcing the police to remove them. The arrest in Manchester of Annie Kenney and Christabel Pankhurst was the first of a long series which included, in the following years, Emmeline Pankhurst herself. In 1907, as a form of protest against the use of violence and the oligarchic leadership of the group, seventy members of the WSPU founded the Women's Freedom League. Their action focused on a refusal to pay taxes and to fill in census modules, although they too sometimes resorted to chaining themselves to the Parliament gates.

In 1910, during Herbert Henry Asquith's Liberal government, a committee of parliamentary members was formed to compose a text on female suffrage that could satisfy all the nation's political forces. Yet the fall of the government delayed the issue once more. Half a million people met in Hyde Park, demonstrating the level of consensus women's right to vote had by then earned within English society. The WSPU's campaign, from 1911 to 1913, was increasingly violent, characterised by assaults on public buildings, arson, low-power bombs, the destruction of post and poisoning of dogs. The government reacted by imprisoning many members and force-feeding those who began hunger-strikes; protests eventually led to the approval of a law (called 'the cat and the mouse act') which freed the prisoners.

In 1912 the proposal of a law for women's right to vote was turned down, exacerbating the radicalism of WSPU militants. The group's differences with other feminist associations became even greater after the beginning of the War, which was greeted enthusiastically by the Pankhursts; the NUWSS continued, unlike the WSPU, to struggle for women's right to vote even during the war. At the beginning of the conflict only Finland and Norway, in Europe, had given women the full right to vote (in 1906 and 1913 respectively), while in the rest of the world only New Zealand (1893) and Australia had done so (with some restrictions that were later completely abolished, in 1902 in the federal state, and in 1908 when the last state, Victoria, voted in favour of women's enfranchisement). During the conflict women gained the right to vote in Denmark and Iceland (1915), in Russia after the 1917 Revolution, and in the Netherlands.

In March 1918 the House of Commons approved, with a score of 385 votes against 55, the Representation of the People Act, which granted the right to vote to women above thirty who owned land. The House of Lords – of which Lord Curzon, the president of the National League for Opposing Women's Suffrage, was a member – approved it with 134 votes against 71. At this point, out of twenty-one million voters, eight and a half million would be women. Only in 1928 did Britain approve a law which put women on an equal footing with men, as citizens with full political rights.

While such changes took place much later in Latin European countries (in France and Italy only after the Second World War; in Spain, apart from a brief period between 1933 and 1939, in 1975), Germany followed the British course. In the years preceding the war it was predominantly Socialist women who were the most active and determined in their demands for the right to vote. Only in 1908 were they allowed to join the Sozialdemokratische Partei Deutschlands, which gained over four million votes in 1912 and became the leading party of the Reichstag. In 1914 the Socialist women who were registered with the party numbered 175,000, while liberal feminism could count on only 14,000 supporters. The Socialist militants and sympathisers, who often disagreed with their party's leaders, decided to mobilise for Women's Day (the first time it took place in Germany was on 19 March 1911). Two years later the leaders of the party attempted to boycott the Day for fear that it might become a 'second' first of May, yet on 3 March 1913 they were forced to agree to it.

The 1918 November Revolution opened a path, in Germany, for universal suffrage. Initially, the October opposition by liberals and Catholics against the Social-Democratic proposal to grant the right to vote to women appeared to be successful. However the Kaiser's escape ended the brief government of Prince Max von Baden, which was followed by an entirely Socialist government led by Philip Scheidemann.

In the United States too, the end of the war created the conditions for the realisation of female suffrage, which was inscribed in the nineteenth amendment of the constitution, approved by Congress on 4 June 1919 and ratified on 18 August 1920. President Wilson had decided to support it in January 1918, after the Congress approved it; however the Senate refused to even discuss the amendment, which was later rejected by three votes. The activities of the National Women's Party in favour of pro-suffrage candidates contributed to create a favourable majority for the November 1918 elections: on 21 May 1919 Congress approved the amendment with a score of 304 to 89, and the Senate did the same five days later (56 votes to 25).

Before the approval of the amendment ('The right of citizens of the United States to vote shall not be denied or abridged by the United States or by any State on account of sex'), most of the Western states had already given women the right to vote locally, while only two had done so on the East Coast (New York in 1917 and Michigan in 1918). The first state to allow women to vote locally was Wyoming in 1869, followed by Washington in 1883, Colorado in 1893, Utah in 1895 and Idaho in 1896. Between 1911 and 1914 the same right was granted in California, Arizona, Oregon, Kansas, Montana and Nevada; in 1918 Oklahoma and South Dakota followed suit.

Why were the Western states so far ahead of the 'cultured' and 'advanced' Eastern ones, when it came to women's right to vote? In large part because the borders between the private and public spheres were thinner; because more women were active (as doctors and lawyers, for example) in what were earlier typically male sectors; because a greater percentage of women were land-owners; because education for women was better and because women were more present in socially relevant activities (libraries, assistance, associations against alcoholism and prostitution). Greater opportunities for the female gender meant a greater probability of gaining the right to vote. The fact that more women worked in male sectors and took part in public activities, which aimed to reinforce traditional family values, appeared to pacify men with regard to the positive effects of female suffrage.

The right to vote locally had often been obtained by stressing the differences between women and men, and by anticipating an improvement in the condition of woman within her 'separate' sphere (family, assistance, education) from the granting of universal suffrage. The approval of the nineteenth amendment constituted instead the recognition and full affirmation of the principle of the 'constitutional' equality between men and women. Not everyone interpreted it this way, and even after the enfranchisement of women many courts, in various states, did not allow women to be part of civilian juries, according to the legal differences between 'states'. If this 'incremental' vision of suffrage 'is coherent with the limitative and orthodox meaning we now give the nineteenth amendment', other courts 'recognised that the previous exclusion of women from the right to vote was based on their asserted inferiority to men, and thus interpreted universal suffrage as a negation of such an assertion'.[200] Despite the fact that many scholars have underlined its limited objective, 'the nineteenth amendment was a product of the revolutionary idea that women share an equal status within a democracy': if considered within a historical context, the recognition of women's equality was 'far more coherent with our national ideals and constitutional values'.[201]

An important chapter of the history of the feminist and suffragist movement took place in Japan, and entwined, during the same years in which universal suffrage was being recognised in Europe, with an idea of 'rights' that is not completely comparable to the European and North American experiences.

The salience of rights in Japanese thought, however, suggests that nineteenth century concepts of rights drew from indigenous as well as imported ideas. To the indigenous value of self-cultivation through education and ethical development was added the important notion that the cultivated person was an individual who was entitled to a respected role in civil society or the public arena and, in turn, to inclusion in the emerging modern state.[202]

Public debate, which was at its apex during the 1920s, focused on the request to grant women the right to vote and on the obligation of the state to protect women. During the Meiji era (1868-1912) the many meanings given to the Western term 'rights', which was associated with a variety of neologisms and translations, underlined Japan's problem of its relations with foreign ideas, as well as with the type of relationships of power each group and individual could enjoy within a modern state. For Japanese women political participation and inclusion in the state (or 'nationalisation', a significant term for the European experience) would have signified a preventive elimination of patriarchal and male sexual privileges.

The dominant idea was that female suffrage was to follow the development of a sense of belonging to the state, as a result of an education capable of combining the ethic objectives of Confucianism with Western-type instruction. Women became active in the field of social reforms (concerning poverty, alcoholism, prostitution) and reinforced their role within the family and civil society as a prerequisite for political rights; at the same time they affirmed the right to participate in order to be – as women, mothers, wives – citizens and thus educate their family to citizenship. Demands for a political right – to vote – were formed on the basis of a relational right (with those who had rights), not an individual one. The practical struggle was represented as the correction of laws regarding political associations and public assemblies (women were excluded from both). This would be a first step towards enjoying an education and a degree of participation sufficient for emerging women capable of facing the role they were assigned within the construction of modern states.

The foundation – during the Taishô[203] period, in 1919 – of the Shin Fu-jin Kyôkai ('New Association of Women') and other female organisations served to unite women, yet also to develop their importance as a group, as a class, as part of the state, and thus as owners of rights (to be protected and included). The struggle to abolish the new Chian keisatsuhô ('Police law for public peace') – which once more vetoed female public participation and presence – was accompanied by the battle to protect women from marriages with men who had sexually transmittable diseases. The 1898 civil code punished adulterous women with divorce and two years of prison, yet it did not allow women to ask for a separation if their husband had contracted sexual diseases during extra-marital relationships. Two petitions on these issues were rejected by the Diet, leading to a stronger inclusion of these requests, within female associations, for the complete achievement of civil rights and of the right to vote.

The achievement of rights in order to become better mothers and wives and to be respected as persons and women in a society freed from patriarchy, polygamy and prostitution: these were the concepts women insisted upon, earning a growing level of consensus within Japanese society. On 26 February 1921, the Diet unanimously recommended the acceptance of female political participation. Barron Fujimura Yoshirô, a member of the Chamber of Counsellors (analogous to the English House of Lords), replied that such a measure was against natural laws, in both a physiological and psychological sense. At first the law was rejected, but it was later approved in August; at this point the feminist movements shifted their attention to the recognition of equality between men and women. On this basis 43 different organisations united, in September 1923, within the Tokyo Rengô Fujinkai ('Tokyo Federation of Female Associations').

The February 1925 electoral law granted universal male suffrage in Japan, yet the question regarding the extension of the right to vote to women returned continuously to public attention and within the Diet's debates. For women the key word was *fusen*, a term that can be written and translated in two different ways: the first means 'universal suffrage', the second 'female suffrage'. The long struggle of Japanese women gained two partial and limited victories in 1931, before nationalist militarism delayed the question until 10 April 1946, when they finally obtained the right to vote.

The dynamics of the struggle for women's rights in Japan is an excellent example of a process that was profoundly different – as in other countries – to men's battle for rights in the second half of the eighteenth century: women's demands appeared to be motivated by 'the desire to participate in power rather than to be protected from its excesses'.[204]

8. *The peace treaty*

When the Paris Conference began, on 18 January 1919, millions of deaths caused by the 'Spanish' influenza were adding to the nine million who had died during the war. This terrible influenza shocked the world between June 1918 and the spring of 1919 (sixteen million people, most of whom were under thirty-five, died in India alone). The countries who suffered most losses during the war had been Germany and Russia, yet it was Serbia that lost most men in proportional terms (35% of the country's combatants).

Although the concept of human rights 'was never mentioned during the Versailles Conference, nor in the Pact of the League of Nations',[205] the Conference was accompanied by high hopes. One diplomat wrote that 'we were not prepared simply for Peace, but for Eternal Peace'.[206]

In the seventh part of the Treaty of Versailles, in the articles 227 to 230, it was established that a special tribunal was to be created specifically in order to judge Wilhelm II of Hohenzollern and that all those who had 'committed acts against the laws and customs of war' were to be accused. These measures were based on the conviction that punishment for the worst violations of the *ius in bello* should accompany the far heavier economic and territorial losses imposed upon the defeated states. Even if limited only to crimes committed by the defeated states, a form of public and international condemnation would have allowed the process which had begun before the war, concerning war regulations, to continue.

The Paris Conference created a commission to identify the responsibility for the war and to agree adequate punishments. This commission was formed of representatives from the victorious states (Britain, France, Italy, United States and Japan), and was soon known as the 'commission of the 15'. Its main objective was to judge those who were responsible for causing the war and, during the conflict, had committed unacceptable crimes. Three different sub-commissions studied the causes of and responsibility for the war, the violations of the laws of war and customs according to the legislation established before the conflict, and ways to identify culprits and the punitive measures to be applied.

The commission's unanimous conclusions were that Germany was to be held responsible for starting the conflict, and that Turkey and Bulgaria had instigated a 'war that was fought by the central empires, and their allies, Bulgaria and Turkey, in a barbaric form and with illegal methods which violated the laws and customs of war and the principles of humanity'.[207]

Violence against the Armenians, considered to be 'primitive barbarianism', was included in the second category of crimes – those against 'the laws of humanity' – while the first category dealt with crimes against enemy soldiers (for example the use of gas). The 1907 Hague Convention was intended to be a juridical reference which could unite the whole commission in a consensus – for at the time there were no juridical norms or deals regarding crimes committed by a state against its own citizens. Indeed, it allowed the prosecution of violations of 'existent laws between civil populations or laws of humanity and dictates of public conscience.' Whoever was considered to have broken such laws, 'however high their position may have been, without distinction of rank, including chiefs of States, who have been guilty of offences against the laws and customs of war or the laws of humanity, are liable to criminal prosecution'.[208] The exact reference was to the so-called Martens clause, which had been inserted into the Convention after its conclusion. The clause allowed the punishment of criminal actions which were not specifically listed in the treaty. Paradoxically, it was precisely the Martens clause which made it impossible to find the solution the commission was seeking.

The attempt by the victorious countries to create an international penal justice court, to punish the political and military leaders of the central empires, was based on the idea that the 1899 and 1907

Hague Conventions had been violated, as well as on the conviction that Wilhelm II was guilty of international crimes. The fact that the alibi of acting on orders from above could not be considered a defence added a new dimension to the juridical development of international law.[209]

In this case it was American resistance that impeded the creation of an international tribunal; the view expressed by state secretary Robert Lansing was that war crimes were to be judged by each state's military tribunals: to oppose the creation of a special court, Lansing used the Martens clause, which made the formation of an international tribunal an accessory measure. Indeed differences on this issue were based predominantly on the choice between an international tribunal and a tribunal formed by only the victorious nations; and on the limits of an international tribunal over the possibility of judging individuals considered responsible for crimes committed by a state or in its name. Apart from the Ottoman leaders of the Union and Progress Committee, who were responsible for the massacre of the Armenians, the problem mainly concerned the German emperor Wilhelm II, and the possibility of judging him on the basis of what some – politicians, diplomats and jurists – believed to be a retroactive use of national and international law. The American veto initially blocked all the work of the commission of the 15, yet later President Wilson himself seemed to encourage the solution adopted by articles 227 to 230 of the Treaty of Versailles. However the President's optimism was halted by Lansing's realism, which soon spread to most European leaders. The eventual result was the 'national' trials in Leipzig and Istanbul. In Leipzig 888 defendants were acquitted out of a total of 900, while six of the remaining twelve were pardoned for having followed orders from above. The remaining six were given light sentences and pardoned just a few years later. In Istanbul the main executers of the Armenian genocide were sentenced to death, most of them by default (one sentence was carried out, but after the nationalistic disorders which followed, no further executions took place).

The French Prime Minister Georges Clemenceau represented, alongside British Premier David Lloyd George and American President Woodrow Wilson, the major powers at play, and was the strongest supporter of drastic and punitive measures against Germany. When commenting on his behaviour, economist John Maynard Keynes – the most lucid critic of the treaty and its consequences – wrote:

> This is the policy of an old man, whose most vivid impressions and most lively imagination are of the past and not of the future. He sees

the issue in terms of France and Germany, not of humanity and of European civilisation struggling forwards to a new order. The war has bitten into his consciousness somewhat differently from ours, and he neither expects nor hopes that we are at the threshold of a new age. [...] The policy of reducing Germany to servitude for a generation, of degrading the lives of millions of human beings, and of depriving a whole nation of happiness should be abhorrent and detestable—abhorrent and detestable, even if it were possible, even if it enriched ourselves, even if it did not sow the decay of the whole civilised life of Europe.[210]

One of the most complicated arguments of the Paris Conference was self-determination, which President Wilson had placed at the very heart of his international policy in his speech to Congress in January 1918. At the end of 1917 Lenin had also theorised on self-determination as the cornerstone of the new Bolshevik government's international relations. The right of each population to independence and the opportunity to choose its own political regime and economic and social development risked destabilising not only defeated countries, but the victors as well, with regard to the populations in their colonies (although Wilson had also mentioned the need to consider the 'fair demands' of colonial governments). The presence in Paris of numerous non-European states (Canada, Australia, New Zealand, South Africa, Japan) and various national groups, who had arrived with the intention of pressurising the major powers and defending their own rights (Arabs, Jews, Armenians, Indians, Chinese, Malese, Kyrgyzes, Koreans, black inhabitants of America and Africa), made the situation even more complicated. After all, the question was already extremely delicate in Europe, given the presence of numerous national minorities on the continent and the need to redefine the national borders of many European countries.

In the name of the right to self-determination, new states were created for the populations of Finland, Estonia, Latvia, Lithuania, Poland, Czechoslovakia, Hungary and Albania. A federal state was created to include Serbia, Slovenia, Bosnia, Croatia and Montenegro. Minorities, who were still present in some of these states despite the attempts to create ethnically homogeneous countries, obtained protective treaties, which also included Jewish and Muslim minorities. However, the problem of self-determination entwined with the more complex racial issue.

The important Japanese newspaper *Asahi* wrote that Japan intended to insist on the 'equal international treatment of all races', because 'no other question is as inseparable and materially intertwined with the permanence of peace in the world than the fair or unfair treatment of a great majority of the world's population'. If President Wilson was not capable of destroying 'the wall of discrimination', then he 'will have spoken in vain of peace, justice and humanity, revealing himself simply to be a hypocrite'.[211]

Rightfully believing that the Senate would never approve an article concerning racial equality, Wilson strained the rules of the commission of the League of Nations (of which he was President) and – although 11 delegates out of 17 were in favour of its insertion – declared the proposal was to be turned down, as it had not been approved unanimously. No regulation actually established any need for unanimity, yet Wilson stated it was required given the delicacy of the argument. As a result the American president became the target of ferocious criticisms by all those fighting for human rights in the United States: William Edward Du Bois, founder in 1909 of the National Association for the Advancement of Colored People (NAACP) and author of the influential work *The Negro* (1915), accused him of having forgotten the promises he had made to black soldiers during the war.

The first pan-African Congress, which Du Bois himself had helped organise, took place in 1919 and asked the powers reunited in Versailles to quickly establish 'home rule' for African populations, following a temporary co-domination by the winning states and local elites. In the summer of that same year, the response to Wilson's actions exacerbated and radicalised the 'race riots' taking place in many Northern and Southern states of the United States (South Carolina, Texas, Washington D.C., Illinois, Tennessee, Nebraska, Arkansas), and opposed white and black people within a context of social crisis, unemployment, high prices and competition for jobs. Black people's demands for equality were considered too radical, and interwoven with the more general 'Red Scare' which had began in 1919.

During this 'Red Summer', the black poet Claude McKay wrote his most famous poem, 'If We Must Die':

> If we must die, let it not be like hogs
> Hunted and penned in an inglorious spot,
> While round us bark the mad and hungry dogs,
> Making their mock at our accursed lot.
> If we must die, O let us nobly die,
> So that our precious blood may not be shed
> In vain; then even the monsters we defy
> Shall be constrained to honor us though dead![212]

9. *The League of Nations*

During the First World War, especially in its last two years, early enthusiasm had been replaced by widespread feelings of disillusion, tiredness and desire for peace. In many countries this contributed to the revival of social conflicts, justified by the harsh conditions of life citizens had to endure. This was the context in which the major European countries – including the democratic ones that would win the conflict – introduced legislative measures which suspended or limited traditional rights, attributing the need to give the government greater powers to the emergencies of war. It had always been considered normal that the 'state of war' changed and limited freedom for citizens; in this case it became the occasion and justification for measures which often had no actual relation to the war, and concerned instead tenser and more radical social dynamics which had been difficult to solve for the governments.

On the outbreak of the war, on 8 August 1914, Britain adopted the Defence of the Realm Act. This act imposed censorship, the requisition of buildings for military purposes and more general measures for social control (the prohibition on selling and consuming alcohol on public transport and during certain times of the day), as well as regulations aimed at preventing support for the enemy (the veto on flying kites, lighting bonfires, buying binoculars and discussing military matters in public) or of saving food for the population (the prohibition on feeding wild animals).

In the United States, on 15 June 1917, the Espionage Act was passed. On the basis of this document Eugene Debs, a three-time Socialist candidate in previous elections, was arrested for 'obstruction to enlistment' (remaining in prison for three years), and 75 newspapers accused of violating the Act were suppressed or deprived of press postal privileges. The victims of these measures were predominantly pacifist, radical and Socialist organisations who opposed the war and were thus compared to the enemies on the other side of the Atlantic.

This law was reviewed and integrated the following year into the Sedition Act, which condemned any hostile, disloyal, offensive or vulgar attitude towards the government, the flag and the army. Hundreds were arrested as members of organisations that were against war and of the Industrial Workers of the World (IWW) trade union, probably the most consistent and determined opposition movement. However, the arrests also affected intellectuals and pacifist or isolationist citizens who dared to openly criticise the government. The necessity of condemning whoever might weaken or harm the morale of a country at war justified the arbitrary and unmotivated use of repressive measures. For example, during the 'Spanish' flu epidemic, which began in the spring of 1918, news about the virus was censored in order not to weaken the morale of citizens and of the troops. The result was of course that many states did not prepare adequate measures to combat the virus.

The Sedition Act was revoked only in 1921, and was a fundamental tool during the so-called 'Red Scare' between 1919 and 1921. The beginning of civil anti-government protests in 1917 was centred on obligatory conscription (which only excluded recognised members of religious sects which prohibited the use of weapons). But from 1919, thanks to the involvement of the National Civil Liberties Bureau, later transformed into the American Civil Liberties Union, the main targets of the state's repression would be 'wobblies' (members of the IWW) and Socialists, considered to be subversives and potential spreaders of Bolshevism and anarchy.

A 1917 law allowed the Minister of Employment to arrest or deport any immigrant who spread propaganda or favoured the destruction of property or the downfall of the American government; whoever belonged to the IWW could not even obtain naturalisation. In December 1919 many foreign-born Anarchists and subversives – including Emma Goldman and Aleksander Berkman – were deported to Russia. The chief instigator of the 'Red Scare' was Minister of Justice Alexander Mitchell Palmer, who in 1917 had refused the position of Minister of War because of his pacifist views (he was a Quaker). Following a series of Anarchist attacks on public spaces, convinced he needed to remove any subversive risk from the American soil and supported by Wilson and public opinion, he authorised the so-called 'Palmer raids' (arrests, round-ups, intimidations, interceptions). These led to the arrests of over 10,000 wobblies and pacifists, radicals and Socialists, Anarchists and Communists (with over 3,000 people arrested in one single night in January 1920). In 1919, in the Ministry of Justice, the General Intelligence Division was created, under the guidance of a young J Edgar Hoover, who would later found and direct the Federal Bureau of Investigation between 1924 and 1972. In just a few months Hoover collected the names of over 150,000 'radical' suspects, an archive which he would use, five years later, to create the FBI.

The war had indeed led to various types of rebellion and revolutionary attempts, which became a constant problem for governments both during the conflict and in the years of post-war reconstruction. In 1916 the 'Easter Rising' for Irish independence was halted by British tanks. Among the Irish nationalist leaders, who were tried and later executed by court martial, was Roger Casement, whose report on the Congo atrocities had helped end Leopold II's colonial regime. WB Yeats dedicated his poem *Easter 1916* to the executed leaders ('I have met them at close of day/ Coming with vivid faces').

In Germany a series of revolutions actually led to the beginnings of a civil war. First the Bavarian Soviet Republic was defeated after just a few months by the regular army, then Ebert's Socialist government in Berlin was challenged by the recently formed Communist Party in an insurrection which ended with a bloody repression: this civil war was a composite one (Socialists against Communists, nationalists against Socialists) which eventually led to the elections of the Constituent Assembly and to the birth of the Republic of Weimar. In Russia the revolution which had defeated the Tsar and led to democracy dragged on for months in a stalemate between two separate powers, aiding the Bolshevik revolution in October and its subsequent creation of a dictatorial one-party government. Long conflicts took place in Italy and Czechoslovakia, Poland and China. In the British colony of India, in 1919, the Government of India Act tried – after the Amritsar massacre – to widen native participation in local assemblies, which were becoming more and more powerful; but the Indian Congress called such measures 'disappointing' and condemned them. The war that many thought would put an end to all wars seemed to have instead taken the lid off a Pandora's box in which social, national, racial and gender conflicts all joined with the problems of post-war reconstruction and the widespread economic crisis. However, the immediate post-conflict period was not characterised only by violence and repressions: many new nations became independent and established their constitutions, as well as the limited but consistent civil and political liberties such a procedure guaranteed. When evaluating the results of the Pact of the League of Nations, the Ligue des Droits de l'Homme noted how the methods and obligations to protect human rights were not the same in each region and country of the world, did not extend universally to everyone, and how there was no clarity regarding the instruments to spread them or to punish their violations: power remained firmly in the hands of the strongest nation-states.[213] And yet:

> never before in history had a peace conference produced so many treaties or programmes with so many provisions about the right of self-determination, the right of minorities to be protected, the right to enjoy life by receiving relief assistance, and the rights of labouring classes, or produced an international organisation formally charged with guaranteeing these particular rights. Never before had the global community made such a direct connection between peace and justice, or been willing to acknowledge such extensive responsibilities. For the beneficiaries, these provisions thus held an extraordinary promise that the future would be different from the

past. For the excluded they provoked a realisation of the necessity
to exert continual pressure and a determination never to give up
until they realised their vision.[214]

The end of the war also led to a series of positive signals: the creation
of the International Labour Office (ILO) and of the Permanent Court of
International Justice within the League of Nations, the revival of the
International Red Cross, through its Committee in Geneva, and the
creation of the League of Societies of the Red Cross, created in 1919 as an
international federation. The League of Nations certainly represented a
generous illusion that world conflicts could be avoided. While the revolutionary tensions and civil conflicts calmed down during the 1920s, the
League was incapable of preventing the French-German-British conflicts
poisoning international relations across the whole of Europe, while also
impeding the continent from finding a common line for its relations with
the United States. Yet about ten years after the end of the war, there
appeared to be signs of greater hope for human rights in the Western
world: the treaty of Locarno, in 1925, which ratified the pacification of
the Western powers through the recognition of national borders (except
for those of Eastern Germany) and Germany's admission to the League
of Nations, and the Briand-Kellogg pact which rejected war as a solution
for international conflicts.

Chapter Five
From Darkness to Light

1. *Life and survival during the great crisis*

'I have seen thousands of these defeated, discouraged, hopeless men and women, cringing and fawning as they come to ask for public aid. It is a spectacle of national degeneration.'[215] These words, pronounced in October 1933 by the Mayor of Toledo, Ohio, speak of a national desperation which was soon to find a resolution. Within three months the United States of Franklin Delano Roosevelt, who had been elected just a year earlier, managed to find jobs for over four million unemployed, thanks to the Civil Works Administration.

The most striking aspect of the great crisis (which began in October 1929 on the New York Stock Market, and soon spread across the Western world) was the sudden and radical impoverishment of the richest and most advanced regions of the world, reduced to a state of misery similar to their pre-industrialisation state. The most elementary social rights suddenly became uncertain. Even the right to life and to an acceptable existence became more of a hope than a certainty for millions of people.

Unemployment was the most macroscopic and terrible symptom of the crisis. 1932 was the climax of the progressive worsening of the situation: the unemployment rate in the United States was 25%, while it had grown to 43.7% in Germany, 31.7% in Denmark, 30.8% in Norway, 26.1% in Austria, 22.8% in Sweden and 22.1% in Britain. According to the League of Nations' statistics the unemployed population of the Western world amounted to 25 million people, without taking into account the millions of partially employed individuals or those who were reduced to a condition of bare survival in the countryside. Most of the unemployed population depended almost completely on public assistance, which was forced to maintain extremely demanding programmes but only partially managed to do so. Hundreds of thousands of people ran up large debts and lost their homes, living in a state of hunger and illness in temporary huts and camps, without any sanitary services.

> I had never before seen such lean and pale faces; not white, but grey. I recognised this lean grey paleness as the true sign of the chronically unemployed: the sign of those who had suffered years of poor nutrition, of sensitivity to cheap imitations of food, of never knowing what a full stomach meant. Many of those faces were covered in red boils. This was also due to the lack of vitamins and nutrition in the food they ate, which had no power over their rust and decay.[216]

This sudden return, even in the homelands of the industrial revolution and democracy, to living conditions more typical of Eastern European nations or agricultural countries, was often accompanied by an equally shocking regression in the sphere of civil and political freedom. This step backwards in the field of individual and collective rights often took place within the boundaries of formal legality, yet was accompanied by new forms of intimidation, violence and widespread illegality which authorities could not, or did not want to, avoid or stop.

The most significant case, which anticipated an overriding tendency of the 1930s, was Italian Fascism. At the end of October 1922 Benito Mussolini was given the task of forming a new government by King Victor Emmanuel III. The Fascist response to the lengthy Italian political and parliamentary crisis (which had lasted since 1919) was successful largely as a result of its cunning political strategies, both on the level of pre-insurrectional mobilisation, as in the case of the March on Rome, and within the institutional sphere. The paradox of the Fascist victory is that the most relevant rights obtained by Italians up to that moment – male suffrage in 1912 and later, in 1918, male suffrage which included illiterate citizens; the establishment of a maximum of eight hours for the working day – had not led to a greater degree of stability in the country. Thus the party that set out to form a government (not based on an electoral majority, but thanks to the fact that the king and political elites held in high esteem its capacity to maintain order) was precisely the party that, gradually, would abolish all the rights won by the country over the course of the previous hundred years.

Many nineteenth century thinkers, including Alexis de Tocqueville, had expressed their concerns over the future of a mass society and democracy. These worries appeared to be confirmed at the moment when mass participation in the public sphere became a reality, especially because such participation was not limited to the vote. On the contrary, the conflicting mass mobilisations of the period favoured alternative parliamentary and governmental solutions to those proposed by the political parties that had the most votes, who were neither capable of maximising their social consensus on an institutional level, nor of minimising the fears surrounding certain radical fringes in their ranks.

Just as nobody within the Italian parliamentary majority and opposition had seriously believed that Fascism could represent an actual danger – to the extent that key figures such as Giolitti, Salandra, Facta, Bonomi, Orlando, Gronchi, De Gasperi and De Nicola had all given their vote of confidence to Mussolini, while Benedetto Croce gave his vote even after the murder of Matteotti – similarly in Germany, ten years later, the ambiguous relationship between the electoral system, social mobilisation and institutional logistics benefitted a solution that would result in the most drastic negation of rights ever realised by a political regime. Adolf Hitler's National Socialist party obtained 2.6% of the votes in 1928; in September 1930 this number had grown to 18.3% and in July 1932 to 37.4%. This was a sufficiently high consensus to obtain the charge of forming a new government from President Hindenburg, on 30 January 1933, after the failure, over the course of just nine months, of two governments led respectively by von Papen and von Schleicher. The Italian and German constitutions were extremely different: Italy was still under the Albertine Statute, which was already out of date when the country was unified; the German Weimar constitution was instead probably the most advanced example of post-First World War juridical and political concepts. Yet neither the former nor the latter were able to block the rise to power of movements which aimed above all to destroy democracy and political rights.

Many of those countries which had only recently become independent also shared serious problems regarding the application of new political and civil rights. Poland had regained its freedom after a century and a half of being divided between other countries, and now found itself at the centre of a territorial conflict between Czechoslovakia, Germany, Lithuania and the USSR, as a result of the fact that 30% of its population consisted of Belo-Russian, Lithuanian, Rumanian, Ukrainian and German minorities. No less than 14 governments had ruled the country between 1918 and 1926, when Marshall Pilsudski's coup d'état enabled the creation of an authoritarian and dictatorial state (initially with only 30% of the votes). Other authoritarian governments in Europe were the regime of Count Bethlen in Hungary, of Cankov in Bulgaria (which had taken power through a coup), the various governments which succeeded one another in Romania and the regime of Alexander I in Yugoslavia, after the 1929 abolition of the local constitution. In all these countries the rights of minorities, although often enunciated in legal terms, progressively became non-existent or were strongly diminished. This is what happened in Poland, to the Magyar (and Ruthenian, German and Slovak) minorities in Romania, to Slovaks and Germans in Czechoslovakia and to Macedonians during the conflict between Bulgaria and Yugoslavia. Indeed in Yugoslavia the conflicts between Serbs, Croatians and Slovenians were the basis for the dictatorship of Alexander Karagjeorgievi.

After the First World War, women appeared to be living through a moment of progress in terms of their participation in the public sphere. They gained the right to vote in Austria, Germany, the Netherlands, Poland and Belgium (with some limitations) in 1919, in Sweden in 1921, and in Burma – the first Asian country to grant such rights – in 1922. The first Latin American country to allow women to vote was Ecuador in 1928, the same year in which the right to vote was granted to English and Irish women. The same measures were adopted by many countries during the 1930s (Costa Rica, Cuba, Uruguay, Bolivia and Brazil). Spain instituted universal suffrage during the republic, before the 1936 military coup and consequent civil war established the regime of General Francisco Franco.

In the United States the racial question was intertwined with problems of immigration and with Madison Grant's Eugenics. Grant, having being defeated by Franz Boas for the leadership of the Association of Anthropologists (Boas favoured cultural anthropology over Grant's physical anthropology), pressured the Immigration Restriction League to establish the 1924 Immigration Act, which included restrictive measures on populations from Southern and Eastern Europe (and prohibited all forms of immigration from Asia). In the Southern states, between 1930 and 1934, over one hundred cases of black people being lynched took place, leading Congress to introduce the Anti-lynching Bill (a similar attempt had been made in 1922). The Bill was boycotted by Southern senators and thus rejected by the Senate.

> The proposal regarding an anti-lynching law – stated North Carolina senator Josiah Bailey – is the herald of a policy deliberately thought up by agitators not to oppose lynching, but with the goal of introducing a policy of interference in local matters. The law on lynching will soon be followed by a law on civil rights. [...] But I must warn you that no administration can survive without us.[217]

Roosevelt, who was afraid of losing support from Southern politicians and of a consequent division within his party which might have endangered his New Deal project, decided not to support the law openly. As a result, the anti-lynching law was rejected. The National Association for the Advancement of Colored People (NAACP), led by James Weldon Johnson during the twenties and by Walter Francis White in the thirties, continued its struggle for civil rights, which had become even more complicated during the Depression. In 1930, thanks to support from the American Federation of Labor, it was able to block John Johnston Parker's nomination to the Supreme Court due to his anti-worker and anti-black positions (this was the first rejection of a presidential candidate in the twentieth century); at the same time the Association was preparing the ground for the first anti-segregation measures through a legal and constitutional battle which helped the NAACP exceed the 500,000 member mark.

2. *From inside the colonies*

The most intense and pioneering mobilisation against colonial power to take place between the two world wars was in the British *raj* (the term indicated both the name of the colonial government and that of the local viceroy). At the beginning of the century the *swadeshi* (an internal protest aiming to obtain autonomy and self-government, called *swaraj* in opposition to the *raj*) had spread across the country, while after the First World War many protests took place against the renewal of the Defence of India Act, an emergency law adopted during the conflict. This new mobilisation was above all the work of the Congress party – whose most important figure was Gandhi – which managed to create a united Hindu-Muslim front against the British by spreading its beliefs regarding the *satyagraha*, a form of non-violent struggle.

The protest which swept across the country during the twenties, following the Amritsar massacre, was characterised by a civil disobedience based on economic emancipation, the refusal of imported goods and the reinforcement of self-rule and faith in the country's own strength. The goal of the protest was the new 1921 Government of India Act. The refusal to pay taxes was accompanied by lack of cooperation in work places and the boycott of local institutions. In the 1923-24 elections the radical fringe of the Congress obtained a large majority (after the massacre of 20 policemen by demonstrators, Gandhi had retired to meditate and began a hunger strike, temporarily abandoning the leadership of the protest). A large number of racial disorders between Hindus and Muslims, euphemistically dubbed 'community contests', took place during the second half of the twenties and linked in with the class conflict between poor peasants and landowners.

At the end of the 1920s the Congress, on Gandhi's suggestion, elected as its leader Jawaharlal Nehru, whose policy was based on *purna swaraj* (complete self-government). On 26 January 1930 the Indians celebrated their first Independence Day, and swore to resist the British dominion until they had achieved total self-government. One month later Gandhi launched the second national *satyagraha* against the taxation of salt, and led a 400 kilometre march of civil disobedience. Nehru was sentenced to six months in prison, while Gandhi was arrested with most of the Congress. The next phase of protests, boycotts and rebellions was marked by the disagreements between Gandhi and Bhimrao Ambedkar, the leader of the 'untouchables'.[218] The Mahatma sought to find a mainly religious solution to the situation (based on the 'redemption' of the untouchables through changes to their food and sexual customs, and on the education of other castes to 'tolerate' them), while Ambedkar wanted the recognition of electoral autonomy in the form of a percentage of members within local representative institutions.

In 1932 Gandhi and Ambedkar reached an agreement, ratified in Poona, which certified the recognition of the untouchables within the Hindu community (as demanded by Gandhi) yet with a fixed number of members within institutions (as requested by Ambedkar). The 1935 Government of India Act tripled the Indian electoral base (35 million people could now vote), increasing the legislative assemblies' powers and conceding a greater degree of autonomy to Indian Ministers within local institutions. The Muslim League, which controlled just one fourth of the offices reserved for Islamic citizens, was to later become – under the leadership of Mohammad Ali Jinnah – the legitimate and rooted political representation of Muslim nationalism. At this point the Congress and League appeared ever more distant, just as the British had predicted; however the nationalistic and autonomist propaganda from both movements allowed them to find moments of unity during the struggle against the British *raj*.

In Africa and in the Middle East, the colonial policy of both Britain and France was to consolidate their positions and reinforce their economic hegemony. Egypt, formally independent since 1922, was still strongly bound to the British Empire. In the competition between the two nations, French governments in Syria and Lebanon only partially compensated for the British ones in Iraq and Palestine, or for the United Kingdom's role in the 1932 unification of Saudi Arabia. In the sub-Sahara regions of the continent, colonial dynamics mostly concerned the seizing of local communities' lands through relations with local tribal chiefs. The British, and especially the French, tried to create reliable local elites (thus encouraging competition between clans and ethnic groups) who would be part of the new ruling classes, who were educated in Europe and were the main point of contact for colonial powers. In Africa nationalism was far weaker than in India, mainly because of the administrative and political units, as well as the actual borders of the states, which had been invented by the colonising countries and often imposed with no respect whatsoever as to geographic morphology or ethnic, linguistic and cultural differences. During this period, local leaders aimed above all to extract for their own clans and tribes as much as possible from the colonial powers, by conceding land to the colonists and guaranteeing the exploitation of all existing wealth.

The most significant episode to take place in Africa between the two wars was the loss of independence of the last free territory of the continent (excluding Liberia): Ras Haile Selassie's Ethiopia. In 1930, during a ceremony which featured many representatives of the Italian government, Selassie was named Emperor by Mussolini, who the Ras deeply admired. The Fascist regime had already re-conquered Somalia (1924-25) and Libya (1928-31), and in Cyrenaica it had committed particularly brutal massacres and crimes against the local populations. Mussolini had been preparing for the Ethiopian adventure since 1932-33, having gained considerable endorsement from the British and French. On 3 October 1935, Italian troops crossed the border between Eritrea and Ethiopia, supported by the Italian air force and artillery. Seven months later, on 9 May, Mussolini proclaimed his empire after the troops had captured Addis Ababa.

The nature of the conquest achieved by Italian Fascism in Africa is described in this comment by a member of the International Red Cross: 'It is not a war, and it is not a massacre. It is the torture of tens of thousands of defenceless men, women and children through the use of bombs and gas'.[219] General Badoglio, authorised by Mussolini, used gas against the enemy army, and against civilians, and would have decided to use germ warfare if Mussolini had not stopped him once the conflict appeared to have been won. Italy was one of the nations which had signed the Third Convention of Geneva in 1925. The Convention, alongside the rights of prisoners of war, had approved a protocol regarding the prohibition of the use of asphyxiating, toxic or similar gases and of viral weapons, thus augmenting the decisions made by the previous Geneva Conventions, in article 171 of the Peace of Versailles and in the 1922 Declaration of Washington. The justification used by Italy – which formally denied the use of gas until the middle of the 1990s – can be found in the pages of the

Popolo di Roma, 3 January 1936: 'We are at war. We would have liked to fight fairly, with the greatest respect for human and international law; yet our enemy, with his terrifying atrocities, forces us to use any means to fight him.'

Haile denounced the use of gas before the League of Nations, stating that over 250,000 people had been killed. Yet the Ethiopian resistance struggled on. On 8 July 1936 Mussolini authorised General Rodolfo Graziani, who had been nominated viceroy of Ethiopia, 'to once more begin and systematically carry out a policy of terror and extermination against rebels and the population. Without a policy of ten eyes for an eye we will not heal this wound in time'.[220] Graziani had allegedly been injured during an attack on 17 February 1937, while celebrating the birth of the Prince of Naples. What followed was a ferocious repression, which led the American ambassador to state he could not remember seeing anything of the kind since the Armenian massacre during the First World War. Amongst the thousands of Ethiopian victims were also five hundred monks from the Debrà Libanòs convent, the most important local institution of the Coptic religion.

In November 1935 Italy was condemned by the League of Nations, yet Fascist violence was hardly weakened by the economic sanctions that were imposed; on the contrary, the regime earned further consensus from the population, borne up by the country's nationalistic pride. After all, the sanctions were almost ridiculous: the embargo was placed on donkeys and camels, while it allowed cars, trucks and petrol to be imported. After the debacle during the Manchurian crisis, the League of Nations had further revealed its limitations. In those same years, a further blow to its reputation came from Spain, which was suffering the terrible tragedies of the civil war. The Western powers were incapable of enforcing the principle of non-intervention which was continuously ignored by the Fascist regimes of Italy and Germany.

During the Spanish civil war terrible atrocities were carried out by both sides (although the violence of the rebel generals' troops was certainly more intense, intentional and programmed). One episode in particular was similar to the Italian violence in Ethiopia. On 26 April 1937 the German planes from the Condor Legion, following Wolfgang von Richtofen's orders, attacked the Basque resistance. The town of Guernica was completely destroyed after a three-hour long bombardment. On 1 May the *New York Times* summed up the horror of the event: 'This peak of cruelty shocks the world more than any barbaric act during any barbaric war.'

3. *Against totalitarian attraction*

In 1936 Mussolini's Italy conquered Ethiopia by using gas and massacring the civilian population, and gave a 'spot in the sun' to King Victor Emmanuel III, who briefly enjoyed the illusion of creating an empire. At the same time Italian soldiers were participating as 'volunteers' in Franco's coup against the Spanish democratic republic. 1936 was also the year in which the Nobel for Peace was assigned to a little-known German journalist, Carl von Ossietzky (however the prize actually referred to 1935, when it had been suspended for a year). The decision by the Norwegian committee led Heinrich Mann to state that 'the conscience of the world' had finally awakened, while Romain Rolland wrote that this was the occasion to 'crown an apostle of peace, determined to the point of martyrdom'.

Certainly the prize assigned to Ossietzky had a very particular political meaning, given that the campaign in his name had begun when he was imprisoned first in the concentration camps of Sonnenburg, and later Esterwegen-Papenburg. He had been imprisoned immediately after the Nazi ascent to power, following the Reichstag fire which marked – at the end of February 1933, a month after Hindenburg had asked Hitler to form the government – the beginning of the anti-liberty laws and of the suppression of all rights won in Germany during the previous century.

Since the First World War Ossietzky had clashed with justice due to his pacifist views and strong criticisms of militarism and its links to the political world. A member and later secretary of the Deutsche Friedensgesellschaft (the German Association for Peace), at the beginning of the twenties he was the foreign editor-in-chief of the 'Berliner Volkszeitung', through which he tried to form a republican, democratic and pacifist political party for the 1924 elections. In 1926 he became editor-in-chief and then director of *Die Weltbühne* ('The stage of the world'), from which he began his struggle to inform the public of Germany's rearmament policy. In 1927 he was sentenced to a month in prison for having criticised the legalisation of paramilitary organisations, and in 1929 he was accused of treason after having revealed military secrets that demonstrated German infractions of the Treaty of Versailles,[221] with regard to the country's rearmament. He was pardoned thanks to an amnesty in December 1932, after having spent seven months in prison in Spandau. Just three months later, the final phase of his persecution by the Nazi regime would begin.

In December 1934, while he was still in the concentration camps – where he was tortured, beaten and forced to undertake hard labour despite the fact he had previously suffered from a heart attack – the campaign to present him as a candidate for the Nobel Prize for Peace was born. In April 1935 Jane Addams officially sent the proposal to Oslo.[222] The furious reaction by the Nazi government, which threatened to view the awarding of the prize to Ossietzky as an intolerable intrusion into German internal affairs, created a division within the pacifist world. On one side were those who continued to support the choice of the German journalist persecuted by the Nazi regime (including pacifist writer Ernst Toller, dramatist Werner Hartung, Albert Einstein, the young Willy Brandt – in exile in Oslo – Bertrand Russell, H.G. Wells, Aldous Huxley, Virginia Woolf, John Dewey, Franz Boas, Charles Beard and Oswald Garrison Villard). On the other side were those who believed that his pacifist merits were not sufficient to merit the prize, as well as those who thought the prize might make his conditions worse, as a result of Nazi vengeance. The first group included Ludwig Quidde, Nobel winner in 1927, while the second was led by a very well-known Quaker, Corder Catchpool, who even managed to visit Ossietzky in the concentration camp, and feared that the Nazi reaction to the prize might worsen both his conditions and those of his fellow prisoners.

The Gestapo documents disclosed after the Second World War reveal, on the contrary, that the regime was deeply worried by the rumours circulating abroad about Ossietzky's condition, to the extent that Goering himself decided to move him to the 'prison wing' of the Virchow Hospital in Berlin, in the spring of 1936. Immediately after the Nobel committee's decision to postpone the assignment of the prize by one year, a controversy surrounding Ossietzky stirred up by Norwegian writer Knut Hamsun – a supporter of Hitler and a bestselling author in his own country – pushed many intellectuals to defend the German journalist and to extend the campaign in his name, which would lead to him winning the prize the following year.

> To be sure, there were mixed motives among all those nominators. To the more political, it was a blow against Hitler and fascism, to many liberals, it was a demonstration for intellectual liberty. To the peace activists who participated, support for their peace principles. But perhaps what made the campaign so successful was that while Ossietzky did indeed symbolise all these causes, the focus of all the effort was upon a human being in torment, not just a symbol, but a man who had fought the good fight and was suffering for his peace beliefs. What if he was not a towering figure in the peace movement? Through the campaign for his prize, his fate did indeed touch the conscience of the world.[223]

In May 1933, when Ossietzky had just been imprisoned and sent to the concentration camps, a Jewish citizen from High Silesia, Franz Bernheim, presented a petition to the League of Nations to denounce the anti-Jewish regulations promulgated in his region, which represented a clear violation of the Convention signed in Geneva by Germany and Poland to protect the civil rights of minorities. The petition analysed above all the effects of the new legislation, which contradicted the German-Polish Treaty of 1922, which aimed at protecting ethnic minorities in High Silesia (at the time under German rule). Bernheim, a resident of Gleiwitz, had been fired, like all Jewish workers, by a German company, as a consequence of the anti-Semitic legislative and administrative norms proposed by the Nazi government as the first act of its anti-Jewish policy.

The petition of a single citizen forced the League of Nations to question whether a state could be accused and sanctioned by a majority of other states over an issue – racial policies – previously left to each country's internal affairs (after all, the United States had refused to ratify their entrance in the League of Nations precisely out of fear of such interference in their policies). In this case, however, the accusation was not against the anti-Jewish laws in themselves, but their application within a region, High Silesia, where the norms were to conform to the Treaty of Versailles or to later bilateral treaties. The dilemma – if defending the rights of a citizen violated the sovereignty of a state – was an explosive question for international relations, and thus the decision of the League of Nations was the centre of much attention.

Many years later, a member of the French delegation to the League of Nations in 1933 – René Cassin, who would later be a relevant figure for the formulation of the Universal Declaration of Human Rights in 1948 – remembered the Bernheim petition as a turning point in the conception of human rights, for the objectives of international law and its ability to defend individuals from the arrogant behaviour of states. It meant the recognition of each single person as a subject of international law, as a bearer of duties yet also due protection and guarantees regarding his/her rights.[224]

The decision of the League of Nations[225] reaffirmed the principles of the protection of minorities and yet was also widely ineffective, as Germany abandoned the international organisation at the end of the year, both in the name of its full national sovereignty and as a protest against French intransigence during the conference on disarmament: 'The petition therefore exposed the League to the dilemma of the protection of the human rights of the citizens of a sovereign state in the face of resistance to the very idea of limiting state sovereignty. It therefore had profound significance on how rights and their protection were conceived in the years before the Second World War'.[226]

The discussion over the Bernheim case underlined the arrogance of Nazi Germany in diffusing its organic and ethnic nationalism based on racial theories. German representative August von Keller, while refusing the resolutions proposed by the assembly, defined the 'Jewish' problem as a mere domestic German concern, and on the contrary demanded the right to defend German minorities living abroad and struggling to maintain their cultural identity. France and Britain intended to defend the treaties on minorities, yet on the other hand they did not want the effects of the Bernheim case to expand any further than the borders of High Silesia.

Only the Haiti delegate, Antoine Frangulis, tried to propose a generalisation of the protection of human rights, by extending the dispositions of article 2 of the treaty on minorities and theorising an International Convention based on the International Declaration of Human Rights, prepared in 1929 by the Institut de Droits International and approved by the Fédération Internationale des Droits de l'Homme:

> there is not only one category of citizens of a State, described as a minority, which deserves attention, but [...] all the citizens of which human communities are made up are entitled to the same freedom and the same protection, and the League of Nations must consider the problem as a whole from the aspects of the rights of man – that is to say, of the rights which men possess as such, whether they belong to a minority or a majority – and it must seek the solutions that are necessary.[227]

The proposal of Frangulis, the Greek jurist who, with the émigré Russian diplomat André Mandelstam, outlined this particularly coherent modern vision of human rights, hardly caught anybody's attention[228] beyond the closed circle of international scholars of law and human rights associations – which were at the time few and hardly influential. The British and French believed that such an outlook might undermine their colonial empire, while Latin American states, led by oligarchic governments or military dictatorships, appeared to be completely unfamiliar with the problem. The Soviet Union, which joined the League of Nations in the Autumn of 1934, was just about to enter (after the murder of Kirov) the era of repression which would soon lead to the Great Terror and the Moscow trials.

4. *Between totalitarianism and democracy*

1937 was the twentieth anniversary of a revolution that was supposed to free mankind from exploitation and injustice, and was the most terrible year in the history of the USSR:

> The Communist dictatorship was accompanied by political repressions, both before and after 1937. It was this year, however, that became, in the memory of the people, the sinister symbol of that entire system of mass murders organised and executed by the state. Evidently this happened because the Great Terror had its own extraordinary characteristics, which predetermined its particular place in history and the enormous influence it would have – and continues to have – on Russia's fate. 1937 meant gigantic repressions involving all regions and all social castes with no exception, from the country's leaders to workers and peasants who were distant from politics. During the 1937-38 biennium, over 1.7 million people were arrested on the basis of political accusations. If we also consider the victims of deportations and those condemned as 'socially dangerous elements', the number of repressed people rises above two million; amongst the arrested, more than 700,000 people were executed. [229]

While this violence was taking place, public trials based on extorted confessions were eliminating what was left of the old Bolshevik class and ridding the state of most of the leaders elected in 1934 during the XVII Congress of the CPSU. The new 1936 constitution, supposedly based on universal suffrage, formally guaranteed each individual's inviolability, freedom of speech, freedom of the press and association, as well as recognising the right to work, rest, education, health, to a home and to social equality. Yet, in reality, no rights were guaranteed in the USSR, a country dominated by the arbitrary decisions of the state and the party, which struck at every family and at all social categories. However, while consciousness of Nazi brutality grew alongside the strengthening of its regime, Communist violence was often ignored or justified.

In May 1938, 150 American intellectuals signed a declaration justifying the Moscow trials and supporting their death sentences. This appeal, signed by figures such as Nelson Agren and Malcolm Cowley, Elizabeth G. Flynn and Lillian Hellman, Irwin Shaw and Richard Wright, warned citizens not to fall under the influence of anti-Soviet propaganda aiming to weaken progressive forces opposing the Fascist menace. Heinrich Mann, who, two months later, would joyfully celebrate Ossietzky's Nobel prize, wrote in September 1936 that 'the Moscow trial and the execution of the sixteen old revolutionaries has shaken the prestige of the USSR [...] yet when conspirators intend to damage the revolution, the state has every right to eliminate them, for the good of the revolution itself, rapidly and without any hesitation'.[230]

In those very same days, in France, an appeal signed by Georges Bataille and Paul Eluard, Jean Giono and Daniel Guérin, Magdeleine Marx and Jacques Prévert, instead demanded the truth behind the accusations of the Moscow trials. This was the objective of the Dewey Commission – an inquiry led by the elderly philosopher – which, during a counter-trial held in Coyoacán, Mexico, deconstructed the evidence and testimonies used in Moscow by the procurator Vyŝinskij to demonstrate Trotsky's treason. With regard to a fair trial, the European and American left-wing were divided between those who justified violations of rights in the name of truth and of the revolution, and those who opposed them by demanding the right to know the truth, in order to continue fighting Fascism without hypocrisy or inconsistency.

A similar, though disturbingly isolated, episode took place during the International Congress of Writers in Defence of Culture, which was held in Paris between 21 and 25 June 1935.[231] The presence of non-Communist writers was, in the intentions of the organisers (the Russian Erenburg and Frenchman Aragon), fundamental for ensuring the event's unifying and anti-Fascist nature. On the second day of the Congress, Robert Musil, after a partially ignored speech in which he invited writers to withdraw themselves from the 'demands' of politics, concluded by reminding writers to hold 'dear also the love for truth; I would like to remark on this because at the moment it is not very strong and what we define culture is not directly using as its own criteria the concept of truth, although no culture can be founded upon an unclear relationship with truth'.

The problem of truth emerged in a dramatic episode that perhaps even Musil was not expecting, on Monday 24 June, the day before the close of the Congress. After a brief speech by Pasternak who praised poetry and happiness, Gaetano Salvemini, the famous anti-Fascist Italian writer and – at the time – Harvard professor, spoke about, in what became an embarrassing moment of truth for the whole Congress, the 'Serge case'. Victor Serge was an Anarchist Russian-Belgian writer, who had lived in France for many years before travelling to Russia to support the Bolshevik revolution, who had been deported and had now been in prison for three years. His French friends, including Magdeleine Marx and Maurice Paz, intended to speak of his detention in a Congress about freedom and culture, and even Gide appeared to want to speak a few words on the most famous political prisoner of the USSR. Salvemini began by protesting against the bourgeois identification with Fascism and by appreciating the Communist individualism admired by André Gide. He then added the following words, provoking scandalised and disapproving reactions:

> I would not feel at ease protesting against the Gestapo and against the Fascist Ovra, if I were at the same time making efforts to forget that a political police also exists in the Soviet Union. In Germany there are concentration camps, in Italy there are islands used as detention places, and in Soviet Russia there is Siberia [...] – Victor Serge is a prisoner in Russia. Fascism is the enemy not only because it is capitalistic, but because it is totalitarian. After centuries of Tsarism we can understand the need for the present totalitarian Russian state only if we hope for its evolution towards forms that are freer, but we must say this and not celebrate it as if it were the ideal condition for human freedom.

The overriding interest, within democratic countries, in violations of rights committed by Fascist states came from the strong fear that Nazi Germany was preparing a new era of war in Europe. Thus not enough attention was paid to what was happening in Russia in 1937, and still less to what was happening even further away during that same year. The Japanese invasion of China, two years before the Second World War began, was not condemned by the League of Nations. Indeed the institution was increasingly and evidently in decline, mostly intent on hiding its failures over the Spanish civil war and the Fascist conquest of Ethiopia, and it was soon abandoned by both Nazi Germany and Fascist Italy. The surrender, on 13 December 1937, of the capital Nanjing was accompanied by a wave of violence which soon involved civilians. About 250,000 people, no more than half of whom were soldiers, were massacred in horrible ways over the course of just a few weeks, after being beaten, tortured and raped. The Nanjing atrocities, almost undocumented for many decades, were the result of a sense of national and racial superiority introduced into the Japanese army by years of propaganda. By mixing together the myths of obedience and the certainty of impunity, this sense of superiority translated into a slaughter which horrified Western visitors in the city, yet never reached the European and North American public.

In the years preceding the Nazi aggression against Poland and the beginning of the Second World War, the two major European democracies were still struggling with the effects of the Great Depression. Britain relied on the Commonwealth, created in 1931 to protect the empire's market, and on tax agreements with the United States, which concluded only in November 1938. In France, the experience of the Popular Front, which had brought the Socialist Léon Blum into the government in 1936 after a wave of strikes and occupations, accelerated a series of governmental measures and trade union agreements which made the country the most advanced state in the world in terms of social legislation: with a working week of 40 hours, freedom of trade union organisation, direct elections of delegates and collective negotiations. But the financial crisis, aggravated by Anglo-American egoism, led to the devaluation of the franc and loss of capital, forcing Blum to leave office in 1938 to be replaced by a new centrist government.

> The corporative egoisms and multiple social resentments led to a general crisis of civic sense at the very moment in which it was most necessary. The fear of the future, born from the crisis, gave way to the fear of war, conceived by some as a civil war. This anguish paralyzed a large part of French society just as the feeling of an irreversible decline had paralyzed the Weimar society. This facilitated the need for a saviour (a marshal) in the same way it had opened, thanks to the mediation of another marshal, the path for the Führer.[232]

5. *The disappearance of rights*

The European political and social scene transformed rapidly after the assault on Poland on 1 September 1939, and the success of the German *Blitzkrieg*. By 1941, just before the Nazi attack on the Soviet Union, the entire European continent was practically under German control, apart from neutral countries (Sweden, Ireland, Switzerland, Spain, Portugal, Turkey). By using its army, Germany imposed its laws, and especially those concerning Jews, 'subversives' and 'antisocial' people, upon the rest of Europe.

Upon its rise to power, the National Socialist government had persecuted its political opponents and those identified as its social or racial enemies by building up legislation which soon overturned the entire Weimar juridical system. Immediately after the dismissal of the parliament, the decree 'for the protection of the population and of the state' declared the Communist Party (and soon all other parties) illegal, and suppressed fundamental constitutional rights. The law implemented on 7 April 1933 to reform the country's public administration excluded 'non-Aryans' and the politically 'unreliable'. Later measures led to the limitation and prohibition of Jews working in certain professions (as lawyers, doctors) and to the restriction of their access to universities. In 1933 a law for the prevention of hereditary disease made it legal to forcibly sterilise all those who suffered from hereditary diseases or mental problems, including schizophrenics and alcoholics.

Although the repression involved generic and arbitrary categories such as anti-social individuals or political enemies, the apex of the new norms was anti-Jewish discrimination. Such a policy was based on a racial philosophy which envisioned citizenship as founded on the *Volksgemeinschaft*, the 'national community', which transcended the individual and in which population and race were supposed to merge. In September 1935 the Nuremberg Laws excluded Jews from citizenship, prohibiting marriage or sexual relationships with Aryans, as well as suppressing their right to vote and excluding them from any public function. The law established that anyone with three or four Jewish grandparents was to be considered a Jew (of 'mixed' race if he/she had two), independently of his/her religious or cultural heritage. A partial formal limitation to this anti-Jewish policy, and in particular to its explicit public propaganda against non-Aryans, was sustained during 1936, when Berlin and Garmisch hosted the Olympic Games, and the regime chose not to portray itself as excessively totalitarian.

The Aryanisation of public administration was followed by that of the German business world. After the November 1938 *Kristallnacht*, Jews were banished from schools, cinemas, theatres and sports fields, and mostly prevented from entering 'Aryan' zones. The Jews were given new identity documents and passports that were easily identifiable from the letter 'J'; they were also obligated to add to their own names Israel, for men, or Sara, for women. During the repression other non-Aryans were categorised with the Jews, such as the 'bastard Rhinelanders' (descendants of German women and Senegalese soldiers from the French occupation army) and, later on, Gypsy populations, despite their Indo-European origins.

Italy, which had passed anti-liberty measures regarding political and civil rights since the 1925 'leggi fascistissime',[233] decided in 1938 to follow the racist direction of its Nazi ally. It must be said that one year earlier Mussolini's regime had already promulgated a series of explicitly racist laws concerning its African colonies, based on a total denial of rights and complete discrimination. The confirmation that Jews did not belong to the 'Italian race', and the juridical measures based on those of Nazi Germany, which were introduced in five royal decrees between 5 September 1938 and 29 June 1939, made Italy one of the leading countries of the racial persecution that was destined to sweep across Europe during the following two years.

It would be a long and complex task to list all the principal violations of rights which were carried out during the Second World War, mostly by the Axis (Germany, Italy, Japan) – although the context certainly facilitated violations of the laws of war and of international laws by the Allies as well. However, the intensity and seriousness of crimes committed during those years would later prove to be decisive for the identification of new systemic directions which, after the war, led to a new culture and practice of human rights. I will summarise these violent events by quoting a work of my own from three years ago:[234]

Amongst the novelties of this war, in terms of violence against civilians, the most relevant certainly concerns the bombardment of cities, carried out for the purpose of weakening the morale of populations – an objective which completely failed – and of destroying industrial establishments that were identified as important for the war. Some successes were obtained in this arena, although completely secondary ones in terms of the war's development. Strategic bombardments were initially used by Germany against England: following the example of the destruction of Guernica, on 14 November 1940 the German air force bombed and destroyed Coventry, with explosive and phosphor-based bombs. This was the most famous episode of a strategy the Germans never abandoned and was soon to be used by the Allies as well.

The Anglo-American aerial offensive in Europe was particularly intense during the last nine months of the war, when 60% of the entire conflict's strategic bombarding took place. After the 1942-44 bombardment of the Ruhr, in 1945 many cities that were not influential on a military or industrial level were bombed: this led to the destruction of Dresden – where 140 thousand people died – while in the Pacific the bombing of Tokyo in March killed over 200 thousand civilians. A new, terrible degree of strategic bombardments was reached at the end of the war, when the first atomic bombs were dropped on the Japanese cities of Hiroshima (on 6 August) and Nagasaki (on the ninth). The nuclear explosions respectively killed 140 thousand and 70 thousand people, but the consequences took their toll on the population for decades to follow.

Civilians were not being massacred only from the air: land armies committed mass murder to terrorise the civilian population, to punish the hate and resistance they encountered, as well as any aid given to partisan fighters. The German troops – mainly the Wehrmacht, not just the special SS troops – were responsible for massacres between 1941-43 on the Eastern front, in 1943-45 in the Balkans (Greece and Yugoslavia) and in Italy (while retreating). In the Pacific it was the Japanese soldiers that carried out massacres against other Asiatic populations deemed racially inferior and against prisoners of war, who were often victims of degrading and inhuman treatments, if not of mass execution. The Nippon officers also enslaved thousands of women – mainly Korean and Chinese – who were used as 'comfort women' by the Japanese troops and abandoned, after the war, to a sad destiny of solitude and ostracism.

Among the massacres of the Second World War a tragic peculiarity concerns the genocide of the Jews, called the Shoah or Holocaust in many cultural contexts.[235] The original nature of this violence - often the violence itself has been classified as a sign of uniqueness, while in truth it is a common element of many historical events - was certainly demonstrated by its scale, by the determination to completely destroy a human group on the basis of arbitrary racial criteria, by the bureaucratic and technical tenacity within the Nazi-designed *final solution*. However, the main peculiarity of this tragedy lies in the perception that what took place was an aberrant moment in human history, in which all forms of violence, exclusion, destruction and ostracism were experimented with at the same time in order to obtain results based on a crazed ideological 'rationality'.

Any moment of the Shoah (from the Nuremberg Laws to the creation of the ghettos, from concentration camps to forced labour to extermination camps, from private violence to gas chambers) is equally representative of the tragedy which led to the death of five and a half million Jewish men and women from all age groups and countries. Yet Auschwitz remains the symbol of the Holocaust and over the years has become the name that summarises all the destructive capacity humanity – modern and educated – can achieve out of hate.

During the war, when the signs of Nazi barbarity were not yet fully evident, democratic states were already proposing to the Allies new solutions for international organisation and for relationships between states. The meeting between the American president Roosevelt and the British prime minister Churchill in Placenta Bay, on 12 and 13 August 1941, aboard the *Augusta* cruiser, led to the creation of the Atlantic Charter, which articulated the principles for a future world order, with ideas such as self-determination, peace, freedom and the rejection of territorial expansions, as well as economic and social improvements, social security, and high standards in the work place. On the basis of the Atlantic Charter, on 1 January 1942, 26 national governments, some of which were in exile, signed the United Nations Declaration,[236] which set up the foundations for the creation of the international institution destined to replace the obsolete League of Nations. 'The 1941 Atlantic Charter' – wrote Nelson Mandela, over 50 years later – 'signed by Roosevelt and Churchill, reaffirmed faith in the dignity of each human being and propagandised a series of democratic principles. Some people in the West believed it was just a list of promises that would not be maintained, however we Africans did not.'[237]

In that same month, twenty days after the declaration of the Atlantic Charter, a meeting took place on Lake Wannsee in Berlin at which some of the most important Nazi officers discussed the forms of the 'final solution' for the Jewish problem. Himmler, following an order from Hitler delivered by Goering, asked his officers to organise the total extermination of the 11 million Jews in Europe.

Thus, in January 1942, one of history's many paradoxes saw the definition of the most terrible violation of human rights – the destruction of an entire community of persons based on an arbitrarily established definition of belonging – overlap with the promise to create a world where no such event could take place.

6. *The four freedoms*

On 6 January 1941 Franklin Delano Roosevelt obviously could not know that eleven months later, on 7 December, the Japanese attack on Pearl Harbour would lead the United States to enter the war. However, the speech he gave that day before the American Congress was already characterised by the clear consciousness that an era was ending and a new one was about to begin.

> In the future days, which we seek to make secure, we look forward to a world founded upon four essential human freedoms. The first is freedom of speech and expression -- everywhere in the world. The second is freedom of every person to worship God in his own way -- everywhere in the world. The third is freedom from want, which, translated into world terms, means economic understandings which will secure to every nation a healthy peacetime life for its inhabitants -- everywhere in the world. The fourth is freedom from fear, which, translated into world terms, means a world-wide

reduction of armaments to such a point and in such a thorough fashion that no nation will be in a position to commit an act of physical aggression against any neighbour -- anywhere in the world. That is no vision of a distant millennium. It is a definite basis for a kind of world attainable in our own time and generation. That kind of world is the very antithesis of the so-called "new order" of tyranny which the dictators seek to create with the crash of a bomb. To that new order we oppose the greater conception -- the moral order. A good society is able to face schemes of world domination and foreign revolutions alike without fear.[238]

The speech was not simply a quotation of traditional freedoms, nor was it just an invitation to nations to cooperate on an economic level and reduce armaments in the future. Roosevelt was trying, with the communicative talent he had already demonstrated with the New Deal, to render in an essential fashion a list of rights that had been trampled on and destroyed by the war in many parts of the world. Thus he identified two 'positive' freedoms – which summarise the historical significance of the American Declaration of Independence – and two of the main dangers which appeared between the two wars (poverty and the fear of war), in order to create a new and more modern freedom from the threats they posed.

Although his speech proved to be the most important example, Roosevelt was not the only one interested in the future of human rights during a period in which the events of the war appeared to have humiliated all the hopes of humanity. In the months preceding Roosevelt's speech, which became famous as the 'four freedoms' speech, one of the best-known English writers, H.G. Wells, spoke constantly about human rights, while proposing a draft which summarised all previous declarations of human rights and established a series of guidelines for the future. Wells had written a letter to *The Times* on 25 October 1939, asking the newspaper to open a debate on the 'objectives of the war', those 'we are fighting for', and answered his own question as follows:

at various crises in the history of our communities, beginning with Magna Carta and going through various Bills of Rights, Rights of Man and so forth, it has been our custom to produce a specific declaration of the broad principles on which our public and social life is based, and to abide by that as our fundamental law. The present time appears to be particularly suiting for another fundamental assertion of the claims of the common man.[239]

Wells created a committee to write the new Declaration of Rights and invited various important figures to join it: amongst them were the president of the House of Lords, Viscount Sankey – the document then became known as the 'Sankey Declaration' – economist Barbara Wootton, winner of the Nobel Prize for Peace in 1933 Norman Angell, and the ex-Viceroy of India, Lord Lytton. Published in February 1940 by the *Daily Herald*, the Declaration was presented by Wells, alongside Salvador de Madariaga, on 12 March in Westminster Central Hall, in front of 3,600 people. The writer also corresponded, concerning these issues, with Jan Masaryk, Chaim Weizmann, Jan Christiaan Smuts, Clement Attlee, Gandhi and Nehru and President Roosevelt himself. Furthermore, he included the Declaration as a separate attachment in four of his books published between 1941 and 1942.

In the months following Roosevelt's speech many books, articles and pamphlets concerning human rights were published.[240] Various associations also began to consider human rights a central theme in their activities: from the Carnegie Endowment for International Peace to the International League for Human Rights, from the World Citizens Association to the British Labour Party, from the Pan-African Movement to the Council on African Affairs, from the League of Colored People to the Congress of Racial Equality.

Between August and October 1944, at Dumbarton Oaks, near Washington, representatives from the United States, Britain, the Soviet Union and China met seven times to study the structure of the international organisation to be formed after the war. Despite the common goal of maintaining peace and security, and the fact that Roosevelt's 'four freedoms' were considered by all as a starting point, each delegation had internal differences between those hoping for an energetic policy based on human rights, and those who envisioned national sovereignty as being impossible to diminish by supranational organisations. Unfortunately the discussions went no further, and although the structure of the United Nations was becoming clearer, the idea of inserting a declaration regarding the respect for human rights was soon abandoned. The new Undersecretary of the United States, Edward Stettinius, had no intention of following such a path, as did State Secretary Cordell Hull, unlike his predecessor Sumner Welles. The United States, Britain and the Soviet Union rejected China's proposal – China had also proposed to assign 'part' of the nation's sovereignty to the international organisation – to strongly underline the equality of all states and races.

Stettinius indicated a willingness to support a general statement of principles about human rights, but no one that would threaten national sovereignty or speak explicitly about racial equality. [...] The British and the Soviet delegations would not even support this statement that took away with one hand what it gave with the other. They feared that a general statement about human rights and fundamental freedoms in the section on general principles for the United Nations would open a Pandora's box and release dangerous forces that would seriously threaten their sovereignty and power.[241]

The draft for the United Nations Charter which emerged from Dumbarton Oaks was lacking 'humanity', as noted by some observers, and owed too much to the political realism many deemed necessary while the conflict was still going on. Although the agreement 'seemed to have little appreciation for the power of the visions of human rights generated during the World War II',[242] such ideas were by then spreading and could no longer be reduced to a mere diplomatic environment, especially in a conflict which many regarded as contrasting incompatible human values and visions.

A month before Dumbarton Oaks the Allies met in Bretton Woods, in New Hampshire, where they created the international financial institutions that were to guarantee economic order after the war: the World Bank to finance development and the International Monetary Fund to reinforce currencies' stability, based on the American dollar. However, most of the diplomatic interest of the Allies was focused on the conference of the United Nations, scheduled for the end of April 1945 in San Francisco. Two weeks before its beginning, the death of President Roosevelt on 12 April appeared to further weaken the possibility of the promotion of human rights becoming a central objective for post-war international order: 'Before the 1945 conference in San Francisco one thing was evident: the main powers were not going to focus their post-war agreements on human rights. It was not in their interest to proceed in this direction.'[243]

On 25 April, when the conference began, in the hall of the San Francisco Opera House, the war in Europe was coming to an end. The new President of the United States, Harry Truman, who was fully aware he could not compete with his predecessor's charisma, introduced himself by stating: 'we must build a new world – a far better world – one in which the eternal dignity of man is respected'.[244] However, it was the representatives of minor delegations who insisted the most, and in the least formal manner, on the attention to rights not being subordinated to geopolitical considerations. Indian representative Ramaswami Mudaliar, who would later become the President of the Economic and Social Council of the United Nations, stated that:

> there is a great reality, one fundamental factor, an eternal verity which all religions teach, which must be remembered by all of us, the dignity of the common man, the fundamental rights of all beings all over the world. Those rights are incapable of segregation or of isolation. There is neither border nor breed nor colour nor creed on which those rights can be separated as between beings and beings. And, speaking as an Asiatic, may I say that this is an aspect of the question which can never be forgotten.[245]

The most numerous block of countries at the conference (21 out of 51), the South American group, held a similar position, demanding that the values expressed in their constitutions and by the thoughts of Simón Bolívar, which were at the basis of many countries' independence, would be implemented. A few months before the San Francisco conference, in February, the inter-American conference on the problems of war and peace had taken place in Mexico City, in the Chapultepec Castle. During the conference much attention was given to the creation of an international justice system and to guarantees regarding human rights and the responsibility of states. The Cuban delegation had even presented two distinct drafts, one regarding an 'International Declaration of the rights and duties of individuals' and the other for a 'Declaration of the rights and duties of nations'.

Another delegate strongly expressed the opinion of 'minor' countries, Carlos Romulo from the Philippines. Romulo had fought in the American army against the Japanese and won the Pulitzer Prize in 1941 for a series of articles on the predicted end of colonialism, as well as participating in the Bretton Woods meetings. Later he would remember how the major powers looked 'at us representatives of smaller countries as if we hardly existed. They behaved as if they owned the world, walking proudly like conquerors in their poorly tailored bell-bottom trousers'.[246]

Alongside the minor delegations, representatives from numerous associations – some religious, some working on human rights, work policies and peace – were present in San Francisco and continued to exercise a considerable degree of pressure on their governments. Their influence, although it cannot be measured, must certainly have been relevant, if we consider how even Stettinius, who had the reputation of being a cynical 'realist', agreed to listen to them and accepted some of their proposals. The leaders of the Joint Committee for Religious Liberty, of the Congress of Industrial Organizations, of the American Association for the United Nations and of the American Jewish Committee, were charged by Stettinius with the creation of a Human Rights Commission: various countries agreed to this, including the Latin American ones, France, India, Egypt and New Zealand.

When the United Nations Charter was approved on 26 June – it was officially introduced on 24 October after being ratified by the first 29 states – many were satisfied with the inclusion, both in the Preamble[247] and in a few of its articles (the first, 55th, 73rd[248] and 76th),[249] of precise references to human rights and the need to protect and strengthen them. The constitution of an International Court of Justice, the judiciary of the United Nations, appeared to signify a further step toward the achievement and maintenance of a new standard for human rights. During the final meeting, President Truman addressed all those who feared that the United Nations would mean the creation of a world government capable of threatening the prerogatives of individual nations, as well as those who thought the positive value of the new international organisation was strongly diminished by the lack of clear norms concerning the regulation of human rights and the punishment for violations against them: 'This Charter, like our Constitution, will be expanded and improved as time goes on. No one claims that is now a final or perfect instrument. It has not been poured into a fixed mould. Changing world conditions will require readjustments – but they will be readjustments of peace and not of war.'[250]

Alongside pressure by non-Western states and non-governmental associations, one factor which certainly proved important for the renewed attention to human rights was the way in which the end of the war had posed the question of justice and punishment for those who were responsible for causing the war itself.

7. The crime of genocide

At the beginning of May, while the United Nations conference was taking place, Britain changed its position on the creation of an international criminal tribunal to judge the Nazi leaders responsible for atrocities and war crimes. The London Charter for the international military tribunal, signed on 8 August, identified the three categories of crimes – war crimes, crimes against peace, crimes against humanity – for which the representatives of the Axis would be judged.

In January 1942, the same month in which the Wannsee conference had confirmed the organisation of the final solution against the Jews, the exiled governments of nine occupied states had sent out the Declaration of St. James, which had foreseen the use of tribunals at the end of the war to try the Nazi criminals who had violated the Conventions of Geneva and The Hague. At the end of that same year Roosevelt, Churchill and Stalin had established that the war criminals would be punished in the very locations where they had committed their crimes, and formed a commission for war crimes within the United Nations.

Until the very end of the war the Allies were divided in terms of opinions and options over the carrying out of 'severe justice': initially the English and Americans appeared to prefer summary executions at the moment of capture, with no trial, while the Soviet Union favoured the creation of a tribunal; later it appeared that Churchill and Stalin preferred summary justice, rather than the public judgement supported by Roosevelt's counsellors, who were worried that the Allies might themselves violate the principles of justice promoted by the United Nations, and thus transform German criminals into martyrs for the German population.

The liberation of the extermination and concentration camps in 1945 (Auschwitz was liberated by the Red Army and Bergen-Belsen, Buchenwald and Dachau were liberated in April by the Anglo-American armies) was decisive in demonstrating the need to show the entire world the crimes of Hitler's regime. Thus jurists from the winning countries set to work to identify the principles and structure of post-war trials.

Behind the entire procedure was a difficult choice between three different options: to persecute the Nazi criminals according to the laws in force when the crimes were committed, which would however legitimise the Nazi regime as a source of laws; to judge them according to the laws of the victorious states, thus entering the minefield of different juridical systems and antithetic conceptions of justice (for example, in the laws of the Soviet Union there were no guarantees for minimum defence measures); or to create a new international law and produce the instruments necessary for its implementation.

The third choice was the path selected by the London Charter, which identified the typology of crimes to be punished (art. 6) and paved the way for the international military tribunal that would hold its most important trials in Nuremberg (a symbolic location, as it was the chosen place for the most important meetings of Hitler's party). The most significant of these trials took place between November 1945 and October 1946.

The three crimes that summarised all the offences committed were: 'war crimes', intentionally identified as the traditional ones (established in Geneva and The Hague) – murder, deportation and mistreatment of civilian populations and enemy prisoners, sacking and devastation of buildings without any military necessity; and two new typologies: 'crimes against peace' (the planning of aggressive wars) and 'crimes against humanity' (the arbitrary and unmotivated persecution of civilians, in violent and discriminatory forms).

The sudden gap created between the 'justice of Nuremberg' and previous judiciary tradition is still at the centre of many historical and juridical debates. On one side all rights bound to the nation-state appeared to become obsolete in favour of universal supranational ones; on the other side such choices appeared to place in doubt the observance of the basic norm of irretroactivity, the criteria of the *nullum crimen, nulla poena sine lege.* During the following years and decades international law would develop in a previously unthinkable fashion, although facing many obstacles – above all those concerning the creation of the Permanent International Criminal Court, opposed mainly by the American states – to its full and coherent implementation under the United Nations.

With regard to the accusation – expressed at the time by one of the defendants, Hermann Goering – of transforming the victor into a judge and the loser into a defendant by using retroactive laws, it must be said that in terms of war crimes the Martens clause had already indicated, at the beginning of the century, the existence of certain 'humanitarian' rules that were rooted in the collective conscience and could not be violated. In other words, and more precisely those of Robert Jackson, Chief Prosecutor for the United States, 'the very essence of the Charter is that individuals have international duties which transcend the national obligations of obedience imposed by the individual state... if the state in authorizing action moves outside its competence in international law'.[251] It was far more difficult to attribute intentions of 'gratuitous destruction' to German bombings of civilian populations, in consideration of the Allies' bombardments of Dresden, Hamburg or Tokyo, not to mention Hiroshima and Nagasaki.

However, more problems needed to be overcome. All modern juridical systems unmistakeably connected the existence of a crime with the will of the culprit, and with his/her full subjective consciousness regarding this will. Thus the problem became one of identifying individual responsibilities – the only ones that could be prosecuted – within state mechanisms which had moved against 'peace' and in favour of exterminations. The solution for the Nuremberg case, which was derived from the Anglo-Saxon juridical tradition and not an aspect familiar to European law, was represented by the categories of 'conspiracy' and 'criminal organisation'. The Nuremberg court declared as such the SS (Schutzstaffel, defence squads, the main paramilitary formation of the Nazi party), the Gestapo (Geheime Staatspolizei, the secret police of the German state), and the leaders of the Nazi party, thus exonerating the government of the Reich and the high command of the Wehrmacht (the German army). The implicit result was to exclude obedience to orders from above as a possible excuse, and on this basis a list of 22 principal criminals was prepared, men whose power extended over various national territories under the Third Reich's control. Territorially localised crimes would instead later be examined by national tribunals.

The solution chosen in Nuremberg – in some ways a compulsory one – was to limit the crimes of Nazism's mass consensus to the conspiracy of a few, by creating an 'intentionalist' interpretative paradigm destined to influence many of the studies about the Shoah: extermination was depicted as the product of a conscious, coherent and systemic project by just a few men, motivated by an unstoppable hate for Jews. The indifference of the majority of the population was assimilated into an obedience obtained by a ruthless dictatorship using violence. Many criticisms have been expressed regarding the 'Nuremberg paradigm', and even some of its supporters have had to recognise that:

> it was not the model of an unbiased international tribunal (that would have required judges from countries which had remained neutral); counts one and two (conspiracy to wage aggressive war and crimes against peace) were novel and infringed the rule against retrospectivity; the fairness of the trial on count three (war crimes) was affected by the ruling against *tu quoque* evidence. But the great achievement of Nuremberg was count four: the crime against humanity – in effect, an ordinary crime committed on a scale of barbarism unimaginable until the Holocaust.[252]

When reflecting upon the destiny of Jews in Hitler's Europe, a Polish and Jewish jurist living in the United States, Raphael Lemkin, first used the term 'genocide' and tried to define this new concept of modern barbarity. Lemkin's groundbreaking work, although now revised and somewhat scaled down, led to the Convention for the Prevention and Repression of Genocide, approved by the General Assembly of the United Nations on the day before the Universal Declaration of Human Rights, 9 December 1948. Scholars who studied the process leading Lemkin to coin such a rapidly successful neologism underlined his attempts, before 1944, to analyse contemporary examples of attempts to destroy ethnic groups (such as the Armenian tragedy during the First World War[253]) and to connect those events to other cases of mass violence committed over the course of human history.[254] The proposal advanced in 1933, during an international juridical conference, to prepare an international treaty aimed at sanctioning as 'barbaric crimes' any attack against national, religious and ethnic groups had been practically ignored, despite the fact that it already corresponded to the new post-war need to reconsider the question of national sovereignty and its intangibility. In the vast volume which introduced the term for the first time, Lemkin wrote that '[it] is intended rather to signify a coordinated plan of different actions aiming at the destruction of essential foundations of the life of national groups, with the aim of annihilating the groups themselves. The objectives of such a plan would be disintegration of the political and social institutions, of culture, language, national feelings, religion, and the economic existence of national groups, and the destruction of the personal security, liberty, health, dignity, and even the lives of the individuals belonging to such groups. Genocide is directed against the national group as an entity, and the actions involved are directed against individuals, not in their individual capacity, but as members of the national group.'[255]

The Nazi policy in Europe was the context which led Lemkin to revive and perfect his juridical proposals and caused the symbolic term to be used. If physical destruction was the most terrible and immediate aspect of the new crime of genocide, it was equally important to identify the biological and cultural components at its foundations, which constituted the historical innovation which inspired Lemkin's work. The Polish and Jewish jurist believed that this innovation was above all characterised by the 'subjective' element, the new moral and juridical perception created by Nazi barbarity. Indeed Lemkin dedicated his efforts to the mission of making the international community both morally and juridically conscious of this innovation and transforming it into an accepted international norm, in order to prevent any possibility of such events being repeated.

The final result, which was codified into the Convention for the Prevention and Repression of Genocide, two years after the first resolution approved by the General Assembly of the United Nations in 1946, was a compromise (although certainly a high-quality one). The document was partially inspired by article 6 of the Statute of the International Tribunal of Nuremberg, which had given a first and fundamental definition of 'war crimes'. The definition included, alongside voluntary murder and violence against prisoners of war, 'the mistreatment, deportation aimed at obligating forced labour, or for any other objective, of the civilian populations in occupied territories [...] the execution of hostages, the sacking of private or public wealth, the unmotivated destruction of cities or villages and devastation not justified by military necessity'.[256]

The Convention was the first document to advance the idea that a crime could exist against a 'group' as such, and that it could constitute a crime before the international assembly of states. This conception was introduced and affirmed forcibly, although some saw the Convention as a threat to national sovereignty (including Englishmen Sir Hartley Shaw-cross and, later, Mr. Davies).[257] Despite various attempts to circumscribe and reduce its meaning, the idea of not speaking of the crime of genocide in the Nuremberg trials prevailed, above all so that it would not be considered only as the product of an armed conflict. The Australian President of the UN General Assembly, Herbert Vere Evatt, underlined the fact that introducing the recognition of the 'fundamental right of each human group to exist as a group'[258] was a significant step forward for international law.

The text of the Convention was written while the impact of the war was still vivid and the tragic fate of European Jews was becoming increasingly clear. The Assembly avoided – after a long discussion – explicitly quoting the Nazi policy of genocide and 'concluded that any reference to the barbarity of the Third Reich would have limited the primary goal of the Convention, the prevention and punishment of genocides by states, whether during periods of peace or moments of war'. Thus only the Preamble spoke of history, yet in a more generic manner: by recognising that 'all historical periods have inflicted terrible losses on humanity' and that it was precisely 'to free humanity from similar hateful calamities that international action was required'.[259]

Substantially the Convention was born historically linked to the decision to prevent a repetition of Nazi violence; yet it went further than that, and re-analysed, in a new light – both morally and juridically – the entire history of humanity, or at least of a part of it. The Shoah was the event that was capable, in its uniqueness, of developing a more general level of consciousness and of proposing a universal evaluation on both juridical and moral grounds.

The Convention on Genocide was approved in its definite form in October 1950 and was officially introduced on 12 January 1951 after being ratified by 20 countries. The list did not include the United States, despite efforts by President Truman to obtain a rapid consensus from Congress. Within the American political, juridical and academic fields there was a widespread fear that American citizens could be accused of crimes over the 'eradication' of Indians during the nineteenth century or to racial 'segregation' in the Southern states.

In the December 1946 resolution by the United Nations, genocide was accepted as a term 'when racial, religious, *political* groups or other types of groups were partially or totally destroyed'.[260] The Russian and Soviet bloc's insistence led to 'political groups' being excluded from the definition approved on 9 December 1948. According to the Polish delegate, they lacked the 'distinguishable characteristics that because of their mutability don't allow for inclusion in the definition'.[261] Additionally, 'cultural genocide' (the destruction of a culture belonging to a human group) was not included. During the debates leading to the elaboration of the Convention another proposal regarding the prohibition of acts aimed to 'destroy the language, religion or culture' of an ethnic, racial, religious group (examples provided included the prohibition on using certain languages in daily life or at school, the destruction of libraries, museums, schools, historical monuments, or the prohibition on accessing such institutions). The proposal was rejected, above all because it was considered too vague – some feared it could have favoured political interferences by other states in the internal affairs of governments accused of committing 'cultural genocide' – and because this subject should be addressed by other international treaties.[262]

8. *A victory of civilisation*

In October 1945, just a few months after the creation of the United Nations, the fifth Pan-African Congress was a demonstration of the progress made in the language of rights. Emerging personalities such as Kwame Nkrumah and Jomo Kenyatta, alongside old fighters like the American Du Bois, demanded independence, respect of human rights and an end to racial discrimination, by signing a 'challenge against colonial powers' which included the following text: 'The delegates of the fifth Pan-African Congress believe in peace [...] If the Western world is determined to rule humanity with force, Africans may also use force, as a last resource, to obtain freedom, despite the fact that force destroys the world.'[263]

The miraculous work leading to the United Nations' approval, on 10 December 1948, of the Universal Declaration of Human Rights, took place in the complex post-war context: a period characterised by both peaceful and armed requests for independence in colonial states, by the urgency of a material and economic reconstruction in which social conflicts were increasing, by the inadequately organised de-Nazification and de-Fascistisation campaigns and by the first signs of the Cold War.

In truth the Cold War influenced the very writing of the Universal Declaration: certainly it is important to note how the final discussion regarding article 1 between members of the third commission of the United Nations began in October 1948, when the Human Rights commission led by Eleanor Roosevelt had started its operations in January 1947. In October 1948, for example, a two-week long tough debate took place over article 3 ('Every individual has a right to live, to the freedom and security of his person'), which everyone had thought would be approved without any discussion: the debate broke out when the Soviet delegate Alexei Pavlov asked for the inclusion of the prohibition of the death penalty. This proposal led to reciprocal accusations between the Western and Eastern blocs: the former accused Communist regimes of limiting personal freedom, while the latter denounced Western governments for their colonialism and racism.

However, the structure built so laboriously by the Roosevelt Commission managed to withstand the impact of the third commission of the United Nations (for Social, Humanitarian and Cultural Affairs), although immediately after the approval of the text, on 10 December 1948, discontent began to grow in both the United States and the Soviet Union because both countries believed the document favoured the ideology and policies of the opposite 'bloc'.

The principal novelty, introduced by one of the main authors of the entire text, was the use of the word 'universal' to describe the Declaration, rather than 'international'. Apart from the problems of minorities and the right to seek asylum, which would have probably caused a break with the Soviet commissars, it can be stated that all elements considered during the commission's discussions to be relevant and pertinent to a new culture of human rights were ultimately included in the definitive text.

The most complete analysis of the Declaration is still probably the work of Charles Malik, the Lebanese intellectual who contributed more than anyone else – alongside John Humphrey, René Cassin and, although in a less significant manner, Peng-chun Chang and Carlos Romulo – to the writing of the Declaration, which he presented himself before the General Assembly of UN on 9 December.

Malik remembers that 'thousands of minds and hands contributed to its formation',[264] and defined the Declaration as a 'composite synthesis' of all the different traditions of rights: explicitly mentioning the heritage of Latin American culture summarised in the Bogotà Declaration on the duties and rights of men (2 May 1948) and of Asiatic wisdom, both Indian and Chinese. According to Malik, the 'negative' roots of the Declaration are to be found in the atrocities of the Second World War, while its 'positive' ones are the 'four freedoms' specified by Roosevelt in 1941: freedom of speech and faith, freedom from fear and from need. Of course these are strongly historicised roots, which may be localised in the tragic experience of the previous years rather than in metaphysical needs or philosophic or religious considerations.

The Declaration had a more relevant moral and political importance than a Convention, which would have been legally binding, yet was also far more difficult to approve and apply. The strength of the text lies precisely in the identification of a common sentiment, a concluded agreement, capable of maintaining its significance even in the face of incapacity or negligence by states to realise and truly apply the principles expressed in the Declaration. The capacity to produce a text able to overcome historical and political contingencies (which were already crumbling, and transforming the wartime alliances) was not just due to the eminent protagonists in the commission, but also to Eleanor Roosevelt's great political-organisational capacity, to her determination to defend certain principles and to her diplomatic and mediatory abilities as leader of the human rights commission. Indeed it was largely thanks to her that the authors focused their attention on the text and voluntarily excluded from their discussions – with a self-discipline worthy of note – the great international questions which were dividing the world during those first two years of the Cold War (the creation of the state of Israel and the war in the Middle East, the partition of India, the Berlin bloc, the rise of Communism in China).

We must underline an important element of the works of the Roosevelt commission: the constant search – although sometimes carried out with ideological bitterness or driven by political interests – to find a lowest common denominator that truly could belong to different cultures and be considered a collective heritage. In 1947 the American Anthropological Association had warned members of the commission against such a daring and apparently impossible effort: 'standards and values are relative to the culture from which they derive so that any attempt to formulate postulates that grow out of the beliefs or moral codes of one culture must to that extent detract from the applicability of any Declaration of Human Rights to mankind as a whole'.[265]

The commission had manifested the intention of achieving its purpose on the basis of two strong convictions: to give a cultural – yet also moral, juridical and political – signal to indicate the end of the era of violence and horror, and that – even if principally based on the language of Western culture – there was a possibility of identifying a series of principles and values belonging to all humanity's major cultures.

The final result ('Human beings are endowed with reason and conscience and should act towards one another in a spirit of brotherhood') did not fully reflect the suggestions of Peng-chun Chang, who stated that it was important to underline the value of individuals not just on their own, but within relationships with other individuals and with the entire human race.

The debate within the United Nations and General Assembly led to the approval of the Declaration with a score of 48 votes in favour and eight abstentions. Yet it was also accompanied by a cultural debate (which would last for many years to come) surrounding the philosophical, anthropological, historical and juridical aspects of the Declaration. The philosophical or religious nature of rights, the natural or positive substance of their eventual common foundations, the characteristics of the universality they demanded and promised, the possible difference between 'fundamental' rights and more generic human rights, the relations between national sovereignty and universal jurisdiction, the relationship between the rights of individuals and collective ones, the necessary and eventually compulsory measures to make the respect of human rights a concrete possibility: these were just a few of the problems behind the approval of the Declaration. And such arguments were often accompanied by further questions:

Are human rights absolute, or must they be conditioned and modified by particular circumstances? What if the right of free speech is used to actually inflame racial hatred, goad class antagonism, arouse religious intolerance, or incite war? What is the precise relationship between individual rights and corporate or social responsibilities? Is any society entitled to expect that every human right will be exercised with responsibility and due regard for the rights of others? Is it possible to establish international normative standards of behaviour norms for the world, while at the same time respecting different philosophical and cultural values? And is there any value in proclaiming a vision of international human rights if means are not simultaneously provided for their implementation? [266]

Chapter Six
Rights Rediscovered

1. *Are universal rights possible?*

In June 1947 the Executive Committee of the American Anthropological Association prepared a document that was sent to the Human Rights Commission of the United Nations, led by Eleanor Roosevelt. The Committee's text posed a question destined to play a crucial part in debates on human rights for many decades, and is still central today in discussions regarding the universality of rights. Starting from the affirmation that respect for the culture of different *human groups* is just as important as respect for the personality of the *individual* and his/her full development as a member of society, the text was an invitation to consider both individuals and their membership of social groups.

According to the Anthropological Association, the past neglect of similarities between cultures had led to disastrous doctrines such as the 'white man's burden', which had encouraged economic exploitation accompanied by the prohibition on local communities managing their own businesses. This political and economic process was later rationalised by theories of the cultural inferiority or 'primitive mentality' of colonised populations, which eventually led to the eradication of their human rights. If an individual realises his personality through the culture he is a part of, then respect for cultural differences is absolutely necessary: individual freedom may not be obtained if the group the individual belongs to is not free. The *Homo sapiens*, stated the Association, is a unique species, and cultural differences are explained by complexity, richness and historical conditions, not by biological diversity.

These considerations, which sounded like a strong criticism of colonialism (an issue the newly-created United Nations Organization could not discuss openly), led to the conclusion that, if values are relative to the culture which generates them, 'ideas of right and wrong, good and evil, are found in all societies, though they differ in their expression among different peoples. What is held to be a human right in one society may be regarded as anti-social by another people, or by that same people in a different period of their history'.[267] If a Declaration of the Rights of Man was possible in the eighteenth century, given the fact that it originated within a largely homogeneous (Western, Anglo-American and French) culture, the twentieth century required a definition of norms that were no longer bound to just one culture or to the aspirations of just one population. According to the anthropologists, the basic principle to be applied was the following: that the standards of liberty and justice should be founded on the recognition that a man is only free when he lives in the way that his own society defines as freedom. Thus 'only when a statement of the right of men to live in terms of their own traditions is incorporated into the proposed Declaration, then, can the next step of defining the rights and duties of human groups as regards each other be set upon the firm foundation of the present-day scientific knowledge of Man'.[268]

The reasonable insistence on avoiding a hegemonic imposition of Western values was accompanied – probably due to the approach chosen – by a de-historicised view in which cultures appeared immobile, and in which 'tradition' could easily be identified by its own equally established and shared 'values'. However, what was being paradoxically left aside was precisely the tragic and head-on clash of values which had just taken place within cultures and civilisations both Western (fascisms versus liberal democracies) and Asian (Japanese militaristic nationalism versus China, Korea, Indochina): such a position completely ignored the political and ideological choices of governments, as well as the constitutions and fundamental laws of each country. For example, was it possible, while during those very months ethnic and religious violence between Hindus, Muslims and Sikhs was increasing in Punjab, Bengal and Bihar, to identify a single model of freedom or justice for one of these three groups and communities? Had not the very notions of group, of community, and consequently of tradition, gone through transformations and dynamics (perhaps not everywhere, yet certainly in most regions) that were different from the immobile schemes suggested by the anthropologists? Had such theories not developed by studying and confronting precisely the cultures least involved in the geopolitical transformations which had transformed the human landscape between the nineteenth and twentieth centuries?

In the same months in which the anthropologists were suggesting that the Human Rights Commission of the United Nations should delay the illusory idea of a truly 'universal' declaration, the cultural agency of the UN, which had just been formed under the name of UNESCO (United Nations Educational, Scientific and Cultural Organization), sent out a complex survey to thinkers and intellectuals within member countries. It asked them to suggest what the relationships between political rights and economic and social rights were; how formulations of human rights and freedom were different in different societies; how the eighteenth century rights had been modified by the industrial revolution and by the First World War; and what the theoretical references, practical extension and guarantees of realisation were with regard to certain rights such as religious freedom, freedom of opinion, of association, of movement and communication.

In the introduction to the 1949 publication on this symposium,[269] the French philosopher Jacques Maritain explained that the book was dedicated to the rational interpretation and justification of those individual rights that society must respect and 'that would be desirable for our time to list in the fullest fashion possible'. Given that the question of human rights involved the entire structure of moral and metaphysical convictions of each individual, a clash between interpretations and justifications was almost inevitable, although a more pragmatic approach might have favoured a convergence without altering theoretical differences, identified by Maritain as a contrast between those who accepted 'natural law' as the basis of human rights, and those who refused it:

> In the eyes of the first the requirements of his being endow man with certain fundamental and inalienable rights antecedent in nature, and superior, to society, and are the source whence social life itself, with the duties and rights which that implies, originates and develops. For the second school man's rights are relative to the historical development of society, and are themselves constantly variable and in a state of flux; they are a product of society itself as it advances with the forward march of history.

Despite this theoretical gap, it was still possible to reach an agreement regarding a declaration and enumeration of rights, given that one did not need to be a follower of Locke to recognise individual rights, nor to be a supporter of Marx to recognise economic and social rights. In this sense the supporters of liberal individualism, of Communism, of a cooperative society, could have made the same list of rights, and could have identified its basic values. Maritain claimed that:

We must not expect too much of an International Declaration of
Human Rights [...] even the noblest and most solemn declaration
could not suffice to restore to the peoples faith in Human Rights.
It is the implementation of these declarations which is sought from
those who subscribe to them; it is the means of securing effective
respect for Human Rights from States and Governments that it is
desired to guarantee. On this point I should not venture to express
more than the most guarded optimism.[270]

Amongst those who replied to the UNESCO questionnaire Mahatma
Gandhi was the person who wrote less, for reasons he explained in a
brief letter. He was convinced that:

all rights to be deserved and preserved came from duty well done.
Thus the very right to live accrues to us only when we do the duty
of citizenship of the world. From this one fundamental statement,
perhaps it is easy enough to define the duties of Man and
Woman and correlate every right to some correspondent duty to
be first performed. Every other right can be shown to be a usurpation
hardly worth fighting for.[271]

The historian E.H. Carr concluded his historical *excursus*, mainly focused
on the French and Russian Revolutions, by observing:

that any declaration of rights which would be felt to have any
validity today must include social and economic as well as political
rights; that no declaration of rights which does not also contain a
declaration of correlative obligations could have any serious meaning;
that any declaration of rights and obligations of the individual in
society should at the present stage be regarded as a declaration of
intention or as a standard to be aimed at rather than as an internationally binding engagement.[272]

Spanish writer and diplomat Salvador de Madariaga, formerly his country's
Minister of Education and Justice in 1933 and now in exile, believed
human rights to be a question of 'the right political relations between the
individual and the society to which he belongs', where the fundamental
basis should be the vaster 'liberty of personal experience' limited only
'for the sake of the individual liberty of others [...] of the nation [...] of
the world community'.[273] From this perspective he suggested including

the right of each citizen to refuse military service in any war that was declared illegitimate by the United Nations Security Council.

Political theoretician and economist Harold Laski, who had led the British Labour Party until just a few months earlier, while remembering that declarations from previous centuries were based on the conflict between individual freedom and the political power and authority of governments, claimed that, in an era characterised by new and different inter-state relations, 'any attempt by the United Nations to formulate a Declaration of Human Rights in individualist terms would quite inevitably fail'. Considering peace the main issue, and given that the time in which every national state could demand its right to sovereignty, with no other limitations than its own will, was destined to end, he concluded that 'a Declaration such as is proposed would do more harm than good unless it was issued in the confident expectation that the members of the United Nations gave to it an unquestionable faith and respect.'[274]

Benedetto Croce was also against the public formulation of a declaration, as he was critical both of the idea of 'natural rights', which he considered useful for the past but now indefensible, and of the idea of historically determined rights, which would lead to the loss of 'the logical base of those rights considered to be universal, which would be reduced, at best, to rights of man *in history*. In other words, they would become rights accepted as such by men of a particular time'. The impossibility of reaching an agreement between the two main schools of thought at the time, the liberal and the authoritarian-totalitarian, made it possible only to theorise 'an international public debate regarding the necessary principles at the basis of human dignity and civilisation', which would certainly crown the liberal current as its victor. Only at that time would it be possible to 'formulate a declaration of certain historical and contemporary rights and needs in some such short form as the Ten Commandments'.[275]

Chinese philosopher Chung-Shu Lo felt the need to summarise the principles of Confucianism and the history of his country, where instead of demands for rights it was more correct to speak of ethical education, in which the prominent role given to the 'good will' of leaders had supposedly led to continuous revolutions within Chinese history. However, he believed it was possible to formulate a declaration of rights for the entire world, as long as it was 'brief yet clear, broad yet concise, fundamental yet elastic, so that it may be interpreted to suit the needs of peoples in different circumstances. For this reason I lay down here only three basic claims, valid for every person in the world, namely: the right to live, the right to self-expression and the right to enjoyment.'[76]

Indian philosopher and educator Humayun Kabir, who would later become a minister in the Nehru government and compile the 1950 UNESCO Declaration on the race question, believed that the period of separate and opposed civilisations had come to its end, and stated that it was necessary to formulate a 'charter of human rights to-day [that] must therefore be based on the recognition of the equal claims for all individuals within one common world'. Kabir thought it was essential to underline this aspect, as the previous Western conception of rights had only theoretically ensured rights for all individuals, while in reality it had conceded rights only to (a limited amount of) Europeans. Thus the West had strayed 'from the theory and practice of democracy which characterised the early days of Islam, which had managed to go beyond distinctions based on race and colour in an unprecedented and unequalled fashion'. Now the main problem was to 'reconcile the conflicting claims of liberty and security', by guaranteeing that each human being may enjoy the minimal means of human existence, such as food and clothing, a home, education, medical and sanitary services. In this perspective 'the rights of the individual should be subordinated to the community to the extent required in order to ensure such rights', while the individual should otherwise be free from any interference by the state or by society. Thus Kabir indicated the decisive importance of political democracy, without which 'the very possibility of economic and social democracy is destroyed. Political democracy is thus the only basis on which the structure of accomplished human rights may grow'. If Kabir's was the 'Islamic' point of view, or at least one point of view within Islamic culture, according to political scientist S.V. Puntambekar the Hindu conception of human rights consisted of:

> ten essential human freedoms and controls or virtues necessary for good life. They emphasise five freedoms or social assurances and five individual possessions or virtues. The five social freedoms are freedom from violence (*Ahimsa*), freedom from want (*Asteya*), freedom from exploitation (*Aparigraha*), freedom from violation and dishonour (*Avyabhichara*) and freedom from early death and disease (*Armitatva* and *Arogya*). The five individual possessions or virtues are absence of intolerance (*Akrodha*), Compassion or fellow feeling (*Bhutadaya, Adroha*), Knowledge (*Jnana, Vidya*), freedom of thought and conscience (*Satya, Sunrta*) and freedom from fear and frustration or despair (*Pravrtti, Abhaya, Dhrti*).[277]

Puntambekar believed that all freedoms needed corresponding virtues, or duties, the same concept expressed by Gandhi; and that the creation and development of this 'new' type of man and citizen was absolutely necessary. He concluded his speech by stating that he too, like all Indians, wanted 'freedom from foreign domination and from the civil war'.

2. *Failure or success?*

The decades which followed the Universal Declaration of Human Rights may be judged – and many scholars have done so – as a period of continuous failure for the Declaration's objectives, or as a period of partial success for its vision, even if one contradicted by contrasting forces and by many obstacles. Jurist Geoffrey Robertson, one of the major British experts on human rights and a Queen's Counsel,[278] entitled a paragraph of his fundamental work *1946-1976: Thirty Inglorious Years*,[279] thus over-turning the famous definition by French economist Jean Fourastié, who had dubbed the three decades after the War the *Trente Glorieuses* to underline the economic miracle which took place during this period. Paul Gordon Lauren, one of the most important American scholars to analyse the 50 post-Declaration years as a unitary block, stated that during the period 'the world had witnessed a veritable revolution in transforming visions of international human rights into reality'.[280]

What may reasonably be observed is that hopes born between the end of 1948 – when the Convention on Genocide and the Universal Declaration were signed – and August 1949 – when the four Geneva Conventions regarding the protection of the injured and prisoners of war, of civilians and women had updated humanitarian principles – were already evidently contradicted by the beginning of the Cold War and by the increasing antagonism between the United States and the USSR. Alongside the clash which had its epicentre in Berlin and in the Soviet 'blocking' of the divided German capital (June 1948 - May 1949), we must also mention the tragedy of central-eastern European (mainly Polish and Yugoslav) and Asian refu-gees. In India and Pakistan 12 million people were forced to flee from the new states, as a result of threats and discrimination.

The profoundly ideological nature of the Cold War, which was fought mainly within the field of communication, language, image and identity, caused a set-back for human rights – the terrain of common values between the clashing powers – which were now used only occasionally and instrumentally to underline contradictions (civil and political rights versus economic and social ones) that in truth had already been identified while the Declaration was being prepared. The prospect of accusing the enemy of violating human rights was an occasional temptation for the two superpowers, but they chose to use this tool sparingly, as both knew they were strongly criticisable, for different reasons, over the respect of the Declaration's articles. The arms race and the escalation of the nuclear threat were indeed in clear opposition to the Preamble of the Declaration and to the historical motivations which, during the alliance between the two countries, had led to the Declaration itself. And yet the Cold War could not stop human rights from sustaining a constant presence, no matter how strongly marginalised or exploited, within international public debates.

The Korean War broke out on 25 June 1950, when seven divisions of the North Korean army crossed the 38th Parallel and, after overcoming the Southern defences, occupied Seoul. This was the first event (and for quite some time the only one) to provoke a reaction by the United Nations. Thanks to the absence of the Soviet delegate in the Security Council (in protest at the denial of a seat to the People's Republic of China), it was decided that the United Nations should intervene against the aggression. On 15 September an offensive led by General MacArthur re-conquered Seoul, crossed the 38th Parallel and on 19 October occupied the Northern capital Pyongyang. At the end of the month support from Chinese 'volunteers' allowed North Korean troops to re-conquer the entire Northern part of the country. Unsuccessful offensives by both sides eventually led, in July 1951, to a negotiation which returned the country to its exact pre-war situation.

The war statistics were terrible. 900,000 Chinese soldiers and 600,000 North Koreans were killed in battle, as well as 400,000 South Koreans and 54,000 Americans. Hundreds of thousands of civilians had been massacred. Out of 30 million inhabitants, two million Koreans had been killed, while five million were now refugees. Millions of people were separated from their families across the border between North and South. Atrocities were committed by both sides in equal measure, while bombardments by the American air force against civilian targets equalled those against Germany during the entire Second World War. It was only much later that the involvement of American soldiers in massacres against civilians emerged, while at the time news immediately came through regarding the conditions of deprivation and violence in the Northern Korean camps, where Chinese 'instructors' brainwashed prisoners' minds.

Occurring a few years after the Second World War, it was not only military conflicts that were the context for mass violence and terrible violations of human rights. The idea that every person – independent of gender, religion and culture – should enjoy the same rights severely undermined the colonial system, although it had not yet been doubted explicitly. Indeed Article 21 of the Declaration,[281] if interpreted correctly, was the nail in colonialism's coffin. On polemical and propagandistic grounds, it was hardly difficult for the Soviet Union and Communist countries to reply to accusations regarding violations of the rights of their citizens by inviting Western countries to observe the violations they had instead committed within their colonies.

Alongside those violations of rights which were a vital part of the very existence and survival of colonies – and even of ex-colonies, as could be observed in the tragic transitions to independence in India and Pakistan – there were many cases in which democratic countries committed inhuman atrocities that were completely antithetical to the culture of rights they claimed to support and defend. An extreme, yet significant, example was the British re-utilisation of the same brutal strategies it had used, before the Second World War, in the Boer War (strategies it had to abandon even before WWII due to the reaction of public opinion). This time information concerning concentration camps and fortified villages (built to deport and isolate civilians from their links to the guerrillas) only partially reached the public, which widely accepted the defensive justifications of the authorities.

The use of concentration camps, which had initially been experimented with in Malaysia to fight the Communists of the Malayan Races Liberation Army, was at its most extreme in Kenya, during the 'state of emergency' declared by British governor Sir Evelyn Baring in October 1952. Almost one thousand people suspected of belonging to the Mau Mau – the rebel movement of the Kikuyu ethnic group, which at its most popular could boast 30,000 members – were victims of unmotivated detention and died in the camps, while 20,000 were killed while fighting or shot casually. Their hands were chopped off, just as in Leopold II's Congo, as proof of the elimination of a rebel. The violence by the Mau Mau against other members of the Kikuyu group accused of collaborating with the British, and in some cases even against white people, generated an atmosphere of justification and silence regarding the repressive British measures: these were revealed for the first time in 1954 by a group of journalists in Nairobi and denounced by a delegation of the Labour Party. The following year future British minister Barbara Castle spoke of a 'police state' in which rights had been violated, killings and torture went unpunished and authorities in charge of justice regularly connived with its violations.

The behaviour of the French within their colonies was different yet showed strong similarities, in particular in Indochina and Algeria. On the same day in which Paris was celebrating the surrender of Nazi Germany,

8 May, in Sètif a vast popular demonstration took place: thousands of Algerians who had participated in the anti-Nazi resistance reunited to place a crown at the feet of the monument dedicated to the city's victims, and to demand independence for their country. The demonstration was simultaneously attacked by soldiers from the French army, troops from the Foreign Legion and colonial militia: according to the most reliable sources, 10,000 people were killed, although the Algerians spoke of 45,000 victims and the report by General Duval estimated more than 150,000 Muslims 'presumed' dead. What took place was an 'unforgivable tragedy' – as it was defined, only in 2005, by the French ambassador in Algiers, Hubert Colin de Verdière – that would be repeated, fortunately with far fewer victims, in 1961, when 200 people were killed during an Algerian demonstration in Paris. The order to attack the demonstration came from the Prefect of Paris (who was later condemned for the organisation of the deportation of Jews during the Vichy government) and the bodies of the victims were thrown into the Seine.

During the Algerian war for independence (1954-62) the French democracy consciously violated some of the fundamental rights of individuals. As recorded in his memoirs, published in 2001, by Brigade Captain Paul Aussaresses, the political authorities in Paris were fully aware of the torture and arbitrary executions of suspected members of the NLF (Algerian National Liberation Front) before, during and after the 1957 'Battle of Algiers', since they had ordered General Massu to re-establish order 'at any cost'. This decay of values in the Fourth Republic and later in the France of General De Gaulle obviously did not take place without clashes. Denunciations of systematic torture appeared in the Catholic magazine *Témoignage Chrétien* in February 1957 and in *Esprit* in April. During the same year Georges Arnaud and Jacques Vergès published *Pour Djamila Bouhired* for Editions de Minuit, dedicated to an Algerian woman sentenced to death after having been tortured. In his preface to the autobiography of Henry Alleg, who had been the director of the newspaper 'Alger Républicain' and – because of this role – arrested and horrifically tortured, Sartre denounced torture 'as a syphilis which devastates this entire era. [...] Today, however, is the moment of Cyprus and Algeria; and Hitler, let it be said, was merely a precursor. Repudiated – sometimes hardly energetically, after all – yet systematically applied behind the façade of democratic legality, torture may be defined as a semi-clandestine institution.'[282]

If European democracies were failing to respect human rights, as seemed to be the case in their colonies, the situation was no better in countries belonging to the Socialist bloc led by the Soviet Union. In Hungary,

Romania, Poland, Czechoslovakia, Bulgaria and Albania this period was characterised by the ban on all non-Communist political parties, by the repression of any opposition and by the religious, social and ideological persecution of anyone considered dangerous by the new regimes. In the USSR the last years of Stalin's dominion were marked by an increase in police brutality and in deportations to work camps, as well as by new persecutions – including a particularly violent anti-Jewish campaign – which were suspended only after the dictator's death. During those same years, in the USSR 'brother' countries, a series of farcical trials, similar to the 1936-38 ones in Moscow, condemned and sentenced to death many of the previous leaders, who were thus forced to undergo the same fate they had imposed on thousands of their opponents during their regimes. The extent and depth of the 'crimes of Stalin' were revealed in 1956, when the new secretary of the CPSU, Nikita Khrushchev, read the delegates of the Party's twentieth Congress a secret report regarding 'illegalities' committed during the previous decades. Just a few months later Khrushchev ordered the brutal repression of Hungarian citizens. Budapest was occupied by Soviet tanks, thousands of Hungarians were arrested and some were even executed without trial.

The post-war period was one characterised by violations of fundamental rights in the United States also. Anti-Communism became the ideological cement of the Cold War period, and in its name the government and agencies for control and repression (from the FBI to the CIA) created measures of collective intimidation and violence which favoured an anti-progressive and anti-liberal attitude within the country. This was the period of the 'witch-hunt', as it has often been called. A time dominated by Republican Senator Joe McCarthy, whose name would be used to define the repressive policy and anti-Communist hysteria of the early fifties. Outside the national borders these policies were led by the CIA, which, following orders from Presidents Truman in 1952 and Eisenhower in 1953, successfully destabilised the Arbenz government in Guatemala. Indeed in 1954 Arbenz was forced to resign and was replaced by a man trusted by the American intelligence, Castillo Armas. The new leader had invaded the country from Honduras with his troops, and instituted a policy of repression, immediately killing hundreds of people without any trials whatsoever. Over the next few decades his government would kill over one hundred thousand people.

Given this widespread atmosphere, it is not surprising that the period was also characterised by frequent attacks on the new international legislation of rights, viewed by many countries as a Trojan horse constructed specifically to weaken national sovereignties. Amongst these there was, of course, the Soviet Union, which feared controls and the release of information about its internal reality; but also the United States, where numerous influential associations (from the American Bar Association to the Daughters of the American Revolution) and powerful Senators and Deputies openly disputed treaties and conventions they believed to be an affront to their nation's independence. Senator John Bricker, while suggesting that the country should withdraw from all international agreements, categorically stated that he did not want 'any international groups, and in particular the one led by Mrs. Eleanor Roosevelt, which prepared the draft of the Convention on Human Rights, to betray the fundamental, inalienable and God-sent rights of American citizens guaranteed by the constitution'.[283]

Even the darkest years of the Cold War should not however be seen as a simple and linear rejection of the complicated compromises achieved in 1948-49 by the Universal Declaration, by the Convention on Genocide and the four Geneva Conventions. Such principles were often included in new constitutions or in fundamental national laws (for example in Costa Rica, El Salvador, Haiti, Indonesia, Jordan, Libya, Puerto Rico, Syria), although they did not prohibit many of these countries from repeatedly violating human rights during the following years. However, it was above all a series of new specific conventions which tried to concretise, specify and further guarantee the values of the Universal Declaration.

The Cold War rendered the constant and threatening confrontation between East and West 'global in geographical scope and affected nearly everything that the United Nations attempted, ranging from such matters as the election of the secretary-general and voting procedures to substantive issues concerning collective security in the face of threats to peace, arms control, and interpretations of international human rights'.[284]

The Convention Relating to the Status of Refugees was formulated in 1951, one year after the creation of the High Commission of the United Nations for Refugees. The Convention is the fundamental legal document for the definition of the status, role and rights of refugees, as well as of states' obligations towards them. In 1952 the Convention on the Political Rights of Women was approved, which obliged member states to yield the right to vote to women, as well as the right to be elected within representative institutions and to participate in public office. Two years later the Convention on Stateless Persons was approved and in 1956 it was the turn of the Supplementary Convention on the Abolition of Slavery, which updated the previous one from 1926; in 1957 the Convention on the Nationality of Married Women was approved, which, on the basis of article 15 of the Universal Declaration ('Everyone has the right to a nationality. No one shall be arbitrarily deprived of his nationality nor denied the right to change his nationality') intended to guarantee that women could not be deprived of or excluded from nationality when they married or divorced.

3. *The decline of colonialism*

In 1955 only five African countries could be considered independent: Liberia (the only state which had always been independent), Ethiopia and Libya, which had previously been subjected to Italian domination, Egypt and South Africa, where the exploitation of and discrimination against the black majority were probably worse than in any other colonial domain. The Charter of the United Nations had recognised the self-determination of populations as a fundamental aspect of the new international order and of the new relations between states, in article 1 (paragraph 2: 'To develop friendly relations among nations based on respect for the principle of equal rights and self-determination of peoples, and to take other appropriate measures to strengthen universal peace') and article 55 ('With a view to the creation of conditions of stability and well-being which are necessary for peaceful and friendly relations among nations based on respect for the *principle of equal rights and self-determination of peoples*').

This was a clear enunciation, yet expressed 'in timid terms that defined it [self-determination] more as an objective to be achieved than as an immediately binding precept'.[285] The first strong formalisation of this principle came only in December 1960, with Resolution 1514/XV adopted by the General Assembly of the United Nations, regarding the concession of independence to ex-colonial countries and populations. The following year a special committee for decolonisation (or 'committee of the 24') was established to implement the previous resolution and guarantee the independence of colonial populations.

As often happened, given the composite nature of the United Nations, when the resolution was approved the process towards decolonisation was actually already well underway, and in truth the UN indication served mainly to accelerate and certify a process which had already begun. This procedure was hardly a simple one, given the fact that both France and England had attempted to preserve their colonial empires despite the openly hostile position of the United States. The anachronistic attitude of these two countries underwent a profound crisis in 1956, at the end of the Suez crisis, although both powers should have perceived the changes in international relations at least one year earlier.

The Bandung Conference of Non-Aligned Countries – promoted by some of the newly independent Asian states (Indonesia, India and Pakistan) alongside Egypt and Yugoslavia – had indeed already affirmed the will to carry forward the process of decolonisation in Africa and Asia in a determined, intense and rapid fashion.

The French defeat in Indochina in 1954, in the battle of Dien Bien Phu, demonstrated the difficulties that even a modern army could face in dealing with the new and original forms of guerrilla and military strategy adopted by populations struggling for independence. The Suez crisis, which had seen the military defeat of the Egyptian Nasser, yet also his political victory, became a symbol of the possibility of defeating British colonialism, and generated an increase in anti-Western tendencies in all countries in the region. Jordan ended its alliance with London, Iraq underwent a coup d'état, followed by the killing of King Feisal II and his family, while in Lebanon a civil war began, that was destined to be a part of the country's history from then on. Immediately after the Dien Bien Phu defeat, the Algerian NLF had declared an insurrection on 1 November 1954, thus beginning a war for independence which would only end eight years later, resulting in at least one million deaths, mostly of Algerian civilians.

Africa was the main terrain for the push given to decolonisation by the events of the early fifties. Already at the end of the forties, during what was called the 'second colonial occupation', the British were planning to create large federate units which could include many territories and eventually be included in the Commonwealth, while the French opted for a policy of assimilation and integration which, at least at the time, only granted the right to vote to a tiny minority. In that same period, thanks to constitutional reforms and the concession of a greater freedom of movement, trade unions were increasing their strength in African countries, leading to a season of strikes and demonstrations, while episodes of resistance and revolts in the countryside were multiplying and would soon be accompanied by sporadic forms of guerrilla fighting and by the creation of the first nationalistic parties.

The first African country to achieve independence was the Gold Coast, where Kwame Nkrumah – educated in the United States and famous for his African struggles in Britain – in the name of a pan-African nationalism based as much on Marcus Garvey as it was on Gandhi, managed to earn a huge consensus for his party, the Convention People's Party, based on a programme of national unity and supported by the most important figures within the country's main communities. In the administrative elections of 1954 and 1956 Nkrumah's party obtained the majority within the main region for the production of cocoa, despite the strong support given by the British government to the Ashanti notables. Having no more direct and strategic interests to defend in the country, and given the lack of a violent opposition to be fought off, Britain realised that it could no longer elude the concession of the rights to self-determination established by the UN Charter (which it had contributed to formulate): in 1957 Nkrumah became the first president of the new state of Ghana.

The situation was far more complicated in Nigeria, given the presence of three dominant ethnic groups in the country's three regions and the territory's richness in raw materials and in petrol. A federal constitution – an attempt to solve the lack of a national majority party – paved the way for the agreements which in 1960 led to the country's independence. The first Nigerian president was Abubakar Tafawa Balewa, leader of the Hausa/Fulani group. In that same year the territories which had agreed in 1958 to become part of the Franco-African Community as autonomous states also obtained their independence from France: Senegal, the Upper Volta, which was re-named Burkina Faso, Cameroon, Chad, French Congo, Dahomey, Mali, Niger, Togo and the Ivory Coast. Guinea, which had refused to enter the Francophone Community, had already become independent in 1958, although the price it had to pay was the end of French aid to the country.

Congo also achieved its independence before the approval of Resolution 1514 by the General Assembly of the United Nations, although it was the result of a process of violence and divisions that was in keeping with the tradition imposed by Leopold II and his heirs. The administrative elections of 1957 were characterised by ethnic and political conflicts which resulted in an increase of violence and disorders during the second part of the year. Thus, in January 1959, the Belgian king, Baudouin, unexpectedly announced the concession of independence within 18 months. The region around the capital Leopoldville was dominated by the party of Joseph Kasavubu, with the Katanga region instead favouring the secessionist party of Moïse Tshombe, while in the area surrounding Stanleyville the strongest party was led by Patrice Lumumba, a radical nationalist who was the paladin of the country's unity. Lumumba won the elections in the spring of 1960 and became the country's Prime Minister, while he nominated his ally Kasavubu as President of the Republic.

A few days later, on 30 June 1960, the date on which the country's independence was effected, Congo had already fallen into chaos: the Katanga region announced its secession, soldiers began committing violent acts against the white population to avenge the humiliations they had suffered during colonialism and Belgian troops entered the country and bombarded the port of Matadi. To end the violence – and avoid the transformation of one of the crucial moments of the decolonisation process into a bloody tragedy – the secretary of the United Nations, Dag Hammarskjöld, convinced the Security Council to authorise the 'Operation des Nations Unies au Congo', approved by resolution 143 in July 1960 in order to:

> oversee the withdrawal of Belgian troops and to help the Congolese government restore law and order; they were not supposed to get involved with Congolese politics in general and the Katangan secession in particular. But this is precisely what happened. Arguably, this was because ONUC's underlying goal was to restore an acceptable degree of Westphalian order by maintaining Congo's territorial integrity, peacefully if possible but by force if necessary.[286]

It was the first mission (only followed much later by UNISOM II in Somalia) to involve the use of force based on Chapter VII of the Charter, and was organised, led and directed under the supervision of the General Secretary, although Hammarskjöld's activity was openly contested by Khrushchev during the autumn 1960 session of the UN General Assembly. After the mission's initial success, however, violence broke out once more and in January 1961 Lumumba, who had been confirmed in office by the parliament, was arrested and later murdered by the Chief of State, General Mobutu. A few months later Hammarskjöld died too, in a mysterious airplane crash: many suspected the plane had been sabotaged, although it was never determined with certainty.

This was the international situation when, on 14 December 1960, the United Nations approved the Declaration on the Granting of Independence to Colonial Countries and Peoples, which recognised 'the passionate desire for freedom of all dependent populations and their decisive role in obtaining their own independence' and the 'burning desire of populations of the world to end colonialism in all its forms', while also declaring that 'the liberation process is unstoppable and irresistible, and in order to avoid a serious crisis we must end colonialism and all associated practices of segregation and discrimination'. Thus:

> 1. The subjection of peoples to alien subjugation, domination and exploitation constitutes a denial of fundamental human rights, is contrary to the Charter of the United Nations and is an impediment to the promotion of world peace and cooperation. 2. All peoples have the right to self-determination: thus they freely determine their political status and pursue economic, social and cultural

development. 3. Political, economic or educational inadequacies should never serve as excuses to postpone independence.[287]

Sierra Leone and Tanganyika became independent in 1961, followed by Uganda, Rwanda and Burundi in 1962, Zanzibar and Kenya in 1963, Malawi and Zambia in 1964. Nearly the whole of Africa had now achieved its independence, except for the Portuguese colonies, which would have to wait a further decade. Many have stated this was the greatest extension and simultaneous obtainment of human rights in world history. The destruction of colonial empires deeply modified the very structure and agenda of the United Nations: this was also demonstrated by the 1961 election of Burmese U Thant as Secretary General of the United Nations.

4. *Non-governmental movements and organisations*

The major transformations generated by decolonisation, best summarised by the December 1960 Declaration on the Concession of Independence, did not automatically solve the problem of discrimination against subjected peoples or groups considered inferior as a result of their ethnic diversity. In 1960, the year that symbolised Africa's awakening, in Sharpeville, South Africa, a new repressive phase of the country's apartheid opened with a terrible massacre, accompanied by norms which went in the exact opposite direction from those espoused by the United Nations. On that occasion, as the South African Commission for Truth and Re-conciliation recognised 30 years later:

> The police deliberately opened fire on an unarmed crowd which had met peacefully in Sharpeville on 21 March 1960, to protest against the new law on passports. The commission also believes that the SAP (South African Police) failed to give the crowd the order to disperse before shooting and that it continued to fire at the crowd while it was escaping, thus shooting hundreds of people in their backs. As a result of this excessive use of force 69 people were killed and over three hundred were injured. The commission also believes that the police did not facilitate medical access and/or assistance to those who had been wounded immediately after the march.[288]

Following this event, the newly independent countries of Africa and Asia asked for an emergency meeting of the UN Security Council, which was openly criticised by the South African Prime Minister Hendrik Verwoerd in the name of national sovereignty threatened by 'international forces'. On 24 January, General Secretary Dag Hammarskjöld told American President John F. Kennedy, who had just begun his term of office, 'that he had been incapable of reaching a "reasonable" agreement regarding racial problems while recently visiting South Africa'.[289] Polemically commenting on his own country's new isolationist and racist policy, Nelson Mandela – who had been arrested for illegal travels and instigating strike action – asserted that 'the Universal Declaration of Human Rights establishes that all men are equal before the law'.[290]

African and Asian countries who wanted to solve the problem of South African discrimination founded a Special Committee on the Policies of Apartheid, which produced the Declaration on the Elimination of All Forms of Racial Discrimination, adopted in November 1963 by the General Assembly of the United Nations. In its first article it stated:

> Discrimination between human beings on the ground of race, colour or ethnic origin is an offence to human dignity and shall be condemned as a denial of the principles of the Charter of the United Nations, as a violation of the human rights and fundamental freedoms proclaimed in the Universal Declaration of Human Rights, as an obstacle to friendly and peaceful relations among nations and as a fact capable of disturbing peace and security among peoples.[291]

Two years later, on 21 December 1965, the Assembly adopted a Convention on the same theme and with the same title (International Convention on the Elimination of All Forms of Racial Discrimination) which entered into force three years later, after 27 countries agreed to integrate it within their legislations.[292]

The awareness that the sixties could represent a new phase for the United Nations was accurately summarised by the Colombian delegate:

> there has been a change of ideas, expressions, attitudes, objectives, even ideals. There has been an awakening in world consciousness regarding a duty that cannot be denied, an awakening of peoples with regard to a clear duty – to reinforce the foundations of justice, of a society based on equality, of states' obligations to promote conditions which may allow every person to fully enjoy such rights.[293]

Such changes were undeniable, just as the dynamism of the United Nations, despite the limits inherent to its structure, was clear with regard to a problem – racial discrimination – which now appeared to be solvable, two centuries after the beginning of the struggle against the slave trade. However, the South African case was not the only obstacle to the realisation, within the legislation of each country, of one of the fundamental principles of the Charter of the United Nations and of the Universal Declaration. Many Western countries were also perplexed, even worried, by a process which had always found its proudest enemies in the Western world. The most obvious case was that of the United States, and not just because of the fact that they signed the International Convention on the Elimination of All Forms of Racial Discrimination later than many other countries (as they did with many other United Nations documents).

In the United States, since the beginning of the fifties, the movement for equal civil and political rights for Afro-American citizens, according to the words of the constitution (in amendments XIII, XIV and XV), had grown significantly. Afro-Americans were still being discriminated against, especially in the Southern states, despite the fact that the abolition of slavery had taken place almost one century earlier.

At the beginning of the twentieth century the Supreme Court had confirmed the right to racial segregation within schools, thus reinforcing the conviction that Afro-American citizens belonged to an inferior category, as theorised by the so-called 'Jim Crow laws' (local or state laws which, after 1876, had allowed the legalisation of racial dis-crimination and segregation in all public spaces: schools, restaurants, transportation, swimming pools, libraries and so on). Afro-Americans could not be members of juries, while convicted black people were sen-tenced with extra-judicial punishments; in many Southern states lynches continued to take place even in the first decades of the twentieth century, often supported by the local police.

In 1909 the National Association for the Advancement of Colored People (NAACP) was founded to legally dismantle the Jim Crow laws, fight segregation in federal offices introduced by President Wilson and to contest racism in public life (an example of such racism may be found in one of the first successful silent films, D.W. Griffiths' *Birth of a Nation*).

After the Second World War, when many Afro-American soldiers fought in the American army, the struggle for civil rights was fully revived, and in 1954 the Supreme Court finally declared that segregation in schools was anti-constitutional. This was the moment in which direct actions by different militant groups fighting for civil rights gave birth to a new, crucial phase of the Civil Rights Movement. Their civil disobedience and non-violent protests were rapidly successful, and managed to involve the entire country in boycotts and demonstrations. The boycott of public transport in Montgomery in 1955 and 1956, following the arrest – for violation of racial segregation – of Rosa Parks, a young dressmaker who had refused to give her place on the bus to a white man, marked the beginning of a new era of struggles. A few years later, in 1960, four students refused to abandon a shopping mall restaurant in Greensboro, North Carolina, and thus essentially invented sit-ins (a direct action which involves the occupation of a public area), a non-violent practice which would later be used in protests all over the world. The new Democratic administration which won the elections in 1960 could no longer ignore the strength of the movement: in June 1963 President Kennedy promised to introduce a law to establish the equal treatment of all citizens, in a speech on civil rights no other President would have had the courage to make in such clear terms. The strength of the movement and the urgency of its aim were further demonstrated by the huge march on Washington, organised during that same year by Martin Luther King and attended by half a million people. The assassination of Kennedy did not impede the parliamentary process concerning these issues; indeed his successor, Lyndon B. Johnson, was able to avoid the blocking of the proposed law by the obstructionism of Southern Senators. On 2 July 1964, the Civil Rights Act banned all forms of discrimination. The Afro-American protest contributed to the affirmation within the law of many principles of the Universal Declaration, and, consequently, of the prohibition of any discrimination based on colour, race, religion, gender or nationality. A further Civil Rights Act, promulgated in 1968, ended discrimination over the rent and sale of apartments, financial support and credit, and within employment.

The early sixties were thus marked by action by major international institutions – including the United Nations – and mobilisation, awareness and pressure campaigns by civil society movements – such as the American Civil Rights Movement – aiming to push governments to accept legislation in accordance with the principles of the Universal Declaration. However, this period in the history of human rights was also characterised by the creation of new associative forms and instruments for mobilisation, protest and pressure on governments. Alongside those who were fighting to bring the rights recognised by the Declaration to all populations and citizens of any colour, gender and religion, were also those who realised that the most ancient and fundamental individual rights were still far from being protected and guaranteed – even in Europe, where the history of human rights had been inaugurated 200 years earlier.

One morning, Peter Benenson, a forty-year old British lawyer, was shocked to read in the *Observer* about two Portuguese students who had been arrested and sentenced to seven years in prison, for having toasted to freedom in a Lisbon restaurant. As he later declared, 'that so enraged me that I walked up the steps of St Martin-in-the-Fields, out of the Underground, and went in to see what could really be done effectively to mobilise world opinion'.[294] The idea of launching a campaign by sending thousands of letters to the Portuguese government from all parts of the globe was certainly an innovative one, although it was not surprising given the lawyer's personal story. Peter was the son of a Colonel of the British army, John Solomon, and Flora Benenson, the daughter of an immigrant Jewish Russian banker, who had basically raised him herself after his father's death. Flora[295] educated Peter privately and entrusted his tuition to W.H. Auden, the great poet who would later marry Thomas Mann's daughter, Erika, to allow her to escape Nazi Germany; later still he would also participate in the Spanish civil war before moving to the United States alongside Christopher Isherwood in 1939 and obtaining American citizenship. Peter later attended the prestigious Eton College, where he organised the Committee for Spanish Aid for the victims of the civil war, and was identified as a 'subversive' after having organised a protest against the high prices of the school's refectory. During those years he was moved by Arthur Koestler's book *Spanish Testament*, about imprisonment within a death cell of a Francoist prison. He then studied history at Oxford University and during the war he organised a collection amongst his friends' families (amassing around four thousand pounds) to allow two young Jews who had escaped Hitler's Germany to reach England. Having obtained his degree, he entered the British Army – where he worked in the Minister of Information's press office – joined the Labour Party and, after the war, was sent by the Trade Unions to Spain as an observer of the activities of local unions, opposed by the Franco regime. In Spain he visited the local prisons, and later criticised the lack of guarantees and fairness within the country's judicial procedures.

After the war Peter worked with his mother, who was amongst those working to provide shelter and food for the thousands of refugee children who arrived in the English capital, from all over the world, in those years. In 1960, declared the World Year of Refugees by the United Nations, he began investigating the possibility of also helping political prisoners. The occasion which prompted this idea was precisely the case of the two Portuguese students, which led him to write an appeal – entitled *Forgotten Prisoners* – published by the *Observer* on Sunday 28 May. The many replies were later published in a column entitled *Appeal for Amnesty*. The article began as follows:

> Open your newspaper – any day of the week – and you will find a report from somewhere in the world of someone being imprisoned,

tortured or executed because his opinions or religion are unacceptable to his government. The newspaper reader feels a sickening sense of impotence. Yet if these feelings of disgust all over the world could be united into common action, something effective could be done.[296]

The campaign launched by Benenson was supposed to last one year. Instead it was the first act of a series of increasingly numerous campaigns promoted worldwide by the organisation he had founded in July 1961, Amnesty International – whose logo is a candle surrounded by barbed wire. Amnesty International became the prototype of what would later be known as NGOs (Non Governmental Organisations), not-for-profit volunteer associations created around specific local, national and international objectives and actions. In 1963 Amnesty International came under the guidance of an international Secretariat, later led by Séan Mc-Bride and then by Martin Ennals, two of the greatest world experts and human rights defenders.

5. *Humanitarian interventions and the re-discovery of human rights*

It is widely held that the late sixties, and more precisely 1967, marked the beginning of the third phase in the life of the United Nations and for human rights. If up until 1954 the main problem consisted in the formulation of norms and concepts, during the following decade international diplomatic efforts multiplied with regard to both the indirect and direct protection of rights, through meetings, debates and publications aimed at identifying the states that were committing severe violations. Thus 1967 marked the beginning of a phase in which the Human Rights Commission of the UN fell under the influence of new independent states, which often reoriented and reprioritised the Commission's activities. On one hand this resulted in the selective protection of certain countries, while on the other it translated into a widening of general interventions to officially introduce the two major treaties adopted in 1966, the Covenant on Civil and Political Rights and the Covenant on Economic, Social, and Cultural Rights.

Although they had been ready for many years, these two major Covenants had been delayed by the Cold War, when the two rival superpowers had fought their own battle on human rights by opposing civil and political rights to social and economic ones, and vice-versa. This is why two distinguished texts, both based on the Universal Declaration, were prepared: the former, mainly supported by Western countries, included

53 articles; the latter, promoted mainly by the Socialist bloc, consisted of 31. With regard to civil and political rights, these documents provided a greater degree of juridical clarity than the Declaration, and extended the number of listed rights; regarding economic and social rights, they introduced clear and strong norms on the right to work, to education and to cultural life: 'Substantially, states wanted to be free to choose which pact to ratify.'[297] The 1967 reorganisation of the Human Rights Commission on a regional basis increased the number of members to 32 (eight from Africa and the Western countries, six from Asia and Latin America, four from Eastern Europe) and seemed to direct the Commission towards a revival of the message of the Declaration – as suggested by the Head of Amnesty International and Secretary of the International Commission of Jurists, Séan McBride – as 'the Charter of freedom of the oppressed and subjugated'.[298]

The question of human rights became more urgent and began a new phase of its existence, especially in relation to the growth of 'Third World'[299] countries. This era was also marked by battles for national liberation in countries that were still not independent, and by popular movements – characterised by a combination of parliamentarianism and guerrilla fighting – which energetically opposed civil or military regimes especially in Latin America. The violation of human rights by countries which still maintained their colonial status, or by authoritarian regimes (often encouraged and supported by the United States), helped to reinforce and legitimise struggles by their governmental opposition, by popular movements and even by guerrilla groups. It must be said that Amnesty International also condemned analogous acts by Communist regimes, which directly inspired certain Third World movements.

A list of the problems and cases regarding human rights which were addressed during the sixties would be extremely lengthy. Amongst the most striking cases were the many victims of the great proletarian Cultural Revolution in China, which were only partially revealed at the time, and the half a million people – mostly belonging to the Communist party – massacred in Indonesia; the violence against the Hutus in Burundi (at least 150,000 victims according to moderate estimates) and the repression in Pakistan following the first free elections in 1970; the American bombing of villages in North Vietnam and Cambodia and the counter-guerrilla actions in Guatemala, which according to Amnesty International killed 30,000 people; General Pinochet's coup d'état in Chile and the invasion of Afghanistan by the Soviet Union. Some violations – such as the My Lai massacre in Vietnam in March 1968 by a company of American marines – were more shocking than others, because they were in evident conflict with the principles professed by the country which committed them. Other ones, like the most terrible episode of the seventies, the genocide of the Cambodian population by Pol Pot's Khmer Rouge, were minimised or justified[300] for many years in ways that could not be explained by mere lack of information, and were instead the result of determined ideological prejudices.

Yet it was during this decade, the most violent of the entire century – if we exclude the two world wars – that the Conference on Security and Cooperation in Europe (CSCE) took place in Europe. The Final Act of the conference summarised the main themes negotiated by 35 countries: security, cooperation and human rights. Regarding human rights the conference established that:

> The participating States will respect human rights and fundamental freedoms, including the freedom of thought, conscience, religion or belief, for all without distinction as to race, sex, language or religion. They will promote and encourage the effective exercise of civil, political, economic, social, cultural and other rights and freedoms all of which derive from the inherent dignity of the human person and are essential for his free and full development. Within this framework the participating States will recognise and respect the freedom of the individual to profess and practice, alone or in community with others, religion or belief acting in accordance with the dictates of his own conscience. The participating States on whose territory national minorities exist will respect the right of persons belonging to such minorities to equality before the law, will afford them the full opportunity for the actual enjoyment of human rights and fundamental freedoms and will, in this manner, protect their legitimate interests in this sphere. The participating States recognise the universal significance of human rights and fundamental freedoms, respect for which is an essential factor for the peace, justice and well-being necessary to ensure the development of friendly relations and co-operation among themselves as among all States.[301]

The Helsinki Final Act was an attempt to revive the dialogue between the West and the East. The conference involved all European countries (except for Albania), Canada, the United States and the Soviet Union. On the theme of human rights it added nothing significant to what had been established by the main international documents, in particular by the two 1966 Covenants, which were officialised only in January and

March 1976, when they were ratified by thirty-five countries. The Covenants, together with the Universal Declaration, actually constituted the International Bill of Human Rights, considered by the United Nations 'a milestone in the history of human rights, a proper *Magna Carta* leading humanity toward a new vital phase: the conscious acquisition of human dignity and value'.[302]

As stated by one of the founders of Human Rights Watch, Aryeh Neier, 'during the seventies, events in different parts of the world altogether inspired the formation of an international movement for human rights'.[303] From the coup in Chile to the Soweto riots and the murder of Steve Biko in South Africa, from the situation in Indochina after the Vietnam war to the growing dissent in Communist countries, for the first time a series of events established respect for human rights as a new ethical foundation for states' internal and international politics. Thus an increasing number of organisations began following the directions provided by the Helsinki resolutions and gave birth to the first properly international human rights movement. Apart from the formation of various 'Helsinki Groups' in different parts of the world, this new tendency was underlined above all by the Nobel Prize for Peace won by Amnesty International in 1977.

Neier, who had become one of the leaders of the American Civil Liberties Union (ACLU) (he had joined the organisation in 1963), became the main instigator of Americas Watch (later transformed into Human Rights Watch) alongside Robert Bernstein and Orville Schell Jr., and year after year he expanded his interest in human rights: from the Soviet Union to Latin America, from Asia to Africa. In his memoirs he wrote:

> In what I consider my most important contribution, I initiated the monitoring of abuses committed in armed conflicts by assessing the conduct of combatants in accordance with the laws of war. Human Rights Watch pioneered in this monitoring and, over time, the international human rights movement broadly followed its lead. A consequence is to make the human rights practices of opposing armed forces a focus of public debate over wars in many parts of the world. Embarking on this path also led me to propose such innovations as the international prohibition on landmines, establishment of the international criminal tribunal for ex-Yugoslavia and, in certain extreme circumstances, advocacy for international military intervention when nothing else will prevent so great a crime as genocide.[304]

Alongside new associations for human rights, the activities of older organisations were also expanding. Ever since its foundation the Red

Cross had identified the fundamental principles of humanitarian action as impartiality, neutrality, humanity, independence, participation by volunteers, unity and universality. During the period of their expansion, between the sixties and seventies, a debate developed within humanitarian organisations between 'purist' positions – those intending to respect the values established by Henri Dunant – and 'pragmatic' ones – those who intended to operate with greater solidarity and believed humanitarian principles were an excessive bind that should be adapted according to actual circumstances. After all, the Red Cross had been struck by criticisms because of its 'silence' regarding Nazi concentration camps during the Second World War.

The decisive moment was represented by the crisis in Biafra, the country formed in 1967 within the Eastern region of Nigeria, which became the stage of a terrible conflict and famine. The Western powers were doubtful whether or not to intervene: although they did not recognise the new state, only France – and humanitarian organisations in various parts of the world – appeared preoccupied by the emergency. In April 1968, while student revolts swept across Europe, the correspondent of the 'Sunday Times' wrote: 'I have seen things in Biafra this week which no man should have to see. Sights to search the heart and sicken the conscience. I have seen children roasted alive, young girls torn in two by shrapnel, pregnant women and elderly people blown into many fragments'.[305] It was during this period that the idea of creating a new organisation, freer than the Red Cross to intervene during a humanitarian crisis, was born, based on the reflections of a group of humanitarian operators – and on their presence in the field during the months after the conflict, which ended with the re-constitution of unitary Nigeria in 1970. Thus Médecins Sans Frontières was founded, an organisation formed in 1971 by French doctors and journalists who believed in a strong *témoignage* in response to the silence of the Red Cross: such a testimony was not intended as opposed to the principle of neutrality (which remained a milestone of all humanitarian activities, with humanity, independence and impartiality), but as a way to make the organisation more committed and active, less diplomatic and compromising. The principle of neutrality was now 'intended as an operative principle, as a means (silence and confidentiality) to reach a goal (efficacious assistance and protection for the victims of war) [...] The interest of victims was the main concern when choosing to speak publicly or not about violations of human rights'.[306]

6. *Specific rights. Hopes and regressions*

The Helsinki Final Act and the ratification of the two Covenants (the Covenant on Civil and Political Rights and the Covenant on Economic, Social, and Cultural Rights) appeared to shine a completely new light on the second half of the seventies. The hopes created by such important and complementary documents added to those produced at the end of the wars in Vietnam and Indochina. At the end of 1976 the United States was close to electing a president, Jimmy Carter, who strongly believed in human rights, a fact that marked a clear difference from the previous Nixon and Ford administrations. In that same year Lelio Basso, the founder of the International League for the Rights and Liberation of Peoples (which in 1974 had led to the Russell II Tribunal and would generate the Permanent Tribunal of peoples three years later), became the advocate of the Charter of Algiers. This document, approved on the 4 July 1976, represented an actual Universal Declaration of the rights of peoples, based upon the 30 articles of the 1948 Declaration.

The fact that the document was approved by many non-governmental organisations, by movements for the liberation of certain countries and by many people involved in the international movements for the defence and promotion of human rights, demonstrates the scope and strength of the public opinion and civil society that were now willing to put pressure on institutions in order to concretise the principles they had articulated and approved. Lelio Basso explained his initiative on the basis of 'the crisis of international law, which has profound causes', also given that 'the number of independent states, in other words the subjects of international law recognised traditionally, has doubled, and the colonies which have become independent, just like Socialist states, cannot recognise the validity of old laws they did not help formulate'. He recognised the legitimacy of the objection: 'who gave the Algiers conference the authority to make this Declaration?', yet he replied that 'the conference spoke in the name of a new order to be established and that would certainly not be installed by the powers of today unless the will and strength of peoples were to impose it'.[307]

The position of Basso was one that sought to reconcile a necessary reference to the universality of rights with an attempt to dynamically modify their historical contents, which had emerged during the Second World War. To do so it shared a strong bond with the concrete actions of collective subjects fighting to realise their own rights through the conquest of political power. Among the supporters of Basso's proposal were non-governmental organisations – mainly committed to the defence of human rights and to humanitarian intervention – and revolutionary movements interested in rights as a tool for their political battles. This coexistence of different approaches to human rights is the clearest sign of the transformation taking place during those years. These changes would result in the rapid decline (accompanied by disillusion, if not actual demise) of revolutionary hopes and projects, and in the affirmation of the culture of human rights as a fundamental basis for contrasting the hypocrisies and interests behind the implementation of the December 1948 Declaration by large and small states alike.

Carter's foreign policy (later criticised as a weakening of American power), was characterised by an unprecedented (in the White House) attention to human rights. His mediation between Egyptian President Anwar Sadat and the Israeli Premier Menachem Begin, during the 1978 Camp David negotiations, was fundamental and led to the ratification of the Panama Channel Treaties, to the full diplomatic recognition of the People's Republic of China and to the SALT II agreements on the limitation of the construction of strategic weapons (these latest agreements were signed in Vienna in 1979).

Carter himself stated:

> Less than five weeks after I became President, we announced our intention to reduce American aid to Argentina, Ethiopia and Uruguay, given the serious violations of human rights committed by their regimes. I declared my intention to treat every American ambassador as my personal rapporteur on human rights: and I asked each of them to take on direct responsibility by writing and preparing their Country Report on human rights.[308]

During the first year of his presidency, this commitment led him to sign both the United Nations' Covenants (which had entered into force the previous year), as well as the American Convention on Human Rights, which created an Inter-American Human Rights Commission. The Commission was to have powers of supervision and control. However, the Convention was never ratified by the Senate of the United States.

In truth those years were amongst the darkest in human history in terms of the respect of human rights. In all Latin American countries – from Argentina to Chile, from Brazil to Ecuador, from Uruguay to Bolivia, from Colombia to Venezuela, from El Salvador to Guatemala, from Haiti to Nicaragua, from Paraguay to Cuba, from Peru to Honduras – human rights were being violated by violent military dictatorships and authoritarian regimes, as well as by the movements which opposed them, incapable of avoiding either the involvement of civilian victims in their battle for freedom, or unmotivated violence and abuses against their enemies.

Those were also the years of the terrible Cambodian massacre, certainly the most neglected and removed, for many decades, from international attention: the tragedy took place between April 1975 – when the Khmer Rouge entered Phnom Penh – and December 1978 – when Vietnamese troops began to conquer Cambodian territory and, one month later, forced Pol Pot and his men to retreat to the mountains. Two million people, the inhabitants of the capital, were forcibly dispersed in the rural zones, in an attempt to create a pre-modern village civilisation, free from any foreign presence and based on a social levelling involving the disappearance of middle classes, intellectuals and professionals. Under the guidance of 'brother number one', as Pol Pot called himself, the intensive social re-modelling by the Khmer Rouge was an extreme radicalisation of past Communist experience which hit the entire population, but above all the Vietnamese, Chinese and Muslim Cham minorities.

The alliance between Communist China and the United States allowed the Democratic Kampuchea of the Khmer Rouge to keep its seat in the United Nations for over ten years (instead of it being reassigned to the People's Republic of Kampuchea); it forced the Human Rights Commission of the UN to ignore a 1,000 page long report on testimonies of the violations and violence committed by Pol Pot's men; it also blocked the numerous requests to create an international penal tribunal to judge the people responsible for the Cambodian genocide; furthermore it prevented any of the documents of the peace negotiations – which began in 1989 and ended in 1991 with the Paris agreements – from mentioning not only genocide but even any crimes against humanity whatsoever. President Carter even condemned the Vietnamese actions and forced an embargo on the new Cambodian government – a policy confirmed by his successor President Reagan.

The second part of the seventies was also distinguished by the Vietnamese 'boat people', refugees from South Vietnam from the Indochinese conflict seeking to escape torture, deprivations and re-education camps where over a million people had been imprisoned without any formal accusation or trial. Between 1975 and 1979 over half a million people abandoned Vietnam – as well as Cambodia and Laos – and chose to face the sea, storms and pirates aboard makeshift boats. Even initiatives such as the 1978 World Conference against Racism organised by the United Nations could not avoid being considerably re-dimensioned by this international situation.

The conference rejected any doctrine based on racial superiority – labelled a 'scientific falsity' – recognised the contribution of all populations to the progress of civilisation and condemned all forms of discrimination. South African apartheid was particularly stigmatised, as an 'extreme form of institutionalised racism', and likened to crimes against humanity. The 1973-82 decade was dedicated (as were the ten years leading up to 2003) to the battle against racism and racial discrimination, in the name of the conviction that economic and social inequalities reinforce discrimination and cultural prejudices.

The process of international reconciliation which began in 1974 with meetings between Brezhnev and Ford (and continued after Helsinki with the signing of SALT II by both leaders) was viewed by the Russian leader as a sort of *status quo* to guarantee Soviet control of Eastern Europe in exchange for the USSR agreeing to not destabilise the Western balance. However, the American defeat in Vietnam and the institutional weakening of the United States over Watergate led the secretary of the CPSU to believe world power relations might be shifting in his favour, and to order a series of actions in Africa and Asia. This explains the USSR's indirect intervention in Angola (carried out by a Cuban contingent) and in the Horn of Africa, as well as the aid given to Vietnam (in the war against Cambodia) and the December 1979 invasion of Afghanistan.

This Soviet policy of aggression beyond its national borders was accompanied by a decrease in repression against nationalistic movements (Ukrainian, Georgian, Baltic ones) and the creation of committees to implement the Helsinki agreements. The most significant victim of these committees was Andrei Sakharov, developer of the Soviet nuclear bomb and from 1970 a passionate defender of civil rights, who was forced into exile in Gor'kij. An analogous event took place in Czechoslovakia, where in 1977 Charter 77 was born, a movement for the defence of all citizens founded by Jiří Hajek and Václav Havel, the playwright unanimously elected President of the Czech Republic in 1989. August 1979 saw the birth in Poland of the first independent and free trade union movement in a Socialist country: the presence, dynamism and growing consensus of Solidarność led Poland to declare the state of war in 1981.

1979 was also the year of the Islamic revolution in Iran led by Ayatollah Khomeini, who combined religious values and traditional principles with revolutionary struggles to destabilise the corrupt monarchy of Reza Pahlavi. Khomeini's fundamentalism roused the population against the monarchy's isolated power, in a process which progressively marginalised the country's liberal and nationalistic forces and aimed to seize power by mobilising political-religious committees and the armed militia of the pasdaran. The construction of an Islamic republic and a theocratic power took place in just a few months and was followed by the siege of the American embassy in November 1979: this event contributed to Carter's electoral defeat against Ronald Reagan.

On 18 December the General Assembly of the United Nations approved the Convention on the Elimination of All Forms of Discrimination against Women (CEDAW), which expanded and improved the previous declaration and aimed to fight:

> any distinction, exclusion or restriction made on the basis of sex which has the effect or purpose of impairing or nullifying the recognition, enjoyment or exercise by women, irrespective of their marital status, on a basis of equality of men and women, of human rights and fundamental freedoms in the political, economic, social, cultural, civil or any other field. (art. 1).[309]

The CEDAW, apart from being the result of the previous decade's feminist struggles for the rights of women in various parts of the world, was also a product of the attempt to transform the general contents of the 1948 Declaration into legally binding instruments for the countries which signed it. Coherently with the new phase of the United Nations, it was decided that rights should now be specified, especially for particularly relevant sectors lacking international norms.

Indeed, during the following decade, two further Conventions were adopted – the 1984 one on torture, and the 1989 one on children – which reinforced the aforementioned tendency, forcing states to choose a position and adhere to proper and binding legal instruments, rather than just to moral principles or an international political order.

In 1981, in Nairobi, the conference Heads of States of the Organisation for African Unity adopted the African Charter on Human and Peoples' Rights, which entered into force in October 1986, after having been ratified by 35 out of 50 African states. The commitment to 'eradicate all forms of colonialism from Africa' was accompanied by attention to 'the virtues of their historical tradition and the values of African civilisation which should inspire and characterise their reflection on the concept of human and peoples' rights'; the goal of eliminating 'colonialism, neo-colonialism, apartheid, Zionism and to dismantle aggressive foreign military bases and all forms of discrimination, particularly those based on race, ethnic group, colour, sex, language, religion or political opinions', 'adherence to the principles of human and peoples' rights and freedoms contained in the declarations, conventions and other instrument adopted by the

Organization of African Unity, the Movement of Non-Aligned Countries and the United Nations.'[310]

Two years later, the second World Conference against Racism, while confirming the objectives the first conference had set five years earlier, also urged states to take measures to fight those ideologies (apartheid, Nazism, Fascism) founded on intolerance, ethnic hatred, denial of fundamental rights; the conference also underlined the double discrimination suffered by women, and encouraged a rapid analysis of the rights of refugees, immigrants and emigrating workers; amongst its main achievements was the creation of a working group for indigenous populations which, after 22 years of discussions and negotiations, led to the Universal Declaration of the Rights of Indigenous Peoples, partially anticipated in 1989 by the Covenant on Indigenous and Tribal Peoples approved by the ILO (International Labour Organization).

In November 1989 the Convention for the Rights of the Child was adopted. It entered into force ten months later (the shortest period to pass between the adoption of a human rights document and the ratifications necessary for its entry into force) after having been ratified by the highest number of states ever (in December 2004 only Somalia and the United States had not signed it; they still have not done so). A few days earlier the Berlin Wall had fallen and the Communist states were entering the phase of their collapse, concluded in 1991 with the disintegration of the USSR. Such a sudden change in international politics had not taken place since the end of colonialism; the path was paved for the recognition of civil and political rights for millions of people in Central-Eastern Europe, previously deprived of them by one-party regimes. When remembering the sacrifices made to obtain this freedom, Havel stated:

> We must also bear in mind that other nations have paid even more dearly for their present freedom, and that indirectly they have also paid for ours. The rivers of blood that have flowed in Hungary, Poland, Germany and recently in such a horrific manner in Romania, as well as the sea of blood shed by the nations of the Soviet Union, must not be forgotten. First of all because all human suffering concerns every other human being. But more than this, they must also not be forgotten because it is these great sacrifices that form the tragic background of today's freedom or the gradual emancipation of the nations of the Soviet Bloc, and thus the background of our own newfound freedom.[311]

7. *New hopes and new horror*

On 25 June 1993 the World Conference on Human Rights organised by the United Nations ended with the approval of a Declaration and a Programme of Action. As stated by the Secretary General of the organisation, Boutros Boutros-Ghali, the general impression was that the conference had launched a 'new vision for a global action for human rights in the next century'. While trying to summarise the significance and results of the conference, he also stated that he was:

> tempted to say that human rights, by their very nature, do away with the distinction traditionally drawn between the internal order and the international order. Human rights give rise to a new legal permeability. They should thus not be considered either from the viewpoint of absolute sovereignty or from the viewpoint of political intervention. On the contrary, it must be understood that human rights call for cooperation and coordination between States and international organisations. [312]

In the name of article 55 of the Charter, of resolution 43/131 adopted by the General Assembly of the UN in 1988 and of the many democratisation missions of the previous years, Boutros-Ghali spoke of the imperatives of universality, guarantees and democratisation. Referring to chapter VII of the UN Charter he then asked to proceed with the creation a permanent international criminal tribunal, and a special tribunal for the violations of international humanitarian law committed in former Yugoslavia since 1991.

The Vienna conference, with its 7,000 participants, representing 171 states and approximately 800 NGOs, was an eloquent testimony of the fact that, 25 years after the first conference on human rights (in Teheran) and 45 after the Universal Declaration, the culture of human rights was once more expanding and spreading to ever larger zones of the globe. The attention given to the rights of women, children and indigenous populations (as well as the request to institute a high commissioner for human rights, thus strengthening the Geneva Centre) was accompanied by the NGO Forum. This institution adopted the slogan 'All rights for everyone' and proceeded to discuss – in an extremely open, often tense and complex, fashion – the main unresolved problems of this new phase for human rights.

Of course the traditional hypocrisy which impeded the analysis of single violations by single countries was still present, and forced the conference to remain at a more general level. The Italian Minister of Justice, Giovanni Conso, stated that national sovereignty, a central element for international relationships, was not to be considered an obstacle to state initiative when faced with events such as genocide or institutionalised racism. Despite these significant limitations many discussions took place, leading to a common conclusion which reaffirmed that 'human rights were universal and indivisible and could not be the exclusive property of any one culture, region or political system'.[313]

The rights to development, to a healthy environment for present and future generations, to the use of technology, to the elimination of poverty, to security against terrorism, to asylum and assistance for refugees: all these rights were accompanied in the final resolution by the rights of women and minorities, by the rejection of unilateral actions by states; and above all by descriptions of the new and increasingly coordinated role of the United Nations. Particular emphasis was placed on the questions of racism, racial discrimination, xenophobia and other forms of intolerance. The conference also rejected practices involving torture and 'enforced disappearances'. Ultimately all states were invited to make public the progress made in the field of human rights, on the occasion of the 50th anniversary of the Universal Declaration.

A controversial theme for the Vienna Conference (and one destined to remain unresolved during the following years) was that of the actual universality of the Declaration, as well as its markedly Western character. A demonstration of the constant and recurring influence of international politics, even on issues that by then appeared to be accepted and incontestable, was the request by some states – China, Singapore, Malaysia, Thailand, Indonesia – to specify the primacy of regional and national particularities (and thus of the principle of sovereignty), rather than international law, with regard to universal characters. The fact that Syria and Cuba immediately joined this 'anti-Western' controversy underlined the fact that this was an attempt to earn freedom – in the name of historical and cultural particularities – from the obligation to respect international mechanisms on rights (ones that had furthermore been ratified by those very same states).

Yet it cannot be denied that this controversy, which placed the problem of 'Asian values' under the international spotlight, did bring to light two of the deepest contradictions and dilemmas of the entire history of human rights: the strong Western imprint of its theoretical foundations and the historically determined character of the evolution of rights in every part of the world, including the West. This theme, which would soon be enriched by many interesting historical and theoretical studies, had been raised in 1993, just a few weeks before the meetings in Vienna, during the

Bangkok conference. In a certainly instrumental and provocative fashion, the Singaporean Prime Minister Lee Kuan Yew had proposed to identify within traditional Confucian ethics the 'Asian values' to be considered as alternatives to certain Western civil and political rights (furthermore, he completely omitted different Asian ethics, such as Buddhism or Islam).

The concluding Declaration of the Bangkok Conference reaffirmed a commitment to respect the principles of the UN Charter and of the 1948 Universal Declaration, yet also emphasised the respect of national sovereignty and the principle of non-interference in other states' internal affairs; it underlined the universality of rights, yet also the need to consider each context and historical dynamic; it recognised the key role of states in the promotion and protection of the human rights of their citizens, and the need for the identification of appropriate structures, procedures and mechanisms with regard to this objective. Rather than choosing to close the question of non-Western values, the Bangkok meetings attempted to include it in the transformation of international relations following the downfall of Communism and many other authoritarian regimes world-wide; while it avoided the opposition of 'Asian values' to the milestones of current human rights, it also theorised a new and more appropriate development for non-Western countries.

The following historical events were however far more rapid than expected by worldwide diplomacies, still intent on trying to re-elaborate such relevant yet unshared themes. The questions of war and genocide, which had given rise to the visions of the Declaration, suddenly returned to the centre of international attention, at the moment when the culture of human rights was beginning to seem a widespread (although not homogeneously interpreted) international common denominator.

In January 1991 the American President George Bush ordered the bombing of Iraq, following its invasion of Kuwait six months earlier. The coalition led by the United States (formed under the protection of the UN) forced the Iraqi army to retreat from Kuwait after five weeks of bombings. Yet it also allowed the retreating army of Saddam Hussein to reorganise and take its revenge through a bloody repression of ethnic and religious minorities (the Kurds and Shiites) who had hoped to establish a democracy in the country.

Between 1992 and 1995 the United Nations sent a series of expeditions to Somalia – the largest one consisted of 20,000 American soldiers – to guarantee the distribution of humanitarian aid to the population, as the country was reduced to complete chaos by a civil war between political factions and tribes. The killings of Pakistani and American soldiers and the impossibility of maintaining any form of order led to the disastrous failure of this international humanitarian intervention. Yet what happened in Rwanda in April-May 1994 was even more horrific when the 'machete genocide' killed 600,000 people (Tutsis and moderate Hutus) in just six weeks, the highest murder rate of all twentieth century massacres. On 21 April, while the massacre was taking place, the Security Council of the UN unanimously voted to pull out the 2,500 UNAMIR men, leaving Canadian general Roméo Dallaire to command only 270 men.

> This book – wrote Dallaire, ten years after the genocide, when presenting his autobiographic volume *Shake Hands with the Devil* – is a cri de coeur for the slaughtered thousands, a tribute to the souls hacked apart by machetes because of their supposed difference from those who sought to hang on to power... This book is the account of a few humans who were entrusted with the role of helping others taste the fruits of peace. Instead, we watched as the devil took control of paradise on earth and fed on the blood of the people we were supposed to protect.[314]

March 1999 marked the failure of pressures by the international community on Serbia to restore the autonomy of Kosovo and on Kosovo nationalists within the UCK to abandon their guerrilla tactics and return to the negotiating table. Following the large-scale repressive actions of the Serb army, which were all too similar to previous ethnic cleansing methods and mechanisms, the United States decided on military intervention and began bombarding Belgrade and the rest of Serbia. The NATO operation was concluded on 9 June, when Milošević and the Serb parliament accepted an agreement that was practically identical to the one they had refused a few months earlier at the Rambouillet conference.

The war killed hundreds of people, caused 40 billion dollars' worth of damage and cost NATO seven billion dollars, as well as turning almost a million people into refugees fleeing towards Macedonia, Albania and Montenegro. As one human rights defender, not prejudicially hostile to military interventions in extreme situations of danger for civilian populations, wrote:

> The Allied powers claimed they began the war for the protection of human rights. In truth, they were dragged to war by an oppressed ethnic minority whose own army also committed violations of human rights. Once led to war, the West proved incapable of stopping the tide of violations against human rights cut loose as a form of response to the intervention.[315]

At the end of 1994, for the first time since the Nuremberg and Tokyo trials, an international court proceeded to judge individuals deemed responsible for war crimes and crimes against humanity. On 14 December the International Criminal Tribunal for the Former Yugoslavia accused Dusko Tadić and Goran Borovnica. The former, arrested in Munich in February 1994, was accused of twelve counts of crimes against humanity, twelve serious breaches of the 1949 Geneva Conventions and ten counts of war crimes. On 7 May 1997 the tribunal declared he was guilty, on the basis of individual criminal responsibilities, of crimes against humanity and violations of the laws of war, and sentenced him to 20 years in prison. Before the start of the trial, writer Juan Goytisolo had told the tale of a young woman who had survived the violence committed by the Serb 'White Eagles' in Visegrad in May 1992. The reportage had been commissioned by 'El País' and included the following passage:

> Some girls tried to kill themselves by jumping from the window where the 'White Eagles' held them in order to rape them. My neighbour and her seventeen year old daughter were raped, their throats were slit and their corpses were thrown into the river. One girl escaped from a house which had been soaked with petrol and set on fire, with no skin, no hair, burnt, a living scar, a ghost, a skeleton. She was saved and is now hospitalised in Ljubljana. 'I live, she said, to testify.'[316]

It took several years of information, analysis and pressure activities by feminist and human rights organisations before in 2001 the decision by the criminal tribunal of The Hague (concerning the events in former Yugoslavia) recognised rape and sexual slavery as crimes against humanity. This position was confirmed by the Security Council of the United Nations on 19 June 2008: resolution 1820 (Women and Peace and Security) established that 'rape and other forms of sexual violence may represent a war crime, a crime against humanity or an element of genocide'.[317]

The criminal tribunal for crimes committed in Rwanda (International Criminal Tribunal for Rwanda, ICTR), based in Arusha, was created in November 1994. In 1997 it began its first trial against Jean-Paul Akayesu, the mayor of the town of Taba, accused of genocide and crimes against humanity. He was sentenced to life imprisonment in October 1998.

During that same year, on 17 July, after a five-week long diplomatic conference, the International Criminal Court Statute – or Rome Statute – was approved with 120 votes in favour, seven against (China, Iraq, Israel, Libya, Qatar, United States, Yemen) and 21 abstentions. The document established a permanent international court to judge individuals responsible for international crimes, genocide, war crimes and crimes against humanity.

The last decade of the twentieth century, which began with a new war and was characterised by civil wars, ethnic cleansing and even genocide, would have appeared to end in hope: represented by this new international commitment (although the hostility between the two greatest world powers certainly reduced its significance). Human rights were once again in the public eye.

One phenomenon above all others has been a major contributing factor to the growing political impact of human rights on the conduct of international relations and the behaviour of governments: the ever more pervasive and readily observable conviction of human beings around the world that they are entitled to the enjoyment of human rights. This phenomenon, I would argue, has taken on almost universal proportions and is attributable to several factors. First is the massive corpus of human rights legislation that the United Nations, its specialised agencies, and various regional organisations have promulgated and publicised over the years. Of equal impact is the growing importance the international community has come to attach to human rights as a priority item on the agendas of international diplomatic conferences and in bilateral and multilateral relations.[318]

Chapter Seven
Human Rights in the XXI Century: Problems and Contradictions

1. *Democratisation and globalisation*

During the last two decades of the twentieth century the growth of democratic countries, or at least of those regimes where crucial democratic elements (elections, political parties, freedom of press) were introduced or reinstated after dictatorships, was strongly related to the question of human rights. The struggle against military dictatorships in Latin America (for example the courageous and influential actions of the Plaza de Mayo mothers and grandmothers in Argentina); the activities and dissent of groups in civil society in Eastern Europe and in the Soviet Union (such as Solidarność in Poland); the battle led by Nelson Mandela from his prison cell to accelerate the end of the apartheid regime in South Africa: all such movements shared a strong relationship with human rights, with those principles recognised in Helsinki in 1975 and constantly reaffirmed by the United Nations during the eighties.

The legacy of the connection between democracy and human rights has been strong, if not always coherent, ever since the nineteenth century, when it found its most significant juridical expression in the formulation of constitutions: the ideal place for rights to be elevated to fundamental and founding principles for rooted and long-lasting democratic states. The values of the Declarations which gave birth to the eighteenth century revolutions were soon incorporated into the American and French constitutions, and provided indications of a possible model for the rest of the world. Naturally constitutions were not always a guarantee of respect for the principles they contained, and the Terror following the French Revolution was a perennial warning in this sense. However, history has also seen dictatorships and totalitarian regimes formulate constitutions based on rights similar to the more advanced democracies – this was the case of the constitution of the USSR which was approved in 1936, shortly before the beginning of the Great Terror – only to ignore such principles altogether: yet another form of deception towards their citizens.

The wave of democratisations of the late twentieth century was generally accompanied by the approval of constitutions – many of which shared a 'rigid' structure – which featured, in their initial articles, a catalogue of fundamental rights largely based on the 1948 Universal Declaration and on successive documents from the United Nations. In that same period, within historical democratic systems, many documents regarding human rights were codified and gained constitutional value: 'This is what happened in many systems based on a British matrix, such as Israel or New Zealand, and ultimately even in Britain itself, with the 1998 Human Rights Act of 1998, as well as in many states which, when 'upgrading' their old constitutions, decided to insert a catalogue of rights (for example in Finland in 1995 and Switzerland in 1999)'.[319] For many scholars the British case is the clearest example of how deeply the culture of human rights has penetrated: to the point of becoming a constitutional declaration that counterbalances the traditional parliamentary power over judiciary power. Having been approved after analogous measures were adopted in the Netherlands and in Canada (two countries where public opinion is particularly active with regards to human rights), the British Human Rights Act:

> unquestionably has the potential for being one of the most fundamental constitutional enactments since the Bill of Rights over 300 years ago. While so much constitutional change in the United Kingdom has been achieved without resort to legislation, this is a deliberate part of a programme of constitutional change by legislation. The Convention, once incorporated, will place respect for human rights at the centre of any legal dispute.[320]

This – often late – insertion of human rights into constitutions offered those countries which adopted it the possibility not only to insert the most classic civil, political, economic and social rights within the new documents, but to also consider 'third' and 'fourth' generation rights: those concerning cultural rights, development, the environment, peace, biotechnologies, privacy and the rights of future generations. Often the subject of rights, consistent within the various Conventions from the late twentieth century, was no longer considered as the rights of an abstract individual, but of a person characterised by his/her environment, 'individualised' in order to underline how he/she is a carrier of rights (as woman, child, immigrant worker, elderly, disabled or indigenous person).

> The consequences of this process led to complex problems, such as the relationship with juridical traditions or local cultures, or the need for the coexistence of rights which may contradict each other and require some adapting. This was particularly evident in the relationship between individual rights and collective rights (such as those of religious and cultural communities), which require continuous modifications. Not to mention that an indiscriminate proclamation of rights often clashes with a need to limit them in the name of public interest, or with the impossibility of actually guaranteeing their respect due to the lack of financial means: thus the risk of empty constitutional proclamations is a serious one, that could lead to the loss of faith in constitutional declarations which often exist only in a theoretical form.[321]

The insertion of lists of human rights in new or upgraded constitutions reinforced the duty of the judiciary power to protect and guarantee those rights against violations, both from private subjects and (more frequently) from organs of the state or from political and administrative subjects. What is generally lacking in these constitutions, and would be the duty of the state, is a reinforcement of preventive measures (educative, cultural or of any other kind); in reality this translates into a purely compensation-based – or, even worse, denunciation-based – formula when facing violations of recognised and sanctioned rights. Doubts regarding the insertion of rights into constitutions are even stronger when we question the relationship between the current globalisation process and human rights. Whether it began, as an innovative and radical transformation, in the seventies or in the nineties (scholars disagree on this point), globalisation is now an undeniable phenomenon, although different opinions, interpretations, justifications or contradictions may be associated with it by individuals and groups.

Globalisation, as has often been claimed, is a system of transnational fluxes of people, goods, investments and information, yet also of ideas and authority; such fluxes are more intense and rapid than in the past, thanks to the information and digital revolution which took place at the end of the second millennium. This growing interrelation between states, markets, peoples and persons was characterised by strong economic (both financial and productive) and technological aspects, and accelerated its political and international expansion after the downfall of Communism and the end of the Cold War. Such an acceleration certainly led to a more rapid gaining of consciousness regarding the transformations underway.

'A globalised world is simultaneously more *connected, cosmopolitan, commercialised* and influenced by *communication. Connection* is a functional parameter of globalisation, involving growing numbers and volumes and an increase of transnational movement of bodies, businesses, information and norms.'[322] Human rights are mostly involved in these movements, whether we are speaking of transnational migrations, global market effects, the international use of information or super-national norms identified to address the *governance* problems of this new historical era.

If we recognise that globalisation is also, necessarily, an era of migrations, the problem of immigrants and their rights (which occupies an entire Convention[323]) becomes a structural one. Indeed this issue appears particularly complex when facing the theme of citizenship. Among the by-products of globalisation is the increase of residents in foreign countries who are not recognised as citizens. This condition – which in Italy has been summarised by politicians and by the media with the incorrect and deeply pejorative term 'clandestine' – may often be the cause of conflicts between state policies and international human rights standards, as established by the 1948 Universal Declaration and by successive acts of the United Nations. In many countries, for example, non-citizens have no right to assistance, instruction, work, security in the workplace, protection for their family, not to mention the right to a dignified life in terms of housing, hygiene, and nutrition. These are all examples in which:

> universal personhood continues to be subordinated to citizenship as a basis for rights. [...] These oppositions between citizens and aliens pose obstacles for migrants' claims to rights based on universal personhood, even within a state that formally supports international human rights norms. [...] This contrast rests in part on liberal notions of contract, consent, and propriety, but also on racial or neocolonial ideologies that underline the continuing division between the First and the Third Worlds. Together, these philosophical strains produce a discursive distinction between citizens and alien workers as mutually exclusive categories and as legally or legitimately unequal in their entitlement to rights.[324]

2. *War and humanitarian interventions*

A strong and widespread pacifist movement, somewhat similar to the one contesting the Vietnam War during the sixties, arose in the twenty-first century, over the armed interventions in Afghanistan and Iraq. Yet during the first years of the millennium only a few hundred people actually mobilised over the terrible violations of human rights taking place in many parts of the globe (in Congo and Darfur, in Chechnya and Tibet, in Zimbabwe and in Burma, just to name a few). And this was true even when attempts were made – as in London, for Darfur – to organise public demonstrations.

The diffusion of the culture of human rights and the constant space given by the media to the violations of rights proved insufficient to make their defence automatic or to provide sufficient grounds for mobilisation. Strong political motivation, such as the active role of the United States or of other Western powers as agents responsible for acts of war and violence, were still, as in the sixties, the most decisive and significant causes of mobilisation, especially amongst young people.

Probably one reason for focusing the protests against the United States, while the mobilisation in favour of human rights in many other parts of the world was severely underestimated, may be found in the instrumental and political use that had been made of human rights to justify armed intervention, war coalitions and military initiatives. Phrases such as 'humanitarian intervention', 'humanitarian interference', 'exportation of democracy', which have been used increasingly since the First Gulf War, have been instrumentally selected by governments and coalitions alike to justify their decisions, provoking reactions which, in some cases, have become the reason to speak of 'imperialism', and even to label human rights a 'neo-colonial' instrument of the West to reinforce and strengthen its global dominion.[325]

Juridical discussions regarding the lawfulness of war were particularly heated during the Gulf War and the armed intervention in Kosovo, and continued to be just as vigorous regarding the wars in Afghanistan and Iraq, although they did not manage to produce any conclusive results or shared decisions in the ambit of international law. According to chapter VII of the Charter of the United Nations, the Security Council may impose measures to reinstate peace and international security, which range from economic sanctions to international military actions.[326]

In April 2004, the executive director of Human Rights Watch, Kenneth Roth, energetically summarised his refusal to consider the intervention by the Bush administration in Iraq as 'humanitarian', now that the falsity of the previously adopted justification – the existence of weapons of mass destruction – was evident.

We are different from a pacifist organisation that may oppose war in any circumstance. We believe there are moments in which war is necessary. There is a duty, especially when facing genocide or an analogous massacre, to use war to stop it. Human Rights Watch has encouraged military interventions to stop similar massacres in many occasions, the most important probably being the case of Rwanda, to try and stop the genocide which took place ten years ago. We had greater success with our humanitarian intervention in Bosnia, to stop the genocide which climaxed with the massacre of seven thousand Bosnians in Srebrenica. Thus there have been moments in which we have asked the international community to intervene militarily to save some lives. Now I come to the problem if the war in Iraq may be justified as a humanitarian intervention, from the perspective of someone who believes in humanitarian actions as a possible option, and would like to be certain that such an option is efficacious when truly needed. It is very difficult to justify the war in Iraq as a humanitarian intervention. Due to this difficulty and to the enormous unpopularity of the war – all over the world and increasingly also in the United States – I fear that these efforts to justify Iraq as a humanitarian enterprise will damage humanitarian interventions as an institution and that it will be even more difficult, in the future, to demand a military action to potentially save thousands of human lives.[327]

While refusing to consider critical factors based on a disinterest in atrocities far worse than those committed by Saddam Hussein, and on the long-term American involvement in the Iraqi dictator's repressive policies, Roth identified 'the dominant criteria for the case to be in the fact that the population to be saved must be facing a current or imminent massacre. If this is not the case it is very difficult to justify a humanitarian intervention'. Such a situation was lacking in the Iraqi case, as was the respect of international humanitarian law, at the moment of the invasion and during the military operations. Equally absent was a multilateral effort legitimised by a majority of states, even if not by the Security Council. After recalling the complex and criticised, yet effective, interventions in Liberia, Eastern Congo, the Ivory Coast and Sierra Leone, the director of Human Rights Watch concluded by expressing his concern that 'the war in Iraq risks undermining the entire project of humanitarianism if we don't seriously recognise that, although humanitarianism is now quoted to justify the war in Iraq, this justification does not stand up to a critical investigation of this case'.[328]

There is a widespread consensus, among international organisations and NGO officials – and scholars – over the fact that, in clearly identified and exceptional circumstances, humanitarian interventions are the only solution to tragic situations; or that, in order to be successful, humanitarian aid must be accompanied, in certain contexts, by a simultaneous military presence. The theories and practice of 'peacekeeping' and 'peace enforcement' have increased the range of interventionist options, often merging with purely humanitarian actions.

The notion of an humanitarian emergency is substantially ambiguous. The same is also true for the terms 'humanitarian disaster' or 'humanitarian crisis'. The use of the adjective 'humanitarian' tends to confuse the cause of the phenomenon with its consequences and may even give the false impression that the answer to the (humanitarian) consequences may contribute to solve the causes (which have a completely different nature). This is particularly true for so-called complex humanitarian emergencies, as obviously in such cases the causes of the crisis are political or military or the result of massive violations of human rights and are certainly not humanitarian.[329]

A comparative study by the Tufts University Feinstein International Center underlined the increasing spread of the idea, within countries that are subjects of humanitarian actions, that sometimes the values of such actions are only formally universal, while in truth they are in conflict with the needs and expectations of the civilian populations of such countries. Furthermore the study revealed the growing danger to the priorities of humanitarian interventions and the risk that human rights might be sub-jugated to more directly political objectives. A greater attention to the needs of and results for those who receive aid, rather than to the consistency or compromises of the provider of aid, would help avoid this risk, as stated by this African proverb:

"Until the lions have their historians, history will always be written by the hunters", or so says the African proverb. Perhaps the time has come to give the lions, the gazelles and even the suffering grass a stake in the debate. In fact, testing the universality of the humani-tarian impulse (and its human rights cousin) at the grassroots level, as we have done in our case studies, has helped broaden our under-standing of contextual issues and how communities look at the work performed by outsiders. Much more work needs to be done in this arena. Caring for war wounded, protecting children and civilians

in war situations, and aspiring for justice and accountability are obligations recognised, in their own ways, in all cultures. This humanitarian substratum is undoubtedly universal. It is the behaviour of leaders and warlords that is problematic, not the dictates of cultures and religions.[330]

One result of the diffusion of a culture of human rights may be observed in the over-emphasising of ethically universal considerations against the more prosaic and contingent character of humanitarian interventions: this process, testified and guaranteed by the development of international humanitarian law has often led to a compromise between humanitarian principles and the political-military logics of conflicts. The mixing of the fields of human rights and humanitarian interventions – which were separated for many centuries – is the result of many factors: such as globalisation, alterations in the means of conflicts, the presence of NGOs, interventions by the United Nations and international organisations. If the essence of humanitarian principles was for a long time considered to be 'non-interference' – the neutrality and impartiality exemplified by the Red Cross – now things are very different: given that 'as belligerents in recent wars have increasingly chosen to ignore humanitarian principles, humanitarians have been forced to rethink the principles of humanitarian action, in effect to challenge this imposition of non-interference'.[331] The refusal by armed forces to recognise the 'limits of war' led to a growing number of humanitarian organisations abandoning the field and withdrawing their operators. Humanitarian agencies are now forced to make choices, or face problems that are in truth political ones (as had been understood by Médecins Sans Frontières since its inception). Yet often they do not possess the parameters (apart from the 'moral' ones, shared by the association) to establish which policy should be adopted or why. The paradox is that often 'the idea of principles of humanitarian action is shifting from something that was intended to regulate agencies, and was thus imposed by the belligerents, to something agencies are trying to use to regulate the belligerents'.[332]

While human rights concern subjects who desire to, or can, actively demand something they feel unfairly deprived of (liberty, justice, dignity, equality), humanitarian actions address passive victims who only desire to be helped and protected. 'Human rights imply a reciprocal relationship between rights and duties. If one has a right, others have the duty to not abuse it and to act in order for it to be considered as such. Donators have no duties. In relationships with a donator, attention is mono-directional and the beneficiary cannot demand it. A donator acts on the basis of a moral impulse, rather than a juridical obligation'.[333] History (especially recently) has proved that this division is not always clear. It was not by accident, indeed, that a juridical context was always sought with regard to humanitarian actions: the objective was to overcome the phase of arbitrary generosity based on a moral or religious, political or ideological impulse, and to instead codify the (legal, although based on a moral cause) duty to provide aid in certain situations.

The variety of situations and contexts of conflicts requiring humanitarian interventions is in itself already a negative response to attempts to identify a single humanitarian model, to be applied in all circumstances. Yet it is important to note that:

> trying to promote the respect of principles is a different policy from choosing a side in a war, yet it is anyhow a policy and as such re- quires political analysis and, above all, political calculations. This is a very different way of thinking than that of most humanitarians, who often feel far more at ease in the absolute and uncompromised morality of their tradition rather than in the utilitarian morality of politics involving the constitution of alliances, agreements and moral compromising, as well as the acceptance of small progress when possible.[334]

3. *Terrorism and safety*

The attack against the New York Twin Towers which occurred on 11 September 2001 seemed to interrupt, or deeply deviate from, reflections on human rights that had developed during the late twentieth century. And it was not simply the logic behind the response of the Bush administration – the preparation of the intervention in Afghanistan and later the 'unilateral' choice to invade Iraq – that led to a redirection of debates regarding war. The very relationships between security and liberty, norms to protect democracy and norms to protect citizens were placed in doubt: this led to a choice of a direction which soon created chain reactions all over the world.

The novelty and unpredictability of the terrorist action – in terms of intensity, objective, means and goals – seemed suddenly to alter the international context inhabited by states and diplomacies, international organisations and non-governmental associations; at the same time the response chosen by the United States reinforced the conviction that a 'clash of civilisations' was not just an extreme academic theory to be used by fundamentalist ideologies: it was a reality that required immediate solutions.

Terrorism menaces society in many ways. There is an evident danger for human life and personal security. Another danger hides within the way society reacts to terrorism. The abominable attacks on the 11 September in the USA and on the 7 July in the United Kingdom have created an atmosphere of fear, in which many people are prepared to put up with severe measures proposed by their governments, even when such measures are incompatible with the standards of international law. However, the battle against terrorism can not be won by abandoning the law and international standards regarding human rights. This tendency will endanger the fundamental values of our democratic society, already menaced by terrorism itself. [335]

The problem of the protection of democracy, or of democracy defending itself, has always been analysed according to three substantial possibilities: a majority menacing the constitution and the guarantees it contains; menaces from anti-democratic minorities; menaces coming from violent and subversive minorities. The models to respond to such dangers have generally been identified in a 'weak' form, where the balance between powers is maintained, and in a 'combative' form, where extraordinary powers may be used. In the background is Karl Popper's reflection on the 'paradox of tolerance':

I do not imply, for example, that manifestations of intolerant ideas should always be suppressed; as long as we can contrast them with rational arguments and keep them under the control of the public opinion, suppression would certainly be less wise than decisions. Yet we must proclaim the right to suppress them, if necessary even with force. […] Thus, in the name of tolerance, we should proclaim the right to not tolerate the intolerant. Thus we should proclaim that any movement preaching intolerance is against the law and we should envision as crimes any incitation to intolerance and persecution, in the same way we consider any incitation to murder, to kidnapping or to reinstate the trading of slaves to be a crime. [336]

Probably the most recent international measure concerning terrorism is the European Council Convention on the Prevention of Terrorism, formulated in Warsaw in May 2005 and officialised in 2007.[337] In article 5 the Convention allows the suppression of 'crimes of public incitement to terrorism'.

The legal, constitutional and political difficulties regarding norms to be adopted against terrorism have generally been associated with the possibility of suspending certain fundamental rights. Although the former secretary of the United Nations Kofi Annan declared that 'upholding human rights is not at odds with battling terrorism: on the contrary, the moral vision of human rights – the deep respect for the dignity of each person – is among our most powerful weapons against it',[338] it is equally true that – especially in the United States and partly also in Britain – the legislations of the major democracies have significantly concerned human rights when applying limitations in reaction to the terroristic aggressions of Al Qaeda.

If, in the case of Britain, it has often been underlined that the 2000 Terrorism Act and above all the 2005 Prevention of Terrorism Act implied limitations to fundamental rights established by the 1998 Human Rights Act, judgements regarding the new American norms – the USA Patriot Act of 2001 and the Patriot Act Improvement and Reauthorization of 2005 – were even more drastic: 'The seriousness of the threats those systems were exposed to led to choices which, by denying the qualitative premises that are at the foundation of Western democratic systems, have probably signified their most terrible loss, almost the paradoxical recognition of the impossibility to defend liberty while respecting liberty'.[339]

Juridical, political and sociological studies have been addressing the definition of terrorism for many decades, often without producing coherent or shared results. In self-explicatory terms, 'in academic environments it is widely accepted that terrorism consists of international acts of violence against civilians, for the purpose of spreading fear amongst the population for political, religious or ideological goals'.[340] We must not forget that terrorism has its own articulated and complex history within the twentieth century (and earlier), ranging from individual anarchic attacks against symbols of power to acts committed during the Second World War by armed civilian groups against occupying powers, from actions within the anti-colonial struggles of the fifties to the wave of assaults, kidnappings and homicides which characterised political struggles in certain European and Latin American countries, especially during the seventies; up to the experiences of the last two decades, which present new modalities in terms of objectives, organisation, types of violence, and which have culminated in international fundamentalist terrorism (of which the actions of Al Qaeda are the most notorious result). It is a phenomenon, as stated by the most authoritative Italian expert on the subject, destined to continue: 'the near and far future will be filled by reappearances of terrorism, we cannot predict which episodes will characterise it, yet it is reasonably certain that they will take place'.[341]

It was the historical and evolutional nature of the transformation and spread of terrorism that modified not only the juridical and political responses to the phenomenon, but also the types of judgement, justifications and attitudes held by public opinion, by governments, by judiciary powers and by international organisations with regard to this argument. It is now known that 'even within a national liberation movement, intentional violence against civilians by members of that movement or on their account would still be an act of terrorism'[342] and as such would be condemned not only on a judiciary level, but also in the sphere of politics, morality and human rights. To underline this change of attitude, which began in the seventies and matured in the eighties, the South African Commission for Truth and Reconciliation decided to show, within its final report, that even terrorist actions committed for just reasons – the struggle to end apartheid – and while fighting 'on the right side' were to be considered serious violations of human rights when they involved civilians in intentional and indiscriminate acts of violence.

If war is now considered a possible response to terrorism – in the rhetoric and senseless form of the 'war against terrorism', led above all by the United States – then it is even more evident that the problem of the definition is instrumental to a predefined political action, rather than to the identification of the actual new and original character of the threat.

> Terrorism is not a public subject (although certain organisations aim to be considered as such) against whom it is logically and materially possible to declare war; and indeed the two military operations unleashed by the American government under the absurd emblem of the 'war on terror' have both been against states and political regimes, Taliban Afghanistan and Saddam's Iraq, accused, with or without foundation, of complicity with terror organisations (yet in the Iraqi case such foundations were completely non-existent). Furthermore, terrorism cannot be 'defeated' in the same way we say a state can be defeated or a regime can be destroyed, nor is the 'defeat' of terrorism necessarily a consequence of the defeat of a state or of a regime.[343]

The difference between war and terrorism, and between conventional wars and terrorist threats,

> is becoming more apparent as time passes. Conventional wars are generally of limited duration. One side eventually wins, victory is declared, and the emergency is over. With the end of the emergency comes a restoration of suspended rights. The threat of terrorism is

never-ending. The emergency thus becomes a permanent state, and the rights that were suspended remain suspended indefinitely.

Such a consequence should not be underestimated, even if, in the American case:

> the only people whose rights have been abridged have been aliens, visitors, foreigners captured in other countries, and a handful of Americans suspected of complicity with terrorism. Virtually all of these people are Muslims and Arabs. The administration's approach has been to deny 'them' their rights in order to protect 'us'. This 'them-us' dichotomy has proved popular with the general public and has generated little broad-based opposition to the emergency measures.[344]

The clear difference between an armed conflict and other situations is what has always determined if a humanitarian intervention is necessary, rather than the mere observance of international obligations for states concerning human rights. The rhetoric of the 'war on terror', analogous to the 'war on crime' and the 'war on drugs', has often made the relative juridical reference to be observed somewhat ambiguous. If it truly were a war it would be possible to kill enemies rather than arrest them, or to imprison them until the end of the conflict. However, it is evident that 'from a juridical perspective even if there were an armed conflict between the United States and Al Qaeda, there could anyway be no such thing as a "war against terrorism". This improper term should be avoided'.[345] It is certainly significant that the Supreme Court of the United States established, in 2004, in the 'Padilla' case, that all prisoners of American military prisons must be judged by a federal tribunal and cannot be taken away from their appointed judge, and in the 'Hamdi' case that 'the state of war is not a blank cheque for the president when we are dealing with citizens' rights'.[346]

If the obligations of a state – which concern human rights – include the security of its citizens, in the case of terrorist attacks the solution is the adoption of measures to protect those who could be victims of such attacks: 'in the choice of its measures the state must consider as its obligation the respect of the rights of those who might suffer because of such measures, especially those of innocent people not involved in terrorism'.[347] Alongside this main duty, however, there is also the guarantee – for all people, with no distinctions – concerning those rights which involve an absolute protection, which cannot be limited even by emergencies such as an armed conflict.

The main right which enjoys this 'absolute' status is the prohibition of torture. According to international law, torture (defined by the Convention against Torture as the cause of violent pain or physical or mental suffering, perpetrated by authorities of a state for such objectives as the obtainment of information or the punishment of individuals) is prohibited in all circumstances. No exceptional circumstance can be invoked to justify torture, not even war or public emergencies.[348]

Besides torture, the right to life, freedom and to a fair trial are those that are usually considered inalienable, alongside the prohibition of slavery, deportation and racial discrimination. And precisely this 'category of cogent (or "imperative") norms has earned a particular importance in the field of the protection of human rights, giving birth to the progressive explanation of an "international" concept of "fundamental rights" based on the formal hierarchic superiority of the normative sources'.[349] As for all other rights, limitations must however follow a clarification of the 'just objective', with a 'legal' proclamation that demonstrates their 'necessity' and 'proportionality' and allows for a non-discriminatory procedure that is in conformity with justice, and thus not arbitrary or taken away from natural judges. Many publications have analysed the extent of violations of such elements by the United States during the 'war on terror': the very names of Guantanamo or Abu Ghraib have become synonyms – embarrassing ones for a homeland of human rights such as the United States – of torture and violations of fundamental rights.

The justification that international norms on human rights impeded the necessary efficacy and speed of actions against terrorism has been widely dismissed over the course of the years, and no verifications have been capable of upholding what have revealed themselves to be political objectives and ideological justifications for the states which decided to limit human rights in order to better fight terrorism. A demonstration of how it is possible to succeed 'in the difficult task of finding a balance between the security of the community and the protection of individual rights'[350] is the case of Canada. The measures taken by the Bill C-36, Anti-Terrorism Act in 2001 and by the Bill C-7, Public Safety Act 2002 were examined in an 'extremely extensive and attended public debate', after which the 'government accepted many of the criticisms, and modified the most controversial dispositions of the originally proposed law'.[351] Although the first decree was essentially symbolic and political, given its substantial practical inefficacy, in the second there was an attempt to harmonise the limitations that it introduced, by safeguarding the relative principles in every situation that did not involve terrorism. In some cases the Supreme Court established that 'the necessity to protect the security of the state cannot involve the expulsion of a foreign citizen, accused of terrorism, to a country where he/she risks being tortured', thus demonstrating 'the commitment of the court to seek a balance between the needs of security and the defence of the principles of law'.[352]

4. *When should genocide be stopped?*

The international community has been trying, for some years, to find a solution to the crimes and violations committed in Darfur, by adjusting the measures to be adopted to the seriousness of the violence and to the danger that still exists for the civilian population.

The almost unanimous recognition that the situation in Darfur was the worst humanitarian crisis of the past years was not a sufficient reason for the constitution of an adequate international intervention: not only on a political-diplomatic level, as regarding 'peacekeeping' or other necessities, but, for a long time, even within the strictly humanitarian sphere.

The massacres of civilians in the country began in 2003 and progressively increased in quantity; soon the number of victims reached a level that – also considering the systems of the massacre – led many observers to define the situation as a demographic catastrophe, a humanitarian disaster and ultimately genocide. In just over a year one third of the population of Darfur, two million people, was forced to flee towards the fields in Chad or to other parts of Sudan. While the World Health Organization and the International Committee of the Red Cross were launching alarmed warnings regarding the number of victims – and projections regarding future ones – a widespread nominalistic *querelle* began: was the Darfur situation to be considered genocide or not?

A tragedy within the tragedy consisted in the fact that, in the case of Darfur, debates did not focus – as would have been preferable – on how to interrupt a continuous and unstoppable mass violence against disarmed civilians, and instead centred on whether or not to use the term genocide for that particular situation. The United States was amongst the first to move in this direction, after a year of massacres, and precisely when the analysis of the Rwandese genocide from ten years earlier reminded the world that the White House had, on that occasion, stopped an intervention by the United Nations that could have avoided or at least diminished the dimensions of the tragedy.[353]

The commission formed by the United Nations – led by Antonio Cassese and including Mohamed Fayek, Hina Jilani, Dumisa Ntsembeza and

Therese Striggner-Scott – began its work on 25 October 2004. At the start of 2005, as the pressure of public opinion seemed to be increasing, the report of the Cassese commission carried the discussion back to the possibility of defining the situation as genocide and underlined the importance of the International Criminal Court opposed by the United States. The main results of the commission can be summarised as follows: regarding the violations of human rights and international law, 'it establishes that the government of Sudan and the Janjaweed are responsible for serious violations and crimes [...] including indiscriminate assaults, murders of civilians, torture, kidnappings, destruction of villages, rape and other forms of sexual violence, forceful moving of peoples [...] against the Furs, Zaghawas, Massalits, Jebels, Arangas and other so-called "African" tribes'. Concerning the accusations of genocide:

> The Commission concluded that the Government of the Sudan has not pursued a policy of genocide [...] The Commission does recognise that in some instances, individuals, including Government officials, may commit acts with genocidal intent. [...] The conclusion that no genocidal policy has been pursued and implemented in Darfur by the Government authorities, directly or through the militias under their control, should not be taken as in any way detracting from the gravity of the crimes perpetrated in that region. Depending upon the circumstances, such international offences as crimes against humanity or large scale war crimes may be no less serious and heinous than genocide.

The consequent recommendations were:

> that the Security Council should refer the situation in Darfur to the International Criminal Court, pursuant to Article 13(b) of the Statute of the Court. [...] The investigation and prosecution of crimes perpetrated in Darfur would have an impact on peace and security. [...] Many of the alleged crimes documented in Darfur have been widespread and systematic. They meet all the thresholds of the Rome Statute for the International Criminal Court. The Sudanese justice system has demonstrated its inability and unwillingness to investigate and prosecute the perpetrators of these crimes.[354]

Since these works by the commission many initiatives have been implemented – the 2007 expedition of a joint mission between the UN and the African Union was renewed in 2008 – yet the international public debate has been incapable of making a strong and efficacious practical decision, nor has it been able to find a shared juridical and political judgement regarding the crimes committed in the African region. Although it is evident that the crime of genocide does not guarantee a more immediate and intense intervention by the international community than any other war crime or crime against humanity, the moral and political weight of the term – the 'G-Word', as it has been dubbed in the debate between scholars – has a power that has often led to nominalistic debates.

In truth many interventions by the two *ad hoc* international criminal tribunals (for former Yugoslavia and Rwanda) attempted to adapt the debate on genocide to the actual – historical and conceptual – context, which has been greatly transformed over the past 15 years. The Arusha tribunal, in answer to the question if what happened in 1994 could truly be considered genocide, stated that 'all this proves that it was indeed a particular group, the Tutsi ethnic group, which was targeted. Clearly, the victims were not chosen as individuals but, indeed, because they belonged to said group; and hence the victims were members of this group selected as such',[355] and that the context of the conflict helped the genocide without allowing the identification of such violent acts as simple acts or crimes of war. What was also particularly important was the underlining of the fact that the Tutsis were not actually an ethnically different group, yet they were perceived as such by the perpetrators of the genocide.[356]

In the trial of Radislav Krstic, brought at The Hague by the tribunal for former Yugoslavia, the Court considered not only the terms of the 1948 Convention, but also the preparatory works that preceded its formulation. After discussing in detail the often fragile and confused boundaries between a policy of genocide and a policy of ethnic cleansing, and analysing the questions of intentionality and of relationships between the physical/biological and the cultural destruction of a group, the Court concluded that, according to international law, what happened in Srebrenica in July 1995 certainly belonged under the definition of genocide, of crimes against humanity and of war crimes.[357]

The innovations of the two tribunals on other aspects relative to crimes against humanity (for example the decisions to consider as such mass rapes and sexual violence committed during ethnic cleansing operations) further demonstrates that the juridical definition regarding these crimes is – and was – strongly bound to the period in which it was formulated. Mass rapes were not even taken into consideration during the Tokyo trials against Japanese soldiers (who had repeatedly committed such crimes) and were not even mentioned with regard to the responsibilities of Allies (and in particular the Soviet and French armies committed many sexual crimes) towards the German and Italian civilian population. This type of crime could indeed never have obtained the juridical recognition by the two *ad hoc* tribunals if many decades of feminist civil battles had not occurred in the meantime, capable of modifying moral common sense and the perception of the basic values of civil coexistence and justice.

How are we to react when facing the eventuality – one which has materialised at least twice during the last 15 years – that massacres and exterminations may have all the characteristics of the 'crime of crimes', genocide? The prospects hardly look encouraging:

> The capacity of industrialised countries to prevent and impede acts of genocide within their own territories should lead them to do something, on an international level, to help those groups which, in developing countries, are instead victims of massacres and destructions. Yet those states, and the entire international community, tend to watch helplessly. With the consequence that the many massacres committed in numerous countries either remain completely unpunished, or are punished by a new government (in the case in which the responsible government has been overturned), or terminate after interventions by another state, certainly not motivated by humanitarian interests.[358]

The presence of bodies of international justice that did not even exist a few years ago should now make it easier to intervene and punish those responsible, once they have been identified and taken to international tribunals. However, within the United Nations and regional and continental organisations that should guarantee a greater possibility of multilateral intervention (even in absence of decisions made on a global level), there is a growing conviction that prevention should be the most important instrument in avoiding future genocides. After all, justice and prevention should be two sides of the same policy aimed at erasing forever the possibility that a government may decide to destroy a group it has selected as its enemy and as an obstacle to its power.

5. *Prevention and protection*

The new century has been characterised by the emergence, as can be read in the 2001 report by the Commission on Intervention and State Sovereignty, of 'the idea that sovereign states have a responsibility to protect their own citizens from avoidable catastrophe – from mass murder and rape, from starvation – but that when they are unwilling or unable to do so, that responsibility must be borne by the broader community of states.'[359]

At the end of 2004, during the debate over the reform of the United Nations, a new document recognised the need for an increased sharing of the responsibility for the protection of citizens, and demanded that it should be 'taken up by the wider international community – with it spanning a continuum involving prevention, response to violence, if necessary, and rebuilding shattered societies'.[360] In March of the following year a report by the General Secretary underlined the need for a collective action to bring together the security of states and that of all humanity.[361] In September the debated and analysed idea of the 'responsibility to protect' was inserted into two paragraphs of the Outcome Document at a meeting of the General Assembly, the 2005 World Summit. In April 2006 a resolution by the Security Council, number 1674 regarding the protection of civilians during conflicts, reaffirmed 'the provisions of paragraphs 138 and 139 of the 2005 World Summit Outcome Document regarding the responsibility to protect populations from genocide, war crimes, ethnic cleansing and crimes against humanity'.[362]

It was the first time that the theme of 'limitations' to the sovereignty of states was addressed in such an explicit and coherent way: such limitations were identified in the subordination to the 'human security' of the peoples each state is responsible for. A strongly debated point within the international community concerned the question if the concept of the 'responsibility to protect' was always to be interpreted in the same way, and if the new documents were actually creating a new international legality, which would transform previous jurisprudence. For example it had been noted that the Commission on Intervention and State Sovereignty 'proposed to take care of the problem of re-characterising sovereignty, in other words of conceiving sovereignty as a responsibility rather than a form of control. Thus the commission used a rhetorical trick: it flipped the coin by moving the emphasis from a right to intervene for humanitarian purposes, which was both politically and legally undesirable, to the less conflictual idea of the responsibility to protect', and by addressing 'the dilemma of interventions from the perspective of the needs of those seeking or needing help (communities seeking protection from genocide, massacres, ethnic cleansing, mass famine) rather than that of the interests and perspectives of those who intervene (those entities which assert the "right to intervene")'. [363]

Differing from the commission, the High Level Panel believed in the reinforcement of the principle of the 'responsibility to protect' only in the case of an armed intervention and only under the control of the Security Council; the Panel also identified five criteria for the use of force (seriousness of the threat, appropriate objectives, last resource, proportioned means and balance of consequences). In the speech of the General Secretary the 'responsibility to protect' 'was no longer envisioned exclusively as a surrogate of humanitarian interventions, but as a strategy to promote the commitment of all nations to respect the state of law and to protect human security'.[364] This was not yet a substantial transformation from the more traditional humanitarian intervention, as there was no reference to the possibility of unilateral actions and the possibility of a military campaign was still left to the authorisation of the Security Council. Only the Outcome Document, which was met with perplexity by countries such as Belorussia, Cuba, Egypt, Iran, Pakistan, the Russian Federation and Venezuela, identified 'a compromise which sought to harmonise the different positions. States avoided the reduction of the idea of the responsibility to protect to a mere moral concept. However paragraphs 138 and 139 of the Outcome Document represent a rather curious mixture of political and juridical considerations, which fully reflected the persistence of the divisions and the confusion regarding the meaning of the concept'.[365] On one hand what appeared to prevail is the idea of a voluntary, and not obligatory, commitment to undertake a collective action based on chapter VII of the Charter of the UN; on the other hand the document also seemed to theorise a solution of unilateral initiatives, even without the support of and legitimisation by the United Nations.

The debate on the 'responsibility to protect' widely appeared to repeat the previous one which took place concerning the intervention in Kosovo, when the supporters of the intervention already considered the use of force for humanitarian purposes to be a part of international law, thus privileging the protection of the citizens of a state rather than the state itself as an abstract entity.

> The concept of the responsibility to protect appears to associate the idea of human security with certain duties, such as the collective responsibility to act when facing serious violations of human rights (prevent, react, re-build). This is a new vision. Up until now these duties were derived, if necessary, from a rather vague concept of solidarity. The connection between protection and responsibility is a step forward, if responsibility is intended in the sense of a positive obligation.[366]

Despite a series of weaknesses and contradictions – including the lack of any form of juridical sanctioning in the case of non-application of the principle of protection – the notion:

may gradually replace the doctrine of humanitarian interventions during the twenty-first century. At the moment, however, many of this concept's proposals remain uncertain from a normative perspective. Thus responsibility to protect is, under many aspects, still a locution seeking a political effect rather than a juridical norm. Further agreements and commitments by states are required in order to transform it into an organisational principle for the international community.[367]

It was not only international documents formulated by the United Nations that implemented or, from a more pessimistic perspective, theorised new relationships between the international community and the sovereignty of single states. Globalisation had already created such relationships, even in terms of human rights, with regard to economic development, financial movements, migration, communication and information. The culture of human rights is not constituted only by norms inserted within conventions or treaties, it is the result of widely accepted standards, of the increasing – and sometimes critical and opposite – participation by governments in the identification of rules and behaviour valid for everyone. The itinerary of this culture, even if we analyse just the past decade, has made it evermore difficult for anybody to hide behind the pure and simple justification of national sovereignty – which was still a widespread defence 20 or 30 years ago. However it is comprehensible that the sometimes instrumental use made of human rights by the United States and other Western powers against 'rogue states', or governments perceived as threats to peace, may later backfire and render them vulnerable to serious and documented criticisms regarding violations committed on the very terrain of human rights.

The decision to analyse the 'responsibility to protect', even though it is still ambiguous on a juridical level and probably dominated by political and moral aspects, indicates a trend which will inevitably be consolidated. The problems which will continue to be pivotal and cannot be solved by any shared principles are substantially those concerning: the relationship between objectives and means; the correct identification of the limit to the moment that must not be exceeded; the rapidity of interventions to prevent the exceeding of such a limit; the articulated prediction of short, medium and long term effects of interventions.

Many humanitarian 'interferences' have taken place during the last decade that should be judged not on the basis of their legitimacy, but of their results. Although such a procedure rarely produces a certain and sound judgement, it however provides elements for evaluation which may be used in the future. The intervention in Kosovo, for example, especially given its methods, was accompanied by a series of serious – even if unintentional – violations of the rights of the previous violators, by the need for the long presence of international military and civil missions in the field and by the dubious legality of the recent international act which gave the region its independence. Just as it is abstract and ideological to claim, on the basis of these premises, that the intervention should never have taken place, it is futile and unproductive to think that it was not instrumental in avoiding a large scale ethnic cleansing and a possible genocide: only by accepting and analysing the contradictions and problems will it be possible to gain useful indications for the future.

The identification of increasingly precise and reliable mechanisms – of 'early warning', for monitoring, for prevention, to identify the limits that must be exceeded before an intervention is necessary – does not guarantee that an intervention may be carried out according to the expected forms, time limits and results. On the contrary, the variables at play are so numerous that each new situation will almost certainly represent an unprecedented and unpredicted scenario. If it is understandable, given the possible effects of direct interventions, that the international community had difficulty deciding which forms of 'interference' to use in tragic situations such as Darfur – where the intervention was late and seriously limited – this certainly remains the most adequate grounds for a discussion; not any longer a debate on the legality of an international intervention widely legitimised by the living conditions of millions of citizens and refugees. In this sense, it's certainly worth remembering the lucid speech written by Antonio Cassese on the occasion of the intervention in Kosovo. The speech was a defence of legality and legitimacy, and also attempted to point out the changes that were occurring within international law – changes that have been further encouraged in the new century by the principle of the responsibility to protect.

In the system of the Charter, as integrated by customary norms of international law introduced during the past 50 years, the respect of human rights and of the self-determination of peoples, although crucial and important, is not sufficient to sacrifice peace. Some may not like this, yet it is the situation *de lege lata*. We cannot however simply limit ourselves to the hope that this dramatic deviation from the rules established by the Charter of the United Nations remains an exception. Once a group of powerful states realises it can subtract itself from the limits imposed by the Charter of the UN and from general international law, and use armed force without suffering any censorship, if not from public opinion, the risk is that a Pandora's box will be opened […]. When facing this enormous tragedy and given the inactivity of the Security Council of the United Nations, entirely due to the refusal by Russia and China to allow the international community to intervene to stop the massacres and expulsions, should we remain inert and watch as thousands of human beings are massacred or brutally persecuted? Should we remain still and silent just because present international law is incapable of providing a remedy for such a situation? Shouldn't the respect for the state of law be sacrificed on the altar of mercy and human compassion? In the international community we are observing the affirmation of the idea that large scale massacres and atrocities may give birth to an aggravated form of international responsibility, which may authorise other states or international organisations to use different counter-measures than those contemplated for ordinary offences. On the basis of this new tendency of the international community, I believe that, within certain rigorous conditions, the use of armed force may gradually be allowed, even without the authorisation by the Security Council. [...] I believe that the task of international law scholars is to indicate the evolutional tendencies of the international community, while observing the actual behaviour of states. In the international community, just like in every other human community, there is a need for conduct parameters aimed at guiding actions by its members. It is certainly not an exceptional fact that new parameters emerge after violations of the existing law. The suggestion of realistic yet cautious behaviour parameters, on the basis of the current tendencies of the international community, may contribute to the realisation of the goal of reducing the use of armed force to the minimum in a community that is evermore inclined to conflicts and massacres.[368]

6. *Justice and reconciliation*

During the nineties the main signs of a new season for human rights were the creation of the two *ad hoc* international criminal tribunals and the beginning of the process which led to the constitution of the International Criminal Court. Unfortunately the creation of these jurisdictional measures followed the perpetration of such horrible violations that the international community could no longer postpone the application of international justice sanctioned by the Charter of the United Nations. In truth, considering that the Nuremberg and Tokyo trials were the legitimate – and probably most functional, given the circumstances – product of 'victor's justice', 'the International Criminal Tribunal for the Former Yugoslavia (ICTY) and the International Criminal Tribunal for Rwanda (ICTR) are the first truly international criminal courts. They were established by the

United Nations Security Council and funded by the regular UN budget under the control of the General Assembly'.[369]

The existence of these jurisdictional mechanisms, apart from their work and their verdicts, has certainly been important on a political and moral level, as the symbol of a growing influence of human rights on international law. The inclusion of rape, for example, as a crime against humanity, in the statutes of both *ad hoc* tribunals and in the statute of the International Criminal Court, as well as in some of their rulings – where violence was considered an instrument of genocide and crimes against humanity – demonstrated the evolutionary process made by international humanitarian law: in the Nuremberg and Tokyo trials sexual violence had not even been discussed. 'Over the past decade, in dozens of trials and appeals, the tribunals have shown that international criminal and humanitarian law can be applied in actual cases – not just a few times, as in Nuremberg and Tokyo, but repeatedly, and in a manner even more rigorous than at the post-World War II trials.'[370]

The most frequent criticisms of the *ad hoc* tribunals – and more recently of the International Criminal Court – concern the slowness of the procedures, the difficulty of making necessary arrests without the collaboration of individual states, the complexity of reaching actual guilty verdicts, and the negative effects these judiciary procedures can have on the pacification and reconciliation processes that are needed in post-conflict situations. Some of these positions are difficult to analyse: probably the detention and trial of Milošević – which remained suspended because of the death of the accused – did reinforce nationalistic feelings and self-pitying attitudes among Serbian public opinion, which was largely incapable of severe self-critical reflection concerning the country's responsibility in the 1992-95 war. It is however equally true that the process aided the understanding of a complex experience which was in need of a moral sanction more than a juridical one; and, on an internal level, it re-inforced democratic tendencies and the supporters of the country's entry into Europe.

If on one hand, the recent indictment of the president of Sudan, Omar al-Bashir, and the arrest of Radovan Karadžić have increased the prestige of the International Criminal Court and of the Tribunal for the former Yugoslavia – which has almost completed its mandate – on the other, these events risk reducing such institutions to symbols of the desire and need for justice rather than proving their worth as instruments for its realisation. However the reduction of these institutions to symbols would be a mistake, especially given the years of work, disagreements and compromises that were necessary to render them functional. International criminal tribunals, as was already noted with regard to the Nuremberg trial, are a monument to humanity's ever-present aspiration to justice, especially after collective tragedies and crimes. Sixty years after Nuremberg:

> the task of international criminal justice remains the same: to achieve justice through reason rather than force; to uphold the basic principles of human rights and due process; to improve compliance with the law; and to eliminate impunity, not through vengeance, but through the rule of law. Work always remains to be done, but with these noble goals as the lodestar, progress is being made, and the expanding universe of international humanitarian law is stronger as a result.[371]

The task of advancing international justice cannot be assigned only to criminal courts, as it should constitute a permanent goal for states, diplomacies, non-governmental organisations, public opinion and all other institutions which share the primary objective of justice. Alongside the (re)birth of organisations for super-national justice – that had existed since the establishment of the United Nations yet excluded during the entire Cold War – these last years have been characterised by the rise of a new type of institution, aimed at accompanying, integrating or replacing the more traditional mechanisms of justice: truth commissions. This new model of alternative (or integrative) justice only came to the attention of jurists, of transitional governments, of international community members and of the public after the establishment of the Truth and Reconciliation Commission of South Africa (TRC). However, historically such organisations were founded much earlier (in Argentina, Bolivia, Brazil, Chile, Chad and Zimbabwe). In Argentina, Chile and Uruguay the chosen solution was an amnesty, due to fear (of a return of military power), divisions within the democratic forces and the belief that it was necessary to reinforce democratic institutions and the state of law. However the Inter-American Court for Human Rights and the Declaration of Vienna later declared the system of amnesty incompatible with certain international conventions, although it was never explicitly prohibited by international law.

In such cases the conflict between the victims' right to justice and the entire society's right to peace and reconciliation were intertwined with political motivations, power relations, evaluations of opportunities and the fear of uncontrollable reactions, not to mention the presence, within the judiciary system, of a significant number of judges who had been involved in violations, corruption and inefficiencies during the years of the dictatorships. In these countries the logic of an amnesty rendered the commissions for truth a mechanism that can hardly be compared with the results of the South African Commission. The struggle of traditional law to respond to massacres and serious violations of human rights through educational tools based on shared moral values, such as dignity and tolerance, has often led to reflections on the possibilities offered by the truth commissions: 'If the objectives are the public recognition of damage and the most comprehensive account possible of what occurred, trials are, at the least, an imperfect means. At the moment a commission for truth is far more adequate for these two objectives.'[372]

Created by the new democratic parliament in 1995, the TRC presupposed that knowledge of the truth of what occurred during the era of apartheid would later advance the possibility of reconciliation between the different South African ethnic, racial and religious groups.

> Commissions for truth generally begin their work from the fundamental assumption that reconciliation depends on the full knowledge and recognition of atrocities by both sides involved in a previous conflict. Without reconciliation there is the danger of violence returning, of diffidence and hate between past contenders, which could threaten the fragile new democracy and the possibility of a lasting peace. [373]

The TRC managed to create a sort of virtuous circle in which fear and atonement, remorse and repentance, menace and compensation mixed together and reinforced each other, and in which the first objective was to uncover as much truth as possible.

The debate which surrounded the TRC, and is still ongoing today (with extremely interesting results), often focused on the relationship between truth and justice, on the possible, necessary or desirable balance between these two elements and on the choices that should or could have been made to place greater emphasis on one or other of the commission's declared objectives. Less attention has been given to the relationship between truth and reconciliation – the two terms which define the South African commission – since it is very difficult to identify and measure the latter: i.e. the degree of solidarity, shared values, moral transformation and commitment to overcome the past and prevent its return.

The TRC was the most significant experience amongst the many cases of commissions for truth: it was the most famous and analysed example, the model which received most criticism and appraisal. However, it was not the only institution, in the Africa of the past ten to 15 years, which attempted to find original paths for the problems of pacification, of justice in post-conflict societies and of reconciliation as a reinforcement for a new-born democracy. Apart from the experiences of Mozambique, Sierra Leone and Liberia, a particularly important example occurred in Rwanda, where, alongside the international criminal tribunal, a system was created on the basis of the tribal and ethnic community structure of the country. This system allowed each community to solve its own conflicts.

Thanks to the strong involvement of the communities themselves, the judiciary system of the 'Gacaca' Courts was formalised by the election of 26,000 honorary judges (men and women, Hutus and Tutsis) for over 11,000 jurisdictions. Thus an imposing justice system, with many levels, was constructed, and made official in November 2002.

The modern model of the *Gacaca* Courts, instituted to repress the international crimes of the genocide period, maintains certain traditional characters. First of all the hearings are completely public and collective (they are held in open locations within the various districts which constitute the Rwandese administrative system). All participants have an equal right to speak. The factual reconstruction of the crime takes place through the testimonies by individuals who participate in the hearing. The system of the *Gacaca* Courts for crimes committed during the genocide is very complex. A first important element was the popular election of the thousands of individuals who have become 'Inyangamugayoi', the judges of these Courts. They should ideally follow the characteristics of the traditional chief who, thanks to his conduct, his integrity and his public legitimisation, has the strength to impose the verdict. Fundamentally the objective of the Rwandese government, when instituting this new system based on traditional mechanisms, was to involve the population as much as possible in the process of re-elaboration of the genocide tragedy. Secondly, the *Gacaca* Courts have a pyramidal structure which, starting from a sort of national jurisdiction, descends to small district courts according to a Chinese box composition. The idea is fundamentally to let the victims speak directly to the perpetrators of crimes (without the mediation of juridical mechanisms and procedures). In particular the confession of crimes is stimulated by reductions of the sentences. [374]

The results obtained by the Gacaca Courts raised doubts and questions which added to the ones generated by the slowness and selectiveness of the *ad hoc* tribunal (TPIR). The problem is not the identification of the unique and substantially adequate model for obtaining justice, for justice now has very little sense if it is not accompanied by real – difficult and complicated – procedures of reconciliation. The culture of human rights must not exclude the many possibilities which have been revealed during the past decade, and must not give to international law only the task of resolving the social, cultural and political conflicts created within a community by serious violations.

A further point of view may be observed in Guatemala, where a commission instituted by the United Nations worked between 1997 and 1998. Here, because of the contingent historical and political conditions – the uncertainty surrounding the peace process, the weakness of the local legal system, internal divisions, and international interferences – a decision was made not to adopt the principle of individual responsibility, but to create a Comisión para el Esclarecimiento Histórico, Verdad y Justicia en Guatemala which 'was to operate in a general context of juridical impunity following the 1996 "National Reconciliation Law", which guaranteed amnesty for all individuals who had committed crimes connected to the political conflict'.[375] Due to these juridical limitations, the commission was forced to analyse the general aspects of war and of crimes against humanity by reflecting on the historical causes and social/cultural aspects of the conflict: thus it reached the conclusion – which would have been difficult to envision in different conditions – that the state violence had been racially determined (above all against the Maya natives) and thus could be considered genocide.

7. Multiculturalism, relativism, clash of civilisations

During the past 60 years, the culture of human rights has been criticised from different perspectives, which often viewed the impossibility of its universalism as a fallacy or as a form of hypocrisy. Cultural relativism, as expressed in the well-known 1947 *statement* by the American Anthropological Association, refused to consider the universality of rights 'self-evident' and instead attributed it to Western ethno-centrism, later polemically defined as cultural imperialism. Following the important work of Huntington,[376] the spread of the idea of a 'clash of civilisations' has often been over-simplified to support political positions that oppose the multicultural dialogue which should supposedly characterise the post-Cold War period. This idea has also often been based on the conviction that only the West, given its history and tradition, truly enjoys a solid and coherent legacy in terms of the culture of human rights. Indeed, according to certain points of view, the culture of human rights is the main and incompatible difference between Western culture and others.

A quick look at Western culture's history is enough to dismiss these theories. During most of their history past European societies enjoyed no tradition of human rights whatsoever. The tradition of religious freedom – which many scholars now believe was originally conceived during the reign of Indian Emperor Ashoka, in the period of Cyrus the Great or during Roman and Greek paganism – was only introduced into the West quite recently, and more precisely at the very moment in which the history of human rights began. And the same can be said about democracy, which only became a widespread tendency in Europe during the twentieth century, when it coexisted with – or was defeated by – totalitarian ideologies and dictatorial regimes founded on principles and disvalues that were also 'typically' Western. Of course we may find the most significant contributions for the formation of a culture of human rights in the thoughts and history of the Western world; yet it would be a mistake to think that such a culture is a natural part of Western culture and that it marked its evolution in a univocal and coherent fashion.

What really did characterise the history of Western culture was the fact that the demands for human rights were often expressed by universalistic languages or inspirations, although in truth they only concerned very limited sectors of the population (males, white men, owners of property), which were the only ones referred to as human beings. However it was precisely that universalistic language, based on philosophical considerations that were deemed to be evident (natural laws), which became an instrument for the widening of the 'historical' limitations of the discourse on rights, up to the point of determining its fundamental transformation in 1948. The Universal Declaration, which extended human rights to everyone, with no distinctions or discriminations, was both the end of an incomplete conception and the starting point for a new phase in which *universalism* was to mean the concretisation of the – finally explained – list of fundamental rights for everyone.

The invoking of universalism did not however signify that such a principle became the standard of Western behaviour. It certainly helped the process of decolonisation, for example, yet it was also completely incapable of preventing this important historical moment being characterised by continuous and profound violations of those rights that had been proclaimed. As many Africans understood, and ironically commented, during that decisive historical experience, 'the love of freedom is universal. Yet so is man's tendency to deny the freedom of his fellow men'.[377]

In 1948, and increasingly in the following decades, the Western programme of human rights was adjoined with other experiences and cultures, which also strongly contributed to the present state of affairs. Just as in the West, other histories and cultures also involved diverse and sometimes contradictory perspectives, values and experiences. It was not a coincidence that many of the first democratic regimes formed during the period of decolonisation explicitly referred to the Universal Declaration and included its fundamental values in their constitutions; while later regimes, which were often autocratic and bloody, demanded their own programme of human rights, autonomous and distinct from the Western one, which they perceived as being 'imposed' by international organisations.

The international political battle fought by many states, which took up positions that were different from those of the main Western powers, was often the occasion of refusing the culture of human rights as partial and Western: on one hand because it appeared to justify the aggressive and hegemonic policies of the United States and Europe (and many states indeed did use it in this sense); on the other because it allowed the legitimisation of aggressive actions against a country's own citizens or those of neighbouring states. On this basis a professor of law at the University of Buffalo, Makau Mutua, defined the 1948 Declaration as an arrogant attempt to universalise a particular series of ideas and impose them upon the three-quarters of the remaining world population. Makau stated that the 'idea of a universality of human rights, which all countries and cultures were to obey, represented the last and most serious example of Western cultural imperialism'.[378] When speaking of human rights as an instrument of American imperialism, as the means of a 'civilisation crusade' in the Third World, and consequently as a 'foreign ideology' for most non-Western societies, the discourse of human rights is instrumentally reduced, for political reasons, to policies of the United States in this twenty-first century.

A relativist position regarding the direct and uniform opposition between cultures does not take into consideration the fact that 'Such "either-or" conceptions of rights, whether directed toward philosophical or political ends, ignore the evolving human rights legal culture based on the UDHR that interprets civil-political and economic-social-cultural rights to be interdependent and indivisible and also disregard precedents and contributions from other cultures'.[380] The past decades have been characterised by the increasing participation, in the sphere of human rights, of personalities, organisations, committees, groups and associations which can hardly be considered exclusively Western. Unless we are to consider as 'plagiarising' anyone - in Africa, Asia, the Middle East – who declares themselves to be in favour of human rights, we must recognise that a large part of the innovative contributions to this field derive precisely, and not by chance, from non-Western cultural settings and from cultural experiences that are the inevitable historical result of globalisation.

We must also not underestimate the fact that, within the contemporary discussion on human rights, there are tendencies – which may certainly be considered uniquely Western – which aim to reaffirm a sort of supremacy of civil and political rights over all others: in other words, privileging first generation rights. This tendency provides important support to whoever sees in human rights the pivot of a necessary – and possible – clash of civilisations; however, it represents the negation of all development of the culture of rights since the Universal Declaration. What is more, there are also those who believe that the specification of rights which took place in the last 20 years is problematic and dangerous: 'The unnecessary proliferation of human rights [...] risks to devalue the very idea of human rights and to subtly weaken every human right'.[381]

The sphere of rights is, now, a ground upon which different positions co-exist – and often oppose each other: not only in the political and diplomatic arena where international documents are produced and measures are taken to address the problems faced by international organisations, but also within the increasingly numerous non-governmental organisations and the study, research and volunteer groups of the world. Now that it has become the 'frank language' of the new century, the culture of rights is also the site of all the difficulties, obstacles and contradictions any subject faces when it achieves a large, yet not completely shared, degree of credibility and legitimacy.

The increasingly frequent use of human rights to justify political, economic and even military actions by states, coalitions and alliances, both in international politics and within single countries, inevitably makes rights an instrument of justification and accusation, and helps to get them accepted or refused on a political level. We should however avoid the level of simplification and trivialisation which, during the Cold War, led to the diminishment of the importance of democracy, due to the fact that democratic states – and in particular the United States – were the ones behaving aggressively and which supported dictatorial and corrupt regimes; and lead to suspicion of any social program (in particular regarding education and healthcare) managed by the state, in order to avoid the risk of legitimising Socialist states.

There are many different historical reasons behind the rise of relativism, although they may be seen as analogous in Africa, the Middle East and

Asia. The failure in these regions of the regimes that were most tightly bound to a Western cultural and economic legacy, or to the attempts to build a secular and socialist form of state, led to the seizure of power by groups and élites, often military or paramilitary ones, which chose to refer to tradition, religion, community customs or clan fidelity to build consensus and legitimacy. The justifications for what were often personal, corrupt and oppressive powers fed a growing anti-Western polemic which, over the years, ended up involving the very culture of human rights many of such countries had embraced during their struggles for independence.

Some African and Asian leaders refuse to accept international human rights standards, claiming that they are cultural values imposed from the outside:

> They are clearly correct if the claim is seen as a recognition that these rights, and the ways in which they are described (and institutionalised), arise out of a particular historical experience in Western Europe and America and that they are part of a constantly worked-over narrative of the legal and political cultures of some of these countries. They were also originally 'universal' only rhetorically and they could coexist without much discomfort not only with both empire and slavery, but with the effective denial of the universal human rights to an "internal" majority.[382]

If the widening of universal rights in the West (where rights are no longer enjoyed only by white male owners of property, but also by women and ethnic minorities) is the result of a cultural transformation, it is also very probable that their acceptance elsewhere is the product of a clash between different cultures within a same tradition. The underlining of the potentiality of rights to become universal is certainly very different from the recognition of their present universality: it is, perhaps, a more historicised and less legalistic way of approaching the question, yet it moves in the opposite direction from the type of relativism which views Western 'rights' and the cultures of 'emerging countries' as incompatible.

Consciousness regarding the necessary coexistence – and possible conflict – between different generations of rights is one of the most important and innovative aspects of these last years. The recognition of the different typologies of rights (individual/group rights, negative/positive rights of liberty, juridical obligations/moral duties) should not however impede the unifying of their multiplicities within a larger and shared vision of human rights. 'In practice as well as in principle, it is urgent to understand the terms in which particular cultures at multiple social levels describe and circumscribe intolerable behaviours and membership in the "human" community enjoying protections. Only with cultural understanding will it be possible to formulate, implement, and protect human rights in a pluralist world.'[383]

All too often the discussion of human rights has forgotten that the culture which developed around them, in history, was also an exercise of philosophical reflections and a unification of struggles for the defence of the marginalised and excluded; an identification of coherent and sound principles and a preoccupation with the recognition and defence of the dignity of individuals; an affirmation of self-evident and logical, rational truths and a form of empathy towards fellow men, above all when they could not enjoy rights which others enjoyed naturally. Thus it would be very important for the confrontation between universalism and relativism, which continues to provide important intellectual proposals, to become further grounded in history and reality. Not as a form of disinterest in philosophical and anthropological debates, but rather to realise that, perhaps, 'there needs to be a middle ground, a pluralist approach, that can negotiate between narrower universalist claims and broader cultural relativist counterclaims and emphases on concrete realities.'[384]

8. *Asiatic, Islamic and African values*

When the Singaporean Prime Minister, during the conference of Bangkok, opposed 'Asian values', based on Confucius's heritage, to Western 'human rights', it was mainly for instrumental purposes. Yet the possible convergence or conflict between the values and principles of different cultures is certainly a real problem. The identification, in different cultures, of contrasting ethical references, has often been considered a justification which strengthens the theory of human rights as a Western product and minimises other cultures' contributions to their formation. The pluralist itinerary chosen by the culture of human rights in the last 50 years cannot, however, avoid the analysis of differences – antithetical or compatible ones – which may exist between cultures with a strong tradition, although it must also be noted that within these cultures an analogous, or even identical, pluralism to that of the Western world may be recognised.

Asian values usually refer to Confucius, while the Taoist or Buddhist heritages are often viewed as variations or reactions based on his thoughts. This great Asian tradition is certainly characterised by an attention to actual human existence rather than to abstract principles; thus its approach to universality has always been very cautious when considering abstract ideas. Differently from Western individualism, the Chinese model has always privileged self-realisation through mutual benefits for members of the community, in a world of reciprocal loyalties, duties and obligations.

Does the recognition (now much stronger than 40 or 60 years ago) of interrelations between the various generations of rights – which should proceed on the basis of balance and harmony – still leave space for an opposition between a culture based on individualism and one based on the rule of the community, be it the family or the state? Although it is true that often individual rights may be in conflict with collective cultural rights, this is mostly true when speaking of indigenous populations, which still represent a difficult and unsolved problem – despite extremely coherent attempts to tackle it – with regard to both Western and Asian states (and multi-national corporations).

The discussion of 'Asian values' was somewhat tainted by the political slant Lee Kuan Yew, the 'Father' of Singapore, tried to give them.

> One cannot gainsay the fact that Confucianism's attraction for Lee is his perception of it as an essentially conservative teaching, which could be supportive of the increasingly authoritarian, law-order-style of politics with which he is identified in Singapore. Nor can we overlook the touch of anti-Westernism in Lee's espousal of Confucian social discipline versus the decadent libertarianism and individualism he sees as undermining the moral fibre of the West. [...] Still it would be a mistake to see no more at work here than a put-down of the West and liberal democracy.[385]

Many scholars have tried, on different grounds, to find values in Confucianism which may constitute a justification for twentieth century rights, despite the fact that historically the discipline developed in China and Asia. Despite the political or cultural instrumentalism which may be used to justify a 'clash of civilisations' or international political conflicts, it is quite evident that a comparison is not only possible, but may even identify relevant points of contact, given that 'Confucian values and Confucian discourse over the centuries have been involved with many of the same issues that have concerned Western human rights thinkers, though in somewhat different language'.[386]

The oft-demonstrated difference between a Western approach, based on rights, and a Confucian one, based on rituals, forgets that many Confucians deemed rituals insufficient to address the problems of late Imperial China. Indeed it is possible to state that the Confucian 'ritual' conception and the Western one may be considered complementary, despite their different goals.

> In most instances, rites can complement rights, providing a moral dimension to interpersonal actions, suggesting additional possibilities above and beyond the legal relations defined by rights. In some instances, rites may even temper the harshness of rights by encouraging individuals to be judicious in their claims and to be considerate of others. […] The rites may help remind us of our moral obligations, our duties, to others.[387]

Confucius believed that the law would make men more quarrelsome, while rituals would create a sense of guilt and lead to greater self-control. His was, however, an extremely hierarchic system which did not allow for the protection of individuals and minorities, although it did generate a sense of belonging to a community and of social solidarity. The present comparison between the Confucian tradition and human rights may lead to the conviction that:

> Most East Asian countries historically much influenced by Confucian culture have demonstrated that the observance of democratic practices and human rights is not incompatible with, and can be beneficially adapted to, Confucian traditions. If obstacles remain to the observance of human rights in China, they are due not to any incompatibility of these concepts or practices with Confucian tradition, but to the misuse of political power in defence of entrenched repressive regimes. [388]

The obligations of a traditional society towards its members (to ensure food and housing, to cure the sick and take care of the elderly), although expressed in different forms, language and conceptualisations, resemble those listed, in Western and modern societies, as socio-economic rights. Although it is true that in one case they are moral obligations while in the other they are often juridical obligations formalised within specific laws, what truly counts, when seeking a possible dialogue between different languages and the historical origins of rights, are the objectives they may achieve in reality. In this sense the universalism of rights is both a work in progress and the statement of a potential sharing.

The position of human rights in Islam certainly represents a more complex problem, despite the fact that certain scholars believe it is only a question of time before their mutual compatibility with Western rights is recognised. Although 'the differences between secular human rights and Islamic rights are indeed conceptually different things [...]contemporary Muslim thought may be able to produce a rights system, that may be based on different ethical and moral premises but not dissimilar to secular human rights declarations in their outcomes.'[389]

In Islam linguistic differences hide possible semantic discrepancies. The term *haqq*, for example, has multiple meanings which include right, but also truth, demand and duty. The most important condition however is the fact that:

> The *sharia* is the source of rights and obligations in Islam. The *sharia* also defines practices of rights as derived from the teachings of the Qur'an, the prophetic tradition (*sunna*), jurists' consensus and reason. Clearly, rights are framed within a religious-moral framework where the omission of a duty/right is subject to religious sanction and its commission results in the acquisition of virtue. The crucial point in the Islamic rights scheme is that God is the one who confers rights on persons, via revealed authority although human authority mediates these rights.[390]

Many different schools of thought clash over both the interpretation of the Koran – and sacred texts – and the very right to provide new interpretations adapting to the present historical era. It is certainly anti-historical, and a result of prejudice, to think that Islamic law is immutable, despite pressure from revivalist Islamists and Western scholars who believe that the immutability of Islam has made this conviction 'so pervasive that even traditional Muslim jurists, who once treated the legal tradition with great subtlety and complexity, have succumbed to such reductionist views.'[391]

In Islamic traditions duty is the basis for any right, as only the completion of the former allows the recognition of the latter. More than the relationship between duties and rights, however, it is useful to analyse the question of conflicts and existing juxtapositions. The main ones concern religious freedom and the rights of women: the possibility of converting to another religion (Saudi Arabia abstained from voting for the Universal Declaration in opposition to article 18); subordination to the husband and, more generally, to the male domain; and discrimination towards non-Muslims. The source of inequalities and of the opposition to certain rights in the Universal Declaration may however be found in the fact that 'in Islam rights and freedom are not considered simply rights of men but products of divinity based on the dispositions of the *sharia* and on Islamic faith'.[392]

Today it is widely believed that the African system of values is different from the Western one, although to homologise the many different experiences within the continent would be a grave denial of reality: 'Restraint is the principle that makes communalism within the family and within the wider society possible. This simply means that a person does not have complete freedom. Individual rights must always be balanced against the requirements of the group.'[393] These linguistic and conceptual differences do not necessarily indicate a negative attitude towards Western culture: the term *ubuntu*, for example, which was crucial for the South African TRC, is a concept which regards the idea of existing only in relation to the existence of others. This is a clear element of a community-based culture, partially opposed to Western individualism, yet it also suggests the possibility of a deeper solidarity that is somewhat close to Western traditions.

A similar linguistic-cultural argument was addressed by the commission led by Eleanor Roosevelt while it was formulating the Universal Declaration. The French jurist René Cassin introduced two fundamental ideas: 'that every human being has a right to be treated like every other human being and the concept of solidarity and fraternity among men'.[394] The principle of the unity of all human races, so tragically violated just a few years earlier, was to find its representation in article 1, which, in this first draft, stated: 'All men, being members of one family, are free, possess equal dignity and rights, and shall regard each other as brothers'.[395] The debate resulted in the addition of the phrases all men are brothers, as they all have reason and are members of a unique family, and so on. At this point Peng-chun Chang contended that another fundamental human attribute should accompany reason; thus he tried to explain the Chinese concept of *ren*, which literally means 'shared mental attitude', but may also be intended as 'sympathy', 'empathy', 'consciousness of one's human companions'. Chang translated it as 'a sympathetic attitude of regarding all one's fellow men as having the same desires, and therefore the same rights, as one would like to enjoy oneself '.[396]

In the final draft Chang's suggestion was inaccurately translated as 'conscience' ('All are endowed with reason and conscience and should act towards one another in a spirit of brotherhood'), but his contribution was substantially accepted in the idea of the individual, a carrier of value for himself yet permanently residing within a network of relations of mutual dependence with the rest of humanity. 'That departure from classical individualism while rejecting collectivism is the hallmark of dignitarian rights instruments such as the Declaration.'[397]

In Africa responsibility is probably a broader concept, with greater family and community connotations than in Western culture:

> African communalism is more than a mere lifestyle. It is a world-view. It may indeed be an exaggeration to claim that the individual in African society is completely invisible within the clan or kin. The point is that problems revolving around individual disagreements and preferences are present but these disputes are resolved not on the basis of a worldview that posits individual autonomy.[398]

As demonstrated by Gellner, even the most passionate cultural relativists have not verified the existence of cultures so radically different that they are incomprehensible to outsiders. Gellner's intuition:

> [has] been strengthened by modern research in evolutionary psychology, socio-biology, primatology, psychiatry, modem cognitive sciences, and neurosciences, which shows rather convincingly that *there* is such a thing as universal human nature, lending credence to the universalist belief that there is an underlying human unity which allows us to devise minimum universal standards applicable to all human beings regardless of their culture .[399]

Cultural relativism's static vision of cultures privileges the immovability of cultures and customs, i.e. continuity, over their constant evolution, and social transformations:

> Instead of using culture as the so-called explanation and justification for all behaviours, it is far more fruitful to analyse (1) whose interests are being served by the "traditional" customs and whose are infringed by them, (2) why some customs are abandoned while others are maintained or resurrected and by whom, (3) who benefits from change in cultural practices versus who gains from maintaining the status quo, (4) who is influencing the direction and the internal dynamics of cultural change and whether such cultural changes might lead to genuine equality and improvement of life to currently marginalised subgroups or individuals or to a further disenfranchisement of the voiceless, and (5) what is the best way in which the universal ideals of human rights could be used to effect change in the nature and dynamics of native power relations in order to produce more equitable results.[400]

9. *The legalisation of human rights*

The transformation of human rights into laws, the transposition of their fundamental principles into juridical rules, the construction process regarding legal norms that may reflect the values expressed by human rights: do these procedures help the spread of the culture of human rights or do they make it more complicated for it to be shared universally? This process is commonly known as 'legalisation'.

The previous question may seem futile and misleading, yet apart from the fact that it has been posed continuously in the history of rights, it remains central to the contemporary formulation of human rights; it also corresponds to the partly ambiguous and contradictory historical character of rights. The commission led by Eleanor Roosevelt discussed at length whether the general text on human rights was to be a *Covenant* – a convention that would have legally bound all nations which signed it – or a declaration, to underline its moral and political inspiration, as well as its guiding role in each government's actual juridical translation of its principles. Much of the strength earned over the years by the 1948 Declaration is due precisely to its 'constitutional' character, which was hard to reject even by states that were not inclined to respect it *in toto*, yet were morally and politically bound by the Declaration with regard to their citizens and to public opinion. Its objective, as Eleanor Roosevelt declared, 'states a common understanding of the peoples of the world concerning the inalienable and inviolable rights of all members of the human family *and constitutes an obligation* for the members of the international community'.[401]

The long process leading to the two 1966 *Covenants* (one concerning civil and political rights and the other on economic and social ones) demonstrated how – when passing from a declaration to a binding treaty – it was not easy to harmonise the needs, reservations and fears of different states, in order to approve an international law that was to become an integral part of those states' juridical systems. It must also be noted that the approval of an international covenant does not prevent the countries which signed it from violating its principles, as can be observed, for example, in the fact that 'the four Geneva Conventions of 1949 have the greatest number of parties of any human rights/humanitarian law instrument. Yet the Geneva Conventions are honoured perhaps more in the breach than in their observance'.[402]

It has often been noted that the history of human rights cannot be reduced to the transformation of its fundamental principles into juridical rules. Some scholars even claimed that '*international*, by its nature, contains traits which alter the nature of human rights provisions. There is a continuous attempt to balance the interests identified by human rights claims with the interests of political community, the state and the nation. That continuous attempt is characteristic of international human rights law.'[403]

Morality and law, just like morality and politics, and politics and law, continuously intermesh, particularly in the history of human rights. Has the legalisation process of rights – i.e. their inclusion, through international laws, in the juridical systems of individual states – led to positive or negative effects for the realisation of human rights? 'There is also the complication of states reserving the right to implement an international human rights instrument only to the extent that it does not conflict with national constitutions and laws. Are these all attacks on the universality of human rights?'[404]

We must consider that in certain cases the refusal to include human rights (as listed in the Declaration) in national constitutions, or the fact that they were not included in some states' juridical systems, was the result of presumed incompatibilities or contradictions regarding the private sphere, which relates to individual existence yet also to community and religious customs. 'This private sphere, which deals with issues such as religion, culture, the status of women, the right to marry and to divorce and to remarry, the protection of children, the question of choice as regards family planning, and the like, is a domain in which the most serious challenges to the universality of human rights arise.'[405]

The problem regarding the incorporation of international principles within national cultures – and legislations – is both a question of agreeing with the principles and of adapting norms, customs and habits that may be in conflict with some of the principles in question. Yet it has also been – and in some cases still is – a problem of reconciliation between those fundamental values and the historical and political moments each state experiences. 'Asian values', for example, were initially introduced within the international public debate as a historical contingency, as a request and reaction by a group of authoritarian governments which demanded to interpret and represent all Asian culture according to its own conflict with the international community, accused of being over-influenced by Western culture; yet in time they also proved to be the terrain for the formulation of actual problems of coexistence, compatibility and potential harmonisation with analogous or contrasting values in historically distant cultures.

For example, it has been observed that:

in some countries of the Southern Cone, for example, human rights were recognised both by constitutional provisions and by submission to international legal obligations, and yet they did not form part of the communitarian and authoritarian discourses of either the left or the right. The Cold War produced a discourse of national security opposed to that of human rights. There was violence of the Left and excessively violent response by the state. The USA provided external support for repression of leftists. In Argentina, Chile and Uruguay the military represented themselves as the guardians of the nation-state with the mission to eliminate its enemies. The military 'contextualised' the concept of human rights in defence of its supposed need to repress enemies of the state.[406]

With regard to 'Asian values', it has been noted that the principles of social order, hierarchy, benevolence, duty and loyalty, indicated as additional or alternative to human rights, are values which:

> if not always intended that of the original proponents, ought to be incorporated into the international human rights discourse if it is to be regarded as more truly cosmopolitan and therefore to work for the global majority. [...] This suggests not only that economic and social as well as civil and political ways should be developed to promote and enforce dutiful behaviour on the part of the powerful in Asia and elsewhere, but also that to exclude these values from international human rights discourse is both to diminish the local effectiveness of so-called 'traditional' modes of governance and to deny to the global majority what little protection global human rights institutions can provide.[407]

Undoubtedly a 'national law – legal institutions, the principle of the rule of law, and particular substantive rules – is essential to assuring that the state operates as the protector rather than a violator of human rights. The ability of citizens to enjoy their human rights unthinkingly, as a matter of course, is largely attributable to an effective national legal system of human rights enforcement'.[408] However, it is equally important to address the question of the cultural compatibility of those rights which are considered fundamental – of their different classification, relevance, identification, linguistic and conceptual declination – by trying to understand if the existing differences are substantial ones, or if they deal with a diversity of customs, habits and norms relative to the private sphere, and its relationship with religions and, above all, with ideologies. Or, furthermore, if such differences are due to political and historical contingencies, in which cultural diversity becomes a means for the affirmation of powerful groups and for instrumental polemics concerning a universality that is refused because of vested interest, rather than innate convictions.

The accelerated process of the legalisation of human rights has strengthened the idea that they arise from juridical texts, and that these documents contain a list of rights rather than their definition. If this were true, a new positivist idea of human rights would emerge, making them valid only when a law enumerates them and establishes appropriate norms for each one. Those who criticise legalisation – or at least this increasing and prevalent legalisation of rights – also believe that, precisely in those places where they become part of the juridical system, this process minimises widespread violations and the lack of protection of human rights; as a consequence it 'suppresses the "subjective experiences" of the victims of human rights violations [...] If the law is too technical and remote, subjective experiences is not self-justifying'.[409]

In certain situations, what may be read as the demand for a right is instead viewed as the defence of dignity or as a community custom in historically and geographically different settings:

> To the extent that culture talk is about dignity and difference, and rights talk about equality and sameness, do we not need a language other than that of the law to express the difference? Finally, how do we ensure that those who claim to safeguard cultural difference do not turn around to impose a cultural dictatorship on their own communities? Put differently, how do we ensure diversity – not just *between* cultures but also *within* cultures – and thus free play for those forces that give cultures their internal dynamism? For those interested in the process of cultural dynamism and cultural change, neither the language of rights nor that of culture is likely to prove adequate.[410]

The advantages of legalisation – 'the practice of formulating human rights claims as legal claims and pursuing human rights objectives through legal mechanisms'[411] – mostly lie in the recognition given to the six most important documents regarding human rights by around 85% of states: the two 1966 *Covenants*, the Convention on the Elimination of All Forms of Racial Discrimination (adopted in 1965 and enacted in 1969), the Convention on the Elimination of All Forms of Discrimination Against Women (adopted in 1979 and enacted in 1981; an optional Protocol was added in 1999), the Convention Against Torture and Other Cruel, Inhuman or Degrading Treatment or Punishment (adopted in 1984 and enacted in 1987), the Convention on the Rights of the Child (adopted in 1989 and enacted in 1991). 'The fact that human rights have been internationally legalised as a complete package rather than a menu from which governments may pick and choose – "All human rights are universal, indivisible and interdependent and interrelated" (Vienna Declaration, paragraph 5) – further strengthens the position of human rights advocates.'[412]

A comparative analysis leads us to agree, in general terms, with those who believe it is possible more so today than in the past to defend, diffuse and fight for human rights, thanks to the legalisation of rights; even when considering the sometimes elusive nature of such actions, which are all too often overpowered by violence and injustice. However, a different answer must be given to those who believe that the juridical character of rights constitutes:

> the main source of their inadequacy. The legalisation of human rights, understood as the positivisation of norms in international conventions and tribunals, national constitutions and domestic courts, exacerbates the tendency of human rights to overlook the wider political, social and cultural context that generates mass violations. This seems to be one of the most severe criticisms of human rights; they operate without sufficient awareness and understanding of the macro-historical context (e.g. apartheid, the Cold War, economical inequality) in which mass violations occur. Since they hold no theory of why violations happen in the first place, human rights institutions are powerless to prevent them in the future. [413]

If logically followed to its conclusion, this position suggests that the process of determining the singular responsibility of those who have violated human rights actually loses the sense of history; and thus that international law, as expressed in the Nuremberg model, should be replaced by a political justice project, in which the central element should be a wide programme of socio-economical redistribution. The lack of such a political and social transformation supposedly even cancels out the – different but not alternative – experiences by the commissions for truth and reconciliation. These criticisms of human rights,[414] despite being different, share a common basis: the attribution to human rights of the will and capacity to transform human society according to their values; as they fail to do so, this supposedly should demonstrate the fallacy of such values, which cannot achieve the objective they have been given, in truth, by the ideology of those very scholars who criticise human rights. They believe human rights should be an instrument for profound social reforms and economic equality, as well as a source of political justice or even of revolution against capitalism and colonial legacies: as they fail to obtain these results, they must be considered tools of propaganda or deceit and must consequently be exposed, deconstructed and even fought against.[415]

Human rights cannot be surrogates for political strategies, social utopias or universalistic ideologies, although most existing fundamentalisms move in this direction. They are the result of a long historical process which has interwoven morality, politics and law in ever-changing ways – and has been increasingly sufficient for historical transformations – in order to correspond to each person's need for equality and justice and for the defence of dignity and those prerogatives which none should deny another human being. These uncertain borders between morality, politics and law have determined a predominantly juridical approach to the argument in a historical phase characterised by the need to communicate and spread the ultimately universal nature of rights. The results of this process have been problematic and, from certain points of view, may appear to have delayed or thwarted the possibility of adapting the reality of rights to their principles.

Today this battle is fought mainly with regard to the different cultures which inhabit the world's many regions. 'The only possible answer is that the achievement of a universal acceptance of the norms of human rights is a process, and different norms occupy different places in this *continuum*. The transformation and acceptance of these norms must ultimately take place within each region and cannot be imposed by external forces', even if 'there are no regional norms on human rights; there are only regional agreements which superintend the conformity to international standards'.[416]

10. *Cultural rights and individual rights: whose freedom?*

Certain problems, concerning aspects of individual existence and its relationship with the life of the surrounding community, refer to rights through a filter composed of beliefs (both religious and ideological), habits and customs. Such customs represent instances of identity for the subjects involved, and their eventual violation is seen by individuals as an offence to their dignity. In our era of globalisation the clash between different cultural identities, and the consequent offences people believe they are enduring, may be important questions only from a relative perspective (although they may be relevant from a political or symbolical point of view). However, the aforementioned clash may also concern questions that are instead central for liberty and justice, and in which human rights may be involved in an ambiguous and complex way.

These problems do not only concern the relationship (increasingly due to globalisation) between the West and 'other' cultures, but also the often contradictory and conflicting values within each culture, including the Western one. After all, the revival of religion within each country's public sphere is a relevant sign of the interruption of the secularisation of society – which had accompanied the advent of modernity – and of a return to religious answers regarding liberty, equality and justice. We must not forget that religious inspiration – and organisations based upon it – was often at the vanguard of the 'practice' of human rights. It has also been stated that 'international human rights law has, in some sense, become the substitute for religion in secular societies'.[417]

Among the problems causing conflicts between the private and public sphere – relative to themes common to both spheres and to rights and dignity – a particularly important one concerns the rights and behaviour of women, often viewed as characteristics of cultural rights or community customs which other fundamental rights could place in doubt.

Women managed to attain the status of individuals and citizens extremely late in history, despite the fact that many of their requests emerged during the first great season of the universalisation of rights. Historically this is due to inferior conditions of economic status, prestige and social recognition, to profound cultural prejudices fed by the male domain, and to a mentality which survived the decline of patriarchal community and family forms. Today, in the era of globalisation, the experiences of women who live in very different economic, social, cultural and political conditions frequently merge, within a world context which considers the rights of women one of the most important factors in evaluating the progress of human rights and identifying macroscopic violations in the sphere of individual rights.

However, the gap between women's formal rights and their actual condition as a disadvantaged 'group' is still very large, as demonstrated by often disturbing statistics – and, in some cases, it is still growing. Despite the fact that it is anti-historical and paradoxical to claim that 'the process of legalisation of human rights has reinforced the subordination of the "victim" of human rights violations, by reinforcing assumptions about difference, including gender and culture differences', there are good reasons – although expressed in a drastic and strongly ideological fashion – to criticise 'attempts to universalise women's experiences primarily along the lines of gender, which perpetuate the exclusions that have been the hallmark of "universalising strategies" since the colonial encounter'.[418] It is certainly true, for example, that the marginalisation and subordination of women in certain developing countries are based on socio-economical conditions which affect most of the population. However, if we 'globally' take the side of the marginalised South against the arrogant West, we should not forget that in many countries of the Southern region women are often even more marginalised and subordinated, due to questions of mentality and culture which aggravate the shared socio-economical conditions.

Those who believe that human rights encourage the idea that freedom and emancipation are based on the objectivity, universality and rationality of law, and that they consequently favour an essentialist approach (by reducing all women to their gender), are observing human rights only through the – important but partial – lens of their juridical realisation. The refusal of the universality of rights as a 'concept which was born from a specific historical and political context,[419] transforms an anthropological banality into a cultural battle (the East's rejection of the 'Orientalism' imposed by the West as part of its self-representation). This perspective does not take into consideration the historical progression of human rights and the fact that the anti-colonial struggles, as well as many non-Western personalities, states and communities, played extremely important parts in the formation of the culture of human rights.

Although questionable as a general discourse, the criticisms by Ratna Kapur (who proclaimed his adherence to the 'postcolonial and feminist postmodernist' theory) are useful when they address certain specific aspects of legalisation such as, for example, those concerning the Islamic veil: 'through different historical and cultural contexts get subsumed in the legal arguments that focus almost exclusively on veiling as an oppressive and subordinating practice that typifies Islam and its degrading treatment of women'.[420] The 'uniform' interpretation of the veil as a symbol of the submission of Muslim women does not consider its role – in some cases – as a symbol of honour or as an instrument to avoid potential molestation, its revolutionary value during the revolt against the Iranian Shah or the fact that in some Islamic countries it is a symbol of female 'empowerment'. The veil, which is essentially a 'private' space, became an object of debate at the very moment it entered the public sphere, perhaps as a result of measures adopted to allow Muslim women to participate to a greater extent in society.

However, the debates regarding the veil which took place in Europe – the most controversial of which probably occurred in France – did not result in a uniform vision of 'Oriental' women as victims of an 'underdeveloped and barbaric' society, envisioned as the opposite of the Western culture of rights.[421] This line of thought is a caricature, based on an almost racist ideology and on a conviction of the superiority of the West; what is more, it represents that point of view most hostile towards the culture of rights as expressed in the West. In Western culture, just as in the 'Oriental' one – or ones – many different and often opposite positions coexist. Their reduction to 'uniformity' may be useful only for those who insist on the idea of a clash of civilisations, or for those who think this is the only way to mobilise scarcely homogeneous populations and cultures within an anti-imperialistic struggle.

Many European states addressed the question of the veil in public in articulate and different ways, and by referring to principles and juridical mechanisms that are hardly uniform. In each of these countries at least two alternative positions opposed each other on this argument. Yet we should avoid viewing this problem as an important aspect of conceptions of human rights. Indeed, the lawfulness and legitimacy of wearing a veil in public hardly constitute a human rights argument, despite the fact that they do certainly address questions of individual freedom, religious freedom, the security of the state and the need for identity to be controlled. The use of the veil is, above all, a question of custom, which gained relevance in terms 'of principles' – as a symbol of freedom of identity – within a particular historical, social and cultural context, characterised by increased immigration from certain zones of the Mediterranean and Asia into Europe, and by the assimilation or integration of second or third generation immigrants.

The debate created by certain cases (and by certain administrative, rather than public or penal, norms) illustrated the problem of wearing – yet also of *not* wearing – the veil, and the oppressive nature of its imposition, in particular upon younger girls, by family-based, paternalistic, cultural and religious pressures. The fact that many of the girls the states were supposedly trying to protect expressed their preference for a symbol of cultural or religious identity, rather than its refusal in the name of individual liberty, made the debate on 'freedom' extremely difficult and complex; indeed fully defendable principles were combined with questions of good sense and opportunity, and were in evident contrast in this particular situation.

Many other specific conflicts concerned different spheres of rights. In India, for example, women's struggle for equality within the family often clashed with religious communities' right to maintain their principles. Individual rights and cultural rights also clashed in the long debate on the unique civil code (UCC): 'The UCC debate is a story about the struggle for women's rights to inheritance, to equal status within marriage and upon divorce; in short, for equality within the family. But the UCC debate is also about the rights of religious communities to their ways of life and the protection of such rights as an integral part of India's democracy'.[422] The situation was further complicated by the fact that Hindu nationalistic right wing parties were the ones demanding the adoption of the UCC, while it was opposed by Islamic communities; and that both types of rights involved were present – in chapter III, within the 'Fundamental rights' section – in the Indian constitution. Another important factor was the significant disagreement between Indian feminist organisations (despite the fact that they were the first groups to demand a unique code, in 1937). Alongside a 'modern' defence of common citizenship and a 'community-based' refusal of cultural uniformity, a third position emerged, which aimed to achieve an internal reform within communities, as an instrument for legislative adaptation. In other words it was decided that civil society, rather than the state, should solve conflicts between rights.

Another important and contradictory case of conflict between different rights in India was the 1994 decision that a husband's verbal divorce, activated through the triple 'talaq',[423] was discriminatory and did not conform to the constitution. In this case, however, women's right to a non-discriminatory divorce coincided with the denial of their right to maintain individual property after the divorce (which had instead been recognised by Islamic divorce).

The problems concerning genital mutilations of women in many Islamic and African countries, the forced suicide of widows in India and the traffic of women and children for prostitution are certainly more pressing issues. The first two cases refer to 'customs' and behaviours that are rooted in local cultures, which are in open conflict with the right to bodily integrity and to life, yet also with the behavioural standards of many citizens of those very same countries. Indeed, before being considered contrary to 'Western' human rights, these practices were already placed in doubt within the local cultures they belong to. The true question, regarding such customs, is what the most rapid and successful strategy to extirpate them would be, given that the recourse to local and regional laws proved to be rather ineffectual.

With regard to sexual trafficking and exploitation, which often result in actual slavery, the 2000 Additional Protocol of the United Nations and the 2002 Convention between Southern Asian States have not so far achieved the hoped-for results. It is certainly true that in some situations the implementation of the new laws has been far more severe on illegal immigration than on the traffic of women and children. Yet the increasing international commitments and the widespread consciousness that these practices are serious violations of human rights can only encourage the future possibility of materially influencing this tragic situation. The recognition that international and regional measures 'have been incapable of offering definitive solutions for the problems of violence and human traffic' cannot become an argument for demonstrating the futility of human rights, or even the worsening effects they supposedly lead to for disadvantaged or marginalised groups. Nor do concerns that 'the legalisation of human rights may change and deradicalise the political content of a social movement'[424] seem to correspond to the truth (although they do partially explain the ideological attitudes of rejection and underestimation).

It is politics which ultimately decides with regard to human rights: the politics of international organisations and the politics of states and governments, two facets of the same global reality. Considering that politics is the art of possibilities and of compromises, it hardly seems to be the most obvious defender of 'principles', as may be seen from its historic results. Nor does it appear able to contest the potential 'tyranny of the majority', as defined by Tocqueville, in order to defend the more vulnerable individuals and groups. The consensus needed by governments, perhaps above all in democracies, is not always a positive factor for those universal values recognised by history as characteristics of the entire human race. Yet the meeting points between politics and law, collective struggles and intellectual/theoretical commitment have always been the terrain of the most tangible and significant results for human rights. Such meetings have been both a form of inspiration and of ratification for movements and struggles involving those who cared to achieve freedom and justice, equality and solidarity.

11. *The human rights revolution*

Human rights first imposed themselves in a coherent and decisive fashion within 'national' revolutions. However, if they are to complete the universalising process which inspired their genesis, human rights must adapt to globalisation and be able to influence its evolution.

Revolutions have always been the product of different forces, not of a single uprising. They represent a moment of unification, the acceleration and understanding of profound developments leading to never-repeatable experiences and intense transformations, within contingent or even episodic circumstances. The French and American revolutions, just like the English one in the previous century, were not caused by a universal need to affirm rights, but by demands for freedom from the homeland or rulers; these demands were accompanied by concrete interests that were economic, justice-related or aimed at limiting privileges: only a disruptive political proposal could truly unite them. Such demands were capable of unifying many different social classes and positions within a unique group which specifically confronted questions of participation, representation and inalienable rights.

The movements and groups involved in those revolutions, mainly the bourgeois class, just like the intermediary institutions they referred to – parliaments, tribunals, churches – found their common denominator and shared language in general principles which summarised the relationship between their values and interests. Their principles were generated by individual and collective daily life experiences – empathy for other human beings – yet also by the theoretical efforts of many thinkers to clarify questions and debates.

The universal inspiration of human rights – for everyone, on the basis of a common belonging – was initially founded on the idea of natural rights; later were added other universal aspirations concerning freedom, equality and justice, and progressively expanded to all classes, genders, populations and groups in a non-linear way, and despite many obstacles and battles which cannot yet be considered completely won. For a long time rights progressed within the borders of nation-states, although international impulses arising from the processes of modernisation emerged almost immediately. In this same period – above all in the last decades of the nineteenth century and the beginning of the twentieth century – rights expanded to the spheres of freedom and to the terrain of economic-social questions. The relevance of these, which rights intend to realise and defend, to human dignity was not an obvious concept, just as the equality of women or slaves were not predictable ideas. This process for the broadening and cementing of rights, no matter how partial or opposed, is still taking place today. It progresses within political decisions that are the result of battles, pressures, compromises, ideal impulses and shared principles; these decisions produce laws, rules and norms which are deemed adequate for the protection, defence, realisation and actualisation of the aforementioned rights.

An important and significant transformation, which cannot be forgotten as the culture of human rights owes its contemporary foundations to those events, took place with the Second World War. The conflict which devastated (not only) Europe was the result of the expansion and success – obtained through a combination of violence and consensus – of regimes which based their ideologies precisely on the denial of rights and of their universality. The clear and simple way in which Roosevelt identified the desirable post-war scenario in his 'four freedoms' speech is an indication of the fact that there was a consciousness – at least in the politician who was most careful of the principles of freedom, equality and justice – that the war had also been a clash between rights and their negation.

To sanction the defeat of those barbaric regimes, an international system was built – in truth it was conceived while the conflict was still taking place – to revive the process which had been interrupted and diverted during the era of totalitarianisms and of the European civil war. This was the context for the universalistic project based on the creation of the United Nations, which produced, through difficulties and with a long-term vision, the 1948 Universal Declaration. The dispositions on human rights within the Preamble and articles 1 and 55 of the Declaration

> constituted, in that historical context, one of the most significant innovations in the scenario of universally participating international organisations: the Pact of the United Nations, for example, stated nothing on the argument. The most significant novelty of the message on human rights which was emerging in the United Nations was above all the idea of the indivisibility and interdependence. [425]

In a certain sense, the definition of the culture of rights and of the peace project within the Charter of the United Nations and the Universal Declaration were ahead of their time. This was immediately demonstrated by the Cold War, which began while the Declaration was still being formulated, when the two superpowers accused each other of violating the rights – either civil and political ones or economic and social ones – that they believed they represented. Furthermore, that culture was incompatible with the political programmes which many governments believed to represent their identity and history as nation-states: above all with colonialism and the racial hierarchy it involved.

The Declaration had the nature of a 'foundation', while successive treaties and conventions were 'inspired' by it: if initially this appeared to be a correction to the lack of a 'catalogue of essential rights' in the Charter of the United Nations, on a historical level it meant that the Declaration acquired a moral and political authority it could never have had if it had been an act containing juridical norms that were obligatory for all members of the UN. The historical process which developed on this basis, alongside the events of the late twentieth century, accelerated and accentuated both the constitution of juridical mechanisms for the realisation of human rights – pacts, conventions, treaties – and the widening of the spheres and the specification of groups that they refer to. The end of colonialism and of many dictatorships, as well as the end of the Cold War and the decline of Communism, suddenly exposed the problems and contradictions of the culture of human rights, and revealed new perspectives on the question of universality and the conflict 'between' rights.

Within a historical period characterised by an exceptional technological development, and by increased interdependence and inter-relations, questions which relate to individual rights – the rights to life and to a dignified death – or to collective rights, such as those of immigrant workers, have a central role within the debate on the relationship between the public and private sphere and between security and rights (just to quote the ones which recently have been at the polemical centre of the debates).

The process of the widespread inclusion of human rights in constitutions coincided with their becoming a part of common sense, sometimes empirically solving the contrast between natural law and positive law, i.e. the enhancement of the moral principles of natural law within positive law.

> The constitutive principles of the juridical system depend, in their contents, on the cultural context they belong to. They express wide concepts which carry great value for humanity such as equality, freedom, justice, solidarity, the person, human dignity, etc. yet the content of these concepts, i.e. their 'conception', is the object of in-exhaustible discussions. No application of the principles can avoid being influenced by this, as constitutional declarations regarding this argument are no more than hints, whose concrete clarifications move within the sense of the history of ideas. Constitutional principles – as has rightfully been stated[426] – should represent a sort of 'common sense' of law, the ground for agreement and mutual sharing of each juridical discourse, the contract to solve contrasts through discussion rather than through oppression.[427]

Attention paid to protecting the principles of human rights is certainly greater today than in the past; yet this has not automatically produced a reinforcement or an acceleration in use of those instruments which may stop violence and offer compensation to its victims. This increase of attention is the result of the widening of international law's prerogatives and interventions via the organisations and conventions mainly instituted by the United Nations. It is politics – both on an international and local level – which often seems to lack the will to apply and realise the principles that have been approved, recognised and often – not always – introduced within local juridical systems. This is owing to the fact that :

regarding the protection of rights, just as in other aspects of associated life, we may observe a shift of power from subjects that have been democratically legitimised (parliaments, governments), to subjects legitimised only on a technical-juridical level (judiciary organs and constitutional law). If we add to this phenomenon the relevant transformation of competences from national systems to super-national entities, which lack democratic legitimisation (for example super-national and international tribunals), the consequence is that democratic powers are now often pushed to the margins of a protection of human rights which is almost entirely assigned to different circuits from the democratic ones.[428]

Is it then necessary to give democracy more importance versus rights, to resize constitutional processes concerning rights, even if they have been the most significant element for their diffusion and actualisation? It must be noted that, during the past few years, characterised by the threats of terrorism and by struggles to combat it, as well as by an increase in immigration, democratic governments have in part voluntarily abandoned the field of protecting human rights, as it was not a competitive argument in terms of electoral functionality and popular consensus. The growing prestige of the main non-governmental organisations – Amnesty International, Human Rights Watch, Médecins Sans Frontières, Oxfam, Save the Children – has not corresponded to an increase of the influence they exert on politics, both internationally and within individual states. However, despite this attitude, governments have often used the rhetoric of human rights to justify their behaviour and decisions.

> An excessive use or abuse of the language of rights may have negative consequences for democratic politics, for interpersonal relations, for individual sense of responsibility and for personal and collective researches regarding the sense of existence. The rhetoric of human rights may indeed ultimately weaken the idea of rights to the extent that it may disappear. History is full of great ideas which disappeared mainly due to their abuse.[429]

It is difficult to state in which way the progress of human rights and their increasing inclusion in constitutions may solve certain new problems emerging in this field. Even democratic politics seem incapable of facing such issues without violating, in the name of the majority, the rights of groups and minorities which are inadequately represented on a political level and can thus only count on the constitution to defend their fundamental rights. Conflicts emerging around symbolic values, collective identities, historic memory, especially if intersected with serious economic and social problems, can become explosive and dangerous. Often they are presented as conflicts between politics and law, between the rights of the majority and limits imposed on dictatorships, between the realm of emotions and the world of reason. If ethics is about intimate relations and strong emotions shared with beloved people (relatives, friends, lovers, compatriots), while morality is concerned with weaker relationships, with human beings as such, especially distant and foreign ones,[430] how can we create a virtuous circle in which strong emotions serve to defend both ethics and morality, i.e. the relationship we have with all human beings? Certainly this 'emotive' difficulty also explains why many human rights associations and organisations tend to use traditionally humanitarian methods, referring to emotional stories about victims and their suffering, rather than a neutral identification of violations according to articles of law and conventions. In a historical period in which politics are more than ever a battleground for emotions – also owing to the vast power of the mass media – constitutional formulations appear to represent the defence of reason; yet they often lack the *appeal* to motivate a strong and widespread defence of human rights.

Human rights can no longer follow the path which has characterised their history since the end of Second World War, unless they are to emphasise their limits and contradictions. Now is the moment for a proper revolution of human rights, which not only places them at the centre of the politics and strategies of international cooperation, but tranforms them into the pivot of a cultural leap similar to those which took place in the late eighteenth century and late twentieth century. In this revolution the identification of the more significant questions should create a debate in which politics and law, history and daily life, the public and private spheres, individuals and communities could all participate in order to make a real contribution and give a concrete possibility to the universality of human rights.

In history human rights arose to limit power, yet by doing so they often legitimised it by assigning it new responsibilities. These dialectics between law and power, united in the field of politics, represent the terrain on which civil society may have the greatest opportunity – as in past centuries – to impose radical transformations in the name of freedom, equality and justice.

Endnotes

[1]N. Bobbio, *Introduzione*, in Id., *L'età dei diritti*, (Torino, Einaudi, 1997), pp. XI-XII.

[2]This is the title of the most complete history book on human rights so far: L. Hunt, *Inventing Human Rights*, (New York, Norton, 2007).

[3]*Ibid*, p.20.

[4]The punishment is proportional to the damage suffered: for murder it corresponds to death, for the murder of a child, the death of the culprit's own child.

[5]Bobbio, *L'età dei diritti*, ibid. p. 54.

[6]P.G. Lauren, *The Evolution of International Human Rights*, (Philadelphia, University of Pennsylvania Press, 1998), p. 5.

[7]L. Henkin, *Judaism and Human Rights*, in 'Judaism. A Quarterly Review of Jewish Life and Thought', 25, 4, 1976, p. 437.

[8]Chung-Shu Lo, *Human Rights in the Chinese Tradition*, in J. Maritain (edited by), Human Rights: Comments and Interpretations, (London, Allan Wingate, 1948), p. 187.

[9]Bobbio, *L'età dei diritti*, ibid. p. 53.

[10]M. Bettini, *Diritti umani e mondo classico*, in M. Flores, T. Groppi e R. Pisillo Mazzeschi (edited by), *Diritti umani. Cultura dei diritti e dignità della persona nell'epoca della globalizzazione*, (Turin, Utet, 2007), vol. I, pp. 400.

[11]E. Pagels, *Human Rights: Legitimizing a Recent Concept*, in 'Annals of the American Academy of Political and Social Science', 442, March 1979, p.58.

[12]http://www.teatrostabiletorino.it/view.php?ID=236&lang=ita.

[13]Bettini, *Diritti umani e mondo classico*, ibid. pp. 402-403.

[14]*Ibid.*, p. 403.

[15]*Ibid.*, p. 405.

[16]*Ibid.*, p. 409.

[17]Titus Livius, *Ab urbe condita*, XXXI, 24, 18.2-5. The text, and relative translation, can be found in the exceptional thesis by Elisabetta Cangelosi, *Diritti umani e mondo antico*, 2008, pp. 122-124, who I would like to thank for allowing me to use it.

[18]Appian of Alexandria, *Roman History* (ϱωναιχα), 8, 19, 128-131.

[19]Bettini, *Diritti umani e mondo classico*, ibid. p. 406.

[20]*Ibid*.

[21]The text I am referring to is B. Kiernan, *Blood and Soil: A World History of Genocide and Extermination from Sparta to Darfur*, (New Haven, Yale University Press, 2007).

[22]S.F. Wiltshire, *Greece, Rome, and the Bill of Rights*, (Norman, University of Oklahoma Press, 1992), p. 25.

[23]Cangelosi, *Diritti umani e mondo antico*, ibid. p. 97.

[24]*Ibid.*, p. 105.

[25]Marco Tullio Cicero, *De officiis*, I, XI, 34-35.

[26]Bobbio, *L'età dei diritti*, ibid. p. 57.

[27]M. Ventura, *Cristianesimo e diritti umani*, in Flores, Groppi e Pisillo Mazzeschi (edited by), *Diritti umani*, ibid. vol. I, p. 244.

[28]Bettini, *Diritti umani e mondo classico*, ibid. p. 408.

[29]M.L. Stockhouse, *Some Intellectual and Social Roots of Modern Human Rights Ideas*, in 'Journal for the Scientific Study of Religion', 20, 4,(December 1981), p. 303.

[30]B. Tierney, *The Idea of Natural Rights: Studies on Natural Rights, Natural Law and Church Law 1150-1625*, (Atlanta, Ga., Scholars Press), 1997; R. Tuck, *Natural Rights Theories: Their Origin and Development*, (Cambridge, Cambridge University Press, 1979); A.S. Brett, *Liberty, Right and Nature: Individual Rights in Later Scholastic Thought*, (Cambridge, Cambridge University Press, 1997).

[31]J. Porter, *From Natural Law to Human Rights: Or, Why Rights Talk Matters*, in 'Journal of Law and Religion', 14, (1999-2000), pp. 84-85.

[32]*Ibid.*, p. 89.

[33]Q. Skinner, *Virtù rinascimentali*, (Bologna, Il Mulino, 2002), p. 37 (quotation from Brunetto Latini).

[34]Q. Skinner, *Virtù rinascimentali*, (Bologna, Il Mulino, 2002), p. 80.

[35]Q. Skinner, *Virtù rinascimentali*, (Bologna, Il Mulino), 2002), p. 121.

[36]F. Petrarca, *De Republica optime administranda liber*, in *Opera quae extant omnia*, Basilea, 1554, p. 420; trad. it. in Opere latine, a cura di A. Bufano, (Torino, Utet, 1975), 2 vol.

[37]Q. Skinner, *Virtù rinascimentali*, (Bologna, Il Mulino, 2002), p. 191.

[38]Cf. M. Villey, *Le droit et les droits de l'homme*, (Paris, Puf, 1983).

[39]Tierney, *The Idea of Natural Rights*, ibid. p. 77.

[40]Stockhouse, *Some Intellectuals and Social Roots of Modern Human Rights Ideas*, ibid. p. 304.

[41]J.N. Figgis, *Political Thought from Gerson to Grotius: 1414-1625*, (New York, Harper, 1960).

[42]The peace of Westphalia ended the Thirty Years' War and the conflict between Spain and the United Provinces. It constituted a basis for the recognition of states, without reference to the dynasties governing them. It also confirmed and amplified the religious tolerance of the peace of Augustus.

[43]S. Bessis, *L'Occident et les autres. Histoire d'une suprématie*, (Paris, La Découverte, 2002), p. 19.

[44]T. Todorov, *La conquista dell'America. Il problema dell''altro'*, (Torino, Einaudi, 1984), p. 60.

[45]*Ibid.*, p. 83.

[46]*Ibid.*, p. 175.

[47]J. Muldoon, *Francisco De Vitoria and Humanitarian Intervention*, in 'Journal of Military Ethics', 5, 2, (2006), p. 133.

[48]*Ibid.*, p. 134.

[49]In 1493 Alexander VI had conceded responsibility of the New World to the Spanish and the Portuguese, with the papal bull *Inter caetera*.

[50]F. de Vitoria, *Political Writings*, edited by A. Pagden and J. Lawrance,(Cambridge, Cambridge University Press, 1991), p. 288.

[51]Muldoon, *Francisco De Vitoria and Humanitarian Intervention*, ibid. p.136.

[52]*Ibid.*, p. 141.

[53]*Ibid.*, p. 3.

[54]*Ibid.*, pp. 8 and 10.

[55]*Ibid.*

[56]D. Zolo, *Cosmopolis. La prospettiva del governo mondiale*, (Milano, Feltrinelli, 1995), p. 99.

[57]Hunt, *Inventing Human Rights*, ibid. p. 117.

[58]G. Oestreich, *Storia dei diritti umani e delle libertà fondamentali* (1968), (Roma-Bari, Laterza, 2007), p. 53.

[59]Oestreich, *Storia dei diritti umani e delle libertà fondamentali*, ibid. p. 55.

[60]Lauren, *The Evolution of International Human Rights*, ibid. p. 15.

[61]C. Cohen (edited by), *Communism, Fascism, and Democracy: The Theoretical Foundations*, (New York, Random House, 1962), p. 436.

[62]Oestreich, *Storia dei diritti umani e delle libertà fondamentali*, ibid. p. 42.

[63]P. Costa, *Lo Stato di diritto: un'introduzione storica*, in Id. e D. Zolo (edited by), *Lo Stato di diritto. Storia, teoria, critica*, (Milan, Feltrinelli, 2002), p. 94.

[64]Hunt, *Inventing Human Rights*, ibid. p. 19.

[65]*Ibid.*, pp. 26-27.

[66]*Ibid.*, p. 34.

[67]*Ibid.*, p. 58.

[68]Costa, *Lo Stato di diritto: un'introduzione storica*, ibid. p. 94.

[69]C. Beccaria, *Dei delitti e delle pene*, (Milan, Feltrinelli, 2007), p. 38.

[70]*Ibid.*, p. 39.

[71]*Ibid.*, p. 78.

[72]*Ibid.*, p. 54.

[73]*Ibid.*, p. 60.

[74]*Ibid.*, p. 62.

[75]*Ibid.*, p. 61.

[76]*Ibid.*, p. 80.

[77]*Ibid.*, p. 81.

[78]*Ibid.*, p. 108.

[79]*Ibid.*, p. 82.

[80]*Ibid.*, p. 69.

[81]T. Todorov, *Lo spirito dell'illuminismo*, (Milan, Garzanti, 2007), p.16.

[82]*Ibid.*, p. 114.

[83]*Ibid.*, p. 53.

[84]S. Sebastiani, *Illuminismo*, in M. Flores, T. Groppi and R. Pisillo Mazzeschi (edited

by), *Diritti umani. Cultura dei diritti e dignità della persona nell'epoca della globalizzazione* (Turin, Utet, 2007), vol. II, p. 717.

[85]After Gregory XVI overlooked the whole problem in 1839 (*In supremo apostolatus fastigio*), it was only under the papacy of Leo XIII, elected in 1878, that the Catholic Church began to explicitly condemn slavery.

[86]O. Pétré-Grenouilleau, *La tratta degli schiavi*, (Bologna, Il Mulino, 2006), p. 177.

[87]J. Wesley, *Thoughts upon Slavery* (1774), available on the website http://gbgmumc.org/umw/wesley/thoughtsuponslavery.stm

[88]'When during the course of human events a population needs to undo the political bindings that held it tied to another one and to assume amongst other powerful players of earth a distinct and equal position, according to natural and divine Law, a fair respect for the opinions of humanity requires that such a population should render explicit what reasons forced it to choose secession': A. Aquarone, G. Negri e C. Scelba (edited by), *La formazione degli Stati Uniti d'America*, (Pisa, Nistri-Lischi, 1961), 2 vol., vol. I, p. 416.

[89]L. Hunt, *Inventing Human Rights*, (New York, Norton, 2007), pp. 21-22.

[90]New Hampshire, Massachusetts, Rhode Island, Connecticut, New York, New Jersey, Pennsylvania, Delaware, Maryland, Virginia, North Carolina, South Carolina, Georgia.

[91]*Thomas Jefferson to James Monroe* (1797), in *The Writings of Thomas Jefferson. Memorial Edition (ME)*, edited by A.A. Lipscomb and A.E. Bergh, 20 vol., (Washington, D.C., Thomas Jefferson Memorial Association, 1903-04), vol. 9, p. 422, available on the website http://etext.virginia.edu/jefferson/quotations/jeff0100.htm.

[92]P. Scholfield, C. Pease-Watkin and C. Blamires (edited by), *The Collected Works of Jeremy Bentham. Rights, Representation, and Reform: Nonsense upon Stilts and Other Writings on the French Revolution*, (Oxford, Clarendon Press, 2002), p. 320.

[93]The *état generaux* were assemblies first united in the Middle Ages, in which the three existing social classes of the time were represented: the clergy, nobility and third state.

[94]D.O. Thomas (edited by), *Richard Price: Political Writings*, (Cambridge, Cambridge University Press, 1991), pp. 119 e 195.

[95]J. Keane, *Tom Paine: A Political Life*, (New York, Grove Press, 1995), p. 315.

[96]*Ibid.*, p. 327.

[97]*Ibid.*, p. 335.

[98]*Ibid.*, p. 386.

[99]*Ibid.*, p. 400.

[100]*Ibid.*, p. 404.

[101]J.-J. Rousseau, *Emilio o dell'educazione* (1762), (Rome, Armando, 1981), pp. 506, 572

[102]*Recueil des pièces authentiques approuvées par l'Assemblée nationale de France*, (Genève, 1789), vol. I, p. 195.

[103]AA.VV., *Cahiers de doléances. Donne e rivoluzione francese*, introduction and notes by P.M. Duhet, (Palermo, La Luna/Editions des femmes, 1989).

[104]*Archives parlamentaires*, 4 July 1793, vol. 68, p. 254, (Paris, 1867-7)2.

[105]Quoted in L. Lacour, *Trois femmes de la Revolution*, (Paris, 1900), p.123.

[106] 'Le Moniteur', 30 October 1793, vol. 18, p. 299.

[107] *Sur l'admission des femmes au droit de cité*, in 'Journal de la Société de 1789', 3 July 1790, n. 5.

[108] 'Le Moniteur', 17 November 1793, vol. 18, p. 450.

[109] M. Wollstonecraft, *A Vindication of the Rights of Woman*, University of Virginia Library, Electronic Text Center, available on the website http://etext.virginia.edu/toc/modeng/public/WolVind.html. Quotations are from chapters 5, 9 and 12.

[110] W.L. Smith, *An Oration Delivered in St. Philip's Church before the Inhabitants of Charleston, South Carolina, on the Fourth of July 1796, in Commemoration of American Independence*, Charleston, S.C., 1796, p. 9.

[111] G. de Staël, *Considérations sur la révolution française*, in *Oeuvres posthumes*, Genève, Slatkine, 1967, p. 178; F.-R. de Chateaubriand, *Le génie du christianisme* (1802), (Paris, Flammarion, 1948), vol. II, pp. 149-150.

[112] C.L.R. James, *The Black Jacobins*, (New York, Vintage Books, 1989), p. IX.

[113] Quotation from A. Fox, *Toussaint Louverture*, (Paris, Gallimard, 2007), p. 120

[114] Quoted in A. Hochschild, *Bury the Chains: Prophets and Rebels in the Fights to Free an Empire's Slaves*, (Boston, New York, Houghton Mifflin, 2005), p. 279.

[115] *To Toussaint l'Ouverture*: 'Toussaint, the most unhappy of men! /Whether the whistling Rustic tend his plough/ Within thy hearing, or thy head be now/ Pillowed in some deep dungeon's earless den; / O miserable Chieftain! where and when/ Wilt thou find patience? Yet die not; do thou/ Wear rather in thy bonds a cheerful brow:/ Though fallen thyself, never to rise again,/ Live, and take comfort. Thou hast left behind/ Powers that will work for thee; air, earth, and skies;/ There's not a breathing of the common wind/ That will forget thee; thou hast great allies;/ Thy friends are exultations, agonies,/ And love, and man's unconquerable mind.'

[116] W. Scott, *The Lay of the Last Minstrel*, (Milan, Giuseppe Crespi, 1829), p. 148.

[117] Cfr. E. Weber, *Da contadini a francesi*,(Bologna, Il Mulino, 1989).

[118] G.G. Byron, *Don Juan*, (Milan, Mondadori, 1982, canto 3, p. 275).

[119] D. Diderot, *Correspondance*, (Paris, Minuit, 1962), t. VIII, p. 16.

[120] *The Writings of Thomas Jefferson. Memorial Edition (ME)*, edited by A.A. Lipscomb and A.E. Bergh, 20 vol., (Washington, D.C., Thomas Jefferson Memorial Association, 1903-04), vol. 14, p. 20.

[121] I suggest reading the poem by William Wordsworth *On the Extinction of the Venetian Republic*, which begins as follows: 'Once did she hold the gorgeous East in fee;/ And was the safeguard of the West: the worth/ Of Venice did not fall below her birth,/ Venice, the eldest Child of Liberty.'

[122] E. Renan, What is a Nation? (1882), in Eley, Geoff and Suny, Ronald Grigor (eds), *Becoming National: A Reader*, (New York and Oxford, Oxford University Press, 1996), pp.52-53.

[123] A. Cassese, *I diritti umani oggi*, (Roma-Bari, Laterza, 2005), p. 16.

[124] A village near the waterfalls of the Seneca river, which had been inhabited by Cayuga tribe and was the location for a Jesuit mission in 1600.

[125] Over one hundred were published between 1780 and 1860.

[126] D.T. Rodgers, *Contested Truths: Keywords in American Politics since Independence*,

(New York, Basic Books, 1987), p. 46.

[127]'Hyperion' and 'Morpheus', in *Mercury and New-England Palladium*, Boston, 18 August 1801 and 2 March 1802.

[128]S. Thoughtfull, 'Something New, – Or, What Next?', in *Euterpeiad*, 2 March 1822.

[129]Cf. N.F. Cott, 'The Bonds of Womanhood: Woman's Sphere' in *New England, 1780-1835*, (New Haven, Conn., Yale University Press, 1977).

[130]'He has never permitted her to exercise her inalienable right to the elective franchise. He has compelled her to submit to laws, in the formation of which she had no voice. He has withheld from her rights which are given to the most ignorant and degraded men--both natives and foreigners. Having deprived her of this first right of a citizen, the elective franchise, thereby leaving her without representation in the halls of legislation, he has oppressed her on all sides. He has made her, if married, in the eye of the law, civilly dead. He has taken from her all right in property, even to the wages she earns. He has made her, morally, an irresponsible being, as she can commit many crimes with impunity, provided they be done in the presence of her husband. In the covenant of marriage, she is compelled to promise obedience to her husband, he becoming, to all intents and purposes, her master--the law giving him power to deprive her of her liberty, and to administer chastisement. He has so framed the laws of divorce, as to what shall be the proper causes, and in case of separation, to whom the guardianship of the children shall be given, as to be wholly regardless of the happiness of women--the law, in all cases, going upon a false supposition of the supremacy of man, and giving all power into his hands. After depriving her of all rights as a married woman, if single, and the owner of property, he has taxed her to support a government which recognizes her only when her property can be made profitable to it. He has monopolized nearly all the profitable employments, and from those she is permitted to follow, she receives but a scanty remuneration. He closes against her all the avenues to wealth and distinction which he considers most honourable to himself. As a teacher of theology, medicine, or law, she is not known. He has denied her the facilities for obtaining a thorough education, all colleges being closed against her. He allows her in church, as well as state, but a subordinate position, claiming apostolic authority for her exclusion from the ministry, and, with some exceptions, from any public participation in the affairs of the church. He has created a false public sentiment by giving to the world a different code of morals for men and women, by which moral delinquencies which exclude women from society, are not only tolerated, but deemed of little account in man. He has usurped the prerogative of Jehovah himself, claiming it as his right to assign for her a sphere of action, when that belongs to her conscience and to her God. He has endeavoured, in every way that he could, to destroy her confidence in her own powers, to lessen her self-respect, and to make her willing to lead a dependent and abject life.'
from Elizabeth Cady Stanton, *A History of Woman Suffrage* , vol. 1 (Rochester, N.Y.: Fowler and Wells, 1889), pages 70-71.

[131]'Oneida Whig', 1 August 1848.

[132] 'The North Star', 28 July 1848.

[133] Island in the South Pacific that was discovered in 1767 by Captain Philip Carteret. In 1790 it became the refuge of the mutineers from the British *Bounty* and of the Tahitians who followed them.

[134] J.H. Dunant, *A Memory of Solferino*, ICRC, (Genere, 1986), p.11.

[135] J. Meurant, 'Inter Arma Caritas: Evolution and Nature of International Humanitarian Law', in *Journal of Peace Research*, 24, 3 September 1987, p. 240.

[136] B.M. Carnahan, 'Lincoln, Lieber and the Laws of War: The Origins and Limits of the Principle of Military Necessity', in *American Journal of International Law*, 92, 2, April 1998, p. 213.

[137] *Ibid.*, p. 215.

[138] *Ibid.*, p. 216.

[139] The 'raglan' sleeve, sown radially around the base of the neck and producing a cut that starts below the armpit and ends beneath the base of the neck, owes its name to Fitzroy James Henry Somerset, the first Barron of Raglan, British Commander during the War of Crimea. The woollen jacket, with a 'V' neck and buttons, extending in length until beneath the thighs, was called a 'cardigan' because it was worn by officers of the British war during the Crimean War, and owes its name to James Thomas Brudenell, seventh Count of Cardigan, who led the charge of the English chivalry.

[140] Quoted in E.T. Cook, *The Life of Florence Nightingale*, (London, Macmillan, 1913), vol. I, p. 236-7.

[141] Cf. H. Small, *Florence Nightingale, Avenging Angel*, (London, Constable, 1998).

[142] Henry Wadsworth Longfellow, amongst the most famous American poets of the time, a translator of Dante and a supporter of the abolition of slavery had just published the verses 'Lo! In that hour of misery / A lady with a lamp I see / Pass through the glimmering gloom / And flit from room to room'.

[143] L. Monteiro, 'On Separate Roads: Florence Nightingale and Elizabeth Blackwell', in *Signs*, 9, 3, spring 1984, p. 520.

[144] *Ibid.*, p. 525.

[145] 'Florence Nightingale as a Leader in the Religious and Civic Thought of Her Time', in *Hospitals*, X, July 1936, p. 82. Ten letters were published in this issue of the periodical.

[146] *John Stuart Mill to Edwin Chadwick*, 7 February 1860, in F.E. Mineka and D.W. Lindley (edited by), *The Later Letters of John Stuart Mill*, (Toronto, University of Toronto Press, 1972). Edwin Chadwick had been the intermediary of this exchange of opinions between Florence and John.

[147] This text was included in *Practical Deductions*, the second volume of the *Suggestions for Thought to Seekers after Religious Truth* written by Florence Nightingale in 1852 and published in 1860.

[148] E. Pugh, 'Florence Nightingale and J.S. Mill Debate Women's Rights', in *Journal of British Studies*, 21, 2, spring 1982, p. 127.

[149] Quoted in R. Strachey, *The Cause: A Short History of the Women's Movement in Great Britain*, (London, G. Bell & Sons, 1928), p. 401.

[150]'Mill to Nightingale', 31 December 1867, in *Hospitals*, X, July 1936, p. 83.

[151]Cf. S. Chodorow et al., *The Mainstream of Civilization*, (Fort Worth,Tex., Harcourt Press, 1994), p. 628.

[152]P.B. Shelley, *Opere*, (Turin-Paris, Einaudi/Gallimard, 1995), p. 161).

[153]Quoted in E.P. Thompson, *The Making of the English Working Class*, (Vintage Books, New York, 1966) p. 761.

[154]P. Bairoch, *Storia economica e sociale del mondo*, (Turin, Einaudi, 1999), vol. I, p. 609 (original edition: Victoires et déboires. Histoire économique et sociale du monde du XVI siècle à nos jours, Gallimard, Paris, 1997)

[155]*Ibid.*, p. 618.

[156]G. Eley, *Forging Democracy. The History of the Left in Europe, 1850-2000*, (New York, Oxford University Press, 2002), p. 5.

[157]Cf. http://www.marxists.org/archive/marx/works/1864/10/27.html.

[158]N. Bobbio, *L'età dei diritti*, (Turin, Einaudi, 1990), p.135

[159]*Ibid.*, p. 115.

[160]A. Cassese, *Violenza e diritto nell'era nucleare*, (Roma-Bari, Laterza, 1986), p. 13.

[161]G. Best, 'Peace Conferences and the Century of Total War: The 1899 Hague Conference and What Came after', in *International Affairs*, 75, 3, July 1999,p. 627.

[162]Cassese, *I diritti umani oggi*, ibid. p. 17.

[163]S. Bessis, *L'Occident et les autres. Histoire d'une suprématie*, (Paris, La Découverte, 2002), p.10.

[164]R. Kipling, *Poems/Poesie*, (Milan, Mursia, 1987), p. 127.

[165]O. Spengler, *Il tramonto dell'Occidente* (1918), (Milan, Longanesi, 1978); J. Ortega y Gasset, *La ribellione delle masse* (1930), (Bologna, Il Mulino, 1962).

[166]G. Le Bon, *Psicologia delle folle* (1895), (Milan, Longanesi, 1980).

[167]G. Dreyfus, a Jewish officer, was arrested in 1894 and accused of treason for having communicated secret information to the German Military Officer in Paris. France was overcome by a wave of anti-Semitism. Two years later another French officer was accused of the same crime and the public opinion split between *dreyfusards* (intellectuals, Socialists, Radicals and anti-militaristic Republicans) and *antidreyfusards* (the nationalistic, anti-Semitic and clerical right wing). The two sides clashed over the issues of anti-Semitism, intolerance and national identity. Writer Emile Zola published a famous article defending Dreyfus, entitled 'J'accuse', in the newspaper *Aurore*. A Colonel, who had added false documents to the dossier on Dreyfus, was discovered and killed himself. In 1899 Dreyfus was pardoned by the President of the Republic Loubet after the War Council had confirmed his sentence. After a further revision he was reintegrated in the army in 1906.

[168]*Bulletin du Premier Congrès universel de la paix*, (Berne, 1901), p. 10.

[169]A. Umiltà, *L'oeuvre de la Ligue internationale de la paix et de la liberté*, (Neuchâtel, Paul Seiler, 189)1, p. 3.

[170]The first published version is in Russian, signed by Ivan Bliokh. Cfr. G. Dawson, 'Preventing 'A Great Moral Evil': Jean de Bloch's 'The Future of War' as Anti-revolutionary Pacifism', in *Journal of Contemporary History*, 37, 1, January 2002, pp. 5-19.

[171]*Bulletin officiel du XVIe Congrès universel de la paix tenu à Munich du 9 au 14 septembre 1907*, (Berne, 1908).

[172]*Sixième Congrès national des sociétés françaises de la paix*, (Reims, 30 mai-2 juin 1909). *Compte-Rendu des séances et documents annexes*, (Reims, 1909), p. 46.

[173]H.R. Fox Bourne, *Civilisation in Congoland*,(London, P.S. King, 1903), p. 213.

[174]M. Kingsley, *Travels in West Africa* (1897), (London, Virago Press, 1982), p. 659.

[175]J. Conrad, *Heart of Darkness*, Electronic Text Center, University of Virginia Library, pp. 69-70, http://etext.virginia.edu/etcbin/toccernew2?id=ConDark.sgm&images=images/modeng&data=/texts/english/modeng/parsed&tag=public&part=all

[176]E.W. Said, *Cultura e imperialismo*, (Rome, Gamberetti, 1998), p. 51.

[177] *Liverpool Daily Post*, 4 April 1902.

[178]K.D. Nworah, 'The Liverpool 'Sect' and British West African Policy 1895-1915', in *African Affairs*, 70, 281, October 1971, p. 349.

[179]E.D. Morel, *Nigeria: Its People and Its Problems*, (London, Smith Elder & Co., 1911), p. XI.

[180]*Parliamentary Debates*, (London, House of Commons, 1903), 4th series, vol. 122, pp. 1297-1298.

[181]Quoted in W.R. Louis, 'Roger Casement and the Congo', in *Journal of African History*, 5, 1, 1964, p. 105.

[182]*Ibid.*, p.106

[183]*Ibid.*, p. 115

[184]M. Twain, *King Leopold's Soliloquy*, (Rome, Editori Riuniti, 1960), pp. 27 e 44-45.

[185]A. Conan Doyle, *The Crime of the Congo*, (London, Hutchinson & Co., 1909), pp. 17-18.

[186] *Chicago Times-Herald*, 20 January 1896.

[187]*Parliamentary Debates*, 1901, XC, 1 March, pp. 179-180.

[188]*Parliamentary Debates*, 1901, XCV, 17 June, pp. 573-577.

[189]S.B. Spies, *Methods of Barbarism: Roberts and Kitchener and Civilians in the Boer Republics January 1900-May 1902*, (Cape Town, Human & Rousseau, 1977), p. 260.

[190]G.B. Davis, 'The Geneva Convention of 1906', in *American Journal of International Law*, 1, 2, April 1907, p. 411.

[191]Cfr. http://nobelprize.org/alfred_nobel/will/will-full.html.

[192]Quoted in A. Schou, *The Peace Prize*, (Stockholm, Nobel Foundation, 1950), p. 20.

[193] *La Correspondance de la paix*, 8 May 1909, p. 2.

[194]Barraute de Plessis, *La Patrie blanche*, (Paris, 1905), p. 6.

[195]T. Mann, 'Thoughts in War' (1914), in *Gesammelte Werke in dreizehn Bänden*, Frankfurt A.M., Fischer, 1974, vol. 13, p. 533.

[196] *The London Times*, 31 July 1917.

[197]E.R. Turner, 'The Women's Suffrage Movement in England', in *American Political Science Review*, 7, 4, November 1913, p. 588.

[198]*Ibid.*, p. 600.

[199]These measures had established a double standard: prostitutes had to be tested for venereal diseases, yet their clients did not.

[200]J.K. Brown, 'The Nineteenth Amendment and Women's Equality', in *Yale Law Journal*,

102, 8, June 1993, p. 2176.

[201]*Ibid.*, p. 2204.

[202]B. Molony, 'Women's Rights, Feminism, and Suffragism in Japan, 1870-1925', in *Pacific Historical Review*, 69, 4, November 2000, p. 640.

[203]A period or era of Japanese history which lasted from 1912 to 1926 and corresponds to the reign of Emperor Yoshihito.

[204]W. Brown, *States of Injury: Power and Freedom in Late Modernity*, (Princeton, N.J., Princeton University Press, 1995, p. 4.

[205]G. Robertson, *Crimes Against Humanity: The Struggle for Global Justice*, London, Penguin Books, 2002), p. 16.

[206]H. Nicolson, *Peacemaking 1919*, (New York, Grosset & Dunlop, 1965), p. 32.

[207]'Commission on the Responsibility of the Authors of the War and on Enforcement of Penalties. Report', in *American Journal of International Law*, 14, 1920, p. 115.

[208]*Ibid.*, p. 117.

[209]Cfr. D. Armstrong, L. Lloyd e J. Redmond, *From Versailles to Maastricht: International Organization in the Twentieth Century*, (New York, St. Martin's Press, 1996), p. 18.

[210]J.M. Keynes, *The Economic Consequences of the Peace*, (New York, Harcourt, Brace, and Howe, Inc., 1919), pp. III.12 e V.176.

[211]'Racial Discrimination to End', in *Japan Times*, 31 January 1919.

[212]'If we must die, let it not be like hogs / Hunted and penned in an inglorious spot, / While round us bark the mad and hungry dogs, / Making their mock at our accursed lot. / If we must die, O let us nobly die, / So that our precious blood may not be shed / In vain; then even the monsters we defy / Shall be constrained to honor us though dead!' (http://www.wsu.edu:8080/~wldciv/world_civ_reader/world_civ_reader_2/mckay.html).

[213]H. Sée, *Histoire de la Ligue des Droits de l'Homme*, (Paris, Ligue des Droits de l'Homme, 1927), p. 174.

[214]P.G. Lauren, *The Evolution of International Human Rights*, (Philadelphia, University of Pennsylvania Press, 1998), pp. 103-104.

[215]Quoted in D.M. Kennedy, *Freedom from Fear: The American People in Depression and War, 1929-1945*, (New York, Oxford University Press, 1999), p. 175

[216]M. Cohen, *I Was One of the Unemployed*, (London, Victor Gollancz, 1945), p. 67.

[217]H. Sitkoff, *A New Deal for Blacks*, (New York, Oxford University Press, 1978), p. 291.

[218]Called *Mahar, Chamar e Chuhra* in North India, and *Paraiyan, Palla, Mala, Holeya* and *Cheruma* in the South, the untouchables are generally indicated as *Dali* or *Harijan*, the terms most used by the English.

[219]L.O. Mosley, *Haile Selassie: The Conquering Lion*, (London, Weidenfeld & Nicolson, 1964), p. 216.

[220]Secret telegram n. 8103 quoted in T.M. Coffey, *Lion by the Tail: The Story of the Italian-Ethiopian War*, (London, Hamilton, 1974), p. 340.

[221]In 1990 the German Supreme Court confirmed the sentence after requests by Rosalinda

von Ossietzky-Palm, Carl's daughter, for the case to be re-examined.

[222]Initially this was to be done by Albert Einstein, yet it needed to be signed by an ex-Nobel winner in the same category. Jane Addams, who had won in 1931, died in Chicago one month after presenting Ossietzky's candidacy.

[223] I. Abrams, *The Multinational Campaign for Carl von Ossietzky*, Stadtschlaining (Austria), International Conference on Peace Movements in National Societies, 25-29 seven 1991.

[224]Cfr. R. Cassin, *La declaration universelle et la mise en oeuvre des droits de l'homme*, in *Recueil des cours de l'Académie de droit international de La Haye*, (Paris, Sirey, 1951), vol. 79, t. 2.

[225]The Security Council of the United Nations asked Germany to stop the violations, while accepting its 'justification' of a mistake having been committed by High Silesian 'authorities', which had misinterpreted German national laws.

[226]G. Burgess, *The Human Rights Dilemma in Anti-Nazi Protest: The Bernheim Petition, Minorities Protection, and the 1933 Sessions of the League of Nations*, Cerc Working Papers Series, n. 2, 2002, p. 6.

[227]League of Nations, 'Minutes of the Sixth Committee', in *Official Journal*, 120, special supplement, 4 October 1933, pp. 32-33.

[228]On the declaration they prepared in 1929 cf. P.G. Lauren, *The Evolution of International Human Rights*, (Philadelphia, University of Pennsylvania Press, 1998), pp. 110 ss.

[229]*Il 1937 e la coscienza contemporanea*, theses elaborated by the Memorial-Italia association in occasion of candidacies for the Nobel for Peace 2007, available at http://www.memorial-italia.it/frontend/?rr=SS_5.

[230]H. Mann, 'Die Revolution', in *Die Neue Weltbühne*, 39, settembre 1936.

[231]For references and quotations relative to this conference cfr. M. Flores, *L'immagine dell'Urss. L'occidente e la Russia di Stalin (1927-1956)*, (Milan, Il Saggiatore, 1990), pp. 238-245. Cfr. also S. Teroni (edited by), *Pour la défense de la culture. Les textes du Congrès international des écrivains Paris, juin 1935*, (Dijon, Eud, 2005), p. 665 (in collaboration with Wolfgang Klein).

[232]C. Charle, *La crise de sociétés imperiales. Allemagne, France, Grande-Bretagne 1900-1940. Essai d'histoire sociale comparée*, (Paris, Seuil, 2001), p. 414.

[233]Fascism's exceptional laws established the existence of the Fascist party only, and left the king, not the Parliament, to control the chief of government's activities; they instituted the Gran Consiglio del Fascismo as the supreme organ of the state, censored the press, led to police control over every association and allowed only Fascist trade unions to exist.

[234]M. Flores, *Tutta la violenza di un secolo*, (Milan, Feltrinelli, 2005), pp.145-147.

[235]For an in-depth analysis of names given to the extermination of the Jewish population, A.-V. Sullam Caimani, *I nomi dello sterminio*, (Torino, Einaudi, 2001), pp. 19-24, 77-101 and 43-51.

[236]The countries which signed the document were: United States, United Kingdom, USSR, China, Australia, Belgium, Canada, Costa Rica, Cuba, Czechoslovakia, Dominican Republic, El Salvador, Greece, Guatemala, Haiti, Honduras, India, Yugoslavia, Luxemburg, Netherlands, New Zealand, Nicaragua, Norway, Panama, Poland and South Africa.

[237]N. Mandela, *Lungo cammino verso la libertà*, (Milan, Feltrinelli, 1995), p. 100.

[238]Cfr. http://www.americanrhetoric.com/speeches/fdrthefourfreedoms.htm.

[239]H.G. Wells, 'War Aims: The Rights of Man', in *The Times*, 25 October 1939.

[240]The Jesuit Wilfred Parsons presented an *International Bill of Rights* to the Catholic Association for International Peace; the Rector of the Law faculty of Southeastern University, Rollin McNitt, proposed an *International Declaration of Human Rights*; Jacques Maritain wrote the book *Les droits de l'homme et la loi naturelle*; exiled Czechoslovakian president Edvard Beneš wrote an essay on *The rights of man and international law*; in the *Public Opinion Quarterly* a study entitled 'Towards an International Bill of Rights' was published; plus many, many more.

[241]Lauren, *The Evolution of International Human Rights*, ibid. p. 168.

[242]*Ibid.*, p. 171.

[243]M.A. Glendon, *A World Made New. Eleanor Roosevelt and the Universal Declaration of Human Rights*, (New York, Random House, 2002), p. 10.

[244]Citato in Lauren, *The Evolution of International Human Rights*, ibid. p.184.

[245]United Nations Conference on International Organization, *Documents of the United Nations Conference on International Organization*, (London-New York, United Nations Information Organization, 1945), 22 vol., vol. I, p.245.

[246]C. Romulo e B. Day Romulo, *Forty Years: A Third World Soldier at the UN*, (New York, Greenwood Press, 1986), pp. 9-10.

[247]'We the peoples of the United nations have determined to save succeeding generations from the scourge of war, which twice in our lifetime has brought untold sorrow to mankind, and to reaffirm faith in fundamental human rights, in the dignity and worth of the human person, in the equal rights of men and women and of nations large and small, and to establish conditions under which justice and respect for the obligations arising from treaties and other sources of international law can be maintained, and to promote social progress and better standards of life in larger freedom, and for these ends to practice tolerance and live together in peace with one another as good neighbours, and to unite our strength to maintain international peace and security, and to ensure, by the acceptance of principles and the institution of methods, that armed force shall not be used, save in the common interest, and to employ international machinery for the promotion of the economic and social advancement of all peoples, have resolved to combine our efforts to accomplish these aims.'

[248]This article, which refers to 'non autonomous territories', is the result of compromises between non-Western countries, which wanted an explicit reference to autonomy and independence, and the interests of the major powers.

[249]Fiduciary administration regimes must 'encourage the respect of the rights of man and of fundamental liberties without any distinctions based on race, language, or religion, and encourage the recognition of the interdependence of the peoples of the world'.

[250]United Nations Conference on International Organization, *Documents of the United Nations Conference on International Organization*, ibid. pp. 715-716.

[251]Citato in G. Robertson, *Crimes against Humanity. The Struggle for Global Justice*, (London, Penguin Books, 2002), p. 234.

[252]*Ibid.*, p. 235.

[253]Cfr. S.L. Jacobs, *Lemkin and the Armenian Genocide*, in R.G. Hovannisian (edited by), *Looking Backward, Moving Forward: Confronting the Armenian Genocide*, (New Brunswick, N.J., Transactions Publishers, 2003).

[254]Cfr. H.R. Huttenbach, 'Toward a Conceptual Definition of Genocide', in *Journal of Genocide Research*, 4, 2, 2002, pp. 167-175; M. Mazower, 'Violence and the State in the Twentieth Century', in *American Historical Review*, 107, 4, pp. 1158-1178.

[255]R. Lemkin, *Axis Rule in Occupied Europe*, (Washington, D.C., Carnegie Endowment for International Peace, 1944), p. 79.

[256]Cfr. E. Greppi e G. Venturini, *Codice di diritto internazionale umanitario*, (Turin, Giappichelli, 2003).

[257]Cfr. M. Lippman, 'A Road Map to the 1948 Convention on the Prevention and Punishment of the Crime of Genocide', in *Journal of Genocide Research*, IV, 2, 2002, pp. 178-179.

[258]*Ibid.*, p. 179.

[259]*Ibid.*, p. 180.

[260]Cursive added by the author.

[261]Quoted in L. Kuper, *Genocide: Its Political Use in Twentieth Century*, (New York, Penguin Books, 1981), p. 26.

[262]A. Cassese, *I diritti umani oggi*, (Roma-Bari, Laterza, 2005), p. 153.

[263]K. Nkrumah, *Towards Colonial Freedom*, (London, Panaf, 1974), pp. 44-45.

[264]H.C. Malik (edited by), *The Challenge of Human Rights: Charles Malik and the Universal Declaration*, (Oxford, Centre for Lebanese Studies, 2000), p.117.

[265]'Statement on Human Rights', in *American Anthropologist*, 49, 4, 1947, p. 541.

[266]Lauren, *The Evolution of International Human Rights*, ibid. p. 222.

[267]'Statement on Human Rights', ibid., 49, 4, 1947, p. 542.

[268]*Ibid.*, p.543.

[269]UNESCO, *Human Rights. Comments and Interpretations. A Symposium*, (London, Allan Wingate, 1949). http://unesdoc.unesco.org/images/0015/001550/155042eb.pdf

[270]*Ibid.*, pp. v, ix.

[271]*Ibid.*, p. 4.

[272]*bid.*, p. 10.

[273]*Ibid.*, pp. 36, 38.

[274]*Ibid.*, pp. 70, 78.

[275]*Ibid.*, pp. 83.

[276]*Ibid.*, p. 187.

[277]*Ibid.*, pp. 192, 200.

[278]In the British system the title of *Queen's Counsel* (previously *King's Counsel*) is given to an elite of top lawyers.

[279]G. Robertson, *Crimes Against Humanity: The Struggle for Global Justice*, (London, Penguin

Books, 2002).

[280]P.G. Lauren, *The Evolution of International Human Rights*, (Philadelphia, University of Pennsylvania Press, 1998), p. 280.

[281]'Everyone has the right to take part in the government of his country, directly or through freely chosen representatives. Everyone has the right of equal access to public service in his country. The will of the people shall be the basis of the authority of government; this will shall be expressed in periodic and genuine elections which shall be by universal and equal suffrage and shall be held by secret vote or by equivalent free voting procedures.'

[282]H. Alleg, *La tortura*, edited by P. Spriano, (Turin, Einaudi, 1958), pp. 14-15. Cf. P. Vidal-Naquet, *La torture dans la République*, (Paris, Minuit, 1972).

[283]*Congressional Record 1952*, 98, pt. 1, Washington, D.C., Government Print Office, 1952, p. 912.

[284]Lauren, *The Evolution of International Human Rights*, ibid. p. 245.

[285]S. Senese, *Autodeterminazione*, in M. Flores, T. Groppi and R. Pisillo Mazzeschi (edited by), *Diritti umani. Cultura dei diritti e dignità della persona nell'epoca della globalizzazione*, Turin, Utet, 2007, vol. I, p. 69.

[286]Cf. http://www.un.org/depts/DPKO/Missions/onuc.htm.

[287]Cf. http://www.gibnet.com/texts/un1514.htm.

[288]*Truth and Reconciliation Commission of South Africa Report*, October 1998, vol. 3, chap. 6, p. 537, available at http://www.doj.gov.za/trc/trc_frameset.htm.

[289]Cf. http://www.un-documents.net/a18r1904.htm.

[290]T. Karis and G. Carter (edited by), *From Protest to Challenge*,(Stanford, Calif., Hoover Institution Press, 1977), 4 vol., vol. 3, p. 731.

[291]Cf. http://www.unhchr.ch/html/menu3/b/9.htm

[292]The only Western countries to sign with this first block were Iceland and Spain, alongside Poland, Hungary and Bulgaria. Italy only signed in 1976; the United States in 1994.

[293]Speech by Clara Ponce de Léon, 16 December 1966, in United Nations/General Assembly, *Official Records, Plenari Meetings, 1966*, 1497th meeting, p. 7.

[294]A. Bennet, 'The Man Who Fought for the Forgotten', in *The Observer*, 27 February 2005 (http://www.guardian.co.uk/uk/2005/feb/27/humanrights.world1).

[295]In 1962 Flora Benenson, during a party in Tel Aviv, told somebody that Kim Philby, who was at the time in Beirut as a journalist, had told her that he was a Soviet spy and asked her to become one herself. Interrogated by Victor Rotschild, an M15 leader, she admitted what occurred but declared she would never testify against Philby. Philby disappeared in January 1963 and sought refuge in the Soviet Union, where he died in 1988.

[296] *The Observer*, 28 May 1961.

[297]A. Cassese, *I diritti umani oggi*, (Roma-Bari, Laterza, 2005), p. 43.

[298]H. Tolley, *The International Commission of Jurists: Global Advocates for Human Rights*, (Philadelphia, University of Pennsylvania Press, 1994), p. 98.

[299]'I created this expression and first used it in the French weekly "L'Observateur" on August 14 1952' (A. Sauvy, *Note sur l'origine de l'expression 'Tiers Monde'*).

[300]For an ideal case, I suggest the article by N. Chomsky and E.S. Herman, 'Distortions at Fourth Hand', in *The Nation*, 25 June 1977; as well as J. Peck (edited by), *The Chomsky Reader*, (New York, Pantheon Books, 1987), p. 291

[301]Cf. http://www.osce.org/documents/mcs/1975/08/4044_en.pdf.

[302]Cf. http://www.unhchr.ch/html/menu6/2/fs2.htm.

[303]A. Neier, *Alla conquista delle libertà*, (Turin, Codice, 2003), p. 188.

[304]*Ibid.*, p. 26.

[305]'Nightmare in Biafra', in *Sunday Times*, 26 April 1968, p. 12.

[306]A. Donini, *Principi umanitari*, in Flores, Groppi and Pisillo Mazzeschi (edited by), *Diritti umani*, ibid. vol. II, p. 1095.

[307]Cf. http://www.leliobasso.it/documento.aspx?id=ec103733449221e8922dbf81e22da6ee.

[308]J. Carter, 'The American Road to a Human Rights Policy', in S. Power and G. Allison (edited by), *Realizing Human Rights: Moving from Inspiration to Impact*, (New York, St. Martin's Press, 2000), p. 54.

[309]Cf. http://www.un.org/womenwatch/daw/cedaw/cedaw.htm

[310]Cf.http://www.centrodirittiumani.unipd.it/a_temi/normedu/004_ua/04_01_01_ita. asp?menu=temi.

[311]Cf. http://old.hrad.cz/president/Havel/speeches/index_uk.html.

[312]http://www.ohchr.org/EN/NewsEvents/Pages/DisplayNewsaspx?NewsID=7906& LangID=E

[313]Cf.http://www.hoboes.com/pub/Prohibition/Comments%20on%20the%20War/ United%20Nations%20Double%20Standard/

[314]Cf. http://www.romeodallaire.com/shake-hands-with-the-devil.html.

[315]M. Ignatieff, *Human Rights as Politics and Idolatry*, (Princeton, N.J., Princeton University Press, 2001), p. 46.

[316]Interview released in J. Goytisolo, Diario da Sarajevo. IV, La memoria dell'orrore, an enquiry translated in *l'Unità*, 4 September 1993, p. 13.

[317]Cf.http://daccessdds.un.org/doc/UNDOC/GEN/N08/391/44/PDF/N0839144. pdf?OpenElement.

[318]T. Buergenthal, 'The Evolving International Human Rights System', in *American Journal of International Law*, 100, 4, October 2006, p. 807.

[319]M. Flores, T. Groppi e R. Pisillo Mazzeschi, *Introduzione*, in Eid. (edited by), *Diritti umani. Cultura dei diritti e dignità della persona nell'epoca della globalizzazione*, (Turin, Utet, 2007), vol. I, p. XXIV.

[320]L. Clements and J. Young, 'Human Rights: Changing the Culture', in *Journal of Law and Society*, 26, 1, March 1999, p. 2.

[321]Flores, Groppi e Pisillo Mazzeschi, *Introduzione*, ibid. p. XXV.

[322]A. Brysk, *Introduction. Transnational Threats and Opportunities*, in Ead (edited by), *Globalization and Human Rights*, (Los Angeles, University of California Press, 2002), pp. 6-7.

[323]The ILO Convention on Immigrant Workers (1975); the UN Convention on the Rights of Immigrant Workers and of their Families (1990).

[324]K. Hill Maher, 'Who Has a Right to Rights? Citizenship's Exclusions in an Age of Migration', in Brysk (edited by), *Globalization and Human Rights*, ibid. pp. 21, 36.

[325]Cfr. A. Gambino, *L'imperialismo dei diritti umani*, (Roma, Editori Riuniti, 2001); S. Zizek, *Contro i diritti umani*, (Milan, Il Saggiatore, 2006).

[326]The one on the interpretation of Chapter VII of the UN Charter, which defines possible measures against threats to peace, including the use of force according to established forms and conditions, is one of the richest and most controversial debates regarding the document.

[327]K. Roth, 'The War in Iraq: Justified as Humanitarian Intervention', in *Kroc Institute Occasional Papers*, 25, 1, 2004.

[328]*Ibid.*

[329]A. Donini, 'Emergenza umanitaria', in Flores, Groppi and Pisillo Mazzeschi (edited by), *Diritti umani*, ibid. vol. I, p. 546.

[330]A. Donini, L. Minear *et al.*, *Humanitarian Agenda 2015: Principles, Power, and Perceptions. Preliminary Report*, (Medford, Mass., Feinstein International Center, Tufts University, September 2006), p. 21.

[331]N. Leader, *The Politics of Principle: The Principles of Humanitarian Action in Practice*, (London, Overseas Development Institute, Humanitarian Policy Group Report 2, March 2000), p. 12.

[332]*Ibid.*, p. 48.

[333]W W. Osiatynski, *Human Rights and Other Values*, manuscript as yet to be published, p. 86 (thanks to the kind permission of the author).

[334]*Ibid.*, p. 50.

[335]D. Kretzmer, 'Il diritto internazionale e la "guerra al terrorismo"', in T. Groppi (edited by), *Democrazia e terrorismo*, Naples, (Editoriale Scientifica, 2006), p. 17.

[336]K. Popper, *La società aperta e i suoi nemici*, Rome, Armando, 1996, vol.I, pp. 346-347.

[337]So far ratified only by fourteen countries out of the forty-six which signed it.

[338]K. Annan, *Fighting Terrorism for Humanity: A Conference on the Roots of Evil*, New York, 22 September 2003, available at http://www.un.org/apps/sg/sgstats.asp?nid=511.

[339]A. Martini, 'Difendere la democrazia da un nemico sconosciuto: il terrorismo', in Groppi (edited by), *Democrazia e terrorismo*, ibid. p. 42.

[340]Kretzmer, 'Il diritto internazionale e "la guerra al terrorismo"', ibid. p.18.

[341]L. Bonanate, *Il terrorismo come prospettiva simbolica*, (Turin, Aragno, 2006), p. 7.

[342]*Ibid.*

[343]M. Bovero, 'Libertà, diritti, guerra. Considerazioni sull'ideologia occidentale', in Groppi (edited by), *Democrazia e terrorismo*, ibid. p. 10.

[344]A. Dershowitz, *Rights from Wrongs: A Secular Theory of the Origins of Rights*, (New York, Basic Books, 2004), pp. 215-216.

[345]Kretzmer, *Il diritto internazionale e la 'guerra al terrorismo'*, ibid. p. 20.

[346]Quoted in H. Duffy, *The 'War on Terror' and the Framework of International Law*, (New York, Cambridge University Press, 2005), p. 442.

[347]*Ibid.*, p. 22.

[348]*Ibid.*, p. 26.

[349]P. De Sena and A. Saccucci, 'Diritti fondamentali', in Flores, Groppi and Pisillo Mazzeschi (edited by), *Diritti umani*, ibid. vol. I, p. 377.

[350]T. Groppi, 'Dopo l'11 September: la 'via canadese' per conciliare sicurezza e diritti', in *Quaderni costituzionali*, XXV, 3, September 2005, p. 577.

[351]*Ibid.*, p. 594.

[352]*Ibid.*, p. 601.

[353]The commander of the *peacekeeping* troops of the UN mission in Rwanda (UNAMIR), Canadian general Roméo Dallaire, once he had understood the situation, asked for more troops from the UN so he could stop the violence. Instead the ones who were already *in loco* were taken away.

[354]*Report of the International Commission of Inquiry on Darfur to the Secretary-General Pursuant to Security Council Resolution 1564 (2004) of 18 September 2004*, UN Doc. S/2005/60, 25 January 2005.

[355]ICTR (International Criminal Tribunal for Rwanda), *Judgement and Sentence vs Jean-Paul Akayesu*, case number Ictr-96-4-T, par. 124.

[356]Paradoxically, during the trial, even the defence claimed that the Tutsis and Hutus were not ethnically different, but belonged to one same race.

[357]*Caso IT-98-33-T*, pp. 197-212, 2 August 2001 (cf. http://www.un.org/icty/glance/krstic.htm).

[358]A. Cassese, *I diritti umani oggi*, (Rome-Bari, Laterza, 2005), pp. 168-169.

[359]International Commission on Intervention and State Sovereignty, *The Responsibility to Protect*, 2001, available at http://www.iciss.ca/report-en.asp.

[360]High Level Panel on Threats, Challenges and Change, *A More Secure World: Our Shared Responsibility*, UN Doc. A/59/565 (http://www.un.org/secureworld/report.pdf).

[361]*In Larger Freedom: Towards Development, Security and Human Rights for All*, UN Doc. A/59/2005, parr. 16-22 (http://www.un.org/largerfreedom/contents.htm).

[362]Security Council, *Resolution* 1674, 28 April 2006, par. 4.

[363]C C. Stahn, 'Responsibility to Protect: Political Rhetoric or Emerging Legal Norm?' in *American Journal of International Law*, 101, 1, January 2007, pp. 102-103.

[364]*Ibid.*, p. 107.

[365]*Ibid.*, p. 108.

[366]*Ibid.*, p. 115.

[367]*Ibid.*, p. 120.

[368]A C. Stahn, 'Responsibility to Protect: Political Rhetoric or Emerging Legal Norm?' in *American Journal of International Law*, 101, 1, January 2007, pp. 102-103.

[369]T. Meron, 'Reflections on the Prosecution of War Crimes by International Tribunals', in *American Journal of International Law*, 100, 3, July 2006, pp. 559-560.

[370]*Ibid.*, p. 578.

[371]*Ibid.*, p. 579.

[372]M. Minow, *Between Vengeance and Forgiveness: Facing History after Genocide and Mass Violence*, (Boston, Mass., Beacon Press, 1998), p. 58.

[373]R R. Nagy, 'Reconciliation in Post-Commission South Africa: Thick and Thin Accounts of Solidarity', in *Canadian Journal of Political Science*, 35, 2, June 2002, p. 324.

[374]E. Fronza and A. Pollini, *La persecuzione dei crimini internazionali:analisi dei modelli giurisdizionali e non giurisdizionali*, Euromediterranea 2003, available at http://www.alex-anderlanger.org/cms/index.php?r=50&k=178&id=769

[375]R.A. Wilson, 'Is the Legalization of Human Rights Really the Problem? Genocide in the Guatemalan Historical Clarification Commission', in S. Meckled-García e B. Çali (edited by), *The Legalization of Human Rights. Multidisciplinary Perspectives on Human Rights and Human Rights Law*,(London, Routledge, 2006), p. 89.

[376]S.P. Huntington, *Lo scontro delle civiltà e il nuovo ordine mondiale*, (Milan, Garzanti, 1997).

[377]L.O. Adegbite, 'African Attitudes to the International Protection of Human Rights', in A. Eide and A. Schou (edited by), *International Protection of Human Rights*, New York, Interscience Publishers, 1968, p. 69.

[378]M. Mutua, *The Ideology of Human Rights*, in 'Virginia Journal of International Law', 36, 1996, p. 589.

[379]M. Mutua, *The Complexity of Universalism in Human Rights*, in A. Sajo (edited by), *Human Rights with Modesty. The Problem of Universalism*, (Leiden-Boston, Mass., Martinus Nijhoff Publishers, 2004), pp. 58-63.

[380]E. Messer, 'Pluralist Approaches to Human Rights', in *Journal of Anthropological Research*, 53, 3, autumn 1997, p. 297.

[381]J. Donnelly, 'Human Rights, Individual Rights, and Collective Rights', in J. Berting, P.R. Baehr et al. (edited by), *Human Rights in a Pluralist World: Individuals and Collectivities*, (Westport, Conn., Meckler, 1990), p. 59.

[382]M. Chanock, '"Culture"and Human Rights: Orientalising, Occidentalising and Authenticity', in M. Mamdani (edited by), *Beyond Rights Talk and Culture Talk. Comparative Essays on the Politics of Rights and Culture*, (Cape Town, David Philip, 2000), p. 19.

[383]Messer, *Pluralist Approaches to Human Rights*, ibid. p. 310.

[384]*Ibid.*, p. 311.

[385]W.T. de Bary, *Preface*, in W.T. de Bary e Tu Weiming (edited by), *Confucianism and Human Rights*, (New York, Columbia University Press, 1998), pp.X-XI.

[386]W.T. de Bary, *Introduction*, in de Bary e Tu Weiming (edited by), *Confucianism and Human Rights*, ibid. p. 24.

[387]R. R. Peerenboom, 'Confucian Harmony and Freedom of Thought', in de Bary and Tu Weiming (edited by), *Confucianism and Human Rights*, ibid. p. 251.

[388] Ching, 'Human Rights: A Valid Chinese Concept?' in de Bary and Tu Weiming (edited by), *Confucianism and Human Rights*, ibid. pp. 79-80.

[389]E. Moosa, 'The Dilemma of Islamic Rights Schemes', in *Journal of Law and Religion*,

15, 1/2, 2000-01, p. 187.

[390]*Ibid.*, p. 193.

[391]*Ibid.*, p. 194.

[392]F. Sabahi, 'Islam e diritti umani', in Flores, Groppi e Pisillo Mazzeschi (edited by), *Diritti umani*, ibid. vol. II, p. 799.

[393]J.A.M. Cobbah, 'African Values and the Human Rights Debate: An African Perspective', in *Human Rights Quarterly*, 9, 3, August 1987, p. 321.

[394]M.A. Glendon, *A World Made New. Eleanor Roosevelt and the Universal Declaration of Human Rights*, (New York, Random House, 2002), p. 67.

[395]*Ibid.*

[396]*Ibid.*, pp. 75-76.

[397]*Ibid.*, p. 228.

[398]Cobbah, *African Values and the Human Rights Debate*, ibid. p. 323.

[399]E.M. Zechenter, 'In the Name of Culture: Cultural Relativism and the Abuse of the Individual', in *Journal of Anthropological Research*, 53, 3, autumn 1997, p. 327.

[400]*Ibid.*, p. 334.

[401]Quoted in C.M. Cerna, 'Universality of Human Rights and Cultural Diversity: Implementation of Human Rights in Different Socio-cultural Contexts', in *Human Rights Quarterly*, 16, 4, November 1994, p. 746.

[402]*Ibid.*, p. 748.

[403]S. Meckled-García and B. Çali, 'Lost in Translation. The Human Rights Ideal and International Human Rights Law', in Eid. (edited by), *The Legalization of Human Rights*, ibid. p. 25.

[404]Cerna, *Universality of Human Rights and Cultural Diversity*, ibid. p. 752.

[405]*Ibid.*, p. 746.

[406]M. Freeman, 'Putting Law in Its Place: An Interdisciplinary Evaluation of National Amnesty Laws', in Meckled-García and Çali (edited by), *The Legalization of Human Rights*, ibid. p. 58.

[407]A. Woodiwiss, 'The Law Cannot Be Enough: Human Rights and the Limit of Legalism', in Meckled-García and Çali (edited by), *The Legalization of Human Rights*, ibid. p. 46.

[408]J. Donnelly, 'The Virtues of Legalization', in Meckled-García and Çali (edited by), *The Legalization of Human Rights*, ibid. p. 76.

[409]Freeman, *Putting Law in Its Place*, ibid. p. 62.

[410]M. Mamdani, *Introduction*, in Id (edited by), *Beyond Rights Talk and Culture Talk*, ibid. p. 4.

[411]Donnelly, *The Virtues of Legalization*, ibid. p. 67.

[412]*Ibid.*, p. 68.

[413]Wilson, *Is the Legalization of Human Rights Really the Problem?* ibid. p. 81.

[414]Cfr. *Ibid.*, pp. 81-85; Wilson is referring in particular to the positions of Mahmood Mamdani, who suggests observing the genocide in Rwanda not through the lens of international law, but through the 'logics of colonialism'.

[415]'Far from being a model for emancipation, human rights are a facade to hide social

and economic inequalities. Human rights are the rights of the bourgeoisie, the rights of the selfish man and of the isolated individual who does not need to depend on others': thus Wilson summarises the Marxist position which is still present in certain debates on human rights (*Ibid.*, p. 82).

[416]Cerna, *Universality of Human Rights and Cultural Diversity*, ibid. p. 752

[417]*Ibid.*, p. 749.

[418]R. Kapur, 'Revisioning the Role of Law in Women's Human Rights Struggles', in Meckled-García and Çali (edited by), *The Legalization of Human Rights*, ibid. p. 103.

[419]*Ibid.*, pp. 106 and 107.

[420]*Ibid.*, p. 107.

[421]*Ibid.*

[422]N N. Menon, 'State, Community and the Debate on the Uniform Civil Code in India', in Mamdani (edited by), *Beyond Rights Talk and Culture Talk*, ibid. p. 75.

[423]In Sunnite traditions, all the husband has to do to divorce is pronounce the word *talaq* ('I divorce you') three times.

[424]R. Kapur, *Revisioning the Role of Law in Women's Human Rights Struggles*, cit, p. 111

[425]A. de Guttry, 'Nazioni Unite', in Flores, Groppi and Pisillo Mazzeschi (edited by), *Diritti umani*, ibid. vol. II, p. 959.

[426]C. Perelman, *Logica giuridica e nuova retorica*, (Milan, Giuffrè, 1979), pp.180 ss.

[427]G. Zagrebelsky, *Il diritto mite*, (Torino, Einaudi, 1992), pp. 169-170.

[428]Flores, Groppi and Pisillo Mazzeschi, *Introduzione*, ibid. p. XXVI.

[429]Osiatynski, *Human Rights and Other Values*, ibid. p. 175.

[430]I am following the distinction between ethics and morality proposed by A. Margalit in *Ethics of Memory*, (Cambridge, Mass., Harvard University Press, 2002).

Index

Lightning Source UK Ltd.
Milton Keynes UK

174666UK00002B/3/P